Praise for *Design Methods for Reactive Systems*

Design Methods for Reactive Systems is a most welcome addition to the literature on systems and software engineering. It is serious and balanced, refreshingly general and hype-free, and is one of the very few books in this area that is not a user manual for a particular methodology. It concentrates admirably on the difficult subject of reactive systems and their behavior, going to considerable lengths to present an impartial view of the main approaches to this subject.

—Dr. David Harel, Dean, Faculty of Mathematics and Computer Science
The Weizmann Institute of Science, Israel

Wieringa's book is one of the most significant design textbooks of the decade. Wieringa uses his undoubted experience in both practical and theoretical design to create a textbook that moves beyond the "statics" of transformational (predetermined) systems to the "dynamics" of reactive systems. In its turn, it lays down the foundations and provides the rationale for a subsequent subject on software product engineering. As such, it fills a very definite need.

—M. Whitelaw, Charles Stuart University, Wagga Wagga, Australia

To use methods well, it's vital to have a good grasp of their conceptual underpinnings. Most books in this area focus solely on notation and don't clarify the important issues. This book is different. It's intellectually rigorous, insightful, and original. In particular, the coverage of UML is far more substantial and reasoned than I have found in any of its "official" texts.

—Daniel Jackson, Laboratory for Computer Science, MIT

This book makes a significant contribution to the software engineering literature. Although the emphasis is on the use of notations to express the functionality of reactive systems, the case studies used throughout the book also highlight the importance of nonfunctional or quality attributes. The summaries included in each chapter are very useful as a shortcut if the reader lacks the time to cover the chapter. The questions and exercises will be useful for instructors and students.

—Dr. Mario R. Barbacci, Software Engineering Institute, Carnegie Mellon University

This book is a primer for reactive system developers. I have worked for over 20 years developing telecom systems and automotive electronics. If this book had been around earlier, it could have helped us avoid many costly problems we encountered.

—Felix Bachmann, Carnegie Mellon University, Software Engineering Institute

Design Methods for Reactive Systems
Yourdon, Statemate, and the UML

Design Methods for Reactive Systems

Yourdon, Statemate, and the UML

R. J. Wieringa

University of Twente,
The Netherlands

MORGAN KAUFMANN PUBLISHERS

AN IMPRINT OF ELSEVIER SCIENCE

AMSTERDAM   BOSTON   LONDON   NEW YORK
OXFORD   PARIS   SAN DIEGO   SAN FRANCISCO
SINGAPORE   SYDNEY   TOKYO

Senior Editor	Tim Cox
Publishing Services Manager	Edward Wade
Senior Production Editor	Cheri Palmer
Editorial Coordinator	Stacie Pierce
Project Management	Dusty Friedman, The Book Company
Cover Design	Yvo Riezebos Design
Cover Image	CNAC/ MNAM/ Dist. Réunion des Musées Nationaux/ Art Resource, NY
Text Design	Lisa Devenish
Illustration/Composition	Interactive Composition Corporation
Copyeditor	Julie Nemer
Proofreader	Martha Ghent
Indexer	Taylor Indexing Service
Printer	The Maple-Vail Book Manufacturing Group

Morgan Kaufmann Publishers
An imprint of Elsevier Science
340 Pine Street, Sixth Floor
San Francisco, CA 94104-3205
www.mkp.com

07 06 05 04 03   5 4 3 2 1

Library of Congress Control Number: 2002112068
ISBN: 1-55860-755-2

This book is printed on acid-free paper.

*To Mieke,
as a wedding present*

S oftware development is difficult in a number of ways. First, it gives rise to artifacts of unprecedented discrete behavioral complexity. We must design those artifacts, and we must understand and deal with the resulting complexities of behavior in the environment—that is, in the subject or problem domain. Second, software lacks the salutary clear-cut distinction between design and construction that is found in nearly all traditional engineering disciplines. There is no clearly recognizable point at which our work switches from creating and analyzing blueprints to pouring concrete or welding metal. The distinction between design and implementation seems desirable and important, but there is no agreement on what it is or how to take advantage of it. Third, in information problems and subproblems we must build and use run-time surrogates for parts of the problem domain—such as a staff database acting as a surrogate for the real world of employees or an object structure providing a surrogate for the real world of lifts and service requests. This surrogacy relationship has spawned a damaging confusion between the reality in the problem domain and its related, but different, surrogate inside the machine.

Partly because of these difficulties, software development has attracted more than its fair share of overoptimistic nostrums and energetically touted panaceas. Even 15 years after Fred Brooks's famous pronouncement, we are all still inclined to look for the silver bullet, for the quick and easy guarantee of success in our work.

This book presents a refreshing but serious and conscientious approach to the work of developing useful software. Roel Wieringa, a philosopher as well as an engineer, is determined to convey understanding along with practice and insight along with information. He is not blinded by ephemeral fashions in notation, but draws eclectically from both new and old ideas and techniques. He looks critically at widely used techniques and notations and judges clearly what should be adopted because it is simple and good, what must be supplemented from another source because it is deficient, and what must be discarded because it is too complicated.

He understands that software development problems are variegated. Not only are there many different kinds of systems to be built, but each system, except the most trivial, must have components and must address subproblems of different kinds. The book contains several case studies, referred to throughout the book and collected in Appendices, which will repay careful reading. Case studies are always difficult for writers about software: too much detail and the point is lost in a mass of daunting complexity; too little and the example conveys nothing. The case studies here are well judged and informative.

He makes insightful comments on the nature of software development as an engineering discipline, on the relationship between formality and precision, and on the distinction between modeling and design. He is not afraid to use an informal rough sketch to lay out a mission statement or a function refinement tree; but he also gives illuminating explanations of the precise semantics of state transition diagrams.

This is surely a book from which everyone engaged in software development—students, practitioners, teachers, and researchers—can learn. I congratulate the author on completing it. I hope it will have the success it deserves and that you will read it with enjoyment and profit.

Michael Jackson
Independent Consultant, UK

PART III **Entity Notations**

PART VI   Software Specification Methods

Appendices

Online Materials (*www.mkp.com/dmrs/*)

Reactive Systems

This book describes methods and techniques for the design of software systems. We look in particular at *reactive* systems, which are systems that engage in stimulus-response behavior. The view of reactive systems I take in this book is wider than that usually taken in the field. In the view taken here, reactive systems include information systems, groupware systems, workflow management systems, enterprise resource planning systems, systems for e-commerce, production control systems, embedded software, interactive editors, and operating systems. It can be argued that even software agents are examples of reactive software systems that are able to respond to events in a goal-driven way. Characteristic of all these systems is that they engage in stimulus-response behavior in order to produce desirable effects in their environment. This book brings together specification techniques and guidelines that have proven to be useful in the design of a wide range of systems engaged in stimulus-response behavior.

Specification or Design?

The question of what is specification and what design has been debated widely in software engineering. The traditional view is that a specification describes what a product will do and that a design describes how it will do it. But this does not help us to distinguish specification from design because, as has been observed by many people, according to this definition one person's *what* can be another person's *how*—that is what is a specification from one point of view is a design from another point of view. In a collaborative problem-solving process one person's solution may be another person's problem. For example, the design decisions about a building concern the general functionality and visual appearance of the building, the materials used, the structure of the electricity subsystem, and so on. Each of these decisions is a solution to a previous problem and is itself a problem to be solved by more design decisions. In this book, I take the view that any creative decision about a product is a design decision. The outcome of design decisions is documented in a specification, and this specification is implemented by a builder. To *design* is to make a decision about a product; to *specify* is to document the outcome of this decision. A specification is a documentation of desired product properties, and these properties may range from external to internal properties.

Specifications are used by builders. Designing and building can occur concurrently, but they are coordinated by documenting design decisions in a specification of what the builder has to build. For example, design decisions about a building are documented in sketches, plans, schemas, blueprints, and so on that are used by builders.

The design decisions treated in this book concern the desired functional properties of a product, namely their desired functions, their behavior and communication properties, and the abstract requirements-level architecture that follows from this. Specification techniques are presented in Parts II to V of the book. Each technique is described in one or two short chapters.

Methods and Techniques

In this book, a specification *technique* is a notation for documenting a design decision. For each technique treated in this book, I describe its syntax and semantics as well as the guidelines for using it, illustrated by a number of small case studies whose specifications are collected in the Appendices. A collection of techniques and guidelines is in itself not a method. In this book, a specification *method* is a collection of specification techniques, guidelines for their use, and in addition a set of consistency rules that tell us how to use these techniques together in the specification of one product design, as well as guidelines about the order in which to use these techniques. Many of the techniques treated in this book are used in different methods. In this book, I describe the use that structured and object-oriented analysis methods make of these techniques. These methods are described in Part VI. Because almost all the techniques used by these methods are described in Parts II to V, the chapters about methods are quite short.

Structured and Object-Oriented Methods

The two major current software design approaches—structured and object-oriented analysis and design—are approaches to reactive system design. Their commonalities are much more significant than their differences. The major difference is the architectural style favored by these approaches. Structured approaches favor a Von Neumann style, in which data storage is separated from data processing. Object-oriented approaches favor, of course, an object-oriented style, in which data storage is encapsulated with data processing. In the design of reactive systems, both styles are useful and they can be mixed.

Jointly, structured and object-oriented methods provide a wealth of design techniques and guidelines for reactive software design. However, these techniques and guidelines are often buried under a multitude of syntactic details of diagram techniques, which makes them unnecessarily hard to use. This is aggravated by the fact that many techniques are sloppily defined. In addition, the design guidelines that come with these techniques are obscured by irrelevant ideological differences between the architectural styles favored by the structured and object-oriented approaches. To be a proponent of one particular style means, all too often, to be an opponent of another, regardless of the utility of a style for the design problem at hand. As a result, useful techniques and guidelines are in danger of being forgotten. This book attempts to rescue useful techniques and guidelines from collective amnesia by treating the techniques and guidelines independently of the methods in which they are used, avoiding the ideological wars that have accompanied these techniques.

The System Engineering Argument

The primary structuring principle used in this book is shown in Figure 1. The System under Development (SuD) is part of a composite system. Together with a number of entities external to the SuD, the SuD realizes the desired properties of the composite system. The SuD itself is decomposed into a number of components, which are themselves systems at a lower level in the hierarchy. The components, the SuD, and the composite system have many kinds of properties, but at each level of this hierarchy, systems have at least these three kinds of properties: They provide services, they have a behavior, and they engage in communications with other entities.

From a design point of view, the composite system is the boundary of the environment relevant for the SuD. The important difference between the SuD and the external entities for the designer is that the SuD is to be designed, but the external entities are given to the designer. They are already there or they are to be bought or they are designed by other people. So the SuD designer has to make assumptions about the external entities and a design of the SuD. The assumptions A describe properties of the external entities and the design specification S describes properties to be realized by the SuD. Jointly, the environment assumptions and the SuD design must be sufficient to show that the desired properties E of the composite system emerge:

A and S entail E

In this book I call this the *system engineering argument.* It is an argument that the composite system has been implemented correctly. The difference with the usual

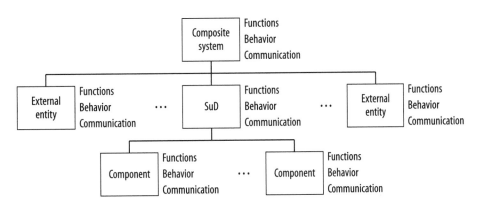

Figure 1 The structuring principle of this book. The System under Development (SuD) is part of an aggregation hierarchy of systems. At every level in this aggregation hierarchy, systems provide services to their environment. These services have behavior and engage in communication.

correctness argument is that the external entities are not designed by the designer. Desired emergent properties not ensured by the external entities cannot be achieved by changing these entities. Given that the external entities are what they are, the desired emergent properties E must be ensured by an appropriate design of the SuD.

The diagram also shows that the SuD can be decomposed into subsystems. At this level, too, the designer may want to give a correctness argument that the subsystems jointly produce the desired properties of the SuD. The techniques used in this book all help in some way to describe the assumptions about the environment, the desired properties of the SuD, and the decomposition of the SuD.

Formality and Precision

The book describes a collection of techniques that range from essentially informal to possibly formal. For example, the mission statement of a system is an essentially informal description of the desired functionality of the system at a high level of abstraction. At the other extreme, an event list of a system is a behavior description that may be informal, but that the designer can formalize if he or she wishes to do so. This book describes the semantic options involved in a formalization of behavior and communication description techniques without choosing a particular formalization. But more important than formalization is *precision:* The expression of what is intended without using redundant words. This book attempts to be as precise as possible without being formal.

Structure of the Book

The book is structured as follows (see Figure 1).

Part I. Reactive System Design. This part explains the concept of a reactive system in more detail and discusses the structure of the environment and the role of the environment in reactive-system behavior. It also explains the framework of Figure 1 in more detail.

Part II. Function Notations. This part discusses notations for describing the functions provided by a system: mission statement, function refinement tree, and service descriptions. These techniques are essentially informal. As shown in Figure 1, we can use function notations at every level in the aggregation hierarchy from the business level down to the detailed software object level.

Part III. Entity Notations. This part discusses entity-relationship diagrams as notations to declare the types of entities in the environment about which the system communicates with its environment. This is very useful as a documentation technique of the meaning of the data that cross the system interface.

Part IV. Behavior Notations. This part introduces state transition tables and diagrams, including statecharts, to describe system behavior. These notations can be used informally, but they can also be formalized. We can use them at every level of the aggregation hierarchy. Formalized versions of the notations tend to be more useful at lower levels of the hierarchy.

Part V. Communication Notations. This part introduces data flow diagrams and communication diagrams to describe communications between systems. Again, they can be used informally, but they can also be formalized. Here too, formalized versions of the notation are more useful at lower levels of the aggregation hierarchy.

Part VI. Software Specification Methods. In this part we look at three methods that use the techniques described on foregoing chapters and then give a bird's-eye view of all these techniques in our design framework.

◆ Postmodern Structured Analysis (PSA) is a mix of Yourdon-style structured analysis with elements of Jackson System Development and object-oriented analysis.

◆ Statemate is a formalized version of structured analysis with an executable modeling tool.

◆ The Unified Modeling Language (UML) is the industry attempt to produce a standard object-oriented software design notation.

We combine all these notations in a design approach called NYAM (Not Yet Another Method) that allows the flyweight to heavyweight use of the notations.

The book includes seven case studies. Four of these appear in the Appendices. The others are smaller and appear in the exercises included at the end of the chapters. Three additional case studies are available at the book's Web site (*www.mkp.com/dmrs*). Most chapters end with questions for rehearsal, exercises, and questions for discussion. Answers to selected exercises and questions appear in Appendix E. (Part of Appendix E appears in the book you are reading now; the rest is available at the book's Web site, *www.mkp.com/dmrs.*) The book includes a glossary and an index in which the number of the page where a term is defined is printed in **bold.**

Audience

The book has two intended audiences. The first audience consists of computer science and software engineering students, who can use this as part of an advanced course on system modeling and design. Although no knowledge of the techniques is presupposed, the effect of reading the text is greatly enhanced if the student has already taken an introductory course covering one or more of these topics: entity-relationship modeling, data flow modeling, and object-oriented analysis. My experience with this text shows that students need to do practical assignments using this material in order to fully understand the meaning and use of the notations treated in the book. However, experience also shows that students start by reading as little as possible and see how far they can get by just glancing at the diagrams. Reading instructions for the hasty student are given in the next section.

For teachers, the book's Web site (*www.mkp.com/dmrs*) contains slides that can be used in the classroom. A password for access to the slides can be acquired from *textbook@elsevier.com*.

The second audience for which this book is intended consists of practicing software and information system engineers, who have encountered some of these techniques in their work practice. This book should enhance their understanding of these techniques and it should extend their repertoire of design guidelines. Readers in this audience are pressed for time and are likely to use this book as a reference manual.

How to Read the Book

A quick way of getting acquaintanced with the book for both groups of readers is to read the half-page introduction to every part and to the Appendices. This should take about ten minutes and it will give the reader a top-level view of its contents. More specific reading instructions follow.

For the hasty student: More thoroughly, you can start reading the book from the beginning. Read sequentially until you get bored with the current part and then skip ahead to the next part, or read until you get bored with the current chapter and skip ahead to the next chapter. This sequential-jump reading process should work for the hasty student. If you really want to bug yourself, do the exercises and check to see if you agree with my answers. And you may discuss the questions for discussion with your colleagues. I have included my answers to them too.

For the hasty professional: As an alternative to reading in sequential jumps, you can use the book as a reference manual of notations and guidelines. If you want to read the book this way, you are probably already familiar with many of the notations described in it and this book should add to your understanding of the notations. Read Part I to become familiar with the design approach of this book. Then read the very brief Chapter 23 to get a bird's-eye view of the techniques discussed in the book. Then refer to the technique chapters if and when you need them.

I should add a warning for the experienced reader: The book contains many new concepts and explains known concepts in a new way. Expect to encounter unexpected relationships between concepts you already know, to view concepts you already know in a new light, and to discover new consequences of things you know. Even if you disagree with my appoach, I hope you will gain new insights from it.

Chapters on guidelines indicate each guideline with a tick $\sqrt{}$. To facilitate the book's use as a reference manual, I have tried to make the chapters on diagram techniques self-contained. Guidelines for one technique can be used without referring to chapters on other techniques. By using the table of contents and the index, you should be able to quickly find the information that you need. All diagrams in the book can be drawn using the diagram editing tool TCM, available at *www.cs.utwente.nl/~tcm*.

Acknowledgements

The book has benefited from discussions with many people. David Harel, Daniel Jackson, and the anonymous reviewers gave very useful comments on an earlier version of the text, which led to a fundamental restructuring of the contents. Michael Jackson has been an agreeable sparring partner for years, ready to disagree with ideas that could not withstand his analytic acumen and always stimulating me to improve my ideas where possible. Felix Bachmann gave very useful comments on all parts of the text. Anthony Hall commented on Part I of the book. Maarten Fokkinga used parts of the text for his course and pointed out numerous difficulties that I had overlooked. David Jansen and Rik Eshuis managed to read and understand many of my earlier versions, and by applying them to case studies showed me what I should have written. Erik Meffert hunted for bugs in my answers to the questions and exercises. A previous version of the text has been read and commented on by Samuil Angelov, Henk Blanken, Rik Eshuis, Maarten Fokkinga, Paul Grefen, Jin-Min Hu, David Jansen, Jan Kuper, Ying-Lie O, and Dulce Pumareja. Their help is gratefully acknowledged. Any remaining errors are, of course, mine.

As any author knows, the revision of a text does not stop when its "final" version is sent to the publisher. Writing a book is like gardening: A never-ending process of removing weeds and of moving plants to various places, where they look better and where you expect them to grow better. My hope is that the ideas in this book will grow in your mind and bear fruit in your practice.

Tim Cox of Morgan Kaufmann imposed an impossible page limit on me, for which the reader should probably thank him. He also imposed a firm deadline, for which my family thanks him.

Dusty Friedman, Julie Nemer, and Margaret Murphy transformed my manuscript into a book at the speed of light—ruining all fax machines at my department. Thanks are due to them for the high quality of the text, graphics, and layout of the book.

The fine balance maintained in my environment between leisure and work—or shall I say love and will—is not due to me but to my partner in life Mieke Poelman, and this is more than I can ever thank her for.

Reactive System Design

Part I introduces the design concepts used in all chapters.

- ◆ Chapter 1. I define reactive systems as systems that, when switched on, are able to create desirable effects in their environment by responding to events.

- ◆ Chapter 2. The environment is structured into subject and connection domains. The subject domain is the part of the world that the system communicates *about;* a connection domain is a part of the world that the system communicates *with*. Subject and connection domains may overlap.

- ◆ Chapter 3. I analyze the structure of the chain of events from an external event to a system stimulus and from the system response to the desired effect in the environment. Examples are given of environment assumptions that we need in order to argue that the stimulus-response behavior of the system will indeed lead to the desired emergent behavior of the composite system.

- ◆ Chapter 4. I distinguish external system properties from system decomposition and partitions system properties into functional properties, quality properties, and other properties. Functional properties are partitioned into desired services, behavior, and communication of the system. This classification of properties provides the primary structuring principle of the book.

CHAPTER 1

Reactive Systems

T his chapter gives examples of reactive systems and contrasts them to transformational systems, listing the characteristics that divide reactive systems from transformational systems. The chapter also lists the four case studies that appear in many examples and describes the three additional case examples that are used in many exercises throughout the book.

1.1 Examples of Reactive Systems

In order to drive home the idea that reactive systems form a very wide class of systems, I start by listing a number of examples of reactive systems, beginning with the usual examples of real-time systems and ending with the not-so-usual examples of e-commerce systems.

A **real-time system** is a system in which the correctness of a response depends on the time at which the response is produced. The response does not consist merely of the production of some output but consists of the production of output at a particular time. The same output produced at the wrong time is an incorrect response. For example, when elevator doors open and nobody enters for 10 seconds, then the doors must close. So the system responds to a timeout by closing its doors. The same output produced at another time—say 5 minutes after the door is opened—is not just inconvenient, it is an incorrect response. Or suppose a controller of a heating tank in a fruit-juice-production plant should switch off a heater within 1 second after a certain high temperature is detected. Switching the heater off at another time would be incorrect. It could lead to a bad juice product, and it might even lead to a disaster.

Often, real-time systems operate under very short time constraints, but this is not always so. Suppose that 1 month before a course starts, a course management system must send a reminder to the course coordinator that it is time to prepare for the next course. The same message sent at the wrong time—say 1 day before the course starts—is a wrong response. Or suppose a salary administration must initiate salary payments on the 25th of every month. The same action initiated on another date would be incorrect or even illegal.

Many real-time systems are **safety-critical.** A safety-critical system is a system whose malfunctioning could lead to loss of life or property. Safety-critical real-time systems that produce output too late may cause harm to their environment; for example, a heart-monitoring system is a safety-critical real-time system.

Some real-time software is **embedded** in hardware systems, such as software embedded in telephones, televisions, and elevator controllers. This usually means that in addition to short real-time demands, there are very stringent space restrictions on the implementation of this software.

Real-time systems are often **control systems,** systems that enforce desirable behavior on their environment. Examples are cruise control, elevator control, and heating-tank control systems. Control systems may also try to direct human affairs. Course management systems and salary administration systems are examples. Another example is a controller for a compact dynamic bus station. Such a bus station consists of a few platforms to which approaching buses are allocated dynamically. An automated control system of such a station must sense the approach of buses, perform the allocation, and then inform the bus driver and the waiting passengers at which platform the bus should park. Of course, bus drivers may refuse to follow instructions and passengers may wander off to other platforms; nevertheless, this system has the basic functionality that any control system has: monitoring events in its environment and sending commands to its environment.

An important class of information-intensive applications with some control functionality consists of **enterprise resource planning** (ERP) systems. These systems provide an integrated set of services to plan the resources needed during a production process. They must register events that occur in the production process and recommend production schedules and may even order necessary parts from suppliers connected to the manufacturer through a computer network. An ERP system thus directs affairs in its environment just as the other systems mentioned do.

Turning to information factories such as banks and insurance companies, **workflow management systems** monitor tasks to be performed in an organization and allocate these tasks to employees working in the organization. In doing this, they enforce a certain life cycle on these tasks. Again, this contains an element of control.

Another example is a **groupware system,** which is a system that provides a distributed infrastructure for cooperation among people that may work at different places and at different times. All groupware systems provide a communication infrastructure. Some groupware systems enforce a certain structure on the dialogs between people, which is again an element of control. Other groupware systems provide videoconferencing facilities, which adds a strong element of real-time functionality.

Yet another class of information-intensive systems that also perform some control consists of **e-commerce** systems. An electronic auctioning system provides a distributed infrastructure in which consumers can meet one another and trade goods, negotiating prices. The electronic auction takes place according to a certain protocol, which imposes a certain behavior on the participants. As another example, business-to-business e-commerce allows businesses to announce their services, find matching partners, and settle on a contract—again a strongly event-driven behavior-intensive activity.

Classic Electronic Data Interchange (EDI) systems provide yet another class of example. It provides the infrastructure for structured data exchange between the organizations. An interesting feature of EDI and e-commerce systems is that parts of social reality, such as requests, promises, offers, payment obligations, and money, are implemented in computers. These systems participate actively in the construction of part of social reality, and they perform some control over their environment.

These examples illustrate that it is not useful to continue thinking in terms of the classic opposition between information systems and control systems. Reactive systems may exert control over their environment, but they also may provide information, facilitate behavior, prevent behavior, facilitate communication, and do many other things. The examples show that a continuous spectrum of types of reactive systems exists that, to varying degrees, can be more or less complex along the following dimensions:

◆ Data complexity

◆ Behavior complexity

◆ Communication complexity

Consequently, a reactive system designer may need specification and design techniques for all of these dimensions.

1.2 Reactive versus Transformational Systems

What divides the examples discussed so far is complexity along the dimensions of data, behavior, and communication; more important from our point of view is what binds together all these examples—that they are **reactive systems.** A reactive system is a system that, when switched on, is able to create desired effects in its environment by enabling, enforcing, or preventing events in the environment. For example, real-time, embedded, and control systems are reactive systems because, when they are switched on, they enforce a certain desirable behavior on their environment. Information systems, groupware systems, workflow management systems, ERP systems, e-commerce systems, and EDI systems are reactive too because they provide desired information and enable communication and collaboration between people or organizations in their environment. Other examples of reactive systems are word processors and operating systems. Reactive systems have a number of characteristics (Figure 1.1):

◆ The system is in continuous interaction with its environment.

◆ The process by which the reactive system interacts with its environment is usually nonterminating. If a reactive system terminates during its availability time, this is usually considered a failure.

◆ In its interaction with the environment, the system will respond to external stimuli as and when they occur. The system must therefore be able to respond to interrupts, even when it is doing something else.

Reactive system	Transformational system
Highly interactive	May interact to collect more input
Nonterminating process	Terminating process
Interrupt-driven	Not interrupt-driven
State-dependent response	Output not state-dependent
Environment-oriented response	Output not defined in terms of environment
Parallel processes	Sequential process
Usually, stringent real-time requirements	Usually, no stringent real-time requirements

Figure 1.1 Characteristics of reactive and transformational systems.

◆ The response of a reactive system depends on its current state and the external event that it responds to. The response may leave the system in a different state than it was before.

◆ The response consists of enabling, enforcing, or prohibiting communication or behavior in its environment.

◆ The behavior of a reactive system consists often of a number of interacting processes that operate in parallel.

◆ Often a reactive system must operate in real time and is under stringent time requirements.

Although reactive systems may provide functionality ranging from control to information provision and communication, they all engage in stimulus-response behavior. Depending on the functionality of the system, a designer of a reactive system may need various techniques for specifying data, behavior, or communication, but in all cases he or she will need techniques for specifying stimulus-response behavior.

Reactive systems can be contrasted with **transformational systems,** which exist to transform an input into an output. Compilers, assemblers, and routines in a library of mathematical functions are transformational systems. The execution of a database query can also be viewed as a transformational system; the query execution maps a query and a database state into a set of data. The entire database server, however, is reactive because it exists to allow its environment to ask queries. A diagnostic expert system is a transformational system; it may enter an interactive dialog to acquire all relevant data about a malfunctioning machine, but when all data are provided, the expert system will produce its diagnosis as output, after which it is finished.

Transformational systems have a number of characteristics:

◆ When a transformational system computes output, it may interact with its environment, but this is only to acquire sufficient information to produce its output and not to maintain a state of affairs in its environment.

◆ A transformational system produces an output and then terminates. If it does not terminate, this is considered a failure.

◆ A transformational system's computations are not interrupt-driven.

- A transformational system has no state that is relevant for external entities. When an external entity sends it an input, it will produce an output that depends only on that input.
- A transformational system's output is defined in terms of its input and not in terms of its meaning for the environment.
- A transformational system's external, observable behavior is sequential. It does not consist of a number of parallel processes.
- Transformational systems usually need not satisfy real-time requirements.

Methods for the design of transformational systems must specify the transformation to be computed by the system, the logical structure of the input and output data, and the algorithm that computes the transformation. The behavior and structure of the environment is not particularly important for these systems. They will perform the same transformation in different environments. A widely used design approach for transformational systems is, therefore, functional decomposition, a method by which external functionality is mapped to internal components of the system.

By contrast, reactive systems are in close interaction with their environment. Design methods for reactive systems must contain techniques to describe the environment and the structure of the interaction with the environment. Functional decomposition is not the only nor the most important design approach for reactive systems; the structure of the environment is at least as important (see Chapter 2).

1.3 Four Case Studies and Three Examples

I use many examples of reactive systems in this book. Four case studies are worked out in Appendices A–D and fragments of these cases are used frequently throughout the book. I introduce these case studies briefly here.

Case study 1: A Training Information System (TIS) for a company, which is used to support the coordination of training courses that the company gives to newly hired employees every month.

Case study 2: An Electronic Ticket System (ETS), which is a software system used by railway travelers to buy tickets. The software is to run on a smartcard when it is inserted in a Personal Digital Assistant (PDA).

Case study 3: A heating controller for a heating tank in a fruit juice plant. The task of the controller is to heat a heating tank filled with juice according to a recipe.

Case study 4: An elevator control system that coordinates the movements of two elevator cages that serve 10 floors. The controller also indicates the location and direction of elevators.

The exercises that appear in many chapters use three additional case examples. For ease of reference, I give the full descriptions here; refer to these descriptions when you need them. (The sources for all these cases and examples are given in the Bibliographic Remarks.)

1. The packaging department of a tea company boxes tea bags in fully automated packaging cells. The tea bags arrive on a conveyor belt and then drop onto a balance, which weighs the bag. A robot arm picks up the bag from the balance and, if the bag's weight is inside a certain interval, it puts the bag in a box. If the weight is outside the interval, it puts it in a separate container. If the box is full, the conveyor belt is stopped and the robot arm replaces the full box with an empty one. After the box is changed, the belt is started again. The device interfaces are as follows. The conveyor belt accepts start belt and stop belt commands. The balance sends a tea bag weight message to the controller when a tea bag drops onto it. The robot arm accepts the commands remove tea bag and put in box and responds to these with a tea bag moved signal, and it accepts a replace box command and responds to this with a box replaced signal. There is an operator that can set the desired weight of the tea bags and the required number of bags in a box. Starting and stopping the packaging cell is outside the scope of the controller. You are to design the software that controls the robot arm and interfaces with the operator. The robot arm has a processor, and the operator has a workstation.

2. A software company needs a bug-tracking database system that allows management to track the status of the bugs in the programs they sell. The workflow of bug handling is as follows. After a bug has been identified, a bug manager assigns the bug to a fixer and to a tester. After the fixer has proposed a fix, the tester tests it. If the fix is found to be incorrect, a problem report is returned to the fixer. If the fix is found to be correct, the bug is reported fixed to the bug manager, who then releases the fix. The desired system tracks the status of a bug and informs the programmers and the bug manager assigned to it of the relevant changes in status by sending emails. There is already an email system in place that can be used for this.

3. In a large chemical company, scientists often need containers for chemicals. Because no one knows where in the company these containers are located, they order new ones from vendors, causing a lot of waste. A solution to this problem is to use a Chemical Tracking System (CTS). This is a software system that allows scientists to request containers of chemicals to be supplied by the chemical stockroom or by vendors. The location of every chemical container within the company, the quantity of the material remaining in it, and the complete history of each container's locations and use is known by the system at all times. The company will save 25% on chemical costs by fully exploiting chemicals already available within the company, by disposing of fewer partially used or expired containers, and by using a standard chemical purchasing process that reduces purchasing costs. The system is able to order chemicals from vendors using an Internet connection. To speed up operations, it gathers up-to-date information from online catalogs of vendors every night and scientists are allowed to purchase chemicals through the system directly, provided that a standard purchasing procedure is followed. When a purchased chemical arrives, it is registered in the system by the stockroom and then put in its desired location. The company administration can also generate all reports that comply with government regulations concerning chemical use, storage, and disposal. The initialization and maintenance of the system are done by the data-processing department.

1.4 SUMMARY

Reactive systems perform state-based nonterminating processes that are interrupt-driven and that interact with the environment in order to enable, enforce, or prevent certain behavior in the environment. They may be subject to stringent real-time requirements and often perform several processes in parallel. Reactive systems may or may not need to handle large volumes of data, engage in complex behavior, or engage in many communications. Different reactive systems have different complexities along these dimensions and consequently different specification techniques are needed to design them. But in all cases, a reactive system designer needs techniques to specify stimulus-response behavior.

Transformational systems perform terminating computations that, when terminated, do not leave the system in a significant state. Functional decomposition is a good design approach for transformational systems. Reactive systems, on the other hand, must be designed from the structure of the environment as well as from the desired system functionality.

1.5 QUESTIONS AND EXERCISES

QUESTIONS FOR REHEARSAL

1. Define the following concepts:

Reactive system

Transformational system

Give examples of these systems from your environment.

QUESTIONS FOR DISCUSSION

2. Which characteristics of reactive systems (Figure 1.1) are present in the tea-bag-boxing controller?

3. Which characteristics of reactive systems (Figure 1.1) are present in the bug-fixing database?

CHAPTER 2

The Environment

Henceforth, we call the reactive system to be developed the **system under development** (SuD). We use this term even for the finished system—when development is finished. When a finished SuD is installed, it is embedded in a network of communicating entities, with which it interacts (Figure 2.1). The network includes devices, operators, maintenance personnel, users, software systems, and other kinds of entities. Ultimately, it includes the whole world, but in practice only a few entities in its immediate environment are relevant for the operation of the system. In this chapter, we look at ways to bound and structure the environment. In Section 2.1, external interactions of a reactive system are viewed as linguistic messages that have a subject and a function and that travel through a communication channel. These three aspects are elaborated in the sections that follow: Section 2.2 introduces the concept of domain, Section 2.3 analyzes the concept of subject domain (the domain consisting of the subjects of messages sent or received by the system), Section 2.4 analyzes the functions that a reactive system can have with respect to a domain, and Section 2.5 discusses the role of a connection domain as communication channel through which messages about the subject domain arrive at or leave from the system.

2.1 External Interactions

To identify the part of the world that is relevant as system environment, it is useful to apply the metaphor that the system exchanges messages with its environment. The term "message" here does not refer to messages passed between objects in an object-oriented software system but refers to linguistic messages passed between the system and its environment. For example, a workflow system communicates with its environment by means of messages about tasks to be performed and actors to perform them, and an elevator control system communicates with its environment by means of messages about passenger requests and elevator arrivals. To completely

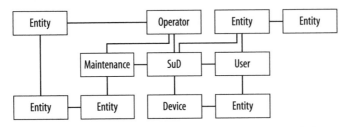

Figure 2.1 The system under development (SuD) is embedded in a network of communicating entities, such as operators, devices, and maintenance personnel.

abstract from the technology used in these message exchanges, imagine that these messages are written on Post-It notes—so external system behavior consists of exchanging Post-It notes with the environment. What can we say about these communications?

◆ The message on each note has a **subject domain,** which is the part of the world that the message is about. Usually, this is the subject of the message. For example, the message "up button pushed on floor 3" received by an elevator controller has as its subject domain the up button on floor 3. If we consider a sequence of messages that form a discourse between the system and its environment, then the subject domain is the topic of the discourse; another term for subject domain that is frequently used is Universe of Discourse.

◆ Each message has a **function** for the sender and receiver. The vast majority of messages received by a reactive system are observations of and queries about the subject domain. The vast majority of messages sent by the reactive system to its environment are confirmations of messages received; answers to queries; or commands, instructions, or recommendations that refer in some way to the subject domain.

◆ Each message has a sender and a receiver. One of these is the system; the other is some entity in the environment. Each message has a communication channel, which is the path through which the Post-It note travels from the sender to the receiver. Sometimes, the note is given directly by the sender to the receiver, in which case we can abstract from the communication channel. In other cases, the communication channel is significant because in it messages may be delayed, lost, or transformed into a format more convenient for the receiver. In these cases, the communication channel is modeled explicitly as a **connection domain.**

Figure 2.2 gives a number of examples. Note that the functions listed in the last column are the functions of the messages, not of the sending or receiving entities. However, one of the communicating parties is the SuD, and it always is the function of the SuD to make these message exchanges possible. We can therefore say that the **function of a reactive system** is the sum of the functions that these messages have for the environment.

Message	Sender	Receiver	Subject domain	Function
"New employee hired"	Personnel officer	Personnel information system	Employee	Observation of subject domain
"Give list of employees with 25 years of service"	Personnel officer	Personnel information system	Employees	Query about subject domain
"These employees have 25 years of service"	Personnel information system	Personnel officer	Employees	Answer to query about subject domain
"Claim received"	Mail department	Insurance claim workflow system	Insurance claims	Observation of subject domain
"Claim to be handled by some actor in class *a*"	Insurance claim workflow system	All actors in class *a*	Claims, actors	Instruction to subject domain
"Pulse rate is *n*"	Heart monitoring system	Nurse	Patient's heart pulse rate	Observation of subject domain
"Move down"	Elevator controller	Elevator motor	Elevator motor	Instruction to motor
"Up button pushed on floor 3"	Up button on floor 3	Elevator controller	Up button on floor 3	Observation of subject domain

Figure 2.2 Messages and their senders, receivers, subject domains, and functions.

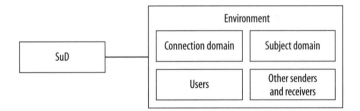

Figure 2.3 Domains found in the environment of a reactive system.

Similarly, the subjects listed in the Subject Domain column are the subjects of these messages, not of the SuD. But because it is the function of the SuD to communicate with its environment about the subject domain, the sum of subject domains of all possible messages exchanged by a reactive system and its environment is called the **subject domain of the reactive system.**

In general, the environment of a system contains various subject and connection domains (Figure 2.3). In the following sections, we explore the concept of subject domain, system functionality, and connection domain.

2.2 **Domains**

Domains are the top-level structuring mechanisms of the environment. In this book, a **domain** is a part of the world that it is for the purposes of the design process convenient to treat as a whole. A domain consists of entities and events that are subject to particular laws of nature and to particular norms and standards. It is often the subject of a particular knowledge area. You might find books about a domain written for professionals, and there is often particular jargon for a domain. If you write the definitions of words describing a domain, there will be more mutual references among the definitions of words pertaining to one domain than references to the definitions of words pertaining to a different domain. Finally, entities within a domain often have more interactions with one another than with entities in other domains, and these interactions often result in a coherent overall behavior.

The domains listed in Figure 2.2 all illustrate these characteristics. The subject domain of a personnel information system consists of the employees of a company and relevant events such as hirings, firings, and promotions. These are subject to particular norms and standards as laid down in labor agreements, contracts, law, and company policies. They are the subject of the professional knowledge of personnel officers. A company dictionary defining all important words for the company would contain a separate section pertaining to employee terminology.

To give one further example, the subject domain of an elevator control system consists of buttons, motors, doors, sensors, and so on and of significant events such as the event that a button is pushed, a motor starts, and a door opens. These entities and events are subject to particular norms and standards as laid down in technical documentation. The entities have more interactions with one another than with other entities, and these interactions result in a coherent overall behavior. There are books written about how to coordinate the entities and events to achieve coherent overall elevator behavior.

2.3 **The Subject Domain**

The subject domain of a reactive system is the union of the subject domains of all messages that cross its external interface. To find out what the subject domain of a system is, ask which entities and events the messages sent and received by the system are about. To count as elements of the subject domain, these entities and events must be identifiable by the system (see Chapter 9).

Looking at various kinds of reactive systems, we find a wide variety of kinds of subject domains. To understand reactive system behavior, it is useful to distinguish three kinds of entities that can occur in a subject domain:

◆ Physical entities, such as devices and natural objects, including people

◆ Conceptual entities, such as organizations, promises, and holiday rights

◆ Lexical entities, such as contracts and specifications

This list is not exhaustive, nor are these kinds of entities disjoint.

2.3.1 *Physical Entities*

Physical entities are entities that have a mass and a location in real space. Figure 2.4 shows a fully physical subject domain. The SuD is a heating controller of a heating

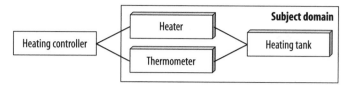

Figure 2.4 A physical subject domain (lines represent communication channels).

tank in a production plant that receives messages from a thermometer and sends messages to a heater, both of which are connected to a heating tank. The lines in the diagram represent connections and do not indicate in which direction messages pass. It is very clear where the subject domain entities exist—in the production plant. You can go there and see them. Note that the system communicates about the subject domain by exchanging messages with some entities in the environment, which may or may not be part of the subject domain. The heater and thermometer act as communication channels between the heating tank and the controller, but, at the same time, if the controller is at all concerned with the reliability of this communication channel, they are part of the subject domain. Some of the messages that are received and sent by the controller are about the heater and thermometer themselves, for example, "Are you still switched on?" and "I seem to have a problem."

2.3.2 Conceptual Entities

A **conceptual entity** is a nonphysical entity that people use to structure their world. Examples are rights, obligations, permissions, prohibitions, claims, and contracts. In addition, a social domain contains conceptual entities such as committees, companies, government bodies, and labor unions. These and many other socially constructed entities are physically invisible but socially very real. Finally, people can play socially defined roles, such as employee, operator, or client. These roles too can be viewed as socially constructed conceptual entities used by people to structure their world.

Workflow systems, groupware systems, EDI systems, and e-commerce systems are used in a social setting. Figure 2.5 presents a typical situation in which we see a mix of people, conceptual entities, and lexical items in the subject domain. The SuD is a personnel information system that receives and sends messages about employees, employee contracts, and the rights and obligations of employees as described by the contract. The system exchanges messages with employee department personnel, and these messages are about employees, their rights and obligations, and their contracts. The system may, for example, be able to answer questions about the right of an employee to take a vacation.

The employee is a person, so we have a social subject domain. The rights and obligations of an employee, on the other hand, are conceptual entities, and so the domain is also partly conceptual. Conceptual entities are invisible. If you enter the

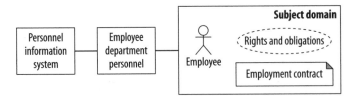

Figure 2.5 A social and conceptual subject domain.

company building and search through all rooms, there is no room in which you will observe a right or obligation. You can see people, chairs, desks and the central heating system, but the rights and obligations are invisible conceptual entities.

But even though conceptual entities are invisible, they are shared among the people in the domain. We share the concepts of the right to vacations, salary, employment, bank account, book-return obligation, production plan, flight plan, insurance, damage claim, and the other zillions of invisible entities that we talk about daily. Modeling a social subject domain always involves modeling these invisible conceptual entities.

Conceptual entities come with **conceptual events,** which are just as nonphysical and invisible. Vacation rights are built up and used, salaries are paid, and obligations are violated or fulfilled. These events too are socially defined constructs that people use to structure their world.

2.3.3 *Lexical Entities*

While walking around in a company building searching for physically visible entities, we see many pieces of paper. One of these may be a copy of the employment contract of an employee, which contains a description of the rights and obligations of the employee. This description is useful evidence that the invisible rights and obligations of the employee exist. It may, for example, describe the rights to vacations and other benefits. The text on this piece of paper is a **lexical item,** by which I mean a physical symbol occurrence. (The lexical item has a complex structure, but this does not concern us here.) The paper and ink are physical, but these are the least important aspects of the lexical item. What is important is the meaning convention by which the contract refers to rights and obligations that are themselves invisible. These meaning conventions should be known to all contract partners. Among others, these conventions ensure that a signed paper contract is an important piece of evidence that these rights and obligations exist.

Lexical items can be copied, and one of the contract copies may be stored in the information system to be manipulated there. In that case, the subject of some of the messages entering and leaving the system is a lexical item stored in the system! This situation is represented in Figure 2.6—there are several copies of the lexical item, and one of them is stored in the SuD. Like all other copies of a lexical item, we can use the copy of the contract in an SuD as evidence that some individual conceptual structure of rights and obligations exists.

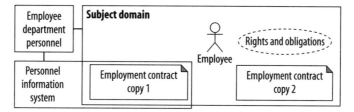

Figure 2.6 A lexical subject domain entity stored in a computer.

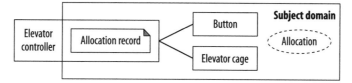

Figure 2.7 A conceptual subject domain entity in a control application.

Conceptual entities can be found even in predominantly physical domains. For example, the subject domain of an elevator controller consists of buttons, elevator cages, and other physical entities (Figure 2.7). There is one conceptual entity in its subject domain—the allocation of a request to an elevator cage. When a request button is pushed, this request is allocated to an elevator cage, which is then to serve this request. The allocation is performed by the controller itself, and the evidence used by the controller that the allocation exists is a record stored in the controller itself. Here are some more examples of domains in which we can find conceptual entities that are represented by lexical entities in the system:

Workflow management systems: Allocation of work to actors.

Groupware systems: Distribution of messages, files, pictures or other kinds of lexical items to a number of participants.

EDI and e-commerce systems: Creation and manipulation of lexical items that represent orders, requests, confirmations, promises, payments, and so on.

Lexical entities can be used to make some invisible conceptual entity observable in the physical world. As we have seen, one possible reason to do this is to provide evidence of the existence of some conceptual entity. Other reasons may be to simply observe or manipulate the item. For example, an editor makes lexical items observable and manipulable (Figure 2.8). There may be several copies of the lexical item, but the ones stored in a computer are considerably more convenient to change than the copies stored on paper. Messages exchanged between the editor and the user are not about the paper copy but about the copy stored in the computer. This is an example of a case in which the entire subject domain is stored in the system itself.

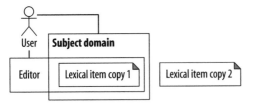

Figure 2.8 A lexical item constructed by the system.

2.4 The Functions of Reactive Systems

The examples given illustrate that the subject domain of a system is closely related to the functionality of the system. This is because the messages that enter or leave the system have a certain function with respect to the subject domain. To paint a very broad picture, we can say that a reactive system can have three kinds of functions:

Informative: To answer questions, produce reports, or otherwise provide information about the subject domain.

Directive: To control, guide, or otherwise direct its subject domain.

Manipulative: To create, change, or otherwise manipulate lexical items in the subject domain.

An informative function does not try to direct the behavior of the subject domain. Typically, the system receives a message about the subject domain from a sender that may or may not be part of the subject domain and responds to that same sender. The message is usually a query or update request, and the response is an answer or update confirmation. In other applications, the message is forwarded to other destinations. We have previously seen that an important use of this function is to provide evidence that some invisible conceptual entity exists or that some invisible conceptual event has occurred.

A directive function constrains or otherwise influences the subject domain. Often the sender of the message and the receiver of the response are different entities in the subject domain itself. Other possible sources and destinations of messages are a system operator and a system client (such as an elevator passenger), who are not in the subject domain. They may, for example, send messages to the system that lead to directives sent to subject domain entities.

A manipulative function constructs and maintains a domain of lexical items. These represent conceptual entities such as texts, graphs, contracts, promises, orders, rights, and obligations. The subject domain of the system consists at least of the constructed lexical items, but may also include the entities that these items refer to (Figure 2.6). The source of the messages about the subject domain is some entity in the environment, such as a system user, and the response is usually an update of the constructed lexical items plus a feedback to the source and possibly to other external entities. As we have seen, the manipulated lexical domain entities are part of the SuD itself.

2.5 **The Connection Domain**

Messages arrive at the system interface from various sources, and they are sent to various destinations. These sources and destinations may be inside or outside the subject domain. Figure 2.9 shows a document circulation system that communicates with entities inside the subject domain (publishers and library members) and outside the subject domain (the librarian). All communications are about subject domain entities such as documents, library members, and publishers. The communication channel with the subject domain introduces delays and potential errors that are significant enough to model the channel explicitly as a connection domain. The communication channel with the librarian is considered reliable and fast enough to abstract from.

The reasons to include a connection domain in your environment model are that the communication channel through which messages pass from source to destination may introduce delays and errors or be subject to important assumptions made by the SuD. Because the communication channel may fail these assumptions and, as a result of this, SuD behavior would be unable to satisfy its requirements, we include the channel in the model as the connection domain.

Figure 2.10 shows a system connected directly to its subject domain. An elevator controller receives messages about events in the life of, among others, buttons and arrival sensors and sends messages to its environment about, among others, motors, doors, and direction indicators. For example, it may receive a message push from button b, and it may send a message start up to motor m. The controller communicates with the subject domain about the subject domain. The communication channel, consisting of wires and registers connecting the controller to its subject domain, is considered reliable and fast enough to abstract from.

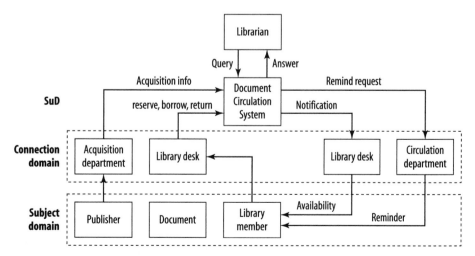

Figure 2.9 A system connected to its subject domain through a connection domain (arrows represent the flow of messages).

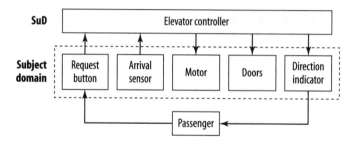

Figure 2.10 A system directly connected to its subject domain (arrows represent message flow).

2.6 SUMMARY

A reactive system exchanges messages with its environment. To abstract from the mechanism of this message exchange, imagine that these messages are exchanged by means of Post-It notes. Each message has a sender and a receiver, one of which is the system and the other of which is some entity in the environment. It also has a communication channel, a subject domain, and a function for the environment.

◆ The subject domain of the message is the part of the environment about which the message gives some information.

◆ The communication channel may introduce significant delays or unreliability, or it may be subject to important assumptions needed by the SuD to fulfill its function. In these cases, it is useful to include the channel in the environment model as a connection domain.

◆ A reactive system that has an informative function provides information about the subject domain. One that has a directive function directs behavior in the subject domain. A reactive system with a manipulative function stores and manipulates lexical items that are part of the subject domain.

The subject domain may consist of physical entities, people, concepts, and lexical items. An important function of lexical items is to make symbolic structure visible. A manipulative system can store and manipulate lexical items.

2.7 QUESTIONS AND EXERCISES

QUESTIONS FOR REHEARSAL

1. Define the following concepts:
   Subject domain
   Lexical item
   Connection domain

2. Can the subject domain of a single interaction be different from the subject domain of the entire system?

3. Can a connection domain of a system be part of the subject domain of that same system?

4. Can the subject domains of the messages sent and received by a system overlap? If yes, give an example; if no, explain why.

5. Explain why a system can contain part of its subject domain.

6. Reactive systems may offer a mix of two or three of the basic kinds of functions—informative, directive, and manipulative. Describe the mix for each of the three example systems:

   ◆ The tea-bag-boxing system
   ◆ The bug-fixing support system
   ◆ The chemical tracking system

QUESTIONS FOR DISCUSSION

7. The subject domain of a reactive system changes when we add functions to or delete functions from the system. Explain this and give an example of each.

8. Identify the subject domains of the following systems, as well as the communication channel by which messages travel between the system and the subject domains. There are usually several possible valid answers, so motivate the answer you have chosen.

   a) An elevator control system
   b) A cruise-control system in a car
   c) A personnel information system
   d) A word processing system
   e) The bank where you have your current account
   f) The account database of your bank
   g) An online bookstore
   h) A supermarket
   i) An EDI system that connects a supermarket with suppliers of diary products
   j) A Web search engine

9. Can the subject domain of company be the same as that of an information system owned by the company?

10. A **workflow management system** (WFMS) monitors and controls the flow of work through an organization. It allocates work to people, makes the relevant applications available, and monitors the progress of a task through the organization. A WFMS is typically supported by a database system (DBS).

Consider the WFMS of an insurance company that handles damage claims and the underlying DBS of insurances. What is the subject domain of:

a) The DBS

b) The WFMS

c) The insurance company

11. Give an example of a system that can be part of its own subject domain.

12. When we open up a computer, we see its physical components, such as a printed circuit board and a ventilator. We do not see the lexical items stored in the computer. So what does it mean to say that a lexical item exists "in" a computer?

CHAPTER 3

Stimulus-Response Behavior

A message that arrives at the system originated at some point in the environment and reached the system by some communication path. And a message that leaves the system travels through a communication path to its destination, where it is expected to bring about a desirable effect. In this chapter, we look at what happens when messages travel to or from the system. Section 3.1 provides examples of the chain of cause and effect in stimulus-response behavior. Section 3.2 defines the terminology of events and actions that I use throughout the book. Section 3.3 examines the way events in the environment lead to stimuli of the system, and Section 3.4 examines the way system responses lead to actions in the environment. In both sections, I give examples of assumptions about the environment that we must make in the specification of desired stimulus-response behavior.

3.1 Cause and Effect Chains

The function of a reactive system is to respond to the occurrence of events or conditions in the environment by causing desirable changes in the environment. It does this by sending a message to the environment, by changing its state, or both. The state change is never an end in itself but is intended to change system responses later on. For example, an elevator controller may respond to a message that a request button has been pushed by storing this information. This is not an end in itself—it is needed later on when an elevator cage arrives at the floor from which the request originates. The elevator controller then uses the stored information to determine whether the cage should stop at the floor.

Generalizing from this and other examples, we get the picture that the system exists to respond to events and conditions in its environment and that these responses should have desired effects in the environment. This is therefore the most general functionality of a reactive system, which includes the three kinds of functions listed in Chapter 2—information provision, direction, and manipulation of lexical items—as special cases. As shown in Figure 3.1, there is a chain of events leading

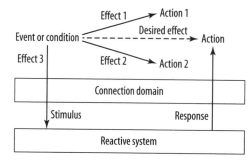

Figure 3.1 The role of a reactive system is to achieve desired effects in the environment by responding to stimuli that originate from events and conditions in the environment.

from the occurrence of events or conditions in the environment to a system stimulus, a response, and a desired action in the environment. Some of the relevant responses occur later, and to bridge the gap in time between stimulus and response the system maintains a state that remembers some of the stimuli that has occurred.

If we abstract from the communication channel from event to stimulus, then the event and the stimulus are identical in our environment model. If we describe the channel explicitly as a connection domain between the event and the system, then the event and the stimulus are different. We can then express in our description that the stimulus occurs later than the event, that an event may not lead to a stimulus, that a stimulus may not be caused by the event it is supposed to be caused by, and that important transformations are applied on the way from event to stimulus. Similarly, if we abstract from the communication channel from response to action, then the response and the action are identical.

Figure 3.1 also shows that the events and conditions have effects even if the system does not exist. The dashed arrow is intended to represent the fact that we need the SuD to produce the desired effect. Introducing the system causes an additional effect of the event, namely the stimulus, and this causes a response that in turn causes the desired action. Here I first give some examples before analyzing the event-action chain in detail. In each example, I list the effects that may happen anyway (effect 1 and effect 2 in Figure 3.1), the stimulus (effect 3 in Figure 3.1), the desired response, and the expected action.

Example 1
- *Event:* A student tells an employee of the student administration that she wants to register for a course.
- *Effects that may happen anyway:* Others hanging around hear what is being said; the employee notices that the student has recently smoked a cigarette.
- *Stimulus for the system:* The employee enters registration data in an information system.
- *Response:* The information system confirms registration.
- *Action:* The employee informs the student that she is now registered.

In a variant without connection domain, the student registers herself by entering the data in the information system at a terminal available for that purpose. Now the event (student informs administration that she wants to register for a course) coincides with the stimulus (data are entered in the information system), and similarly the response coincides with the resulting action.

Example 2
- *Event:* Time has come to print the list of registered students.
- *Effects that may happen anyway:* None.
- *Stimulus:* An employee of the student administration asks to print the list.
- *Response:* The system prints the list.
- *Action:* The employee gives the list to the teacher.

Again, a version without connection domain can be designed too.

Example 3
- *Event:* An elevator cage arrives at a floor with an outstanding request.
- *Effects that may happen anyway:* A small amount of heat is generated, a sensor closes, a current flows through a wire, and a click sound is generated.
- *Stimulus:* The elevator controller receives a signal about the arrival.
- *Response:* The controller sends a stop signal to the motor.
- *Action:* The motor responds by starting a slowdown process.

This example shows that one entity's response is the other entity's stimulus.

Example 4
- *Condition:* The stock in a supermarket store falls below a certain level.
- *Effects that may happen anyway:* A supermarket shelf becomes empty; customers see that the product is almost out of stock.
- *Stimulus:* Through its point-of-sale terminals (POSTs), the information system of the store detects the low stock level.
- *Response:* The information system responds by sending an order to a supplier.
- *Action:* The supplier receives the order.

This is an example in which the response consists of creating a lexical item.

Looking at these and other examples, we find that the effects of an event or condition are due to

- Laws of nature
- The technical specification of previously installed devices
- Properties of people
- Procedures that people must follow
- Rules that people have defined for conceptual entities

This list follows the kinds of subject domain entities introduced in Chapter 2. Laws of nature concern the behavior of physical entities, including people. If an effect occurs due to a law of nature, then we believe that it is certain to occur. The specifications of devices concern the behavior of physical devices. If an effect occurs due to the specification of a device, it will occur most of the time, assuming the device is not broken. But if we trust our devices, we will ignore this possibility. The behavior of people is governed not only by the laws of nature, but also by procedures defined by (other) people. If an effect occurs due to procedures to be followed by people, we should definitively consider the possibility that these effects do not always occur. If rules defined for conceptual entities are written down and accessible and understandable for all stakeholders, then these rules are pretty certain to produce their effects. For example, there are rules that define an employee's salary, his or her vacation rights, and so on. A salary administration may make mistakes in applying these rules, but if the rules are accessible and understandable to all stakeholders then some interested party will probably discover the mistake. However, if the rules are incomprehensible, then any mistakes may never be discovered and events may cause unwanted effects.

3.2 Events, Conditions, and Actions

Let me now define some key terms. An **event** is something that happens in the world. Examples of events are kicking a ball, pushing a button, switching on a light, the occurrence of a deadline, and stock becoming low. Events are discrete, meaning that we disregard the intermediate states of the event and consider it to be atomic. With respect to time, events are considered to happen instantaneously. Events may be physical or conceptual. Kicking a ball is a physical event; hiring an employee is a conceptual event. An event usually causes a state change in the world.

A **condition** is a state of the world that persists for some nonzero period of time. Examples of conditions are that an elevator motor is on, that a student is registered for a course, and that you are reading this book. The difference between events and conditions is that a condition is a state, whereas an event causes a state change. And a condition persists for some time, whereas an event is considered to be instantaneous.

Note that we have the habit of describing an event by describing a condition, such as stock level is low. What we really mean in such cases is the event that the condition becomes true: when stock becomes low. Like all events, this is instantaneous. When we say that a condition occurs, we really mean that the condition has just started to become true, which is an event.

Events are called **actions** when we view them from the point of view of the initiator of the event. For example, when an intended passenger pushes a button of an elevator system, this is an event from the point of view of the elevator system, but it is an action from the point of view of the user. When an elevator cage opens its doors, this is an event for the passenger, but an action of the elevator system. The distinction between actions and events is the same as that between output and input: What is input for one system is output for another system.

With respect to a reactive system, we can distinguish two important kinds of events, external events and temporal events. An **external event** of a system S is an event that occurs in the environment of S, to which S is expected to respond. Pushing a floor button of an idle elevator system is an external event for the elevator controller because the controller must respond to it by sending an elevator car to the floor where the button has been pushed. If the floor button is pushed a second time, before the first event has been responded to, this is not for most elevator controllers an external event because no extra response is needed to this second request. Only if the elevator system is required to respond to it, for example by sending a second elevator car, is this an external event. And if two people bump into one another in front of the elevator door and start to chat, this is an event; however, it is not an external event for the elevator controller because it is not expected to respond to it.

An external event is a discrete change in the condition of the environment. As we have seen, we can name this change in two ways: by giving a name to the change itself or by giving a name to the condition that changes.

◆ A **named external event** is an event in the environment that is given a unique name. Examples: close door, start motor, receive insurance claim.

◆ A **condition change event** is an event in the environment that is given a name by describing the Boolean expression that changes its truth value as a result of the event. Examples: The event that pressure becomes too high is the event that the predicate pressure > limit changes from false to true, and the event that stock becomes too low is the event that the predicate stocklevel ≥ minimum changes from true to false.

The second kind of important event is the temporal event. A **temporal event** is the passage of a significant moment in time to which the system is expected to respond. For example, if 5 seconds after the doors of an elevator are opened, they must close, this is a temporal event. The system must respond to the temporal event 5 seconds passed since opening by closing the doors. As a counterexample, the occurrence of the time when one of the elevator passengers should attend a meeting is not a temporal event for the elevator system (but it is for the passenger).

3.3 Events and Stimuli

A **stimulus** of a system is an event at the interface of the system caused by the environment. By analyzing a stimulus, the system can discover whether an external or temporal event has occurred. The stimulus itself is an event, but it is usually not the external event responded to. The stimulus is an observation event, one in which the external event is observed. Like all observations, this observation may be mistaken. External events occur somewhere in the environment; stimuli occur at the interface of the system. The list of examples in Section 3.1 contains ample illustration of this. In all these examples, the stimulus may contain a mistake.

Example 1: The employee of the student administration may enter the wrong data in the system.

Example 2: The employee may request that the wrong list of participants be printed.

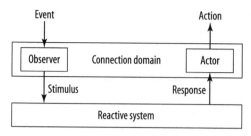

Figure 3.2 Observers and actors are part of the connection domain.

Example 3: The arrival sensor of an elevator cage may send a wrong signal to the controller.

Example 4: The POST in a supermarket may make a mistake in registering the sale of an item and therefore send an incorrect message to the information system.

In all these cases, there is an **observer** of the event that informs the system of the event occurrence. To revert to the metaphor of the previous chapter, often we regard the observer of the event as the sender of the message. Observers can be people or devices. If it is a device, we often call it a **sensor.** Observers are part of the connection domain (Figure 3.2).

3.3.1   *Assumptions about Observers*

In the communication path from some external event to the reactive system, things may go wrong. The observer may be activated by events other than the relevant external event, and it may fail to communicate the occurrence of the relevant external event to the reactive system. To make this point clear, suppose that a production cell must cut a long metal plate into shorter pieces. Figure 3.3 shows a plate-cutting controller, connected to its subject domain, consisting of metal plates, by a photoelectric cell as sensor and a sheet cutter as actuator. The plate arrives on a conveyor belt and the arrival of the beginning and end of the long plate is sensed by the photoelectric cell. What are the events that the controller must respond to? It must respond to occurrences of the events:

◆ The beginning of a metal plate arrives.

◆ The end of a metal plate arrives.

However, the controller can make only the following observations:

◆ On signal received from photoelectric cell

◆ Off signal received from photoelectric cell

The cell itself only responds to the following stimuli:

◆ Close

◆ Open

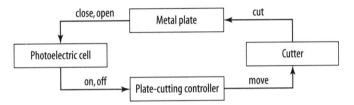

Figure 3.3 A stimulus is used to infer which event has occurred.

The stimuli received by the plate-cutting controller are observations of the relevant external events only under the following assumptions:

◆ The photoelectric cell is functioning properly.

◆ The photoelectric cell is stimulated only by the arrival of the beginning or end of a metal plate.

If the system has no way to validate these assumptions, but nevertheless always acts on them, then the activation of the sensor by other means, for example because someone blocks the sensor with his hand, will cause the controller to respond as if the beginning or end of the plate had arrived; it will command the cutter to cut a plate. The only way for the controller to validate its assumptions about the photo-electric cell is to use another sensor that is able to sense the same external event. Of course, this second sensor is subject to assumptions that are similar to the first.

3.3.2 *Event Recognition*

The plate-cutter example illustrates that reactive systems must interpret the stim-uli that arrive at their interface as observations of events. This interpretation may involve no extra computation, as in the plate-cutter example, or, in other cases, it may involve computations by the system. Suppose that, in addition to the arrival of the beginning and end points of a metal plate, the plate controller must respond to occurrences of the following event:

◆ A point arrives where the sheet must be cut.

Assume, for example, that there are no visible marks on the sheet itself marking where it must be cut. Then the system must infer the occurrence of this event by responding to the arrival of the plate by recording the point in time at which this stimulus occurs and by using information about the speed with which the plate moves under the cutter. The internal computation process in which the occurrence of an external event is derived from data provided by stimuli and stored data, is called **event recognition.**

Event recognition is a very common process in software systems. For example, if a library member turns up at the library counter with a book that he or she wants to borrow from the library, the library database system will check whether the member is registered with the library and is permitted to borrow books, and whether this particular book can be borrowed. All of this is part of a process to recognize the

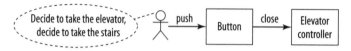

Figure 3.4 Unobservable events.

occurrence of the event **request to borrow a document**. The event recognition process takes place inside the system. The event to be recognized takes place outside the system, in the subject domain.

3.3.3 Unobservable Events

Sometimes it is not possible to observe the external event that the system is supposed to respond to. For example, ideally, an elevator controller should respond to events such as:

◆ Potential passenger decides to take the elevator.

◆ Passenger decides to get out at floor 3.

However, the elevator controller can only observe the close stimulus, which is received from a button (Figure 3.4). Assuming the button is in working order, this stimulus is caused by a push event. The controller makes the further assumptions that this is caused by a potential passenger who has decided to take the elevator and that the potential passenger will not change his or her mind. But there is no way for the controller to validate these last assumptions. The button may have been pushed by a practical joker, or the potential passenger may have changed his or her mind and taken the stairs. There is no number of additional sensors that can create more certainty for the controller about this. Because the assumptions about the potential passenger cannot be validated by the controller, the controller is not able to observe the relevant external events. Hence, elevator controllers are designed to respond to events that they can observe—pushing buttons—and these events are interpreted as requests from potential passengers. In case you are wondering, this is the reason why in Figure 2.10 the passenger is not part of the subject domain of the controller. However, a description of communications in the context of the controller may very well include a passenger to make clear that a push event is assumed to be caused by a passenger. The reason for excluding passengers from the subject domain is that the controller cannot identify passengers.

3.3.4 Observing Temporal Events

The system can observe the passage of time by means of clocks. But note that a clock is not a sensor; time does not consist of events to which the clock responds by ticking. A clock is a machine that indicates the time, and it does this by keeping up with the passage of time. However, like a sensor, a clock may be wrong. Clocks are used to indicate the time, but they may indicate the wrong time.

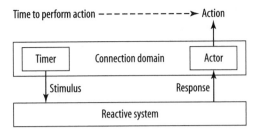

Figure 3.5 Temporal events are not caused by any particular event, and they do not cause any other event. The system must use a stimulus sent by a timer, which is a clock that generates a stimulus when the temporal event occurs.

A **timer** is a special kind of clock that watches for one particular temporal event. Suppose an elevator door must close if its entry sensor has not been activated for a period of 10 seconds. This is implemented by using a timer that ticks 10 seconds starting at the moment the doors are completely open and that is reset every time the door entry sensor is activated (see Figure 3.5). So the desired behavior,

◆ Close when the entry sensor is not activated in a period of 10 seconds.

is transformed into an assumption about the timer and a different behavior:

◆ The timer is assumed to tick once per second.

◆ The door controller must close the door at the 10th tick of the timer.

3.4 **Responses and Actions**

A reactive system responds to an external or temporal event by updating its state or producing an output. Eventually, the updated state leads to a different output than would have occurred without the update. An **output response** of a system is an event at the interface of the system, caused by the system. By producing an output response, the system produces desired effects. When there is no chance of a misunderstanding, I will simply talk of a response when I mean "output response."

The desired effect of a stimulus may consist of one or more desired actions, to be caused by several responses. For example, when a task arrives at a workflow system, the desired effect is to allocate this to an actor and to track the progress of the task through the organization. The allocation of the task to an actor occurs in one atomic response. Tracking the task through the organization is a process that itself consists of several stimulus-response pairs. As another example, when a floor button of an elevator is pushed, the immediate response of the elevator controller is to allocate this request to a cage. The rest of the desired effect consists of a complex process that may consist of starting a motor, sensing arrival of a cage at a floor, stopping a motor, and opening doors. The desired effect of an event may take a period of time to materialize.

There is often a significant communication channel from output response to desired action, which is modeled by means of a connection domain (Figure 3.2). The connection domain, then, contains **actors,** which are entities that can sense the output response and cause the desired action. Actors introduce delay, unreliability and possibly conversions on the way from response to action. Actors can be people or devices; if they are devices, we also call them **actuators.**

3.4.1   *Assumptions about Actors*

Just as we must make assumptions about observers, we must make assumptions about actors. Consider the document circulation system mentioned in the previous chapter (Figure 2.9). The production of a reminder by the document circulation system will produce the desired effect only if the circulation department sends this message to the library member. Or take a heating controller of a heating tank in a fruit-juice-production plant. The controller can send on and off signals to the heater of the tank, but this will achieve the desired effect only if we assume that the heater is functioning correctly. The response will lead to the desired effect only under the following assumptions:

◆ The heater is functioning properly.
◆ The heater is commanded only by the responses of the heating controller.

This mirrors assumptions about stimuli that we identified in Section 3.3.1.

3.4.2   *Response Computation*

Just as events must be inferred from stimuli, responses must be inferred from desired actions. If the document circulation system senses the condition that a library member has not returned a document on time, then the desired effect to be achieved is to remind the member that he must return the document. If that is the desired effect, the appropriate response is to collect the relevant data, format them, and print them. These computations are motivated by the desired action. Similarly in the heating controller example, because the desired action is to heat up the fruit juice, the controller infers that it should send an on signal to the heater.

In both cases, there is a response computation that is motivated by the goal of causing a desired effect. Note that this is the inverse of the relation between stimuli and events. Whereas at the input side an event is inferred from a stimulus, at the output side a response is inferred from the desired effect. The common factor is that stimuli and responses are both interpreted in terms of an environment model.

3.4.3   *Unrealizable Actions*

Just as some events may be unobservable by the system or its observers, so some actions may be unrealizable by the system or its actors. For example, the desired effect of a request sending an elevator to a floor is that the passenger who made

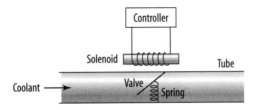

Figure 3.6 An external device (the solenoid) and the entity it is connected to (the valve) by means of a physical influence.

the request enters the elevator. But the controller can only ensure that an elevator cage with the requested direction of service stops and opens its doors. It is then up to the passenger to enter the elevator cage. This is another reason why passengers are outside the subject domain of the controller. Again, the underlying reason for excluding an action such as passenger enters from the subject domain is that the controller cannot identify these actions. Because there is no realizable causal chain from an SuD response to a passenger enters action, there is no reliable connection between the identity of a response and the identity of this action.

A dramatic example of what happens when we ignore the distinction between realizable and unrealizable effects is the near-meltdown of the nuclear reactor that took place in 1979 at Three Mile Island. The near-meltdown occurred when the level of coolant in the reactor vessel remained low for a number of hours. The level remained low because an automatic relief valve remained open (Figure 3.6). The valve was opened by energizing a solenoid and it was closed by a simple spring. The control software correctly assumed that the response switch off solenoid caused the solenoid to switch off; but it incorrectly assumed that this caused the valve to close. There was a second actor in play—the spring. The near-accident occurred when, after the solenoid was switched off, the spring got stuck and the valve remained open. This could have been detected if the controller had had access to a sensor that sensed the position of the valve or the flow of the coolant.

3.5 SUMMARY

The function of a reactive system is to respond to events in its environment by causing desired effects in the environment. This subsumes the three basic kinds of functions identified in Chapter 2—information provision, direction, and manipulation. The chain of events from cause to effect starts with an external or temporal event, which leads to a stimulus, which leads to a response, which leads to a desired action. A named external event is an external event that has a unique name. A condition change event is an external event in which a condition becomes true.

On the way from external event to stimulus, we may find observers (people or sensors) that may cause delays and errors and perform data conversions. Temporal events are observed by timers. On the way from response to action, we may find actors (people or actuators) that, again, may introduce delays, errors, and conversions. A specification of stimulus-response behavior will make assumptions about the correct behavior of observers and actors. If these assumptions are not satisfied, the stimulus-response behavior of the system does not necessarily lead to the desired event-action pairs in the environment. Events and actions occur in the environment of the system, but the recognition of events and computation of responses are part of the system.

The subject domain of the system is bounded by what its observers can observe and what its actors can bring about. Unobservable events and unrealizable actions do not belong to the subject domain. To better understand the desired system behavior, we may include them in our environment communication model, as we did with elevator passengers, but they are not part of the subject domain.

3.6 QUESTIONS AND EXERCISES

QUESTIONS FOR REHEARSAL

1. Define the following concepts:

Event and *action*

External event and *temporal event*

Named external event and *condition change event*

Stimulus and *response*

Observer and *actor*

2. Explain why we need event recognition and response computation in a reactive system.

3. Are temporal events observable? Explain.

QUESTIONS FOR DISCUSSION

4. A reactive system is linked to its subject domain by a connection domain. It is part of a loop that runs from events through the connection domain to the system and then back again from the system through the connection domain to the desired action. In each of the following examples, identify:

   i) The subject domain event being responded to

   ii) The subject domain entity (or entities) in whose life the event occurs

   iii) The observer used to pass information about the event to the system

   iv) The desired subject domain action

   v) The subject domain entity (or entities) in whose life the action will occur

   vi) The actor used to pass the information about the desired action to the subject domain

Write down any assumptions that you are making about the subject and connection domains, if you think these are relevant. Mention only observable events and realizable actions.

a) *System:* An elevator control system. *Stimulus:* Reception of a up_request signal from floor 1. *Response:* Send motor_down signal to motor 3.

b) *System:* A word processor. *Stimulus:* Reception of delete signal. *Response:* The cursor moves left, erasing the character at the position that it moves to.

c) *System:* A bank account database. *Stimulus:* Reception of a command update account 345 with 567 euros from the line connected to terminal 999. *Response:* Add 567 to the balance field of the record that holds account 345 and send a confirmation to a line connected to terminal 999.

d) *System:* An EDI system connecting the information system of a supermarket with the production information system of a supplier. *Stimulus:* The EDI system receives a signal that the number of milk packages in the store has fallen below 100. *Response:* The EDI system issues an order to deliver 300 milk packages.

5. The following systems respond to events in their subject domain. For each system, mention an event that you would like the system to respond to but that is nevertheless unobservable by the system, and mention an event that the system is able to respond to instead, plus an observer of the event.

   a) A car cruise control

   b) A library document circulation information system

   c) An elevator control

   d) A workflow system

   e) An email system

6. The following systems cause actions in their subject domain. For each system, mention an action that you would like the system to cause but that is nevertheless unrealizable by the system and mention an event that the system can cause instead, plus an actor that realizes this.

   a) A patient monitoring system used in an intensive care unit, showing vital data of patients to a nurse

   b) A library document circulation information system

   c) The information system of a supermarket that maintains current stock from minute to minute and that is used to ensure that there are always sufficient items in stock

   d) A Web shop (a Web page with product catalog and transaction facilities)

   e) An email system

7. "An actor (or observer) cannot be a subject domain entity." Give an argument why this is true (in one sense) and an argument why it is false (in another sense).

8. Is a stimulus always caused by an external event?

CHAPTER 4

Software Specifications

To design a reactive system, we must describe its environment, specify the requirements of the SuD, and specify a decomposition. Section 4.1 examines the way in which the SuD together with external entities realizes the desired emergent behavior of a composite system. Some examples of informal system engineering arguments are given. Section 4.2 classifies the desired SuD properties into decomposition properties and external properties and classifies the external properties into functional properties, quality attributes, and other kinds of properties; this book focuses on functional-property specification and on decomposition specification. Section 4.3 returns to the environment and shows what happens to a system specification if certain environment assumptions are not satisfied; we see that some SuD properties that were previously desirable may become neutral or even undesirable when environment assumptions become false. In Section 4.4, the stimulus-response specifications of SuD properties are placed in the larger context of operational specifications.

4.1 The System Engineering Argument

The SuD forms a composite system together with other entities (Figure 4.1). This composite system may be designed, such as an elevator system, a juice-tank heating controller, an electronic ticket system, or a business training department. Or it may be an evolving system not designed by anyone in particular, such as a market, an Internet-based interest group, a value chain, or a group of people playing a distributed software game. In either case, it is a **system,** a collection of elements that interact to form a whole. The composite system has properties that emerge due to the interaction of its components. For example, due to the introduction of the SuD as a component, the composite system may become more reliable, become more efficient, become faster, become able to handle a larger volume of requests, make fewer mistakes, experience more fun, or make more profit. Or the SuD may produce negative contributions—it may make the composite system less stable, less

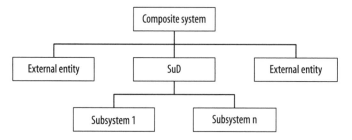

Figure 4.1 The system hierarchy.

predictable in behavior, more unreliable, or less able to fulfill its mission. For better or worse, the composite system has properties that emerge from the interaction of its components.

We try to build into the SuD properties that interact with those of its external entities in such a way that the desired composite system properties emerge. If S is a specification of the desired properties of the SuD, we should be able to produce an argument of the following form:

S and A entail E

where A is a description of the collection of assumptions about the external entities and E is a specification of the desired emergent properties of the composite system. The assumptions A include the laws of nature, the technical specifications of devices used, and the procedures to be followed by people. Here are some examples.

◆ If (S) the TIS allows the registration of unexpected participants and (A) at the start of a course the company training department keeps staff on hand who can register unexpected participants, then (E) the department will be able to handle newcomers efficiently.

◆ If (S) the heating controller can heat juice in a tank according to recipe and (A) operators are able to change recipes, then (E) the juice plant can deal with new kinds of fruit juices in a shorter time than was possible previously.

◆ If (S) the ETS allows travelers to buy tickets through their PDAs and (A) travelers have PDAs that can interface with this system, then (E) the railway company can reduce operating costs by selling tickets through the ETS.

The assumptions about the environment are called "assumptions" because the specifier of the SuD has no control about making them true. The decisions of the specifier concern the SuD, not the environment.

I call the argument that S and A entail E the **system engineering argument.** In top-down system engineering, we specify the desired system properties, decompose the system, and then allocate and flow down the system properties to the system components. Here we look at the same process in a bottom-up direction. Our task is not to design the composite system but to design one of its parts, namely the SuD. The system engineering argument gives us the rationale for the SuD having certain properties—it should have certain properties in order to realize the desired properties E of the composite system. But the system engineering argument makes clear that the properties of the SuD themselves do not suffice to realize the emergent properties E. We need the properties A that are assumed about the environment too.

4.2 Specifications

A **specification** of the SuD is a description of the desired properties of the SuD. It is useful to distinguish two kinds of properties of the SuD:

- **Requirements** of the SuD are the desired SuD properties needed to achieve the desired properties of the composite system. The requirements are motivated by the properties of the composite system.
- **Constraints** are the desired SuD properties imposed by the environment; these are the bounds within which the requirements must be realized.

Requirements feel like goals to be achieved by your design. Constraints feel like design decisions made by others that limit your design freedom. For example, the heating control system may have a requirement that it heats tanks filled with fruit juice according to recipe, and it may have a constraint that it runs on Unix platforms.

A second distinction to make, applicable to both constraints and requirements, is between the external properties and decomposition properties of the SuD (Figure 4.2). External properties, in turn, can be divided into groups that I call **aspects.** Examples of aspects, shown in Figure 4.2, are functional properties; quality attributes; and also legal, social, and economic aspects. In this book, we concentrate on functional properties only. A system **function** is the ability to create a desired effect in the environment. In this book, we distinguish three aspects of system functionality: service, behavior, and communication.

- A system **service** is an interaction that creates a desired effect in the environment. Every service has a triggering event and, when executed, has done something valuable for the environment: delivered an economic value, satisfied a need, achieved a goal, and so on. Reactive systems deliver their services by means of

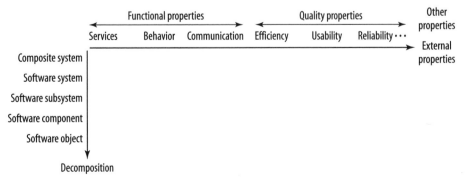

Figure 4.2 Kinds of properties of the SuD.

stimulus-response behavior. The relationship between functions and services is this: Whereas a function is the ability of a system to create a desired effect in its environment, a service is a particular interaction that does create a desired effect. So all services are functions, and each function is realized by means of one or more services.

◆ System **behavior** is the ordering of product interactions in time. Reactive system behavior is always a sequence of stimulus-response pairs.

◆ System **communication** is interaction of the system with entities in its environment. Communication is dual to behavior. Communication channels connect a collection of (sub)systems into a structure so that they can interact, and behavior is the ordering of these interactions over time. In a communication event, two or more entities share an event. If there is a sending event that precedes the receiving event, we view these as two communication events: one in which the sender communicates with the communication channel and one in which the communication channel communicates with the receiver. Compare this with posting a letter and retrieving a letter from your mailbox.

Systems usually have basic services to which a designer can add features. A **feature** is an incremental functionality defined on top of a service that is already available, thus defining a more elaborate service. For example, a basic service of an elevator controller is to deliver passengers to their requested floors. An added feature is to return an elevator cage to a home floor when the cage is empty. An additional feature that can be defined on top of this is that in the morning the home floor is the ground floor, but in the evening the home floor is at the top of the building.

A **quality attribute** is an aspect of functionality that indicates how valuable this function is for the environment. For example, suppose the TIS has a function for the course coordinator to download data about participants from the personnel information system. The usability, efficiency and reliability of this function are aspects that indicate how valuable this service is for the course coordinator.

Sometimes a quality attribute really is a cost for some stakeholder that must be kept as small as possible. For example, the maintainability and portability of a function indicate what the cost of providing this function is for the system maintainer. When we say that maintainability is high, we mean that the cost of maintenance is low.

There are even more aspects relevant for software specification, including ergonomic, social, legal, and financial aspects. These are not mentioned in Figure 4.2 and I will not deal with them in this book. (This does not mean that they are not important; they can be very important.)

As the decomposition dimension in Figure 4.2 shows, a software system may itself be part of a higher-level composite system, and it may be decomposed into subsystems, components, and software objects. The hierarchy in Figure 4.2 gives just one example of partitioning in software decomposition levels. Other aggregation levels can be useful too.

The three functionality properties that we focus on reappear at every aggregation level. (Other properties reappear at every level too, such as reliability or interoperability.) This is illustrated in Figure 4.3.

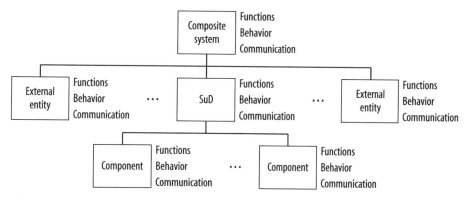

Figure 4.3 The aspects of service, behavior, and communication occur at every level in the aggregation hierarchy.

4.3 The Role of Assumptions

We need assumptions about the external environment in order to show that the properties of the SuD lead to the desired composite system properties. The system engineering argument can be used as a guideline for design decisions:

> If the environment satisfies assumptions *A*, then in order to produce emergent properties *E* the designer decides that the system should have properties *S*.

This allows the designer to justify the properties by the system engineering argument that *A* and *S* entail *E*.

What if the environment does not satisfy *A*? Then the design decision is not justified—it may or may not be desirable that the software has properties *S*. This depends on what properties emerge in this case and whether these properties are desirable, undesirable, or neutral. Here are some examples using those given in Section 3.1. The lists of assumptions given are not complete, but they do give an indication of how much is assumed.

Example 1
- *Desired property:* When the system receives a student request to register for a course, according to the data of the system there is still room for an additional student, and the student is permitted to follow the course, then the system responds by registering the student.
- *Assumptions:* The employee entering the data does not make mistakes, the person requesting registration is really this student, there is no other way to register for the course, and the data about registrations are correct and complete.
- *What if some assumptions are false?:* Then the property is not desired.

Example 2
- *Desired property:* When requested by an employee, the system prints a list of course registrations.

◆ *Assumptions:* The request by the employee is done when registration is closed, and the printed list is given to the teacher.
◆ *What if some assumptions are false?:* Then it is not certain whether the property is still desired.

Example 3
◆ *Desired property:* When an elevator controller receives a signal that an elevator cage arrives at a floor where it should deliver a service, the controller sends a stop signal to the elevator motor.
◆ *Assumptions:* The arrival sensor is activated by the cage and not by static electricity or some other phenomenon, the stimulus is caused by this sensor and not by anything else (e.g., there is no crosswiring), the response arrives at the appropriate motor and not anywhere else (again no crosswiring), the motor is currently on, and when the motor receives the signal it will stop.
◆ *What if some assumptions are false?:* Then it is desirable that the system does *not* have this property. Instead, it should start an emergency procedure.

Example 4
◆ *Desired property:* When the supermarket information system receives a message that stock is low, it will send a reorder to the supplier.
◆ *Assumptions:* The message is sent by a POST, the POST is in good working order, the POST operator is honest and does not make mistakes, the data in the system really represent the stock level, the order sent to the network does indeed arrive at the supplier, and there is a contract between supermarket and supplier that makes this a legally valid order.
◆ *What if some assumptions are false?:* Then the property may still be desired, but probably the system should do other things as well, such as checking the POST transactions against inventory data.

These examples show that requirements carry assumptions with them that are often unstated. When the assumptions on which the requirement for a software property S is based are false, then S may still be desired, S may have to be supplemented by other desired system properties, or it may be desirable that the system *not* have S but does something else.

The examples also illustrate that certain types of assumption occur again and again:

Subject domain assumptions: Assumptions about entities, events, and processes in the subject domain.

Connection domain assumptions: Assumptions about observers, actors and other entities, events, and processes in the connection domain. In particular it is assumed the stimulus is indeed caused by a certain event and that the response does indeed lead to the desired action.

Data assumptions: The data about the subject domain are assumed to be correct and complete.

The two domain assumptions concern the laws of nature, properties of devices, behavior of people, or normative structures (e.g., contracts) in the subject and connection domains of the system. Because all data in the system come, ultimately, from the environment, the data assumption is really shorthand for the assumption that so far in the history of the system, people and devices in the environment have done what they are expected to do. In other words, we can always replace the data assumption by the assumption that the environment behaves as expected.

4.4 Operational Property Specifications

An **operational specification** of a property is a specification of a set of reproducible operations that can be executed by different people to find out whether or not the property is present in a system, even if these people have conflicting interests. The key phrase is "even [with] conflicting interests." Designers, builders, customers, and users have different interests. The designer may want to produce a technically advanced design, the builder may want to implement a feasible specification, the customer may want an affordable design, and the user wants a design that is easy to use. For an operationally specified property, there is a test that they can all do and agree on the outcome—either the SuD has this property or it does not have this property.

Stimulus-response specifications are an important class of operational specifications. In a stimulus-response specification, S has the form

$$s \wedge C \Rightarrow r$$

where s is a stimulus, C is a condition on the system state, and r is a response. The design process consists of decisions about r. If we plug the stimulus-response form of S into the system engineering argument, we get the following template for design decisions.

> ◆ If
>   — the environment satisfies assumptions A,
>   — the system receives stimulus s, and
>   — the system state satisfies condition C,
> ◆ then
>   — in order to achieve emergent properties E
>   — the designer decides to let the SuD produce response r.

If decisions are made this way, the designer can justify the stimulus-response specification by the system engineering argument that A and $(s \wedge C \Rightarrow r)$ entail E.

The assumptions A that cannot be observed or guaranteed by the system must be guaranteed by the environment of the system—by the devices, users, operators, and external entities of the SuD. Condition C, on the other hand, is a condition on the state of the system itself. As we see later, when we look at ways to describe system behavior, if we want to describe stimulus-response pairs in transactional form, we need a system state to be able to define the desired response.

Not all operational specifications are in stimulus-response form. Here are two other examples that are not in stimulus-response form, but are nevertheless operational:

◆ If the temperature is in range R and humidity is in range H, then if we apply force F to one end of this beam it should be deformed less than 2 micrometers.

◆ At least 80% of the users of this ticket machine should be able to use this machine within 5 seconds without reading the instructions.

The first specification is not in stimulus-response form because it gives a relationship between variables. The second specification is not in stimulus-response form because it gives a statistical property. Yet both are operational because people with conflicting interests can perform operations that give an answer independent of their interests.

Quality attributes such as usability and maintainability are often called non-functional properties. Saying that something has a nonfunctional property has the connotation that whether this property is present cannot be objectively decided. I avoid the term "nonfunctional" because it emphasizes an uninteresting distinction, namely the distinction between functional and other properties. The important distinction is not between kinds of properties but between *specifications* of properties—that is, whether or not a specification has been operationalized. If a specification is not operationalized, then it is a specification of an intention that the SuD have this property. It is all right to specify intentions, but a consequence of having a property specification that is not operationalized is that, when the SuD is delivered, the supplier and the customer may get into a dispute about whether the property is present. I recommend that SuD specifications be operationalized as much as possible.

4.5 SUMMARY

The SuD achieves desired effects in its environment by cooperating with other entities in its environment. This cooperation produces emergent properties of the composite system of which the SuD and its external entities are a part. The specification of desired SuD properties must be justified by both the assumption of properties of the external environment of the SuD and by the desired emergent properties of the composite system.

System properties can be classified into requirements and constraints; the SuDs must have both. Requirements are desirable because we need them to achieve the desired emergent properties of the composite system. The system must satisfy constraints because the environment imposes them.

Both constraints and requirements can be classified into external and decomposition properties that can be specified independently from one another. External properties can be grouped into aspects, such as functional, quality, social, ergonomic, and legal aspects. We distinguish three functional aspects: services, behavior, and communication. A function is the ability of a system to create a desired effect in its environment. A service is a function that consists of an interaction, so that it has a definite starting point; behavior is the ordering of interactions in time; and communication is the way in which the interactions of systems are connected in shared events. We can define additional functionality, called a feature, on top of a service that is already available.

Whatever its external properties, a software system may be decomposed into subsystems, lower-level components, and software objects. Other hierarchies are possible too. Whatever the hierarchy, at each level we see elements that, again, have all the aspects that we mentioned: functional aspects, quality aspects, and other aspects such as ergonomic and legal aspects.

When we specify the properties of a software system, we usually make assumptions about the environment that, when falsified, may invalidate the requirements. A property that is desired when the environment satisfies an assumption may be undesirable when the environment does not satisfy the assumption. The general form of a system requirement is therefore: If the environment satisfies assumptions A, the system receives stimulus s, and the system state satisfies conditions C, then it should produce response r. In this formula, the system cannot guarantee or even check assumption A, but it has the responsibility to check C.

Stimulus-response specifications are an example of operational specifications. A specification of a property is operational when it describes a procedure reproducible by different people with conflicting interests and nevertheless yields the same answer—the SuD either does or does not have this property. It is recommended that all desired system properties, including all quality attributes, be specified operationally.

4.6 QUESTIONS AND EXERCISES

QUESTIONS FOR REHEARSAL

1. Define the following concepts:
   Requirement
   Constraint
   Function
   Service
   Feature

2. What is the structure of an assumption-requirement specification? Give an example.

3. What is the structure of an operational specification?

4. Explain how stimulus-response specifications can be used in an operational specification.

QUESTIONS FOR DISCUSSION

5. Consider a coffee machine. We can put in ground coffee and water and switch it on. When switched on, it heats the water and pours the water through the ground coffee so that coffee drips into a pot. We can take out the pot at any

moment to pour coffee from it. Separate the functional properties of the coffee machine into three: functions, behavior, and communication.

6. Suppose that in a particular situation the assumptions of an assumption-requirements specification are not satisfied. The system manufacturer argues as follows:

> Your specification has the form:
>
> (*) If assumption then requirement.
>
> Now, because your use environment does not satisfy the assumption, (*) is vacuously true.
>
> Therefore, my system satisfies your specification (*).

How would you counter this argument? Explain your answer.

7. For each of the following requirements, state whether or not it can be put in operational form. Explain your answer.
   a) The system shall register borrow, extend, and return events.
   b) The system shall respond to any update request within 2 seconds.
   c) The system shall be easy to learn.
   d) The system shall be interoperable.
   e) The system shall only use well-understood concepts at its user interface.

8. Is an operationalized requirement the same thing as a test for the finished product? Explain your answer.

9. Suppose we have refined a set R of nonoperationalized requirements into a set R' of operationalized requirements. Does R' give the designer sufficient information to design a system decomposition such that the system will satisfy R'? If so, explain why. If not, explain why we had to go to the trouble of refining R into R'.

PART II

Function Notations

In these three chapters, we discuss three important parts of a functional system specification: the mission statement, the function refinement tree, and service descriptions. Because you should reach an agreement with the customer about these specifications, they should be made understandable to all.

- ◆ Chapter 5. The mission statement is a high-level description of the purpose and scope of the system that links desired system functionality to the goals of the composite system. System functionality is circumscribed by stating the system purpose, its major responsibilities, and things the system will not do.

- ◆ Chapter 6. The function refinement tree refines this description to pieces of functionality, called services, that have a definite starting event and a value for the environment. The root of the function refinement tree represents the system purpose; the leaves represent system services.

- ◆ Chapter 7. Service descriptions describe these pieces of functionality in language understandable to both the customer and designer.

CHAPTER 5

Mission Statement

The mission statement is the highest-level description of desired system functionality. Whenever you write any system specification at all, whether or not the system is reactive, it should include a mission statement and you should verify it with your customer. Section 5.1 describes the format for a mission statement. Section 5.2 shows how the mission statement should be related to business goals and a business solution specification. Section 5.3 then derives from this the guidelines for writing a mission statement.

5.1 Notation

The **mission statement** of a product is a high-level description of the purpose and scope of the product. It states the reasons why someone should want to pay for the product. Figure 5.1 gives an example mission statement for the Training Information System (TIS).

As we have seen in Chapter 2, the purpose of a reactive system is to create desired effects in the environment, such as to provide information about the subject domain, to direct the subject domain, or to manipulate lexical items. A mission statement relates this to goals of the environment. A mission statement contains a statement of purpose, which should make clear to what top-level environment goal the system contributes. For example, the goal of the company using TIS is to give introduction courses to newcomers every month. Accordingly, the primary purpose of TIS is to support the coordination of these courses. This relates the desired properties of TIS to business goals. There are higher-level business goals, but the one stated here is the highest-level goal to which TIS contributes.

The environment goals can be decomposed into subgoals, such as course preparation, registration, and wrap-up, and accordingly the TIS purpose is refined into three major responsibilities: to support course preparation, registration, and wrap-up. A **responsibility** of a product is a requirement that the product contribute to the achievement of an environment goal. For example, it can be the responsibility

```
┌─────────────────────────────────────────────┐
│ Name:  Training Information System          │
│                                             │
│ Acronym:  TIS                               │
│                                             │
│ Purpose:  To support the management of monthly │
│    introductory training courses           │
│                                             │
│ Responsibilities:                           │
│    • To support course preparation, including allocation of │
│      participants to groups and printing badges │
│    • To support course handling (unexpected, absentees) │
│    • To support course wrap-up              │
│                                             │
│ Exclusions:                                 │
│    • The system will not check the data of unexpected │
│      participants with the Personnel Information System. │
│    • The system does not support the allocation of speakers │
│      to groups.                             │
│    • The system will not support the allocation of groups to │
│      rooms.                                 │
└─────────────────────────────────────────────┘
```

Figure 5.1 Mission statement for a Training Information System.

of a product to allocate participants to courses, to sell railway tickets, or to control a heating tank. Responsibilities contribute something valuable to the environment. A responsibility is a relationship between the system and some desired effect in the environment. We can always say "it is a responsibility of the system to achieve ⟨some environment goal⟩." A responsibility usually corresponds to a group of services.

In more detail, a mission statement can consist of the following elements.

Name. It is always useful to give the product a name—to exist is to have a name. Some people like to include a fancy acronym too.

Purpose. The purpose of the product is to contribute to the achievement of goals in the environment. A statement of purpose should describe this contribution abstractly and concisely. Qualifications and refinements come later.

Composition. It can be useful to indicate what the product is going to consist of: software, databases, hardware, people, procedures, or even complete organization units. Figure 5.2 shows the mission of the ETS, which contains a composition statement.

Responsibilities. The refinement of the purpose into responsibilities is directly linked to the refinement of the environment goal into subgoals. The statement of responsibilities states that the system is going to contribute to the achievement of these subgoals. Each responsibility is described in one or two sentences. This helps to clarify the meaning of the statement of purpose.

Exclusions. There are infinitely many things that the product will not do. As part of the process of expectation management, it is useful to write down some of the responsibilities that the product is not going to have. Each exclusion is described in one or two sentences.

Name of the system: Electronic Ticket System (ETS)

Purpose: To provide capability to buy and use tickets of a railway company using a Personal Digital Assistant and a smart card

Composition: ETS consists of software distributed over the traveler's smart cart and PDA, the conductor's PDA and a central computer of the railway company

Responsibilities of the system:
- To support ticket buying
- To support ticket usage
- To support ticket refunding

Exclusions:
- The system does not perform travel planning.
- Each ticket sold by ETS is for one person and one trip (single or return).

Figure 5.2 Mission of the Electronic Ticket System.

The mission statement is an important tool in expectation management. The customer, user, designer, programmer, tester, and all other stakeholders should keep the system mission in mind during the design process. If this is not done, the mission may drift and gold-plating may occur. And in due time, different people may think that the product has different purposes, which is a recipe for disappointment. For example, if the customer thinks the system is designed to allocate speakers to groups, then a system that satisfies the TIS mission in Figure 5.1 falls short of customer expectations.

5.2 Relating System Purpose to Environment Purpose

The mission statement is the most general specification S of the SuD that we can use in the system engineering argument

A and S entail E

where E describes the desired emergent properties of the composite system and A describes the assumptions needed about the environment of the SuD. So, to find the mission statement, we should find the desired properties E of the composite system first.

5.2.1 Design Levels

To find the desired properties of the composite system of which the SuD is a part, it helps to partition the design activity into layers, as shown in Figure 5.3. The figure

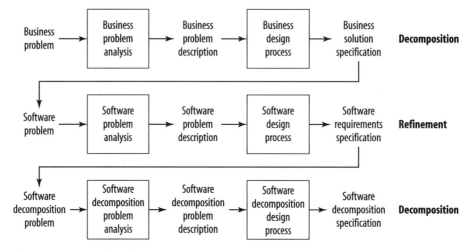

Figure 5.3 Levels of problem solving in software product design. Finding the software product mission statement is an outcome of software problem analysis.

partitions the situation into three aggregation levels: the composite system, the SuD, and the decomposition of the SuD. Any SuD is always embedded, through one or more layers of aggregation, in a social system. To make things concrete, we consider the situation in which the composite system is a business. At each level, there are particular problems that must be analyzed before solving them.

◆ At the business level, there are business problems to solve. In this problem-solving process, business designers will analyze the business goals, objectives, strengths, weaknesses, threats, and opportunities and generate business solutions. Finding business goals is part of the problem-analysis process at the upper left corner of Figure 5.3.

◆ The SuD is part of the solution that business designers came up with. The business solution specification should describe the use environment of the SuD, that is, the entities that the SuD will interact with. It should also include a project charter, which circumscribes the part of the world that you can design.

   The business solution is the software engineer's problem. Software problem analysis is an analysis of the business solution, which should result in at least a mission statement of the SuD. The problem-solving process in the middle layer is a refinement process because you add more detail to an abstract business-level specification of the SuD without decomposing the SuD. It is also a design process because adding more detail consists of making choices between practical alternatives: what events the SuD should respond to, what interaction protocols to follow, which formats these interactions should have, what exactly the subject domain of these interactions is, what devices the SuD communicates with, and so on.

◆ For completeness, the diagram includes one more layer: finding a good decomposition of the SuD.

Figure 5.3 illustrates that a solution at one aggregation level is a design problem for the next lower level.

5.2.2 Goal Analysis

A crucial activity in software problem analysis is business-goal analysis. Both the business problem and the business solution concern a goal structure that can conveniently be summarized in a business goal tree. A **goal tree** is a tree in which a top-level goal is recursively decomposed into subgoals such that the conjunction of the subgoals entails their parent goal. Figure 5.4 gives an example. This is relevant not only for information systems but also for different kinds of reactive systems; Figure 5.5 gives an example of business goals in the context of the heating controller.

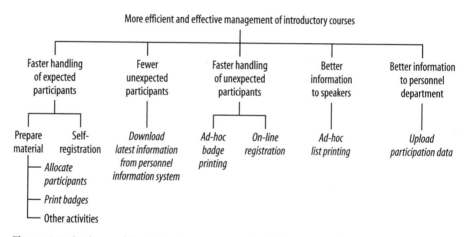

Figure 5.4 Goal tree of the TIS business context. The TIS must contribute to the goals printed in italics.

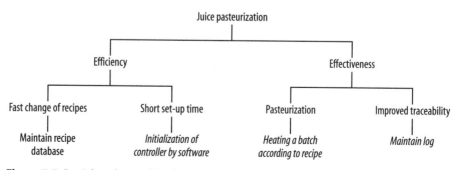

Figure 5.5 Partial goal tree of the fruit-juice-production plant. The heating controller must contribute to the goals in italics.

Each level in a goal tree can be viewed as a description of the desired emergent properties E of the business. For example, the tree in Figure 5.4 shows that the root business goal of the training department (to improve its effectiveness and efficiency) decomposes into a number of more concrete goals, which can be further decomposed until we reach goals to be achieved by means of the TIS. The goals in which TIS plays a part are printed in italics. They are achieved by some cooperative activity between training department personnel and TIS, to be specified more in detail later.

The lower levels in the goal tree should be more operationalized than higher levels. For example, the TIS cannot directly contribute to the root goal of Figure 5.4, More efficient and effective management of introductory courses. This goal is abstract and its achievement is hard to measure. But ad-hoc badge printing, a leaf of the goal tree, is a goal that TIS can handle. Because the leaf goals are achievable goals to which components of the business solution should contribute, I also call them **solution goals.**

The meaning of a goal tree is this: Lower-level goals are the means to higher-level goals. More formally,

If node g has children $g_1, \ldots, g_n$, then achieving $g_1, \ldots, g_n$ is sufficient for achieving g.

Often, we find that a lower-level goal contributes to several higher-level goals. For example, maintaining a log of heating processes is useful for traceability (a business goal), but also contributes information to improve safety (another business goal). If a lower-level goal has more than one higher-level goal as parent, then the goal tree is not a tree but a graph. Nevertheless, to emphasize the fact that there must be a root goal and that goals are decomposed into subgoals, we continue calling it a tree. Multiple occurrences of the same node in a tree are marked with an asterisk.

When we operationalize the goals lower in the tree, they turn into the desired properties of solution components. The goal tree is thus a representation of a business-level system engineering argument that shows how properties to be achieved by the solution components jointly realize the root business goal. It is not the software engineer's task to produce this argument; it should be produced by the business designer. It is the software engineer's task to analyze and understand the argument, however. The software engineer can then produce the lower-level system engineering argument that the properties of the SuD plus assumptions about its external entities jointly suffice to achieve the solution goals.

We can extract the following guidelines from our discussion.

√ Collect business goals and organize them into a means-end tree, such that the children nodes jointly realize their parent node. One lower-level goal may contribute to several higher-level goals.

√ Lower-level goals should operationalize higher-level goals.

√ Grow the tree until you reach the goals to be achieved by the SuD.

5.3 **Guidelines for Finding a Mission Statement**

5.3.1 *Statement of Purpose*

The software specifier's problem consists of describing a software product that contributes to the solution goals. So the problem to be solved by TIS is to provide support for the activities printed in italics in Figure 5.4. Extracting from this a statement of purpose, we get the statement of purpose shown earlier in Figure 5.1:

> To support the management of monthly introductory training courses.

Note that we have now changed the topic from the business to the SuD because we have descended one level in the design hierarchy of Figure 5.3. The statement of purpose is the top-level goal of the SuD, not of the entire business. It characterizes the role the SuD plays in the business solution.

√ Write a statement of purpose that summarizes the business solution goals to be realized and that can finish the statement: "The purpose of the product is to...."

5.3.2 *Responsibilities*

The list of responsibilities refines this problem statement. A simple way to list the responsibilities is to just write, "It is a responsibility of the SuD to contribute to g," where g is any of the solution goals. But that would organize the system responsibilities according to the logic of business goals. There are other ways to organize the system responsibilities:

√ Organize systems responsibilities according to
— The business goals they contribute to
— The business process in which they are used
— The external entities that are needed to exercise the responsibilities
— The kind of added value they deliver to the environment

The responsibilities of TIS (Figure 5.1) have been organized according to the business process to be supported: course preparation, course giving, and course wrap-up.

The reason why the structure of business goals may not be the best organization for the system responsibilities is that we now get to details not considered at the business level. The analysis of the use environment leads to an identification of the business processes to be supported, the entities to be interacted with, and the services to be provided by the SuD. This is the first step from the software problem to the software solution.

It is difficult to make a list of responsibilities at the outset, when the desired functionality of the SuD has not yet been analyzed. The responsibilities summarize the functions of the SuD, and it is therefore natural to develop the list while writing the list of all the system functions (see Chapters 6 and 7).

√ Write the list of responsibilities in conjunction with writing the list of functions of the SuD.

5.3.3 *Composition*

The mission statement lists the boundary of your design freedom by indicating the functionality of the SuD. Each software project always has a charter that tells you what part of the world you may change and what part of the world you must treat as given. Among other things, the charter tells you what ingredients you can use to build the system. This means that you can use the charter to find the first approximation of the system composition.

√ Use the project charter to find a global description of the SuD composition.

5.3.4 *Exclusions*

The list of exclusions is an important tool in managing customer expectations and keeping these expectations in line with what the designer will deliver. It is not written at the start of the software project but during the entire specification project and later. Whenever there is a decision not to include some functionality in the system, document this decision in the mission statement.

√ Write down the reason why a particular functionality or responsibility has been excluded from the scope of the SuD.

It may be useful to distinguish functionality that has been excluded from the first version of the SuD but that will be included later from functionality that will be excluded from all versions of the SuD.

5.4 SUMMARY

The mission statement is a tool to keep all stakeholders' perception of the product purpose constant and to manage their expectations. The statement should be derived from an analysis of business goals, the project charter, and the use environment of the system. The analysis of business goals should lead to a goal tree in which the leaf goals include the goals to be contributed to by the SuD. The statement of purpose summarizes these goals. The list of responsibilities refines the purpose. The statement of the system composition is a high-level characterization of the system boundary and the list of exclusions illustrates this by giving particular examples of properties that the SuD will not have. The list of exclusions is an important tool in expectation management.

5.5 QUESTIONS AND EXERCISES

QUESTIONS FOR REHEARSAL

1. For responsibilities,

◆ What is the difference between a function and a responsibility of a product?

◆ What is the relationship between product responsibilities and environment goals?

EXERCISES

2. Consider the Chemical Tracking System (CTS) described in Chapter 1.
   a) Draw the business goal tree of the company.
   b) Identify the activities to be supported by the CTS.
   c) What is the purpose of the CTS?
   d) What are its responsibilities?
   e) Are there any exclusions you can identify right away?

3. Write a mission statement for the tea-bag-boxing controller described in Chapter 1.

4. Write a mission statement for the bug-fixing database system described in Chapter 1.

QUESTIONS FOR DISCUSSION

5. Write a mission statement of the following products.
   a) A sedan car
   b) A public coffee machine that you regularly use (a machine in which you insert money and receive a cup of coffee)
   c) The word processing software system that you regularly use
   d) The organization unit in which you currently work

CHAPTER 6

Function Refinement Tree

A function refinement tree refines the system purpose into individual services. The tree may refine these further into atomic transactions. We can view the tree as a shopping list of things that the system must do. Section 6.1 discusses the possible representations of a function refinement tree as a tree or as an indented list. Section 6.2 gives guidelines for constructing and validating the tree.

6.1 Notation

A **function refinement tree** is a hierarchical list of system functionality that refines the system purpose to the level of individual services. Figure 6.1 shows a function refinement tree of the Training Information System (TIS) example. Figure 6.2 shows the same tree in indented list form.

Each node in a function refinement tree represents a function of the product for its environment. For example, as we can see in Figure 6.1, it is a function of TIS to support course preparation; in order to provide this function, the TIS has another function, namely to download a list of joiners from the personnel information system.

Figure 6.3 lists the terminology we use to describe system functionality. As defined in Chapter 4, a system function is an ability of the system to produce a desired effect in the environment. The most general function description of the SuD is the mission statement. This is listed at the root of the tree.

The mission is refined into a number of responsibilities, which are the contributions of the SuD to environment goals. A responsibility description always mentions an environment goal to which it contributes. A responsibility may not have a definite starting point and may not be identifiable with a definite interaction. For example, support the coordination of introductory courses and course preparation support do not have a particular start event nor do they consist of a particular interaction that delivers the desired effect.

Figure 6.1 Function refinement tree of the Training Information System.

Figure 6.2 Function refinement tree of the Training Information System in indented list form.

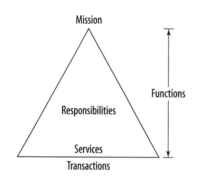

Figure 6.3 Terminology of function refinement.

Responsibilities can be further refined into services, where a system service is defined in this book as a useful interaction between the SuD and its environment. It has a definite starting point, consists of an interaction, and delivers an identifiable added value to the environment. For example, Download list of joiners is a service of TIS. The concept of a service is fuzzy because it is defined in terms of what the user of the system finds valuable.

A service may be an atomic transaction, but it may also be a scenario consisting of many transactions. A transaction is an atomic interaction between the system and its environment. "Atomicity" means that we abstract from any intermediate states of the transaction. Some transactions are already services in themselves because they do something valuable for the environment. Others are not services, but they are part of services.

A function refinement tree represents a refinement relation with the following meaning:

◆ The higher-level function explains why a lower-level function should be present.

◆ The lower-level functions explain what a higher-level function does for the environment.

For example, Figure 6.1 explains that the TIS must be able to print badges because it must support course preparation; and it must support course preparation because it must support course coordination. Conversely, the SuD supports the coordination of introductory courses by supporting course preparation, registration, and wrap-up; and it offers course preparation by being able to download a list of joiners, to allocate joiners to groups, to print badges, and to print lists of group members.

What the tree does *not* represent is a decomposition of the product. A function refinement tree is best viewed as a structured checklist of things the system must be able to do. Function refinement is an activity at the requirements specification level in Figure 5.3; it refines the mission into services without decomposing the system. The strategy of functional decomposition, on the other hand, is a decomposition strategy and belongs to the lowest level in the design hierarchy of Figure 5.3; it is a strategy to partition the SuD into components.

A function refinement tree has several uses in a design process.

◆ It is a simple representation of the SuD that should be understandable to all stakeholders. Little training is required to understand it. This makes it an important tool in communicating a shared vision and therefore in expectation management.

◆ It is an implementation-independent representation of the SuD that helps to keep your design options open. If you use it to represent the functionality of an existing system, it opens up alternative implementation possibilities. If you use it to represent desired functionality of a new system, it avoids premature implementation decisions.

◆ It bounds the functionality of the SuD and relates it to the system mission. This should prevent gold-plating and function drift, processes by which you end up with functionality not motivated by the mission statement.

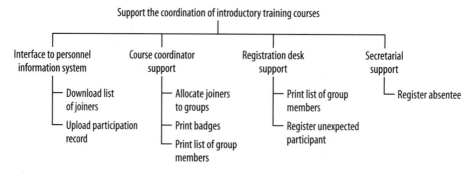

Figure 6.4 Desired user functions: same functionality, different presentation.

◆ It allows you to give a high-level version of the system engineering argument, in which you show that a system with these functions should contribute to the solution goals of the business solution. There is insufficient detail to list assumptions about the environment; this should be done when the functions are specified in more detail (see Chapter 7).

The layout of the tree is the subjective preference of the stakeholders. Even the intermediate nodes between the root and the leaves are matters of subjective preference. Discussing the functionality of the SuD with a different customer may very well lead to a different function refinement tree because that is the way the new customer prefers to see the world. For example, in discussion the functions of TIS with a different customer, we may end up with a tree of user functions shown in Figure 6.4, which partitions the functions according to user rather than according to coordination stage.

We may find that some service can be presented as a daughter of two different nodes. For example, in Figure 6.4, Print list of group members occurs twice, once as a coordinator support function and once as a registration desk support function. We mark this function with an asterisk and duplicate at the relevant nodes of the tree. This turns the function refinement tree into an acyclic directed graph. It is a directed graph because each edge connects a parent and a child and these roles cannot be interchanged; it must be acyclic because it is impossible for a functionality to be refined directly or indirectly into itself.

6.1.1 *Connection with Other Notations*

The root of the tree should be labeled by the statement of system purpose as listed in the mission statement. The system responsibilities listed in the mission statement should be present in the tree, but, as we have seen, we may end up with a tree in which the children of the root are not labeled by the responsibilities listed in the mission statement. If you do not want this, then list all children of the root of the function refinement tree as responsibilities in the mission statement.

6.2 **Design Guidelines**

6.2.1 *Construction*

There are many sources for a function refinement tree: the business goal tree, the system mission statement, information about the intended use context of the system, information about the current system, and so on. To find the desired system functions in this mass of information, it is useful to make some distinctions.

√ Distinguish the properties of the product from the properties of the design and the development process of the product. The ability to provide a service is a product property; the requirement to deliver the system before a certain deadline is a process property.

√ Distinguish the product requirements from the product constraints. Requirements are properties needed to contribute to the desired emergent properties of the composite system; constraints are properties forced on you by the solution environment.

√ Within product requirements, distinguish the properties that consist of a value delivery from the properties that the product must have to deliver this value. The first are true external requirements; the second are properties of a solution.

√ Within the value-delivery product properties, distinguish the services, which are interactions that deliver a value to the environment, from the quality attributes, which are indications of how much value is delivered and to whom.

√ Distinguish the primary services, which are defined independently from one another, from features, which are incremental pieces of functionality.

√ Identify the services that support the primary services, such as maintenance, database administration, maintaining up-to-date information, backup, and recovery.

√ Check that the services start with a triggering event and deliver something valuable to the environment. The triggering event and delivered value jointly identify the service. If you find two triggering events or two different kinds of value delivered, you are probably dealing with two different services.

√ Organize the functions in a tree and relate them to the responsibilities by asking why each function should be there. The answer to this question should be a higher-level function, leading up to the responsibilities and system purpose stated in the mission statement.

As an example, consider the heating controller. Figure 6.5 shows the mission statement. Suppose, from various sources, we obtained the list of desired properties shown in Figure 6.6. The list contains the three business goals that were identified in the goal tree of the juice production plant plus other properties that have been collected from various other sources. To the customer, all of these are things that the system should do. How do we find the desired system functions?

Name: Juice heating controller

Purpose: To control the heating process of fruit juices in a heating tank

Responsibilities:
- To initialize itself with batch data and heat the batch according to recipe
- To report on the heating process
- To maintain safe conditions in a tank

Exclusions:
- Filling the storage tanks with juice
- Transferring pasteurized juice to the canning line

Figure 6.5 Mission statement for the heating controller.

P0 Initialize with batch data.

P1 Heat a batch according to recipe to the desired temperature and for the desired duration.

P2 Monitor temperature in a heating tank.

P3 Maintain a log of each heating process.

P4 Watch for critical conditions. When these occur, raise an alarm or shut down the heating process.

P5 Stop the system upon request of the operator.

P6 The system should run in any plant of the factory.

P7 The system should run on the current NT and the planned Linux platforms.

P8 The system should be up and running within two months.

P9 The system should be developed using the company's in-house development method.

P10 There is a development budget of $60,000 available. The maintenance budget is yet to be determined.

P11 Mean time between failures should be a year.

Figure 6.6 Desired properties of the heating controller.

First, we drop the process properties P8–P10. Second, we drop the constraints P6 and P7. Third, we drop P2, monitoring the tank temperature; this is a task that is not in itself valuable, but that must be performed in order to perform another service (heating the heating tank), so we drop it from our list. P11, mean time between failures, is a quality property that cannot be refined into services, but is an aspect of many services that we will eventually identify. So we are left with P1, P3, P4, and P5 as the functional properties. This list does not contain any features defined

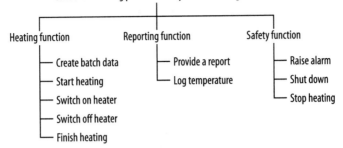

Figure 6.7 Function refinement tree of heating controller.

on top of primary services. We then look at each of the properties in turn, asking whether it is a service, whether it can be refined, and under what responsibility it could fall.

P1, Heat a batch of juice according to recipe: This is a service because it has a starting point and delivers a value, as required by our guidelines. However, we can still refine it into lower-level functions. One of these is actually P0, the initialization function. We refine it into a number of services, as shown in Figure 6.7.

P3, Maintain a log of each heating process: This is included because it contributes to the business goal of maintaining traceability. Discussion with the customer causes us to identify a more general reporting responsibility, of which this is a special case (Figure 6.7). Logging is still a separate function, however, because it takes place at different times and with a different frequency than reporting. In other words, it is triggered by different events than the reporting service.

P4, Watch for critical conditions: This is really a responsibility that must still be refined. We identify two services, Raise alarm and Shut down, to be executed under particular conditions.

P5, Stop the system, turns out to be a refinement that we call Stop heating belonging to the Safety responsibility, with P4.

The result is presented as a tree in Figure 6.7.

A function refinement tree should not grow too deep. There are two guidelines about growing the tree.

◆ Refine the tree at least to the level of system services.

◆ Do not refine the tree further than the level of transactions.

For example, the function refinement tree of the heating controller includes some transactions (under the Heating function) but all other leaves are services. The tree of TIS in Figure 6.1 contains transactions at its leaves.

The identification of transactions and services plays a central role in these guidelines. But, as I have said before, the concept of a service is a fuzzy one. What is considered a service by one user may not be valuable to another user. Two frequently used guidelines to identify services are:

◆ An interaction that a customer is willing to pay for is a service.

◆ An interaction after which users feel they can go away and have a break is a service.

Using low-tech tools. An easy way to find a function refinement tree during a group session is the following. Write a desired functional system property on one Post-It note and stick it to a table or a wall for everyone to see. Continue doing this, writing one property per note. Then, together with the customer, organize the functional properties so that the children of a function show what the system does to accomplish this function, and the parent of a function explains why the system performs these activities.

There are high-tech tools available to do this, which may require you to sit in a darkened room, using machines that need noisy ventilators and heat up the room. Post-It notes allow you to discuss functional requirements in daylight and in a quiet and cool room.

Stop refining the tree when the description of a more refined function would not be easily understood by all stakeholders. The tree is a means of communication, not an architecture for a system. It is a subjective construct, the result of negotiations with the customer about what the customer wishes and the designer thinks can be realized. Different groups of stakeholders will produce different trees.

6.2.2 *Validation*

A few simple checks on a function refinement tree are the following.

◆ Going up in the tree (toward the root), we show why a function should be present in the system; the system mission acts as the ultimate motivation.

◆ Going down the tree, we show which detailed functions must be present to realize a more abstract function.

◆ The function refinement tree is consistent with the list of responsibilities in the mission statement.

◆ The tree has not been grown beyond the level of atomic transactions.

◆ The tree includes all services to be delivered by the system; these are at the leaves or close to the leaves of the tree.

◆ The list of system services suffices to achieve the solution goals listed in the business solution specification.

6.3 **SUMMARY**

A function refinement tree refines the product purpose in one or more steps into services. The tree is related to the business goal tree because each function must contribute to the achievement of some solution goal. The function refinement tree can be used as a means of communication with the customer to manage expectations, keep implementation options open, and restrict the functionality of the system to functions that can be motivated in terms of the product purpose.

6.4 QUESTIONS AND EXERCISES

QUESTIONS FOR REHEARSAL

1. What does it mean to refine a function in subfunctions?

EXERCISES

2. Make a list of functions of the tea-bag-boxing controller.

3. Make a list of functions of the bug-fixing database system.

4. Make a list of functions of the CTS.

QUESTIONS FOR DISCUSSION

5. Make a function refinement tree of the following products. (See Exercise 5 in Chapter 5 for the mission statements.)

    a) A sedan car

    b) A public coffee machine that you regularly use (a machine in which you insert money and receive a cup of coffee)

    c) The word processing software system that you regularly use

    d) The organization unit in which you currently work

6. "There is a relationship between a function refinement tree and the internal decomposition of the system." Give an argument in favor of and an argument against this claim.

CHAPTER 7

Service Description

A service of the SuD is an external interaction with a triggering event that delivers an identifiable added value to the environment. Section 7.1 describes the format in which we describe services, and Section 7.2 gives some guidelines.

7.1 Notation

Services are described by giving four pieces of information:

Name

Triggering event: Some event in the environment that causes the SuD to deliver the service. As explained in Chapter 3, events can be external or temporal, and external events can be named events or condition-change events.

Delivered service: The effect on the environment of delivering the service. The description should make clear to the customer that this effect is valuable.

Assumptions: Assumptions made on the environment. As explained in Chapter 4, without these assumptions, the effect may not be valuable.

For example, Figure 7.1 lists a service of the elevator controller that clearly contributes to the composite system goal of easy travel between floors of a building. It does not list any assumptions, not because there are none, but because the service specification does not depend on them. (We discuss the reasons to include assumptions later.)

A service description has the same uses as a function refinement tree:

♦ To share an understanding of the desired system services among all stakeholders.

♦ To specify system services in an implementation-independent way.

♦ To bound the functionality of the system.

♦ To produce the system engineering argument that these services, under these assumptions, produce the desired emergent properties of the composite system.

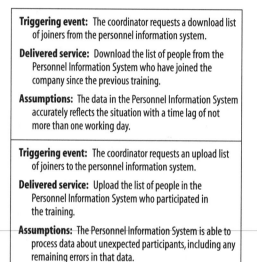

Figure 7.1 The delivery service of the elevator controller.

Figure 7.2 The download and upload services of the Training Information System.

Figure 7.2 shows two service descriptions of the TIS that include assumptions. The reason to include them is that the service descriptions would be different if the assumptions were falsified; in other words, the argument that a system with these services would contribute to the composite system goals depends on the truth of these assumptions.

7.2 **Guidelines**

It is tempting to give detailed information about services too early. We could give details about all possible behaviors and communications that take place during the execution of a service; we could state exactly what the pre- and postconditions of the service are; we could give details about the data formats exchanged and about user interfaces; we could give details about the frequency and volume of interactions, the geographical location where the service should be delivered, and the user population; we could give the requirements on user documentation and help-desk support instructions; and so on. I recommend that this information be given only after you have described the services. Our service descriptions are value-oriented; that is, they emphasize the utility of the service for the user.

In addition, if you want to give any of the more detailed information later on, ask yourself the questions that you should ask about any piece of design documentation that you produce: What is providing it worth, who will read it, how often will they read it, and who will miss it if it is not there?

Figure 7.1 describes one of the two major services of an elevator controller—delivering services to a requested floor. Observe the following:

- The event occurs in the environment. If we ignore the wires connecting the button to the controller software, then we can identify this event with a stimulus of the controller.

- The delivered service is described in terms of what happens in the environment. The environment of the controller consists of buttons, doors, elevator cages, and passengers.

- The effect can only be realized by a complex scenario in which several stimulus-response pairs take place. It will take significant time to realize the effect. When we describe behavior in more detail (see Part IV), we will break this down into atomic interactions.

- The effect mentions a quality attribute, acceptable waiting time. This will have to be made more precise before the customer will buy this system. For example, the manufacturer could guarantee a maximum waiting time of 90 seconds at 80% contract load of the cage.

To select the relevant assumptions from a potentially infinitely long list of assumptions, use the following guidelines.

- Should the requirement be different when the assumption is false? If so, it is relevant.

- Can the SuD observe whether the assumption is satisfied? If so, drop the assumption and incorporate it into the stimulus-response specification.

- Can the SuD itself ensure that the assumption will be satisfied? If so, drop the assumption and add functionality to the system that ensures that the assumption is satisfied.

- When the requirements depend on the assumption, the SuD cannot observe whether the assumption is satisfied, and also the SuD cannot ensure that it is satisfied, then can we at least be certain that the environment ensures that the assumption is satisfied? If not, include the assumption in your specification.

- Even if you can be certain that the assumption is satisfied now, can you be sure that it is satisfied in the future? If not, include the assumption in your specification.

For example, consider the TIS, which downloads data from the personnel information system about employees who have joined the company since the previous introduction course. The assumption is that the personnel information system has recent data about employees that are up-to-date within, say, 1 day. If this assumption is not valid, the TIS may have to deal with a lot of unexpected participants who joined the company after the most recent update of the personnel information system. That changes the requirements on the TIS because it must now handle an unexpected number of last-minute registration in a short time under deadline pressure (typically a few minutes before the course starts). The TIS can do nothing to observe the truth of the assumption or to ensure that it is true. If we cannot be sure that the environment satisfies the assumption, we should include it in the relevant service description (Figure 7.2).

Now take a different assumption—that the names of unexpected participants that are entered in the TIS on the spot are spelled correctly. If this assumption is false, then we would like the TIS to do something about it. What can TIS do to observe whether the assumption is true? It may offer a screen at the registration desk visible to the participant, so that he or she can check whether the name is spelled correctly and tell the registration desk officer if it is incorrect so that the officer can correct the name. But what if an error slips through? The TIS cannot observe whether the names are spelled correctly. We may not assume that all names are spelled correctly, and so we must assume that the TIS sometimes unknowingly uploads misspelled names to the personnel information system. There is nothing the TIS can do to ensure the validity of this assumption, so we add it to the upload service description (Figure 7.2).

As a final example, Figure 7.3 shows two services of the heating controller.

◆ The response to the **start heating** command of the operator

◆ The logging of the temperature, triggered by a temporal event. If an execution of P1 starts at time t_0, then this service is to be triggered at time t_0, $t_0 + 10$, $t_0 + 20$, ..., until the execution of P1 terminates.

Name: P1. Heat batch according to recipe.

Triggering event: Operator command "start heating batch b according to recipe."

Delivered service: Upon reception of this command, the controller ensures that a heating process takes place in the heating tanks in which b is stored, according to the recipe of b.

Assumptions: There is a batch in the heating tank.

Name: Log temperature.

Triggering event: When an execution of P1 starts, and then every 10 seconds during this execution of P1.

Delivered service: The controller records the measured temperature in each tank in which b is stored.

Figure 7.3 The heating and logging services of the heating controller.

The logging service also illustrates another phenomenon, namely that the definition of one service refers to another service. This indicates that the logging service is really a feature defined on top of the basic service of heating a heating tank.

These examples illustrate the two most important guidelines for writing service descriptions:

◆ Describe a service as you would explain it to the customer.

◆ Link your description of the effect of the service to the workflow of the user of the SuD.

7.3 SUMMARY

A service description should clarify what the added value delivered to the environment is and which assumptions about the environment, if any, have been made. Typically, if these assumptions are not satisfied by the environment, then it may not be desirable for the SuD to provide the service. A service description should in addition state what the triggering event of the service is.

7.4 QUESTIONS AND EXERCISES

QUESTIONS FOR REHEARSAL

1. Explain why it is important to describe the value delivered by a function before giving other details.

2. What is the role of assumptions with respect to function descriptions?

EXERCISES

3. Consider the following function of the tea-bag-boxing controller: Place teabag in box or in waste container according to weight. Describe this function according to the template in Section 7.1, adding information from the description in Chapter 1 as necessary.

4. Consider the following function of the bug-fixing database system: Register test report and inform programmer and bug manager. Describe this function according to the template in Section 7.1, adding information from the description in Chapter 1 as necessary.

QUESTIONS FOR DISCUSSION

5. In the following pairs of descriptions, one is a description of behavior as it can be observed and the other indicates the value of the activity for the environment. Which one is behavioral and which one is value-oriented?

a) Sweeping versus cleaning the floor

b) Lighting the room versus switching on the light

c) Setting your preferences versus clicking on the OK button

d) Stopping at a floor with a floor request versus allowing a passenger to get in

6. A description of the delivered value of a service gives you more design freedom than a description of the required behavior of the service. Explain.

7. The following description of a service of the CTS includes details that should be excluded. (See Chapter 1 for a description of the system.)

> The Requester specifies the chemical to request, either by entering its chemical IS number or by importing its structure from a chemical drawing tool. The system can satisfy the request either by offering the requester a new or used container of the chemical from the chemical stockroom or by letting the Requester place an order to an outside vendor. (Wiegers 1999, 133)

a) Simplify the description to a minimal form that still tells the customer why this is a valuable function.

b) What kind of information did you drop?

c) The description omits some important information that is needed to understand why the service is valuable. Which information is missing?

PART III

Entity Notations

The messages exchanged between the system and its environment are about the subject domain. The descriptions of the system purpose and responsibilities, and of the desired system services, also refer to the subject domain. To understand the meaning of these descriptions, it is useful to describe the subject domain in more detail.

- ◆ Chapter 8. I introduce entity-relationship diagrams (ERDs) as a notation to describe which types of entities can exist in the subject domain and how many of them can exist.

- ◆ Chapter 9. I give guidelines for finding an ERD of the subject domain.

- ◆ Chapter 10. I show how to write dictionary entries. The meaning of key terms in the mission statement and service descriptions should be understood by both the customer and designer. Many of the key terms in these descriptions refer to the subject domain; therefore, I include the chapter on writing dictionary entries in this part. Note, however, that the dictionary contains more terms than just subject domain terms and that not all subject domain terms need be included in the dictionary because they are already described elsewhere. For example, the technical documentation of devices may already define important terms. My second reason for including the chapter on writing dictionary entries in this part is that definition by genus and difference (treated in Chapter 10) corresponds closely to defining taxonomic subject domain structures (see Chapter 9).

CHAPTER 8

Entity-Relationship Diagrams

We use an entity-relationship diagram (ERD) to represent the decomposition of the subject domain of a system into entities. An ERD represents two things:

- Which types of entities can exist in the subject domain
- How many of them can exist

In rare cases, we use ERDs to represent components of the SuD, such as the structure of data in the system. Unless otherwise stated, whenever you see an ERD in this book, you can assume that it represents the decomposition of the subject domain into entities.

Figure 8.1 shows an ERD of the subject domain of the heating controller. A rectangle in an ERD represents an entity type. Attributes are written in a box compartment below the entity type name. Lines represent relationships that are used to represent relative cardinality properties. For example, Figure 8.1 says, among other things, that the heating controller subject domain consists of heaters, thermometers, heating tanks, batches, and recipes and that batches have an identifier batchID and are characterized by the amount of fluid in the batch. Each batch is related to one or two heating tanks and at any time, each heating tank is related to at most one batch.

In this chapter, we look at the different elements of an ERD in detail. Section 8.1 introduces the concepts entity, entity type, attribute, and cardinality property. Section 8.2 introduces relationships as a way to express relative cardinality properties and defines the concept of association entity. Section 8.3 defines static and dynamic specialization of entity types.

8.1 Entities and Attributes

An **entity** is a discrete identifiable part of the world; examples are tables, chairs, rocks, kings, presidents, businesses, committees, promises, contracts, traffic signs, and texts. Saying that entities are discrete means that we can collect them in a

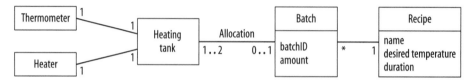

Figure 8.1 Entity-relationship diagram of part of the subject domain of the heating controller.

set. We can count the number of tables in a room, the number of cabbages in a refrigerator, the number of committees installed by your manager, and the number of promises you made yesterday.

Saying that entities are identifiable means that counting how many entities there are does not depend on the state of the counted entities. Each entity has an identity that remains the same under changes of state. Painting the chairs in a room changes their state, but does not change the number of chairs in the room. Updating the balance of a number of bank accounts changes the state of the accounts, but does not change the number of bank accounts.

A counterexample to the concept of a discrete entity is water. Water is a mass, not an entity. We cannot count water; however, we can measure how much water there is in a container. In general, we can ask how many entities there are, but we must ask how much of a mass there is. Thus, we can count how many tables there are in a room, but it is nonsensical to ask how many water there are in a room. Rather, we measure how much water there is in a container, and we can count the number of water containers in a room. It is possible to represent water-holding containers in an ERD because containers are entities; it is *not* possible to represent the water in these containers in an ERD because that water does not have an identity. Very much related to this, we can add masses such as water together and get a mass of the same type. By contrast, if we put entities together, we get a set of entities, which itself is an entity of a different type than its elements.

8.1.1 *Entity Types*

Each entity is an instance of a concept and we always refer to the entity by using this concept. For example, when I say, "Look at this heating tank," I use the concept of a heating tank to direct your attention to what I am looking at. Concepts are shared by people to structure and direct their perceptions and their conversation. Examples of concepts are Heating tank, Elevator cage, Name, Enter, and Exit. Computer scientists call concepts **types** and say that the entity referred to when I point at a heating tank is an **instance** of the type Heating tank. We represent an entity type in an ERD by a named rectangle, as in Figure 8.1. The rectangle may be split into two, in which case the upper part is used to write the type name and the lower part is used to declare a list of attributes (explained next). We always write entity type names with an initial uppercase letter followed by lowercase letters, numbers, or spaces. Attribute names start with a lowercase letter, except if they are Boolean, in which case they too start with an uppercase letter.

All instances of a type share certain properties. For example, all heating tanks have an identifier, a volume, and a date last cleaned; are located in a particular building, and are painted grey; can stand temperatures up to 300 degrees Celsius; bend in a certain way under pressure; are owned by the juice production company; and last at least 10 years. Some of these properties can be represented by a value. These are called **attributes.** For example, Figure 8.1 shows that recipes have three attributes: name, desired temperature, and duration. Other properties, such as that the tanks bend in a certain way under pressure, are not represented by attributes in this book, but we can add these as comments to the ERD if we wish.

The following definitions help to clarify entity types.

- The set of all possible instances of an entity type E is called the **extension** of E. For example, the extension of the Heating tank is the set of all possible heating tanks in the subject domain, including those that exist now, those that have existed in the past, and those that may exist in the future.

- In each state of the world, zero or more entities of a type actually exist. The **current extent** of an entity type is the set of currently existing instances of that type. So the current extent of Heating tanks in a particular subject domain consists of the heating tanks in that domain. Note that the current extent of a type is always a subset of the extension of the type.

- The **intension** of an entity type is the set of all properties shared by all instances in its extension. Describing the intension of an entity type is very informative. We may for example be told that the intension of Heating tank is the set of properties {has a volume, has a heater, has a thermometer, can stand a temperature up to 300 degrees Celsius, is cleaned regularly}. This exactly determines what is and is not to be considered a heating tank—that is, if it does not have a thermometer, then according to this definition it is not a heating tank.

- An entity type usually has infinitely many properties in its intension. For example, if it is the property of all heating tanks that they can stand temperatures up to 300 degrees Celsius, then they can also stand temperatures up to 299 degrees Celsius, 298 degrees Celsius, 200.1 degrees Celsius, and so on. It is impossible to list all these properties in a definition. The **defining intension** of an entity type is a usually small set of properties that we use to define the entity type. The defining intension of an entity type is the list of attributes and other properties that we declare in an ERD.

8.1.2 *Absolute Cardinality Properties*

An **absolute cardinality property** of a type is a set of natural numbers that indicates how many instances can exist at the same time in the subject domain that we are modeling. For example, if entity type E has the absolute cardinality property {4, 5, 6, 9}, then at any time there are either 4, 5, 6, or 9 instances of E.

An absolute cardinality property of an entity type is expressed in the upper right corner of the name compartment. For example, Figure 8.2 gives a part of the subject

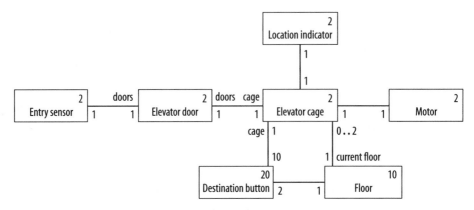

Figure 8.2 Entity-relationship diagram of part of an elevator system.

domain of the elevator controller. It says that the subject domain contains two cages, two motors, 20 destination buttons, 10 floor buttons, and so on.

A cardinality property is represented by a cardinality expression with the following syntax.

- $n_1 . . m_1, \ldots, n_k . . m_k$ stands for $\{n_1, \ldots, m_1\} \cup \ldots \cup \{n_k, \ldots, m_k\}$.
- $n . . *$ stands for the infinite set of numbers $\{n, n + 1, \ldots\}$.
- n (on its own) stands for the set $\{n\}$.
- $*$ (on its own) stands for the set of natural numbers $\{0, 1, 2, \ldots\}$.

To avoid overburdening a diagram with a large number of stand-alone asterisks, we omit these as we wish. So, the absence of a cardinality constraint means the same thing as the presence of a stand-alone asterisk.

In this book, all cardinality properties are **snapshot properties,** not historical properties. A snapshot property is a property of the current state of a domain at any arbitrary time. A historical property is a property of the history of the domain at any arbitrary point in time. For example, in the life of an elevator system, a motor may be replaced, so the historical cardinality of Motor in Figure 8.2 is $*$, which means that at any time a motor may already have been replaced any number of times. Nevertheless, at any time, there are exactly two motors in the system.

Another way of putting this is that an absolute cardinality is a property of current extents. If $|S|$ denotes the number of elements in a set S, then for an entity type E we have $|extent(E)| \leq |extension(E)|$, and if c is the absolute cardinality property of E we have $|extent(E)| \in c$.

8.2 **Relationships**

A **relationship** between entity types is a set of tuples of instances of these types. The number of types connected by a relationship is called its **arity.** Relationships of arity 2 are called **binary.** A binary relationship is represented by a line connecting

Figure 8.3 Possible labels of a
binary relationship line.

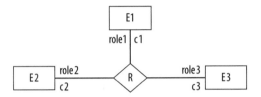

Figure 8.4 Two ways of representing the same relationship.

Figure 8.5 Representation of relationships with
arity higher than 2.

two entity-type boxes, as illustrated in Figure 8.1. Binary relationship lines may be
labeled by the following information (Figure 8.3).

◆ A relationship name R. Relationship names always start with an uppercase letter.
   The name is optionally labeled by a triangular arrow that represents the direction
   of reading the relationship. As Figure 8.4 illustrates, this makes the reading direction independent from the way the boxes are placed with respect to one another.

◆ A **role name** can be added at each end of the line. This represents the role played
   by that entity in the relationship. An example is current floor in Figure 8.2. Role
   names start with a lowercase letter.

◆ A relative cardinality property can be added at each end of the line. Examples
   are c1 and c2 in Figure 8.3 (see above).

In order not to overload the diagram, we can omit any of these names if doing so
does not introduce ambiguity. Relationships of arity 3 and higher are represented
by a diamond, as illustrated in Figure 8.5.

We use relationships in an ERD for two purposes: to express relative cardinality
properties and to define association entities.

8.2.1 *Relative Cardinality Properties*

A **relative cardinality property** says how many instances of one entity type can
exist for each existing entity of some other type. A relative cardinality property is
expressed by placing a cardinality expression at the end of a relationship line. For
example, Figure 8.1 says that for each existing heater there is exactly one existing

heating tank and vice versa. It also says that each heating tank has at most one Allocation relationship with an existing batch and that each existing batch has an Allocation relationship with exactly one or two existing heating tanks. Note that cardinality properties say something about existing entities; they are about extents, not about extensions. A heating tank may be linked to any possible heater, but in any state of the domain it is linked to exactly one existing heater.

Note again that relative cardinality properties are snapshot properties; they are about states of the subject domain, not about histories. Over time, a heating tank will contain many different batches—at different times. But at each particular moment, it will either be empty or contain a batch.

Suppose in Figure 8.3 that we omit labels R, role1, and role2 from a relationship line. Then the diagram still represents information, but much of the intended meaning is implicit. The line should be read as follows:

> For each existing instance of E1 there are c2 existing instances of E2, and for each existing instance of E2 there are c1 existing instances of E1.

Cardinality properties in an ERD may be mutually inconsistent. For example, Figure 8.6(a) gives an inconsistent fragment of an ERD of the subject domain of the elevator controller: Because there are three sensors and two doors, there cannot be a one-one relationship between them. Figure 8.6(b) gives a fragment of the ERD of the subject domain of the ETS. The intended meaning of the diagram is that a payment is made from a bank account and that a refund can be made on behalf of the payment. The comment defines a property that the two paths from payment to account should commute. p.from is called a path expression and denotes the account reachable from a payment p through the from role. p.refund.account is also a path expression and denotes the account reachable from p through refund. (Path expressions are explained in Chapter 10.) The commutativity property says that the two paths should lead to the same account. This cannot be the case if for each payment there is one account but for each refund there are two accounts. (Yes, the example is contrived.)

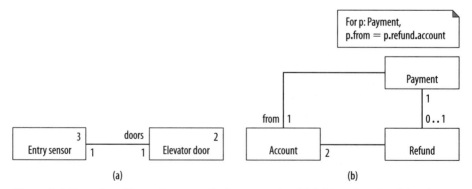

Figure 8.6 Examples of inconsistent cardinality properties. (a) Subject domain of the elevator controller—inconsistent absolute and relative cardinality properties. (b) Subject domain of the Electronic Ticket System—inconsistent relative cardinality properties.

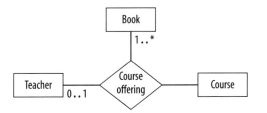

Figure 8.7 Example of cardinality constraints for a ternary relationship.

We should beware of inconsistencies when there are both absolute and relative cardinality properties in a diagram or when there are loops in the relationships. Because the elevator subject domain model Figure 8.2 contains absolute and relative cardinalities and contains loops, it must be checked carefully for inconsistencies. The loop between Elevator cage, Destination button, and Floor would be inconsistent if it were required to contain commutative paths. Happily, it does not contain commutative paths. The intended meaning of this part of the diagram is that for each cage, there are 10 destination buttons and each of these buttons is related to a floor. Traveling the other path, each elevator cage has at each moment exactly one current floor, and each floor has exactly two destination buttons related to it (one for each of the two elevator cages). These two paths are not equivalent, and so there is no inconsistency.

Relative cardinality properties of ternary relationships are harder to understand. In fact, most cardinality properties for relationships with arity higher than 2 cannot be expressed in an ERD. Figure 8.7 expresses the following constraints:

◆ Each existing (Book, Course) pair is related to at most one existing teacher.

◆ Each existing (Teacher, Book) pair is related to any number of existing courses. (There is an implicit asterisk constraint in the diagram.)

◆ Each existing (Teacher, Course) pair is related to at least one existing book.

With some effort, this can be translated into understandable sentences. This is left as an exercise to the reader (see Exercise 6 at the end of the chapter).

ERD diagrams can express only cardinality properties and, in the case of ternary relationships, not even all kinds of cardinality properties can be expressed. If you want to express any other property, add it as a comment to the diagram.

8.2.2 Association Entities

If a relationship itself has attributes, then it is called an **association entity.** This is represented by connecting an entity box by a dashed line with the relationship symbol, as illustrated in Figure 8.8. The relationship between a juice and a recipe is called a Mixture and it has a percentage as an attribute. The figure expresses the facts that a recipe consists of one or more juices and that each of these juices has a

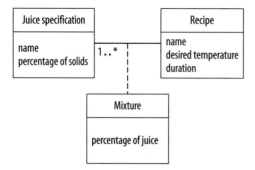

Figure 8.8 Binary association entity.

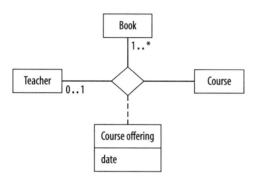

Figure 8.9 Ternary association entity.

certain percentage in the recipe. Association entities of higher arity can be declared as well, as shown in Figure 8.9.

What is the difference between an association entity and a "normal" entity? The difference is in the way we identify them. A relationship is identified by the entities that participate in it, whereas a "normal" entity has its own, independent identity. For example, in Figure 8.1, batches and heating tanks have their own independent identities. We can give an identifier to these entities, such as a serial number. The Allocation relationship between them, on the other hand, does not have an independent identity. When we want to talk about a particular allocation, we must say, "Take the allocation between batch b and tank t." The same is true for association entities. In Figure 8.8, a Mixture is identified by referring to the recipe and juices of the mixture. And in Figure 8.9, we identify a Course offering by identifying a teacher, book, and course.

8.3 **Generalization**

If the extension of an entity type E_1 is a subset of the extension of another type E_2, then we say that E_1 is a **specialization** of E_2 and that E_2 is a **generalization** of E_1. Instead of specialization and generalization, we use subtype and supertype.

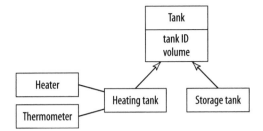

Figure 8.10 Two generalization relationships.

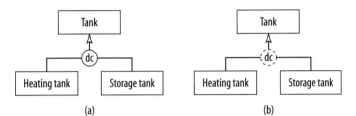

Figure 8.11 Static and dynamic specialization. (a) Static specialization—migration between subtypes is not possible. (b) Dynamic specialization—migration between subtypes is possible.

Figure 8.10 gives an example. The diagram says that a Heating tank is a Tank and that a Storage tank is a Tank. It also says that heating tanks are related to heaters and thermometers, but that storage tanks are not. Finally, the diagram says that all heating and storage tanks have a tank ID and a volume. Because a subtype extension is contained in the supertype extension, all properties shared by all supertype instances are also shared by all subtype instances. This is called **inheritance.**

Note carefully that generalization is a relationship between extensions and not between extents. Remember that the extension of a type is the set of all possible type instances, but that the current extent of a type is the set of currently existing type instances. It is possible that in a particular state of the world, the set of existing tanks equals the set of existing heating tanks.

Suppose that entities can change type. For example, suppose a tank starts its life as a heating tank and, after some years, it is used as a storage tank. If this can happen to all tanks and if, conversely, every storage tank can become a heating tank, then the set of all possible Heating tank entities equals the set of all possible Tank entities, and also the set of all possible Storage tank entities equals the set of all possible Tank entities!

To express properties such as these, we add some notation. Figure 8.11(a) shows three entity-type boxes connected by a generalization arrow that passes through a circle labeled dc. This circle is called a **static specialization node.** It can be labeled as follows:

◆ A d means that the subtype extensions are mutually disjoint; that is, extension(Heating tank) ∩ extension(Storage tank) = Ø, where ∩ denotes set intersection and Ø denotes the empty set.

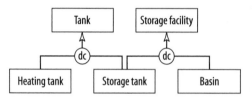

Figure 8.12 Multiple generalization.

◆ A c means that the subtype extensions jointly cover the supertype; that is, extension(Heating tank) ∪ extension(Storage tank) = extension(Tank).

So Figure 8.11(a) means that each tank is either a heating or a storage tank, and that it stays so forever.

Figure 8.11(b) shows a dashed circle called a **dynamic specialization node.** This means that instances can migrate between subtypes. The node can be labeled with the same letters as the static specialization node, but these have different meanings. Remember that at any time, extent(E) is the set of currently existing instances of E.

◆ A d means that at any moment, the current subtype extents are mutually disjoint; that is, extent(Heating tank) ∩ extent(Storage tank) = ∅.

◆ A c means that the current subtype extents jointly cover the supertype; that is, extent(Heating tank) ∪ extent(Storage tank) = extent(Tank).

So Figure 8.11(b) means that at any time, each existing tank is either a heating or a storage tank, but that a tank may sometimes be a heating tank and sometimes a storage tank. The implication is that the extensions are equal, or

extension(Heating tank) = extension(Storage tank) = extension(Tank)

The dashed circle does not allow us to express constraints on the sequencing of type changes. For example, perhaps a heating tank can turn into a storage tank, but not the other way around. Sequencing constraints on type changes can be expressed using behavior description techniques (see Part IV). They cannot be expressed in an ERD.

A single specialization node only allows multiple specialization. To represent multiple generalization use the convention shown in Figure 8.12.

8.4 SUMMARY

An ERD consists of nodes, which represent entity types, and edges, which represent relationships. Nodes and edges can be annotated with cardinality expressions that represent absolute or relative cardinality properties. These are snapshot properties, not historial properties. Entities have properties that can be represented by attributes, whose names can be listed in a box compartment below the entity-type name. A relationship whose instances have attributes is called an association entity.

A special kind of relationship is the generalization relationship, represented by an arrow with an empty head. The inverse relationship is called specialization. If E2 is a generalization of E1, then all instances of E1 are instances of E2. We may use a generalization node to express the properties of disjointness and covering of the subtypes, expressed by labeling the generalization node with a d for disjointness and a c for covering. If the node is dashed, migration between subtypes is possible; if it is solid, migration is not possible.

8.5 QUESTIONS AND EXERCISES

QUESTIONS FOR REHEARSAL

1. Define the following concepts:
   Entity
   Attribute
   Relationship
   Association entity

2. Define the following concepts:
   Type
   Instance
   Extension of a type
   Extent of a type
   Intension of a type

3. Define the following concepts:
   Absolute cardinality property
   Relative cardinality property

4. Define the following concepts:
   Generalization of a type
   Static generalization
   Dynamic generalization
   Disjointness of a set of specializations of a type
   Covering of a set of specializations of a type

EXERCISES

5. A company gives in-house courses to its employees. The teachers of each course are employees as well. Figure 8.13 gives an ERD. Suppose that one course offering may be given in several rooms simultaneously, with one teacher per room. Change the model to represent this. Be sure to make your model represent the fact that one teacher cannot teach in two rooms at the same time.

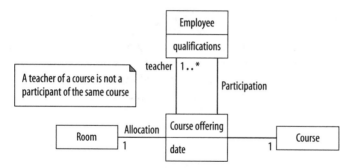

Figure 8.13 A model of courses, participants, and teachers.

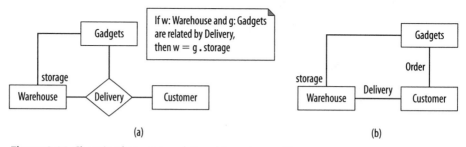

Figure 8.14 Choosing between a relationship and an entity.

6. Rephrase the cardinalities of Figure 8.7 in understandable English.

7. Figure 8.14 shows two ways of modeling the situation that a gadget is delivered to a customer from a particular warehouse where such gadgets are stored. One of them is wrong. Which one? Explain your answer.

8. Suppose we change the meaning of a cardinality property, so that it expresses the number of entities that exist or have existed in the past. Change the cardinalities of Figure 8.1 to reflect this new interpretation of cardinality property.

QUESTIONS FOR DISCUSSION

9. a) Suppose that currently all heating tanks in our factory are grey. Does this imply that this property is part of the intension of the type Heating tank?

   b) If extension(E1) ⊆ extension(E2), then intension(E2) ⊆ intension(E1), and vice versa. Explain.

10. Russian army tank number 1967 was the first one to enter Prague in 1945 and is now a monument. Make a model of the generalization relationships (if any) between Car, Vehicle, Monument, and Tank.

CHAPTER 9

ERD Modeling Guidelines

E ntity-relationship models are used to classify and count entities in the subject domain. This chapter gives guidelines on how to do this. Section 9.1 shows that the boundary of the subject domain is determined by the messages that cross the interface of the system. The identifiable entites referred to by these messages constitute the subject domain. Section 9.2 gives guidelines for distinguishing entities from attributes, and Section 9.3 gives guidelines for distinguishing entities from relationships. These are modeling choices that are guided, again, by a consideration of what has an identity underlying the changes in the subject domain and how this identity is structured. Section 9.4 gives guidelines for classifying entities in a taxonomic structure; identity considerations are crucial in defining a taxonomy, too. Section 9.5 shows how to validate a model.

9.1   The Subject Domain Boundary

One of the first problems to solve is to determine the boundary of the subject domain. The solution is simple: To have a criterion of relevance for the subject domain, you need to know what system functionality is. This is because the messages received or sent by the system refer to the subject domain. So to find the subject domain, find these messages and see what they are about. For example, the elevator controller responds to the following messages, among others:

- ◆ Up-button on floor 3 has been pressed.
- ◆ Entry sensor of cage c activated.

And it sends the following messages, among others, to the environment:

- ◆ Switch off light in button b.
- ◆ Turn off motor m.

The nouns in these messages refer to subject domain entities.

Name: Deliver passengers

Triggering event: A passenger pushes the destination button for floor F in an elevator cage.

Delivered service: The controller ensures that the elevator cage gets to floor F and allows the passenger to leave the cage. Average waiting time at 80% contract load should be no more than 60 seconds.

Figure 9.1 The delivery service of the elevator controller.

But what if you do not yet know what the messages received and sent by the system are? To get a first approximation to the subject domain, you can turn to the service descriptions (see Chapter 7) to see what they refer to. For example, Figure 9.1 shows a service description of the elevator controller that we have seen before. This gives us a first indication of what might be in the subject domain: passengers, buttons, floors, and elevator cages. (We know from Chapter 3 that passengers are outside of the domain, but then this is only a first approximation.) Of course, subsequent analysis may uncover additional entities, and some of the entities just listed may turn out to be irrelevant or unobservable. But at least we have a place to start. This gives us two guidelines for finding the boundary of the subject domain:

√ To find out where the subject domain is, find out what entities the messages received and sent by the system refer to.

√ To get a rough idea where the subject domain is, find out what the service descriptions of the product refer to.

What kinds of entities can we find in the subject domain? There is a rich variety of them.

√ Include in the subject domain the following kinds of entities:
—Natural bodies
—Devices
—People
—(Parts of) organizations
—Conceptual entities
—Lexical items

This list is not exhaustive nor are the kinds disjoint. Chapter 2 gives more examples of these kinds of entities. Natural bodies are physical entities other than devices and people, such as buildings, agricultural fields, and animals. People, devices, and natural bodies are all physical entities and they have properties described by the laws of nature, such as that they expand when heated and drop when not supported. Organizations are groups of people working for a shared mission; examples are a business, a supplier, a customer, and a government department. The world is surprisingly full of invisible conceptual entities, such as property rights, obligations to produce a deliverable, permissions to perform a task, and allocations of tasks to actors. Lexical items are physical symbol occurrences; an example is a written recipe for fruit juice.

The guidelines given so far tell us what things to include. The next one tells us what to exclude:

√ Exclude from the subject domain entities that are not identifiable by the SuD.

We saw in Chapter 3 that we should drop entities from the subject domain that the SuD cannot get reliable information about or that it cannot reliably control. The underlying reason for this is that the SuD cannot identify these entities. For example, it is tempting to add Passenger to the subject domain ERD of the elevator controller because it is really a central entity, needed to understand the purpose of all transactions. However, we use the ERD to represent the entities referred to by the messages that cross the SuD interface. These messages must contain identification information of these entities so that the SuD can keep the different entities apart and can recognize the same entity when it is referred to twice. The subject domain ERD does not express our understanding of the messages but it instead expresses which identifiable entities in the subject domain the SuD knows about. Because the elevator controller does not know the identity of the passengers, they are not part of its subject domain. If, in a different application, passengers are required to identify themselves to the controller before using the elevator, then they would be part of the subject domain of the controller.

We will see later (Chapter 18) that it is all right to include passengers in a context diagram of the controller, which shows where messages come from and where responses go to. In fact, such a context diagram can be useful to show where the unreliability of the connection between the source and destination of a message is introduced.

9.2 **Entities versus Attributes**

When should we model something as an entity and when as an attribute? To find this out, we consider the desired system functionality. An individual in the subject domain should be modeled as an entity if the system should send or receive information about it. Attribute values, on the other hand, *are* the information sent or received by the system.

√ If the system needs to send or receive information about an individual, the individual is an entity.

√ Information about an entity is represented by means of attribute values.

Entities are the things the SuD communicates information about; attribute values are the information communicated about the entities. In a database, entities are the things that the database stores information about and attribute values are the information stored about entities.

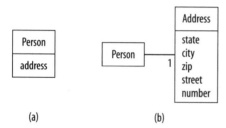

(a)   (b)

Figure 9.2 Modeling an address as an attribute or as an entity type. (a) Address as an attribute. (b) Address as an entity type.

For example, Figure 9.2(a) represents an address as an attribute value and Figure 9.2(b) represents it as an entity type. If a postal service changes the zip codes—and this has been done—then in model (a) this cannot be distinguished from a move to another address, whereas in model (b) it can be distinguished from a move to another address. This is because in model (b), a change in zip code is a change in the state of an address entity. And, as we have observed, changing the state of an entity does not change its identity. In model (a) we cannot even talk about the difference between zip code changes and address changes. For many applications, model (a) is a sufficiently refined view of the subject domain. But if we need to exchange information with the system about changing zip codes, then we need model (b). For example, a direct mail application needs to know when people moved as opposed to when their zip codes changed because only in the first case will they be interested in advertisements for, say, new furniture.

The same difference between entities and attribute values can be viewed from another angle. An attribute value is just that—a value. For example, an attribute of Floor may be number, with possible values from 1 to 10. These values have properties—for example, they are natural numbers, some of them are prime, some are odd and some are even, and they are all nonnegative. All of these properties are derivable from the value themselves. We do not have to store them. They are **derivable** properties, in the sense that all properties of the number 10 can be derived by symbol manipulation without making observations of the real world. By contrast, the fact that you live at a certain address cannot be derived from anything. You need to make an observation of the real world to find out what your address is. It is a **nonderivable** property. The property value might be different, and you need to make an observation to find out what the property value is. If we only need to refer to the derivable properties of something, then we can model it as an attribute; but if we need to refer to contingent properties, then we model it as an entity.

√ An entity has nonderivable properties; an attribute value only has derivable properties.

The distinction between derivable and nonderivable properties is not dependent on the desired functionality of the system but on our dictionary. If we can use the definitions of terms in the dictionary to determine the value of an attribute, then the attribute is derivable. If we need to observe the domain to find the value of an attribute, it is nonderivable.

9.3 Entity versus Relationships

When should we model an individual as an entity and when as a relationship? We have encountered the criterion for this already when discussing the difference between association entities and normal entities in Section 8.2.2:

√ A relationship is identified by its participating entities.

√ An entity has its own, independent identification criterion.

Consider the ERD in which we model the mixture of juices in a recipe. In Figure 9.3(b), this is represented as an associative entity (i.e. a relationship), and therefore it is identified by a juice specification and a recipe. This means two things:

◆ For each Mixture instance, there are exactly one juice specification and one recipe that it relates.

◆ For each pair consisting of a juice specification and a recipe, either there currently is one Mixture instance or there is none; it is impossible for there currently to be more than one Mixture of this juice specification in this recipe.

This expresses what we want.

Contrast this with the result if Mixture is modeled as an entity type, as in Figure 9.3(a).

◆ We had to add two cardinality properties to ensure that for each Mixture instance, there is exactly one juice specification and one recipe that it relates.

◆ For each pair consisting of a juice specification and a recipe, there may currently be many mixtures; it is possible that there are currently more than one mixture of this juice in this recipe.

This is clearly not what we want to express. To see what happens, remember that an entity has an identity independently from its state. Because in Figure 9.3(a), juice

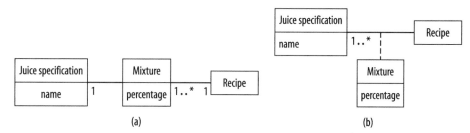
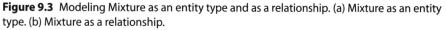

Figure 9.3 Modeling Mixture as an entity type and as a relationship. (a) Mixture as an entity type. (b) Mixture as a relationship.

specifications and mixtures are both entity types, this model allows the following state of the subject domain:

extent(Juice specification)	extent(Mixture)	extent(Recipe)
(s1, ...)	(q1, percentage: 40)	(r1, ...)
(s1, ...)	(q2, percentage: 50)	(r1, ...)

This is possible because q1 and q2 are two distinct identifiers. In Figure 9.3(b), this is not possible because quantities are identified by juice specification and batch. In Figure 9.3(b), an instance of Mixture has an identifier of the form (s1, r1) for a juice specification s1 and a recipe r1, and an extent of Mixture containing two copies of (s1, r1) is not possible because an extent is a set. It is not possible to repair Figure 9.3(a) by adding a cardinality property.

Generalizing, if we model a relationship R between $E_1, \ldots, E_n$ as an n-ary relationship, then for each possible combination of existing instances of $E_1, \ldots, E_n$, there can exist at most one relationship instance. This is a global property that cannot be modeled by a cardinality property.

9.4 Taxonomic Structures

9.4.1 Rules of Classification

Classifications have the tendency to grow over the years as new kinds of entities are introduced in the subject domain. Consider the classification of documents shown in Figure 9.4, taken from one of the libraries of a small university in Amsterdam. What does the class Nonbook document contain if classes such as maps, globes, and photos (clearly not books) are recognized as separate classes? The library contains books that are handwritten manuscripts. Is any book that cannot be borrowed for a day or for 1, 2, or 3 weeks a handwritten manuscript? And what is the difference between maps and atlasses? Is a map with a cardboard protection around it an atlas? Are two maps with a cardboard protection around it an atlas? And so on.

The document taxonomy is a classification of a supertype, Document, into a number of subtypes. Earlier we represented this by connecting the supertype with a set of subtypes through a specialization node. There are a number of simple rules of classification applicable to such a structure that have been known for centuries. I first state these rules and then explain and illustrate them.

√ For each specialization node there should be a **specialization attribute,** which represents a single crisp and unambiguous classification principle.

√ At any moment, the extents of the subtypes of a specialization node should have a comparable size.

√ The specialization should be informative; that is, a subtype should have a larger intension than its supertype.

1 Book (3 weeks)	20 Collection *Jurid. Europeana*
2 Book (2 weeks)	25 Non-book document
3 Book (1 week)	30 Photo
4 Book (1 day/weekend)	31 Globe
10 Periodical (3 weeks)	32 I.O.S. publications
11 Periodical (1 week)	33 Report of the Central Bureau of Statistics
12 Periodical (1 day/weekend)	34 Annual economic government report
15 Map	35 Other economic periodicals
16 Hand-written manuscript	40 Microfiche (book)
17 Atlas	41 Microfilm (book)
18 Reports of parliamentary debates	42 Microfiche (periodical)
19 Legal periodicals	43 Microfilm (periodical)

Explanations:
- Books and periodicals are subdivided according to the period that they may be borrowed.
- The collection *Juridicae Europeana* contains legal periodicals.

Figure 9.4 A taxonomy of documents.

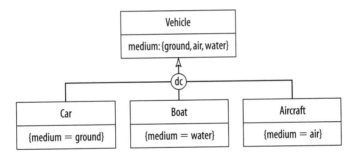

Figure 9.5 A classification attribute. The value of the attribute for the subtypes is added as a comment within curly brackets.

The specialization attribute. If we divide vehicles into cars, boats, and airplanes, then the specialization attribute is transport medium, with the possible values ground, water, and air. The recognition of this attribute makes clear that we may have forgotten some subtypes of Vehicle, such as spacecraft and subways, and a distinction between underwater and water-surface vehicles. Figure 9.5 shows how we can represent this in an ERD, by writing the values of the specialization attribute for the subtypes as comments within brackets.

The definition of a specialization attribute should satisfy a number of constraints.

◆ It should represent a single classification criterion. As a counterexample, classes 1–12 in Figure 9.4 represent two criteria—one in which books are distinguished from periodicals and one in which several different borrowing periods are distinguished.

◆ It should be a crisp criterion. Crisp is the opposite of vague. A classification criterion is vague if it allows the classification of an entity in two or more classes. For example, the distinction between maps and atlasses is not as crisp as it could be. Some entities may be both a map and an atlas. Another example is the classification of people into those who are tall and those who are not tall; there is a grey area of people who are more or less tall.

◆ It should be unambiguous. There are crisp classification criteria that are still ambiguous, such as a classification of documents into those that are about statistics and those that are about economics. Some documents are clearly about statistical economics.

The principle of comparable size. This says that the subtypes of a supertype should have extents that are usually of the same order of magnitude. A classification of people into those that live in Amsterdam versus the rest of the world is suspect because the two classes have a very different size.

The principle of informativeness. This says that we should learn something when we hear that an entity is an instance of a subtype. For example, if we partition books into those that can be borrowed for a day, a week, two weeks, and three weeks, these four subtypes of Book contain no information other than the borrowing period—these subtypes are not informative. They should be modeled by an attribute borrowing period of books. By contrast, the classification of a document as a book or a periodical is informative because there is extra information that we get from this. A book has an author and a publication date; periodicals have editors, not authors, and they have a publication frequency.

Using these guidelines, we can rationalize the document classification of Figure 9.4. This is left as an exercise for the reader (see Exercise 13 at the end of the chapter).

9.4.2   *Static versus Dynamic Specialization*

A static or dynamic specialization node connects a number of subtypes with a supertype. In a static specialization, the subtypes are viewed as special cases of the supertype. For example, in Figure 9.6(a), we partition Vehicle into Car and Airplane.

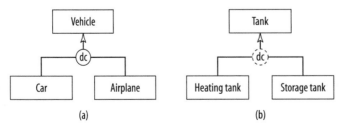

(a)   (b)

Figure 9.6 Dynamic versus static specializations. (a) Static specialization. (b) Dynamic specialization.

Suppose, for the sake of example, that cars never turn into airplanes and that airplanes never turn into cars. Then in this model, a car and an airplane are special cases of a vehicle.

In a dynamic specialization, by contrast, the subtypes are viewed as states of instances of the supertype. Consider Heating tank and Storage tank, modeled as dynamic specializations of Tank in Figure 9.6(b). This means that a heating tank can become a storage tank and vice versa. It would be conceptually incoherent to say that a tank changes its identity when changing subtype. If the identity did change, then it would not be a case of subtype migration but rather a case of destruction of one instance followed by the creation of another. By saying that an instance migrates from one subtype to another, we imply that the identity of the instance does not change—what changes is its state. Being an instance of Heating tank is a possible state of a tank.

Another property of subtype migration is that in this migration, the extent of two subtypes change, whereas the extent of their supertype does not change. When a storage tank becomes a heating tank, the set of existing tanks does not change. Contrast this with a static specialization. In Figure 9.6(a), the creation or deletion of a car (or an airplane) is also the creation or deletion of a vehicle. A change in the extent of a static subtype entails a corresponding change in the extent of the supertype.

This leads us to the following guidelines for distinguishing static and dynamic subtypes.

√ If an instance migrates between dynamic subtypes, it does not change its identity but, instead, its state.

√ If the extent of a static subtype changes, the extent of its supertype changes correspondingly.

9.4.3 *Classification and Counting*

Identification and classification are deeply intertwined. If I ask you to count the number of heating tanks in a plant, you must know what a heating tank is. Without the concept of a heating tank, you do not know what to count as a heating tank. This means that the definition of the entity type Heating tank should include sufficient information to allow us to recognize a heating tank when we see one, and to count heating tanks when we see more than one. (We discuss definitions in Chapter 10.)

For now, consider what this means for subtyping. Is a passenger a person? Not for all counting purposes. If Passenger is a subtype of Person, then a passenger *is* a person. Counting passengers is then the same as counting people. If we say that our airline company carried 6000 passengers today, we are saying that 6000 different people traveled by one of our airplanes. If this is not what we mean, then either we should say what we do mean or we should change our model of the subject domain. Let us first try to say what we mean.

Figure 9.7(a) models Passenger as a dynamic subtype of Person. This means that a person sometimes is a passenger and sometimes is not, and that each time that a person is a passenger it is the same passenger—because it is the same person. If we stick to this model, we have to think about what it is that happened 6000 times today. Did someone enter one of our airplanes 6000 times with the intention of being

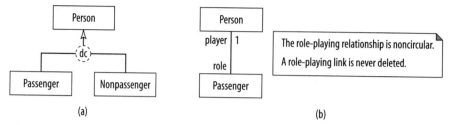

Figure 9.7 Dynamic subtype versus role type. (a) Passenger as dynamic specialization of person. (b) Passenger as role of person.

transported? This is hardly an observable event because the passenger's intention is not observable. Were 6000 tickets used today? Or rather, because one ticket may be used twice on the same day, were there 6000 different tickets used today? Does this include the case in which someone leaves the plane for an hour during refueling and cleaning? By the way, what is a day here? A flight from Amsterdam to Tokyo crosses the date line, lands in Anchorage, and then returns to the previous date. It is surely possible to give a clear definition of what it is that happened 6000 times and in which time period this happened. But we are a long way from the model of Figure 9.7(a).

Clearly, before we can say how many Xs there are, we must know how to recognize an X when we see one and how to count Xs if there are more than one. This is as true for us as it is true for software. If a software system receives or sends messages about instances of an entity type, it must be able to recognize and count these instances. This gives us the following guidelines for defining entity types.

✓ If a software system receives or sends information about a subject domain entity type, then
  —a **recognition criterion** must be defined that tells us how the software product can recognize an instance.
  —a **counting criterion** must be defined that tells us how the software product can keep different instances apart.

The defining intension of the entity type should provide us with both criteria. And if E_1 is a subtype of E_0, then the counting criterion of the two types is the same, but the recognition criterion of E_1 extends that of E_0. Only a subset of the instances of E_0 qualify as an E_1.

9.4.4 Subtypes versus Roles

Let us now take the other route and change our model of passenger. Modeling a passenger as subtype of person is only useful if we want to represent the fact that each passenger is identical to a person. This is interesting for counting purposes and also for recognition purposes: Each passenger has all the properties shared by all people and some more. But if we are not interested in representing this, we can take an easier way out, which is to model passenger as a separate entity type. This

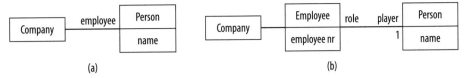

Figure 9.8 Reifying roles. (a) A person playing a role for a company. (b) A reified role allows us to attach attributes to it.

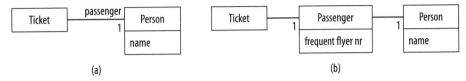

Figure 9.9 The relationship behind the passenger role. (a) A person playing a passenger role. (b) Reifying the passenger role to attach attributes to it.

is illustrated in Figure 9.7(b). Each passenger is a role of a person, and this role-playing relationship never changes. This model tells us that passengers have their own recognition and counting criteria. These should be defined in the dictionary (see Chapter 10).

If we model an entity type as a role of another entity type, we lose the identity between the role and its player, and therefore we lose inheritance. When we model a passenger as a subtype of a person, then person properties are inherited by passengers. For example, if a person has a name, then a passenger does too. But if we model a passenger as a role of a person, then a passenger has no name. Instead, the player of the passenger has a name.

We have seen earlier that an entity plays a role in a relationship. Is that the same concept of role? Yes, it is. Figure 9.8(a) shows a person playing an employee role with respect to a company. There is no place in this model to attach employee information. Perhaps this person plays two employee roles for two companies—or even for the same company. If we want to attach information about the role, we reify it as an entity type, as illustrated in Figure 9.8(b). This has the advantage of our being able to attach attributes to the role.

So behind every role there is a relationship. The relationship behind the passenger role is shown in Figure 9.9.

9.5 Validation

9.5.1 Consistency

To validate an ERD, we first check whether the diagram is consistent. An ERD with its accompanying property descriptions is intended, by its author, to be a description of the subject domain. If the description is inconsistent, then the author made a mistake—there is no possible subject domain described by it. We have seen earlier that relative and absolute cardinality properties can be mutually inconsistent and that commutative paths through the diagram can contain mutually inconsistent relative cardinality properties (see Figure 8.6).

We can use formal specification techniques and software tools to find out whether an ERD and its accompanying property descriptions are consistent. The application of these tools and techniques requires us to formalize the ERD and its accompanying property descriptions. This falls outside the scope of this book. For most diagrams, using formal techniques is overkill, but for subject domains where security is an issue, such as in the subject domain of the Electronic Ticket System (ETS), it may be cost-effective to use formal techniques to check the quality of our descriptions. In most domains, informal analysis and inspection of the ERD is the way to check consistency.

9.5.2 *Checking Validity by Elementary Sentences*

If a diagram with its accompanying property descriptions is consistent, we know that it is possible that it describes a subject domain. But we still have to check whether it represents *our* subject domain. One way to do this is to translate the diagram into simple sentences and ask domain specialists whether these sentences are true. For example, the subject domain model of the heating tank controller can be translated into the following sentences:

◆ A batch of juice has exactly one recipe.

◆ A recipe may be applicable to any number of batches.

◆ At any time, a heating tank has at most one batch allocated to it.

◆ At any time, a batch is allocated to either one or two heating tanks.

◆ Each heating tank has exactly one heater.

And so on. Showing these sentences to a domain specialist should give us a strong indication of whether this model correctly represents the subject domain.

9.5.3 *Checking Validity by Snapshots*

A second way to check whether an ERD correctly represents the subject domain is to produce possible snapshots of the domain described by the model. Take the subject domain of the ETS, part of which is shown in Figure 9.10. It says that a ticket belongs to a route that consists of several rail segments, each of which is between stations. Tickets can be stamped for use and for refund. Each such stamp is made on a particular segment of a route. So far, so good.

One possible domain snapshot allowed by this model is shown in Figure 9.11. Showing this to a domain specialist will elicit cries of disagreement: A ticket cannot be used before it has been bought! A conductor cannot issue a use stamp and a

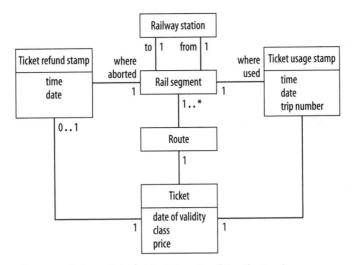

Figure 9.10 Part of the subject domain of the Electronic Ticket System.

Ticket	Route	Segment	Usage stamp	Refund stamp
(t1, April 2)	Return Enschede-Apeldoorn	Enschede-Apeldoorn	March 31	None
(t1, April 2)	Return Enschede-Apeldoorn	Apeldoorn-Enschede	April 1	April 1

Figure 9.11 A snapshot of the ticket subject domain of Figure 9.10. The table shows a ticket t1 with its data of validity, containing two use stamps and one refund stamp.

refund stamp for the same ticket and the same segment! A return ticket must be used within one day! These responses cause us to add as many properties to the diagram in writing.

9.5.4 Identification

Having validated the ERD and its attached property descriptions against the subject domain, we must apply a third kind of check. Does the ERD represent the types of entities identified by the messages that cross the system interface?

For example, Figure 9.10 shows part of the subject domain of the ETS. Does it represent all entities identifiable by ETS? To check this, Figure 9.12 shows the functions of the ETS. The subject domain ERD of Figure 9.10 clarifies what a ticket, a use stamp, and a refund stamp are, but does not mention travelers or conductors. These entities are not part of the subject domain because there is no way, at least in our case study, that the ETS can know their identity. In our case study, the ETS does

---

Name: Sell a ticket.

Triggering event: Traveler requests to buy a ticket.

Delivered service: Allow a traveler to buy a ticket at any time and place chosen by the traveler.

Name: Show a ticket.

Triggering event: Traveler requests to view a ticket.

Delivered service: Display ticket attributes to the user.

Name: Stamp a ticket for use.

Triggering event: Conductor requests to stamp an unused part of a ticket for use.

Delivered service: Mark the requested part of the ticket as used.

Name: Refund a ticket.

Triggering event: Conductor requests to refund an unused part of a ticket.

Delivered service: Cause the unused part of a ticket to be refunded to the traveler and make this part of the ticket invalid.

Figure 9.12 Functions of the Electronic Ticket System. Travelers and conductors are not authenticated by ETS.

not authenticate them and so passengers and conductors are not part of the subject domain of the ETS. The ETS communicates with conductors and passengers, but not about them. To repeat a point made earlier, the context diagram of the ETS, which shows the entities with which ETS communicates, does represent conductors and passengers (see Chapter 18).

9.5.5 *Validation Summary*

We have reviewed four ways to validate a subject domain ERD.

√ To check whether the ERD can represent any subject domain at all, check whether the model is consistent. Check in particular the mutual consistency of the cardinality constraints. If consistency is critical, it may be cost-effective to use formal techniques for consistency checking.

√ To check whether an ERD represents the subject domain, translate it into simple sentences and validate these with domain specialists.

√ Alternatively, to check whether an ERD represents the subject domain, make one or more snapshot models and validate these with domain specialists.

√ Check whether the ERD represents the part of the world referred to and identified by the messages that cross the system interface.

9.6 SUMMARY

The modeler of the subject domain must balance two criteria to determine where the boundary of the subject domain lies: On the one hand, the subject domain should include the entities about which the system sends and receives messages; on the other hand, it should exclude entities that the system cannot identify.

ERDs have three basic elements: entity types, relationships, and attributes. The difference between an entity and an attribute is that the system receives or sends information about entities, but not about attributes. The difference between an entity and a relationship instance is that an entity has its own, independent identity, whereas a relationship is identified by the participant entities.

Entity types can have taxonomic relationships determined by the inclusion relation between extensions or extents. A dynamic or static specialization should be defined using a crisp and unambiguous specialization attribute that partitions the supertypes into subtypes that at any time have extents of comparable size. Subtypes should have a larger intension than their immediate supertype.

A static specialization does not allow migration between subtypes. If a subtype instance is created, this is also the creation of a supertype instance. A dynamic specialization allows migration between subtypes. Through migration, the extent of a subtype can change while the extent of the supertype remains constant.

If the SuD needs to communicate about a certain type of subject domain entities, then there should be a recognition criterion by which the SuD can recognize an instance of the type when information about it arrives and a counting criterion by which it can keep two different instances of the type apart. The recognition and counting criteria should be part of the definition of the type.

Saying that E_1 is a subtype of E_0 implies that the recognition criterion of E_1 selects a smaller class of entities than that of E_0, but that the counting criterion of the two types are the same. If we do not want the counting criteria to be the same, we can model E_1 as a role of E_0. E_1 is then an independent entity type with its own counting criterion and with an existence dependency on E_0.

9.7 QUESTIONS AND EXERCISES

QUESTIONS FOR REHEARSAL

1. What is the difference between:
   - ◆ an entity type and an attribute?
   - ◆ an entity type and a relationship?
   - ◆ a dynamic subtype, a static subtype, and a role?

2. When do we need a recognition criterion and a counting criterion for a type? Why do we need them?

3. Explain why the identification criterion of a subtype is the same as that of a supertype, but the recognition criterion of the subtype is different.

EXERCISES

4. Consider the following functions of the tea-bag-boxing controller. The list of functions is basically the list of controller responsibilities:

   ◆ Allow operator to set required tea-bag weight.

   ◆ Allow operator to set maximum tea-bag count.

   ◆ Place tea bag in box or in waste container according to weight.

   ◆ Replace full box by empty box.

   What is the subject domain of these functions? Make an entity model.

5. Consider the following functions of the bug-fixing support system:

   ◆ Register assignment of bug to programmer and tester, and inform them by email.

   ◆ Register bug fix and inform tester by email.

   ◆ Register test report and inform programmer and bug manager by email.

   ◆ Register bug release.

   What is the subject domain of these functions? Make an entity model.

6. Consider the functions of the CTS described in Chapter 1. What is the subject domain of these functions? Make an entity model.

7. Often, an entity accumulates a number of attribute values over time. Consider the following case.

   > An agricultural field has a location, size, and a certain kind of soil. At a certain time, it lies fallow, and then it starts accumulating attributes. First, it is decided what crop to plant this year, which seed to use for this crop, and which seed manufacturer to use. The crop is then sown. Now the field has a crop. Next, the crop is harvested. Now, the field has a yield too. And independent of this, fertilizer may be distributed over the field and, every time this happens, the field has a fertilizer on it.

   There is a temptation to model this in an ERD with attributes that have initial value null and that will get a value in the future. Examples are the attributes crop and yield. But this is bad practice because null values have many different meanings. Some of the frequently occurring meanings are "unknown," "nonexistent," and "not applicable." There are no sound manipulation rules for null values. The accumulation of values over time can be modeled without using null values by the standard process of creating entities and links between entities. Make an ERD of the field subject domain in which you avoid the accumulation of attributes.

8. Consider the following subject domain.

Passengers can book flights on an airplane. Each flight consists of a number of hops, and each hop is a trip from an airport to a destination airport. Each airport has a unique abbreviation and a name. Each hop has an estimated duration. Flights have a unique number and an estimated duration. Each flight is flown periodically, at different dates and times. Accordingly, hops are flown periodically at different dates and times. All hops of one flight are flown by one airplane. Passengers actually book flight instances, not flights in general. Each booking has a booking number. After a booking has been made, a ticket can be created, with its own ticket number. And when a ticket exists, seat assignments for the different hops of the flight can be made. The bill for a ticket may be sent to a person other than the passenger. This other person may be a company or, in general, any legal or natural person.

Make an ERD of this subject domain. Write down all the domain properties that you cannot express in the diagram.

QUESTIONS FOR DISCUSSION

9. Explain why Passenger and Conductor are not entities in the ETS subject domain.

10. Consider an information system that contains the train schedule of the Netherlands, plus information about deviations from the schedule that is made available through the Web to travelers. Using this system, travelers can find the shortest route from their point of departure to a destination, and they can find out about current delays. Which of these following entities are in its subject domain and which are outside? Motivate your answer with respect to the observability of the entity and the relevance of the entity for the information system.

a) Railway station

b) Rail track

c) Traveler

d) Railway connection

e) Rail car

11. An ERD of the subject domain of an elevator system control must represent buttons. Discuss the reasons to model this as in Figure 9.13(a) and the reasons to model this as in Figure 9.13(b).

12. a) An ERD of the subject domain of a course management system must contain information about students and the exams they take. Discuss the reasons to model this as in Figure 9.14(a) and the reasons to model this as in Figure 9.14(b).

b) Two alternative models are shown in Figure 9.15. Discuss the relative merits of Figure 9.15(a) and Figure 9.14(a) and the relative merits of Figure 9.15(b) and Figure 9.14(b).

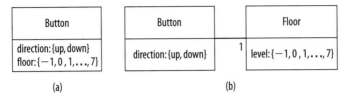

(a)   (b)

Figure 9.13 Two models of buttons and floors.

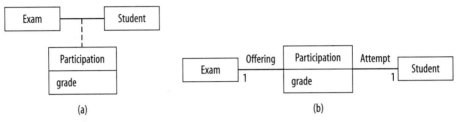

(a)   (b)

Figure 9.14 Two models of students and exams.

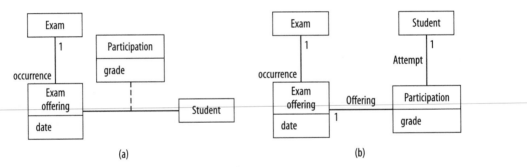

(a)   (b)

Figure 9.15 Two more models of students and exams.

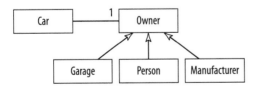

Figure 9.16 A model of car ownership.

13. Improve the document taxonomy in Figure 9.4, taking the principles of classification into account.

14. Figure 9.16 shows a model of car ownership.

   a) At least one entity type in this model is really a role that some entity is playing with respect to some other entity. Which entity or entities are roles?

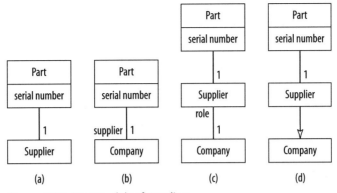

Figure 9.17 Four models of suppliers.

b) Explain why the model is wrong.

c) Provide an improved model that deals with roles more appropriately, and explain why you think it is better.

15. Figure 9.17 shows four models of parts and suppliers. Ask the following questions for each of these models:

a) Is a supplier identical to a company?

b) Can a supplier have additional attributes in addition to those of companies?

c) Can a supplier be identified independently from a company?

Discuss in which situation you would want to use each model.

16. Is a wrecked car still a vehicle? Which criteria do you use to answer this question?

CHAPTER 10

The Dictionary

T he ERD of the subject domain should be viewed as a visual supplement to a dictionary. The dictionary contains definitions of all important terms that appear in the assumptions made about the environment and in the specification of the SuD. The subject domain ERD illustrates the definitions of terms that refer to the subject domain. In this chapter, we look at the structure of the dictionary and give guidelines for writing dictionary entries. Section 10.1 describes the domain ontology used throughout the book. In our domain ontology, a domain consists of individuals and properties of individuals. This motivates the syntactic classification of terms given in Section 10.2. Section 10.3 explains the syntax of path expressions. We use path expressions to refer to entities in the ERD. Section 10.4 distinguishes extensional definitions from intensional definitions and discusses the structure of intensional definitions. Section 10.5 gives guidelines for writing intensional definitions.

10.1   Domain Ontology

An **ontology** is a metaclassification. A domain ontology tells us what kinds of things can exist in a domain. Our classification of terms into syntactic categories is motivated by a particular domain ontology, that is sketched in Figure 10.1. A subject domain consists of entities and timed event occurrences. Entities are individuals that have a duration, and timed event occurrences are individuals that are instantaneous. For example, an event such as push(b: Button) can be instantiated by applying it to a particular button, say b0. This gives us event occurrence push(b0). This occurrence can occur infinitely many times, which we can distinguish by the time of occurrence:

◆ push(b0) at 8:30:55

◆ push(b0) at 8:31:01

And so on. These are timed event occurrences.

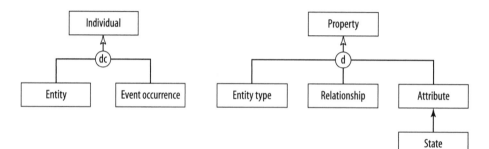

Figure 10.1 An ontology of the subject domain.

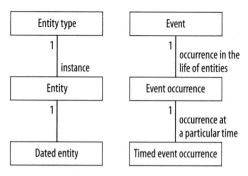

Figure 10.2 Events are types.

Timed event occurrences are instantaneous individuals, just as entities are persistent individuals in the domain (Figure 10.2). The collection of individuals that makes up the subject domain is dynamic. Over time, it grows and shrinks. The counterpart of a timed event occurrence is a dated entity, which is an entity that has a particular start date and a particular end date of existence. However, there is a crucial difference. In our ontology, we exclude the reincarnation of entities. So an entity can exist once, and after its end date it can never exist again. By contrast, an event occurrence can happen again and again. Because I want to abstract from the time of existence of entities and the time of occurrence of events, the individuals in our ontology are undated entities and untimed event occurrences.

The individuals in the subject domain have properties, some of which are defined in an ERD. For example, each entity has a type, it may have relationships with other entities, it may be in a state, and it may have attributes. This subdivision of properties is not exhaustive because there are other properties, not local to entities.

10.2 **Syntactic Categories**

We distinguish here only a few simple syntactic categories that are very closely linked to our ontology.

Identifier. An identifier is a proper name of an individual. We can use identifiers to uniquely identify entities and timed event occurrences. We will require identifiers to satisfy the following two properties.

- *Uniqueness.* Within a domain, at any time, an identifier is a proper name of at most one individual.
- *Immutability.* Once an identifier is the proper name of an individual, it is never reassigned to another individual. Even if the individual does not exist anymore, the identifier is not reused.

I call these two properties the **identifier requirements.** In our diagrams, we distinguish identifiers by underlining them. Note that whether or not something is an identifier depends on the subject domain. The serial number, say 123, of an elevator motor produced by company A is an identifier in the subject domain of company A. But another production company B, which produces tables, may use the number 123 as the serial number for one of its tables. So the number 123 is not an identifier in the world as a whole because it is not uniquely assigned as a proper name to one individual only.

Predicate name. A predicate name refers to the presence or absence of a property of individuals in a domain. Predicate names can have arguments, where an argument is a reference to an individual. When its arguments are filled in, the predicate evaluates to true or false. For example, in the elevator example we define Closed(d) as a predicate name that is true when door d is closed. We write a predicate name with an initial uppercase letter. An ERD introduces three kinds of predicates. (There are other predicates, but these are not introduced by an ERD.)

- **Entity-type name.** We use the entity-type name as a predicate name as follows. If Heating tank is an entity-type name in an ERD, then we can write Heating tank(t) to indicate that t is a heating tank. Heating tank(t) is true if t is a heating tank; otherwise it is false. Entity-type predicates are the only predicates to accept any kind of argument. If b is a batch of juice, then Heating tank(b) is a valid expression and it will evaluate to false.
- **Relationship name.** Similarly, we can use a relationship name as a relationship predicate as follows. If in an ERD Allocation is the name for a relationship between Batch and Heating tank, then we can write Allocation(b, t) to indicate that batch b is allocated to tank t. Allocation(b, t) is true if b is allocated to tank t; otherwise it is false. The arguments of a relationship predicate are typed. So if r is a recipe and m is a thermometer, then Allocation(r, m) is an illegal expression. The components of a relationship are not ordered in an ERD, and so Allocation(b, t) is equivalent to Allocation(t, b). To distinguish an argument, we should label it with the corresponding role name that appears in the ERD, or, if there is no role name, with the corresponding type name in the ERD, such as in Allocation(b: Button, t: Heating tank). However, in this book I usually omit the role name because it is clear from the context.
- **State predicate name.** A state predicate is a Boolean property of an entity. For example, elevator doors d can be in states Opened and Closed. In the first state, that Opened(d) is true and Closed(d) is false. In the second state, the truth values are reversed. State predicates have exactly one argument and they are

typed. So if f is a floor, Closed(f) is an illegal expression. State predicate names start with an initial uppercase letter.

Attribute name. Any unary property of an individual is called an attribute. For example, an elevator cage has the attribute planned direction with the possible values up, down, or none. Then at a certain time, planned direction(c) = up may be true. Attribute names start with an initial lowercase letter, except state predicates, whose names start with an uppercase letter.

Event name. Identifiers, predicate names, and attribute names all refer to parts of the state of a subject domain that have some duration. An event name refers to instantaneous events in the subject domain. For example, we can define arrive(c, f) to refer to the arrival of elevator cage c at floor f. An event name starts with an initial lowercase letter.

Predicate, attribute, and event names all accept identifiers and variables as arguments. If we write Heating tank(23) to indicate that the tank named 23 is a heating tank, then 23 is an identifier of a heating tank. If we write Heating tank(t) to indicate that some individual t is a heating tank, then the letter t is a variable and we can fill in an identifier for t.

Variables are not defined in the dictionary. They are given a type to indicate what kind of identifiers can be filled in for the variable. Identifiers should be defined in the dictionary, unless it is totally clear what they mean to all stakeholders. For example, in planned direction(c) = up, c is a variable that refers to a cage and up is an identifier that refers to a particular direction. Presumably, we do not need to define the meaning of up.

10.3 Path Expressions

We often use **path expressions** to define words. A path expression is a sequence of names separated by dots, starting with an entity identifier or with an identifier variable. We use the following conventions in path expressions. Let e1 be an entity of type Etype1 (Figure 10.3).

◆ Then e1.etype3 refers to the set of all instances of Etype3 related by R3 to e1. In path expressions, type names are written with an initial lowercase letter.

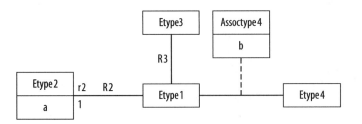

Figure 10.3 Path expressions.

Elevator door	doors	Elevator cage			Location indicator
Opened	1	planned direction:{up, down, none}		1	number: Natural
Closed					

Figure 10.4 Using path expressions.

◆ If the entity at the far end of the relationship plays a named role, as does **Etype2**, then we must use that role name instead of the class name in the path expression. So e1.r2 refers to the entity related to e1 by R2.

◆ If a path expression evaluates to a singleton set (a set consisting of exactly one element), then the expression refers to the object in this set. So e1.r2 refers to a single entity. We can therefore write e1.r2.a, which refers to the value of a for this entity.

◆ e1.assoctype4 refers to the set of all links of type Assoctype4 between e1 and instances of Etype4.

◆ If Assoctype4 is a one-one relationship, then there is exactly one link in which e1 participates and e1.assoctype4.b refers to the value of b of this link.

We now have two equivalent ways to refer to the values of attributes. If c is an elevator cage in Figure 10.4, then, using a path expression, we can write c.planned_direction = up. Or we can write planned_direction(c) = up, as we did earlier. Path expressions are more convenient if we refer to attribute values of other entities: c.location_indicator.number = 3.

We have three ways to say that a predicate is true. If d is an elevator door, we can write d.Opened = true, Opened(d) = true, or simply Opened(d). Again, when referring to attribute values of other entities, path expressions are convenient: c.doors.Opened = true.

Finally, note that in our diagrams I often use names that consist of several words, but that I use underscores when these names are used in path expressions. The reason for this is that diagrams are easier to read without underscores, and path expressions are easier to read with underscores. Just view a space and an underscore as two synonyms.

10.4 Extensional and Intensional Definitions

When you ask a fruit-juice-plant operator to define a heating tank, he will probably stare at you, look around, and point at a heating tank, saying, "That is a heating tank." If you press for a definition, the operator will become aware of the fact that you do not understand even the simplest concepts related to fruit juice production. But chances are that he will not be able to describe the concept either. Nevertheless, as we have seen, there must be some criterion you can use to recognize a heating tank when you see one, and there must be some criterion you can use to count heating tanks, when you see more than one.

People usually give an extensional definition of the concepts they work with in everyday practice. An **extensional definition** of a word is a list of examples of individuals to which the word applies. This is a good way to define an identifier. When asked which heating tank the identifier 123 refers to, the operator will walk up to a tank, point at it and say, "This one."

But although extensional definitions are easy to give, they are not effective for concepts with a large extension. We can only give a small list of examples of any concept, whereas the complete extension of all possible instances of a concept is usually infinite. And a small list of examples does not uniquely determine the intension that we have in mind. If I give you three examples, such as 3, 5, and 7, what is the concept that I am giving an example of? Odd numbers? Prime numbers? Numbers smaller than 10? Numbers larger than 2? There are infinitely many concepts of which these three numbers are examples. An extension does not uniquely determine an intension.

An **intensional definition** of a concept is a small list of properties shared by all and only the instances of the concept. So all instances in the extension of the concept have all these properties, and each individual outside the extension does not have all these properties. It may have some of them, but not all of them. Here is an example.

> **Heating tank.** Entity-type name. A tank with a heater and thermometer, in which juice can be heated. Heating tanks can stand pressures up to 10,000 Newton/m^2.

This tells us what a heating tank is: It is a particular kind of tank. It also gives us the defining properties of heating tanks: They have a heater and thermometer, can be used for heating, and have a maximum pressure. Note that heating tanks have infinitely many properties: They can stand pressures of 0 Newton/m^2, 0.1 Newton/m^2, 0.2 Newton/m^2, 0.3 Newton/m^2,..., 0.01 Newton/m^2, 0.11 Newton/m^2, 0.21 Newton/m^2, 0.31 Newton/m^2, and so on. The intension of the concept of a heating tank is infinite, but most of the properties in the intension are not necessary to recognize or count instances of a concept. The properties listed in an intensional definition are the **defining intension.**

10.5 **Guidelines**

10.5.1 *When to Define a Term*

You should consider defining all terms used in an ERD of the subject domain. The one and only reason to define a term is to improve the understanding of the readers of the specification documents. Unreadable or superfluous definitions defeat this purpose. Here is an unreadable definition.

> **Beneficial owner.** The beneficial owner is the person who is the owner of the income for tax purposes and who beneficially owns the income. Thus, a person receiving income as a nominee, custodian, or agent for another person is not the beneficial owner of the income.

> Generally, a person is treated as the owner of the income to the extent it is required under U.S. tax principles to include the amount paid in gross income on a tax return. A person who is the owner of that income is considered the beneficial owner of that income unless that person is a conduit entity whose participation in a transaction can be disregarded. Generally, the principles of section 7701(I) and Regulations section 1.881-3 apply to determine if a person is a conduit entity.

This is taken from form W-8BEN of the U.S. Department of the Treasury, Internal Revenue Service, version of October 1998. It is one-half of the full definition. It gives an indication of what a beneficial owner is, but also leaves plenty of room to haggle about particular boundary cases. The primary purpose of the definition is *not* to make the reader understand what a beneficial owner is but to close off exits that people have taken to avoid paying tax.

Here is a superfluous definition.

> **push(b: Request button).** A request button b is pushed.

We do not need a definition to tell us this. More generally, many terms used in the subject domain are probably already defined in the technical documentation of the domain. For example, in an elevator subject domain, it probably is not necessary to define terms such as elevator cage, button, and motor. It is clear what these terms mean and, besides, these devices come with technical specifications that explain in detail what these entities are.

Sometimes, we should define a term to avoid misunderstanding, but there is no definition. For example, in a library information system we may want to define Title as

> **Title.** Any item that is published.

This is not good enough; it ignores unpublished materials. Let us try this one:

> **Title.** Any identifiable item of text.

This ignores video and sound material, globes, and atlases. So let us try again:

> **Title.** Any identifiable item of information.

Well, this makes every chapter, every paragraph, and every sentence in a book a title. So we settle for this one:

> **Title.** Anything declared to be a title by the library.

The term "Title" is said to have an **open texture,** which means that it has no crisp boundaries and may shift its meaning over time as new technologies appear, as people develop new habits, and in general as the social and physical context of the term evolves. Terms with open texture cannot be defined intensionally. Unfortunate as this may seem, this is actually useful for concepts that evolve over time. And we can still give an extensional definition that gives an impression of the intended meaning, but leaves open what the intension is exactly. We can, for example, improve our definition of "Title" as follows.

> **Title.** Anything declared to be a title by the library. Examples are books, internal reports, manuals, videotapes, and maps.

Many terms have open texture. For example, the term "boat" cannot be defined except by giving examples. When surf planks were invented, judges had to determine whether or not these were boats. If a surf plank is a boat, the laws of water traffic are applicable and you need a license to be permitted to steer a surf plank. If it is not a boat, this is not necessary. In the Netherlands, surf planks were ruled by high court not to be boats, and so in the Netherlands you do not need a license to use them.

We may also include a definition in the dictionary to make it clear that we actually attach very little meaning to it. For example, the Training Information System (TIS) manipulates data about employees, but it does not do any check on who is or is not an employee. So we include the following definition in the dictionary:

Employee. Entity-type name. Anyone registered by TIS as participant of a course.

This implies that as far as TIS is concerned, any record downloaded from the Personnel Information System or entered manually at the registration desk contains employee data.

Sometimes, a term may seem to have an obvious meaning when it does not. Here is an example.

planned direction(c: Elevator_cage). Attribute. The preferred direction in which c will depart after closing its doors. If there are no requests in the preferred direction but there are requests to be served in the opposite direction, then the cage will depart in the opposite direction.

This may not be what we expected, so it is useful to include this definition in the dictionary.

Summarizing, we have the following guidelines for defining a term:

√ Define a term to improve the understanding of the readers of the specification documents.

√ Define a term with open texture extensionally, by giving a number of typical examples and agreed counterexamples. The definition should also indicate who determines whether the term is applicable to an individual case.

√ Include a definition of a term if the meaning deviates from what the reader might expect.

√ Do not include a definition if it is already given by available documentation.

10.5.2 Definitions by Genus and Difference

A definition of an entity type should provide us with a recognition criterion, which tells us how to recognize an instance when we see one, and an identification criterion, which tells us how to count instances if we see more than one. The classic way of doing this is definition by genus and difference. A definition of a term by genus and difference mentions a general class and then says which subclass this term stands for. Here is an example.

Without genus	With genus
A compiler translates source code into object code.	A compiler is a program that translates source code into object code.
A catamaran has two hulls.	A catamaran is a boat with two hulls.
A heating tank heats juice.	A heating tank is a tank with a heater and thermometer in which juice can be heated.
Joiners recently joined the company.	A joiner is an employee that recently has joined the company.
A ticket represents the passenger's right to make a trip by train.	A ticket is a lexical item that represents the passenger's right to make a trip by train.

Figure 10.5 Examples and counterexamples of definition by genus and difference.

> **Arrival sensor**. Entity type. A sensor in an elevator shaft that is activated when an elevator cage approaches a floor.

The genus is Sensor; the difference is in an elevator shaft that is activated when an elevator cage approaches a floor. The definition of Heating tank given earlier is another example.

Often, the genus of a concept is omitted in a definition because it is thought to be too obvious to mention. This is a mistake because the genus is only obvious to those who already know the meaning of the defined term. Figure 10.5 gives some examples and counterexamples.

A definition by genus and difference defines a taxonomic structure in which the genus is the supertype and the defined concept a subtype. The genus and difference should have the following division of work:

√ The genus provides the identification criterion of the entity type.
√ The difference provides the recognition criterion of the entity type.

10.5.3 *Operational Definitions*

An operational definition of a term gives a procedure that can be followed by anyone to determine whether the term has been correctly applied to a given case. For example, the definition of the concept of a heating tank, given earlier, can be operationalized as follows.

> **Heating tank**. Entity type. A tank with a heater and thermometer attached. The heater can be recognized by red, blue, and black wires leading up to it, and the thermometer can be recognized by its rectangular shape.

Within the domain consisting of all heating tanks in a production plant, this can be a perfectly operational definition that can be used by anyone to unambiguously determine whether a particular tank is a heating tank. It may not work in the neighboring factory because the heating tanks have other thermometers there, but it is operational in this one.

Here is a second example.

> **Idle(c: Elevator cage).** State predicate. c is stationary, its position is such that the cage floor is exactly at the level of a building floor, its doors are closed, and the direction indicator at its current floor is off.

This is not an entity type and the definition is not by genus and difference. But it does provide us with sufficient information to be able to observe whether an elevator cage is idle.

When we define an entity type that has no supertype in our model, we cannot use definition by genus and difference, but we can still operationalize the concept so that we know how to recognize and count instances. Take the definition of an elevator door.

> **Elevator door.** Entity type. A door connected to an elevator cage. It may consist of two halves. When the elevator is idle or stationary at a floor, an elevator door can only open and close jointly with the floor doors for that cage at that floor.

This is not a definition by genus and difference, because the word "door" used in the definition is not defined in the same dictionary. But the definition tells us enough to know what an elevator door is (recognition criterion) and how to count elevator doors (identification criterion).

10.5.4 Abbreviations and Correspondence Rules

A third way to classify a definition, independent of whether it is an operational definition and from whether it is a definition by genus and difference, is to see whether it is an abbreviation or a correspondence rule. An **abbreviation** is a definition that reduces the meaning of a word to the meaning of words defined elsewhere in the same dictionary. To determine whether an individual is an instance of the defined concept, you do not need to make observations of reality; you just need to look up words in the dictionary. If a word is an abbreviation, it denotes a concept that we can already describe using words defined in the same dictionary. A **correspondence rule,** by contrast, does introduce a new concept. A correspondence rule relates the defined word to reality by telling us which observations to make to see whether an individual is an instance of the defined concept.

Here are two examples of abbreviations.

> **Opened(c: Elevator cage).** State predicate. c.doors.Opened is true.

> **Downstream(b: Request button, f: Floor, c: Elevator cage).** Predicate.
> ◆ If c.direction = up, then b.floor.number > f.number.
> ◆ If c.direction = down, then b.floor.number < f.number.

The first definition introduces an elevator cage predicate that can be derived from a door predicate. Derivable terms are indicated in the ERD by prefixing them by a slash, as shown in Figure 10.6. The second definition tells us that if the current direction of a cage is up, the floor of a button is downstream of f if it is higher than f.

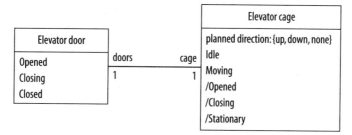

Figure 10.6 Derivable terms.

If the current direction of a cage is down, the floor of a button is downstream of f if it is lower than f. This does not introduce a concept that we cannot already describe using words defined in the same dictionary, but the word "Downstream" makes our descriptions a lot easier to write and read.

Here are two examples of correspondence rules.

> **Allocation(b: Request button, c: Elevator cage).** Relationship predicate. A request from b has been allocated to c and not yet been served by c.

> **Arrival sensor.** Entity-type predicate. A sensor in an elevator shaft that is activated when an elevator cage approaches a floor. If s is an arrival sensor, we say that Arrival_sensor(s) is true.

These definitions tell us which state of reality is denoted by these words. They use words not defined in the same dictionary, and they tell us which observations to make to see whether an individual is an instance of the concept.

10.6 SUMMARY

We define terms in a dictionary when this makes our specification easier to read and improves the understanding of the reader. We distinguish identifiers from names of general concepts. Names of general concepts are partitioned into predicate names, attribute names, and event names. Three important types of predicate names are entity-type names, relationship names, and state predicate names.

This division into syntactic categories is based on an ontology of individuals and properties. There are two kinds of individuals: entities, which persist over time, and event occurrences, which are instantaneous. Three important classes of properties are being an instance of an entity type, having a relationship, and having an attribute. A state is a particular kind of attribute.

If we define a term extensionally, we give a number of examples. This does not suffice to determine its extension, but this is useful to define the meaning of an identifier and it is also useful to indicate the meaning of an open textured term.

If we define a term intensionally, we give a part of its intension, called the defining intension. Such a definition indicates how we can recognize an instance when we see it and how we can count instances when we see more than one. A good way of doing this is definition by genus (which supplies the identity criterion) and difference (which supplies the recognition criterion). We should operationalize definitions so that it is clear to anyone how to determine whether a term is applicable to a given case.

Many definitions are just abbreviations of complex terms. They do not introduce new concepts but make specifications easier to write and read. Other definitions are correspondence rules. These tell us which observations to make to determine whether an individual is an instance of the defined concept.

10.7 QUESTIONS AND EXERCISES

QUESTIONS FOR REHEARSAL

1. What are the identifier requirements?

2. For extentional and intensional definitions,

- ◆ Explain the difference between extensional and intensional definitions.
- ◆ When is it useful to define a term extensionally?
- ◆ Do we list the complete intension of a concept in an intensional definition?

QUESTIONS FOR DISCUSSION

3. Which of the following attributes are identifiers? For the attributes, tell what each identifies.

a) A key of a database table

b) A passport number

c) A personnel number in a company

d) A social security number

e) A Unix process number

f) An Ethernet address

g) An Internet domain name

4. Some of the following terms are open-textured; others have a crisp meaning. Of those that have an open texture, explain why you think this is so, give an extensional definition, and indicate who would decide in particular cases whether the term is applicable or not. Of those that have a crisp meaning, give a definition by genus and difference.

a) Chair

b) Assembler

c) Employee

d) Car

PART IV

Behavior Notations

This part of the book describes behavior notations. Behavior and communication are two complementary functional aspects of the services provided by the system. Behavior concerns the ordering of interactions in time; communication concerns the information exchange between systems during interactions. All behavior notations can be used at various degrees of formality, ranging from rough, incomplete sketches to fully formal executable descriptions.

◆ Chapter 11. I introduce event lists and state transition tables (STTs), which are tabular notations for behavior. These are easy to use and can grow to any size because we can simply continue on the next paper. However, they do not represent the structure of behavior very well.

◆ Chapter 12. I introduce the two major state transition diagram (STD) techniques: Mealy diagrams, used in Yourdon-style structured analysis, and statecharts, used in Statemate and most object-oriented methods. Any STT can be transformed into an equivalent STD and vice versa. Unlike STTs, STDs cannot grow to any size because paper size is finite. However, they can represent the structure of behavior rather well.

◆ Chapter 13. I list the choices to be made if we want to give precise semantics for STTs and STDs. These choices must be made if you want to be able to execute an STT or STD. This chapter can be skipped if you do not want to make the meaning of behavior descriptions precise.

◆ Chapter 14. I summarize the behavioral modeling and design guidelines for STTs and STDs, giving examples of the use of behavior notations for modeling desired behavior in the environment, for assumed behavior in the environment, and for desired system behavior.

CHAPTER 11

State Transition Lists and Tables

S tate transition lists and tables are a simple means to represent the behavior of any system with a finite number of states. By the addition of variables, we can even represent the behavior of systems with infinitely many states. We use state transition lists and tables to represent

- The desired behavior of the composite system of which the SuD is a part.
- The desired behavior of the SuD itself.
- The assumed behavior of the environment.

Section 11.1 discusses event lists, which are simply informal lists of descriptions of events and their effects. The effect of an event may be a simple state transition or it may be a complex scenario consisting of many possible state transitions. Section 11.2 looks at a formalized version of event lists, state transition tables (STTs), that can be used to describe atomic state transitions. Section 11.3 looks at a special kind of STT, called a decision table, in which we describe the possible actions caused by an event that does not cause a state change. There are other tabular notations for behavior than those treated in this chapter. For pointers to the literature, see the Bibliographic Remarks.

11.1 Event Lists

An **event list** is a finite list of event descriptions and, for each event, a description of its effect. Figure 11.1 shows an event list of elevator button behavior. Buttons are part of the elevator subject domain and the controller relies on this behavior in order to create desired effects in the subject domain. For example, when an elevator cage arrives at a floor to deliver a passenger, the controller will send a light off(b) signal to the appropriate button. The event list in Figure 11.1 then says what the effect of this signal is assumed to be: The button will switch off.

> **Light on(b).** If b is not already in state On(b), then it enters state On(b). Otherwise, nothing changes.
>
> **Light off(b).** If b is not already in state Off(b), then it enters state Off(b). Otherwise, nothing changes.

Figure 11.1 An event list that represents the assumed subject domain behavior of the elevator controller.

Event	Desired effect
A passenger pushes a destination button in cage c.	The request is confirmed to the passenger by lighting up the button.
	If c is idle at another floor, its motor starts in the direction of the requested floor. While c moves, its location indicator is set to the current floor. When c arrives at the requested floor, it stops and its doors open.
	If c is idle at the requested floor, its doors are opened.
	When no one has passed the door for some time, the doors close.

Figure 11.2 Event list entry describing desired subject domain behavior for an elevator cage, assuming that the cage starts in an idle state.

Note that an event list entry looks like a dictionary entry, but that its intention is very different. If we choose to write down dictionary entries for the keywords used in the event list, they might look like this:

> **light off(b: Request button).** A signal received by connector B1 of the button.
>
> **Off(b: Request button).** The state in which the button LED does not emit light.

It is not possible for these dictionary entries to be true or false. They are not descriptions of button behavior but agreements on how we choose to use words to describe that behavior. The event list, on the other hand, is a description of button behavior that may be true or false. If button b is broken, then after light off(b), it may still be in state On(b).

Figure 11.1 describes the assumed subject domain behavior. It is not the responsibility of the elevator controller to ensure that this behavior takes place. Figure 11.2, on the other hand, gives an entry in an event list describing the desired subject domain behavior that must be brought about by the controller. It is not yet a complete description because it assumes that the cage starts in an idle state. Note that the effect is a complex scenario that may evolve in different ways and that will take some time to unfold. An important part of elevator controller design consists of working out this specification of desired subject domain behavior, until we know exactly what the desired effects are that the controller has to bring about.

A final example of an event list is shown in Figure 11.3. Here the events are stimuli of the controller, and the effects are responses and state updates of the controller. This list must be read in the context of a software specification, which

Stimulus	Current controller state	Desired effect
pass doors(c)	Opened(c)	• c.state := Opened
	Closing(c)	• open doors(c) • c.state := Opened
10 seconds after the most recent execution of c.state := Opened	Opened(c)	• close doors(c) • c.state := Closing

Figure 11.3 Some stimuli and desired responses of the elevator controller.

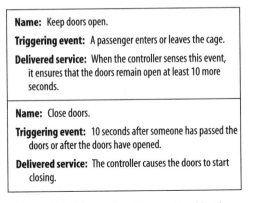

Figure 11.4 Stimulus and response referred to in the event list in Figure 11.3.

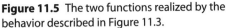

Name: Keep doors open.

Triggering event: A passenger enters or leaves the cage.

Delivered service: When the controller senses this event, it ensures that the doors remain open at least 10 more seconds.

Name: Close doors.

Triggering event: 10 seconds after someone has passed the doors or after the doors have opened.

Delivered service: The controller causes the doors to start closing.

Figure 11.5 The two functions realized by the behavior described in Figure 11.3.

would tell us that pass doors(c) is a stimulus received from a door sensor of elevator cage c (Figure 11.4). The controller states Opened(c), Closing(c), and Opened(c) are the states in which, according to the data stored by the controller, the doors of cage c are opened, closing, and closed, respectively. The desired responses consist of updating this state and producing output responses.

Note that an event list of desired system behavior is similar to a list of system service descriptions. For example, the event list in Figure 11.3 shows controller behavior that realizes the two functions listed in Figure 11.5. The difference is that a service description describes the added value delivered by the system, whereas a system response description, as do all effect descriptions, describes a **scenario** in which the system is involved—a nonatomic behavior, consisting of a number of states connected by state transition, triggered by events. The relationship between the two descriptions is that the scenario description tells us *how* the system delivers its added value. Because a service description does not refer to all possible events and states during a scenario, it is typically less detailed than a stimulus-response description.

Summarizing, an event list describes the effects of events. An event can be any of the three kinds of events identified in Chapter 3: a named event, a condition change event, or a temporal event. The effect of an event is a behavior consisting of more events and states. There are three kinds of behavior that we can describe with an event list.

◆ Behavior in the subject domain that we assume to take place. The list entries have the form (subject domain event, assumed effect in the subject domain).

◆ Desired subject domain behavior that the system must bring about. The list entries have the form (subject domain event, desired effect in the subject domain).

◆ Desired system behavior. This is also called a **stimulus-response list.** The list entries have the form (stimulus, desired effect on the system). In Unified Modeling Language (UML)-related system design approaches, this is often called a *use case.* I avoid this term because it wrongly suggests that desired system behavior is always initiated by a user.

In all three cases, the effect can be described at various levels of detail.

Transactional effect. An effect is transactional if it consists of one state transition of whatever we are describing (the subject domain or the system). In some cases, the effect is that the domain or system enters a next state and no other action is performed. This is shown in Figure 11.1. In other cases, the effect consists of performing an action without changing state. (We see examples of this later in this chapter.) In the general case, a transactional effect consists of both a state change and other actions, as shown in Figure 11.3. The format of a transactional effect description is therefore (actions, next state). The desired effect in each entry consists of a state update, and in some entries an additional action is performed. A **transactional event list** is an event list containing only transactional effect descriptions.

Scenario effect. A scenario effect consists of a scenario that involves several state transitions. An example is the list entry in Figure 11.2. A **scenario list** is an event list containing scenario effect descriptions.

The transactional effect of an event is nondeterministic if it describes a choice between state transitions. For example, in Figure 11.3, the effect of pass doors(c) is

If Opened(c), then c.state := Opened, but if Closing(c), then open doors(c) and c.state := Opened.

This is nondeterministic because there are two possible outcomes. However, the effect of an event in each state is still deterministic, as shown in Figure 11.3. For transactional effects, we therefore usually factor out the current state description, so that we get a list entry of the form

(event, current state, effect)

An event list entry in scenario form can always be expanded into an event list in transactional form because we can describe a scenario always as a collection of possible states and state transitions. This transformation turns the event list into a state transition table.

11.2 State Transition Tables

A **state transition table** (STT) is an event list whose entries have the following form:

(event, current state, actions, next state)

If the event and action occur at the system interface, they are called the *stimulus* and *response*, respectively. Each entry of an STT describes a state transition. Figure 11.6 shows a state transition table equivalent to the event list of Figure 11.3.

An STT can be abbreviated by grouping all entries with the same stimulus, as has been done in Figure 11.6, or by grouping all entries with the same state, as shown in Figure 11.7. Figure 11.7 is a representation of Figure 11.1 in STT form. We can

Stimulus	Current controller state	Controller response	Next controller state
pass doors(c)	Opened(c)		Opened(c)
	Closing(c)	open doors(c)	Opened(c)
10 seconds after the most recent execution of c.state := Opened	Opened(c)	close doors(c)	Closing(c)

Figure 11.6 State transition table of some stimuli and desired responses of the elevator controller.

Current button state	Event	Next button state
On(b)	light off(b)	Off(b)
	light on(b)	On(b)
Off(b)	light on(b)	On(b)
	light off(b)	Off(b)

Figure 11.7 State transition table for request buttons, grouped per state.

Initially		close doors(c)	Closing(c)
Stimulus	**Current controller state**	**Controller response**	**Next controller state**
pass doors(c)	Opened(c)		Opened(c)
	Closing(c)	open doors(c)	Opened(c)
10 seconds after the most recent execution of c.state := Opened	Opened(c)	close doors(c)	Closing(c)

Figure 11.8 Adding an initial state.

Stimulus	**Current controller state**	**Controller response**	**Next controller state**
temp(c)	Not heating and $c < d - 5$	switch on	Heating
	Heating and $c > d + 5$	switch off	Not heating

Figure 11.9 The current state may contain conditions on event parameters. This table contains two entries. The scope of a variable is one entry.

add an entry in an STT that indicates an initial state and, optionally, an initialization action, as shown in Figure 11.8.

An STT entry can contain variables, as illustrated by all examples given so far. If a variable can have infinitely many possible values, we can give a scheme for an infinitely long list. The type of the variables should be clear from the definitions of the events and conditions in the dictionary. The scope of a variable is restricted to one entry. Basically, a variable is bound to a value by the event and current state, and it has this value when updating the state and performing the other actions listed in the entry. This means that the entry for a current state can contain conditions that include the actual event parameters and state variables of the system or domain described by the table. For example, suppose that the heating controller has a state variable d that represents desired temperature and that it receives an event temp(c) in which c is the current temperature of the heating tank. Then the response to temp(c) depends on the value of the event parameter. See Figure 11.9.

11.3 Decision Tables

In some cases, the behavior described by an STT is stateless, so all that we have is a simple transformation of stimuli into responses. Figure 11.10 shows a STT for the event arrive(b, c), which occurs when elevator cage c arrives at a floor for which button b generated a request. The dictionary of the elevator controller subject domain

Event	Current state	Action
arrive(b, c)	Destination request(b, c) and Atfloor(b, c)	• stop motor(b, c) • open doors(c) • light off(b)
	Forward request(b, c) and Atfloor(b, c)	• stop motor(b, c) • open doors(c) • light off(b) • show direction (c)
	Outermost reverse request(b, c) and Atfloor(b, c)	• stop motor(b, c) • open doors(c) • light off(b) • reverse and show direction(c)

Figure 11.10 A transformation table for stateless behavior.

says that there is a destination request for that floor if the request button for that floor inside the elevator cage has been pressed. There is a forward request for that floor if an up (or down) button has been pressed at that floor and the elevator cage is traveling up (or down). There is an outermost reverse request for elevator cage c at a floor if c is currently traveling in direction dir, there is a floor request at that floor for the reverse direction of service, and there is no request to be served by c downstream in the direction dir. For each of these three cases, the table describes what actions must be performed. There is no state transition described. Presumably, this is described elsewhere, in another STT.

We call this a **transformation table** because each entry merely shows how an input event is transformed into an output action without changing state. Note that several entries in a state transition table may be applicable simultaneously. For example, there may be a destination and a forward request for the same floor. The actions for these cases are then combined and executed jointly. In general, we should check whether conditions that can occur together have actions that are mutually consistent. This can be done by means of a decision table.

A transformation table can be transformed into a **decision table** by factoring out all conditions and specifying what should happen in each possible combination of conditions. Figure 11.11 shows a decision table for the transformation table in Figure 11.10. The leftmost column shows three conditions in the upper part and several actions in the lower part. Each column to the right of the double bar shows a combination of conditions in the upper part and indicates the actions to be performed for this combination in the lower part. When Forward request(bf, c) is true, it is not important what the truth value of Outermost reverse request(br, c) is, which is indicated by a dash. The decision table spells out all possible combinations of conditions left implicit in the STT of Figure 11.10. This helps in discovering possible inconsistencies among the decision rules.

bd, bf, br: Request button c: Elevator cage					
Destination request(bd, c) and Atfloor(bd, c)	T	F	T	F	T
Forward request(bf, c) and Atfloor(bf, c)	F	T	T	F	F
Outermost reverse request(br, c) and Atfloor(br, c)	F	–	–	T	T
stop motor(c)	×	×	×	×	×
open doors(c)	×	×	×	×	×
show direction(c)	×	×	×		
reverse and show direction(c)				×	×
light off(bd)	×		×		×
light off(bf)		×	×		
light off(br)				×	×

Figure 11.11 Decision table for arrival actions, equivalent to the transformation table in Figure 11.10.

Each column of a decision table indicates a (condition, action) pair. For example, the last column of the table expresses the pair

◆ If Destination request(bd, c) and Atfloor(bd, c) and Outermost reverse request(br, c) and Atfloor(br, c)

◆ then stop motor(c), open doors(c), reverse and show direction(c), light off(bd), light off(br).

The variables are declared on top of the table and are local to each column. Because each column indicates a combination of truth values of the three conditions, we must take care to keep variables apart that may have different values. The button identifiers have been given different names because a destination request, forward request, and outermost reverse request may all originate from different buttons. But because the conditions concern requests that are allocated to the same cage, the variable c is shared among the conditions.

11.4 SUMMARY

An event list is a list of events with their effects. It can be used to describe assumed or desired behavior in the subject domain or to specify desired system behavior. An event list entry of a desired system behavior tells us what behavior ensues when a certain event occurs. Whereas a service description tells us what value is delivered by the system, an effect description tells us what scenario occurs to deliver this value.

An event list entry can describe transactional or scenario effects. A scenario is an interaction that consists of several state transitions; a transaction is a single state transition. A list entry in scenario form can always be expanded into a list of transactional entries.

A nondeterministic list entry can be disambiguated by extracting from the effect description sufficient information about the current state in which the event occurs. The list entry thereby gets the form (event, current state, effect), where different (event, current state) pairs have different effects.

A STT is a list of quadruples (event, current state, action, next state), possibly extended with an initialization action and initial state. All entries in an STT are transactional. In a transformation table, the entries do not depend on the current state and the entries are really decision rules that describe which actions occur in which conditions. These rules can alternatively be represented by a decision table.

11.5 QUESTIONS AND EXERCISES

QUESTIONS FOR REHEARSAL

1. For event lists,
   ◆ What is the difference between an event list entry in transactional form and in scenario form?
   ◆ Why can an event list entry in scenario form be transformed into a list of entries in transactional form?

2. Explain how a nondeterministic event list entry can be disambiguated.

3. For STTs,
   ◆ Are the entries in a STT in transactional form?
   ◆ What is the form of the entries in a next-state table?
   ◆ What is the form of the entries in a stateless transformation table?

4. What is the relationship between a column in a decision table and a row in a stateless transformation table?

EXERCISES

5. Make a STT of the different states and events in the life of a bug as monitored by the bug-fix support system.

6. Consider the following function description of the tea-bag-boxing controller.
   ◆ **Name:** Remove tea bag from balance.
   ◆ **Triggering event:** Tea bag drops on balance.
   ◆ **Delivered service:** The controller ensures that the tea bag on the balance is placed in the box if the weight is OK and in the waste container if the weight is not OK. If the box becomes full, it is replaced by an empty one.

◆ **Assumptions:**

— There is a tea bag on the balance.

— The box and waste container can still accept tea bags.

— Tea-bag removal is fast enough for the robot arm to be able to remove the next tea bag.

This is sufficient as a function description, but does not give all scenario details. Expand the service description into a STT. *Hints:* Assume that the controller has three state variables—required, max, and current—that represent the required tea-bag weight, the maximum tea-bag count in a box, and the current number of tea bags in a box, respectively. Assume also that the triggering event is tea bag arrives(w), where w represents the weight of the tea bag. Take the simplistic view that w should be equal to required.

CHAPTER 12

State Transition Diagrams

S tate transition diagrams (STDs) consist of a collection of nodes that represent states, connected by edges that represent state transitions. They are useful to represent the structure of behavior consisting of a small number of states. By the addition of variables, they can even be used to represent behavior consisting of an infinite number of states. Like STTs, we use STDs to represent

♦ The desired behavior of the composite system.

♦ The desired behavior of the SuD itself.

♦ The assumed behavior of the environment.

Because STDs are used for such different purposes, we often talk of just the "behavior" described by the STD, without saying whether this is domain or system behavior.

We discuss here two variants of STDs: Mealy diagrams and statecharts. Section 12.1 introduces the Mealy diagram, which is one of the oldest notations for stimulus-response behavior. Section 12.2 shows how the expressive power of STDs can be extended by means of local variables. Almost all our example STDs (Mealy diagrams and statecharts) contain local variables. Section 12.3 discusses statecharts.

12.1 Mealy Diagrams

Figure 12.1 illustrates the constructions allowed in a Mealy diagram. Figure 12.2 shows an equivalent STT. The diagram shows the desired behavior of a heating tank controller. The rounded rectangles represent states and the arrows represent state transitions. A state transition arrow must have a label of the form:

event expression [guard expression]/action expressions

Any of these elements can be omitted, but the slash must always be present. The event expression denotes a named event or a temporal event, the guard expression

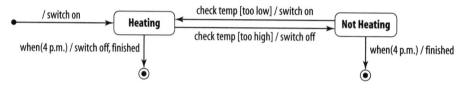

Figure 12.1 A Mealy diagram of desired heating tank controller behavior.

Initially		switch on	Heating
Stimulus	**Current controller state**	**Controller response**	**Next controller state**
check temp	Heating and too high	switch off	Not heating
	Not heating and too Low	switch on	Heating
when(4 p.m.)	Heating	switch off, finished	Final
	Not heating	finished	Final

Figure 12.2 A state transition table equivalent to the Mealy diagram in Figure 12.1.

denotes a condition, and the action expressions denote a collection of actions to be executed. The guard expression can be a combination of more elementary conditions, using the Boolean operators and, or, and not. If the guard expression is absent, as in e/a, we take this to be shorthand for e[true]/a. Multiple action expressions are separated by commas if they are executed simultaneously and by semicolons if they are executed sequentially.

The meaning of an arrow $S \xrightarrow{e[g]/a} T$ is that when the behavior is in state S, the event e occurs and the guard g is true, then the actions a are performed and the behavior changes from state S to state T. When the event occurs but the guard is not true, the actions are not performed and the transition does not happen. For example, if the event check temp occurs when the heating controller is in state Heating and the condition Too high is true, the action switch off is performed and the next state is Not heating.

The initial state of a diagram is pointed at by an arrow departing from a bullet, possibly labeled by an initialization action but not by an event or guard. There must be exactly one initial state in a diagram. A final state is represented by a bull's eye (a bullet within a circle). There may be any number of final states (including none) in a diagram. In Figure 12.1, when the end time 4 p.m. occurs and the controller is in state Heating, the controller responds by sending a switch off and a finish message. When it is in state Not heating, it only sends the finish message.

An STD has an interface determined by the events, guards, and actions that appear in the transition labels. Events and guards are inputs provided by the environment; actions are outputs sent to the environment. For example, the STD in Figure 12.3(a) has an interface as shown in Figure 12.3(b). This interface can be made explicit by drawing a communication diagram for the STD (see Part V).

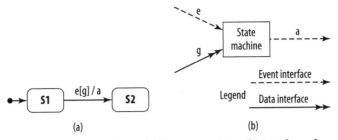

Figure 12.3 STD interfaces. (a) A state transition. (b) Interface of the transition.

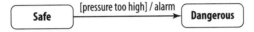

Figure 12.4 A transition triggered by a condition change event.

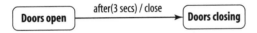

Figure 12.5 A transition triggered by a relative temporal event.

Any of the three types of events introduced in Chapter 3 can trigger a transition.

◆ A **named event** is a discrete change in the condition of the world that we have given a name.

◆ A **condition change event** is a change in the truth value of a Boolean expression. The condition change events represented in a Mealy diagram are the events that a guard changes its truth value from False to True. For example, in Figure 12.4, if the described behavior is in state Safe when the condition pressure too high becomes true, then an alarm is raised and the transition is taken.

◆ A **temporal event** is a significant moment in time. An **absolute temporal event** is denoted when(t) for a time point t, for example, when(January 1, 2000). In Figure 12.9 (see Section 12.2), when the absolute time e arrives, the controller enters a final state. A **relative temporal event** is denoted after(t) and consists of the end of a time period t. For each temporal event, we indicate at what point the period starts. In a Mealy diagram, the relative time periods start when a state is entered. For example, Figure 12.5 represents a transition triggered 3 seconds after the state Doors open is entered.

If there is no named event trigger, then when the preceding state is entered, a choice is made whether or not to make this transition. For example, Figure 12.6 shows two transitions, one without guard expression and one without named event

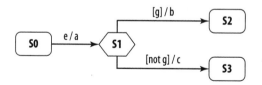

Figure 12.6 An eventless transition.

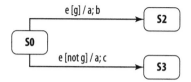

Figure 12.7 A decision state. This state cannot be eliminated if the value of guard g is affected by action a.

Figure 12.8 Simplification of Figure 12.7, applicable when the guard g is not affected by action a.

trigger. The absence of a guard expression is equivalent to presence of [true], so if the behavior is in state S0 and e occurs, then the transition to S1 is made. What happens next? There are two cases to consider.

◆ g *is false when the behavior enters state* S1. In this case, nothing happens. The transition to S2 is made at a later time, when g becomes true.

◆ g *is true when the behavior enters state* S1. In this case, the behavior makes the transition to S2 as soon as possible and b is performed. This behavior is equivalent to a single transition from S0 to S2 labeled e/a; b, where ; (semicolon) denotes sequential execution.

S1 is called a **decision state** because, upon entering this state, a condition is tested to decide whether or not to make the outgoing transition. Figure 12.7 shows a frequently used construction for decision states. The decision state S1 is represented by a special hexagon symbol to draw attention to the fact that it is used to make a decision. We need this construction when the condition tested by g is affected by action a, but we cannot predict in advance what the value of g is going to be. So when S1 is entered, this condition is tested and the appropriate transition is made.

In order to keep an STD simple and understandable, decision states should be avoided where possible. For example, if the value of g is already available when e occurs, then Figure 12.7 can be simplified to Figure 12.8.

12.2 **Variables**

A Mealy diagram may have local variables, which may be tested in guards and updated in actions. Figure 12.9 generalizes Figure 12.1 by using variables, where the variable d represents the desired temperature, t represents the actual temperature of a heating tank, and e represents the absolute time when heating should stop. Figure 12.10 shows the equivalent STT.

The presence of variables refines the interface of an STD. The diagram in Figure 12.9 can accept infinitely many events receive temp(t), one for each possible value of t. It also requires values for d and e, which must be provided by the environment (Figure 12.11). Interface information is important because, by looking at the STD, we cannot see where the values of these variables come from or, if the STD changes them, where they go. This information must be supplied by a communication diagram (see Part V).

The values of variables are bound when an event occurs and remain bound to that value during one transition execution. For example, suppose the controller is in state Heating, d has value 90, and the event receive temp(96) occurs. Then the transition to Not heating is made, with t = 96 and d = 90. Suppose that, for some reason, the environment then makes d change its value to 95 and after that the event receive

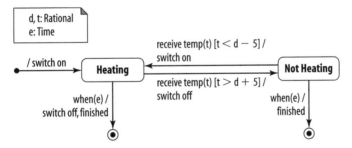

Figure 12.9 A Mealy diagram with variables.

d, t: Rational e: Time			
Initially		**Switch on**	**Heating**
Stimulus	**Current controller state**	**Controller response**	**Next controller state**
receive temp(t)	Heating and t > d + 5	switch off	Not heating
	Not heating and t < d − 5	switch on	Heating
when(e)	Heating	switch off, finished	Final
	Not heating	finished	Final

Figure 12.10 A state transition table equivalent to the Mealy diagram in Figure 12.9.

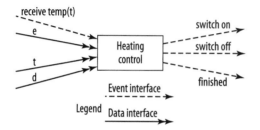

Figure 12.11 Interface of the Mealy diagram in Figure 12.9.

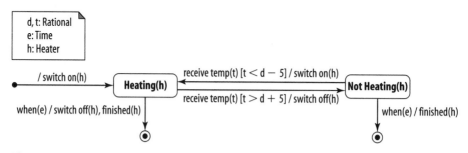

Figure 12.12 A Mealy diagram with an identifier variable.

temp(90) occurs. Now the transition to Heating is made, during which t = 90 and d = 95. This illustrates that a variable binding has a lifetime of one transition execution.

We sometimes introduce **identifier variables,** which are exceptions to this binding rule. An identifier variable is a variable that ranges over entities and is used to parameterize an STD that describes the behavior of any of these entities. Figure 12.12 shows an STD with an identifier variable h: Heater that is bound to one and the same heater in the entire diagram. The intention is that an identifier variable ranges over an entity type defined in an accompanying ERD. Because h is used to parameterize the STD, the diagram is shorthand for a set of STDs, one for each possible value of h.

12.3 **Statecharts**

Statecharts extend Mealy diagrams with three techniques: state reaction, state hierarchy, and parallelism.

12.3.1 *State Reactions*

With each state, we can associate an event list that defines reactive behavior in that state. Each event list entry has the usual form: event expression [guard expression]/action

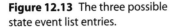

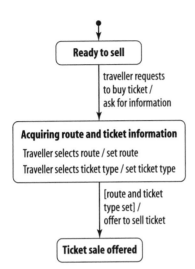

Figure 12.13 The three possible state event list entries.

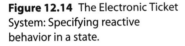

Figure 12.14 The Electronic Ticket System: Specifying reactive behavior in a state.

expression. We distinguish two special events:

◆ entry occurs when the state is entered.

◆ exit occurs when the state is exited.

Figure 12.13 shows the three formats for state event list entries.

State event lists are useful in specifying behavior that does not cause state change. Figure 12.14 shows a fragment of the dialog between the Electronic Ticket System (ETS) and a traveler that contains two event-action pairs in the state Acquire route and ticket information. As usual, the entries in a state event list are not ordered.

State reactions and state transitions differ in important ways in the treatment of entry and exit responses. In Figure 12.15, when e occurs in state S1, then b is performed; but when g occurs, the response consists of three actions performed in the following order: c; d; a. And when f occurs, the response consists of c, even though c is not a label of the transition.

State reactions add the possibility of nondeterminism, as illustrated in Figure 12.16. What happens if e occurs in state S1 and g is true? Different methods

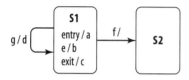

Figure 12.15 Hiding behavior in a state.

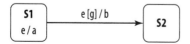

Figure 12.16 Nondeterminism between a transition and a state reaction.

that use statecharts may use different conventions. Statemate and the UML, both discussed later in this book, use the convention that the transition has priority over the state reaction. So when e occurs and g is true, the response is b and the next state is S2. Of course, when e occurs and g is false, the response is a and the next state is S1.

12.3.2 State Hierarchy

The states of a behavior form a hierarchy if being in one state implies being in another state. This allows us to represent transitions that leave a set of states by a single arrow leaving a higher-level state. An example is shown in Figure 12.17, which shows that the state of heating a heating tank is also a state of monitoring a heating tank. The temporal event when(e) takes the controller out of the Monitoring state and, hence, out of all the substates of Monitoring. If a state S0 is partitioned into substates S1, ..., Sn, then exactly one of the substates must be designated the **default state,** represented by the initial state arrow.

Now that we have a state hierarchy, a behavior can be in several states at once. If the behavior is in state S, it is also in all superstates of S and it is in exactly one substate of S. A **basic state** is a state without any substates. A **configuration** is a maximal set of mutually consistent states. Two states are mutually consistent if the behavior can be in both states at the same time. For example, in Figure 12.17 Heating is consistent with Monitoring and inconsistent with Not heating. Note that switching off the heater is an exit action of Heating, but switching on the heater cannot be an exit action of Not heating. (Why?)

Because a configuration may contain many states, we often merely list the **basic configuration.** This is a maximal set of mutually consistent basic states. So far, a basic configuration contains just one element, but when we introduce parallelism (see Section 12.3.3) a basic configuration can contain more than one state. The basic configuration gives sufficient information to construct the whole configuration.

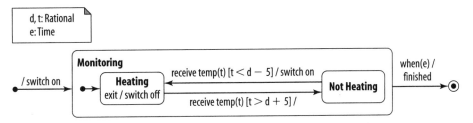

Figure 12.17 A simple state hierarchy.

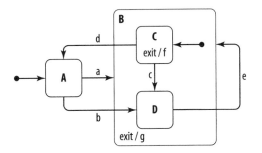

Figure 12.18 A complex state transition structure.

Figure 12.19 Nondeterminism between two transitions.

Transitions can now cross state boundaries. This allows us to create complex structures, especially when they are combined with entry and exit actions. Take the example in Figure 12.18. The following table gives a possible trace of events and responses:

Event	Current configuration	Action	Next configuration
a	A		B, C
c	B, C	f	B, D
e	B, D	g	B, C
d	B, C	f, g	A

Note that the transition triggered by **e** causes **B** to be exited and entered and hence triggers the exit action g.

State hierarchy also offers a new possibility for nondeterminism, as illustrated in Figure 12.19. What happens when the behavior is in configuration {S0, S1}

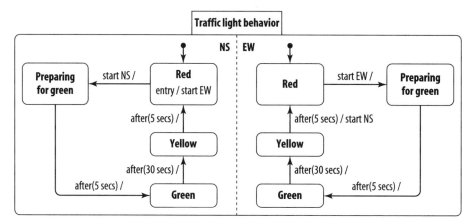

Figure 12.23 Event broadcasting.

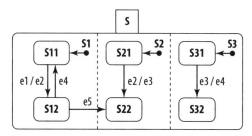

Figure 12.24 A statechart with a multistep response.

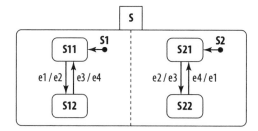

Figure 12.25 Event broadcasting with an infinite loop.

Multistep responses may be interfered with by events produced by the environment. For example, when e5 occurs just after e1, this may cause the behavior to move to basic configuration {S11, S22, S31} (Why?), thus disabling any remaining responses to e1.

Another problem with multistep responses is that they may lead to an infinite loop. Consider Figure 12.25. When event e1 occurs in basic configuration {S11, S21}, then the behavior goes through a sequence of configurations that brings it back to the same configuration, and this goes on forever.

12.4 SUMMARY

A state transition diagram is a collection of nodes connected by arrows. The nodes represent states and the arrows represent transitions. The transitions are labeled e[g]/a, where e denotes a named triggering event or a temporal event, g denotes a guarding condition that must be true for the transition to be made, and a denotes a collection of actions that is executed when the transition is taken. Any of these may be absent. If g is absent, it is assumed to be true always. If e is absent, the transition is made as soon as both the source state is the current state and g is true. The event in which g changes its truth value is a condition change event. A transition without a named triggering event can be used to represent a decision that depends on the preceding action.

An STD can contain variables that can be tested in guards and updated in actions. Events and actions may also have parameters. The variables along a transition are bound when the transition is made and this value is local to that transition. The only exception to that are identifier variables, which are global to a diagram.

An STD has an interface. The triggering events and guards are inputs provided by the environment of the behavior, and the actions are outputs to the environment. The values of variables are supposed to be provided by the environment and updated variables may be outputs to the environment. The precise interface of an STD is defined in a communication diagram.

Statecharts extend Mealy diagrams with state reactions, state hierarchy, and parallelism. A state reaction is defined by an event list attached to a state. Two special events that can be used in this list are the entry and exit of the state. In case of conflict, transitions have priority over state reactions.

State hierarchy arises when being in one state always implies being in another state. This is used in Statemate to represent emergency exits from a process and in the UML to represent specialized behavior. In case of conflict between two transitions leaving a state at different levels in a hierarchy, Statemate prefers the higher-level transition and the UML prefers the lower-level transition.

Parallelism can be used to represent parallel behavior in one diagram. One process can test the state of a parallel process using the in(State) predicate. Actions generated in one component may trigger transitions in all parallel components. This is called event broadcasting.

12.5 QUESTIONS AND EXERCISES

QUESTIONS FOR REHEARSAL

1. Which kinds of events can trigger a transition in an STD? How are these represented in an STD?

2. There are two kinds of temporal event. Describe these.

3. There are two events that can trigger a transition that has no named event trigger. Which events are these?

4. A transition without named event trigger can be used to model decisions. Describe the situations in which this is unavoidable.

5. What is the difference between an identifier variable and other variables in an STD?

6. What are the two differences between a state reaction and a state transition?

7. Define the following concepts:
   Default state
   Basic state
   Configuration
   Basic configuration

8. For parallelism,
   ◆ Describe the meaning and use of the in(State) predicate.
   ◆ What is event broadcasting?

EXERCISES

9. Explain why it would be wrong to include switch on as exit action of Not heating in Figure 12.17.

10. Make a table with a trace of the state transitions of the traffic-light system in Figure 12.23, starting from the arrival of event start NS in configuration Red, Red. Follow the trace until you leave the NS.Red state for the second time. Each entry of the table must contain the event being responded to, the current configuration, the next configuration, and the action performed.

11. Section 12.3.3 shows a trace of the diagram in Figure 12.24. Give the trace that would happen if e5 occurred after e2 occurred but before e3 occurred.

12. There are two ways to represent a state: as a node in a STD or as a value of a variable. Figure 12.26 shows a STD with two variables, one explicitly represented by variable x, with possible values hot and cold, and the other nameless, represented by the two nodes of the STD and with possible values Hi and Lo.

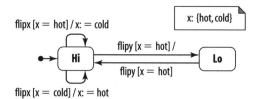

Figure 12.26 A STD with a named and an unnamed state variable.

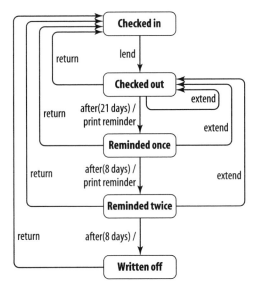

Figure 12.27 A Mealy diagram for a lending library.

a) Make a statechart with two parallel components that represents each variable by a parallel component of the statechart. One component is called x and has states Hot and Cold; the other is called y and has states Hi and Lo. Assume that x is initialized to Hot. Does this statechart represent the same behavior as the Mealy diagram in Figure 12.26?

b) Make a STD with one state and four state transitions, each of which represents one update of a variable. Does this diagram represent the same behavior as the Mealy diagram in Figure 12.26?

13. Figure 12.27 shows a statechart for a book-lending process. A book is either in or out, and when it is out the library can remind the borrower to return the book or extend the loan. If a borrower does not respond to the second reminder, the book is written off. (No doubt you can think of numerous improvements to this simplistic process, but let us keep this process simple for the exercise.)

a) Use state hierarchy to reduce the number of return and extend arrows in the diagram.

b) Use a local variable to count the number of reminders. Take care that this variable has a correct value at all times.

c) When a book is not checked in, it can be reserved. When it has been reserved, its loan period cannot be extended. Add a parallel Reservation process to the diagram in which this is expressed.

A third choice to make when introducing activity states is what happens when the substate reaches its final state. Again there are two options.

Global termination semantics. Final states are global. So when A reaches its final state, the behavior as a whole terminates. This is the choice taken by Statemate.

Local termination semantics. Final states are local. So when A reaches its final state, it waits in this final state until e occurs and then makes the transition to B. This is the choice taken by the UML. An arrival in the final state of an activity state is called a **completion event** in the UML.

This means that in the UML, drawing the bull's eye outside node A gives it a very different meaning, namely that it is the final state of some higher-level activity state.

An interesting case arises if the arrow from A to B does not have a named event trigger. In that case, the UML semantics says that the transition is made when A reaches its final state. Such a transition is called a **completion transition,** and it is triggered by the completion event of the source state.

13.3 **Pre- and Postconditions**

Consider the STT in Figure 13.3. Entry 1 says that when e(x, y) occurs in a state where P(x) is true, then in the next state Q(x) is true. Does that mean that P(x) becomes false in the transition, or does it mean that it does not change its truth value? And does it mean that Q(x) must be false in the current state, or does it mean that it can have any truth value in the current state? When looking at the table, many people would say that Q(x) can have any truth value in the current state and that P(x) does not change in the transition. But when looking at the "equivalent" diagram (Figure 13.4), people tend to say the opposite: In the transition, P(x) becomes

	Current state	Event	Action	Next state
1	P(x)	e(x, y)	a(x, y)	Q(x)
2	P(x)	f(x, y)	a(x, y), b(y)	R(x)
3	R(y)	a(y, z)	b(y)	P(y) and not R(y)
4	R(y)	e(y, z)	b(y)	R(z)
5	R(x)	e(x, y)	c(x)	P(x) and not Q(x)

Figure 13.3 A state transition table (the entries are numbered for ease of reference.)

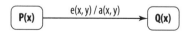

Figure 13.4 An STD "equivalent" to entry 1 in Figure 13.3.

false and Q(x) becomes true. All STDs shown in Chapter 12 should be interpreted this way.

In this book, we treat the current and next-state descriptions in a STT as pre- and postconditions of a transition. A **precondition** of a state transition is a condition that must be true in any source state of the transition; a **postcondition** of a transition is a condition that must be true in any target state of the transition. With this interpretation, entry 1 in Figure 13.3 means that in the current state, Q(x) can have any value and that in the next state, P(x) can have any value. If we do not want this, then we should say so explicitly, for example, by writing P(x) and not Q(x) as precondition and Q(x) and not P(x) as postcondition.

But if we have to write down the truth values of all propositions in the current and in the next state, the STT entries will become very large, thus obscuring the meaning of the transition. There are two things we can do to save ourselves from writing large table entries.

First, some predicates change by implication and we do not have to write this explicitly in a state transition table. We can write **derivation rules** separately from the STT to do this. For example, suppose

For all x, Q(x) → not P(x)

For all x, P(x) → S(x)

where → should be read as "implies that." If this is part of the known properties of the entity whose behavior we are describing (the subject domain or the system), then entry 1 tells us that in the current state S(x) will be true and in the next state P(x) will be false. If we use the STT as a description of subject domain behavior, then these rules are part of our subject domain description. If we use the STT to describe desired system behavior, then these rules are part of our system specification. Rules such as these tell us what should be true in the current state for a transition rule to apply and what changes as a result of applying the rule.

Second, we can save ourselves from writing large entries if we make a blanket assumption that anything not mentioned in an entry that is not implied to change remains unchanged. We call this the **frame rule.** This term refers to animated cartoons, in which there is a background that remains unchanged from one frame to the next. For example, suppose that there is an as yet unmentioned property T(x). Entry 1 in the STT does not mention it, and there is no rule that relates it to properties P(x) or Q(x). Then the frame rule says that whatever value T(x) has in the current state, it will have the same value in the next state.

We should be careful in applying the frame rule when several state transitions can occur at the same time, as in statecharts with parallel components. A predicate unchanged in one transition may be changed in a parallel transition. The frame rule does not apply to individual transitions but rather to steps of concurrently executed transitions (see Section 13.5).

First, we look at two interpretation rules for STDs. STDs express more information than STTs because we assume the following interpretation rules for STDs:

◆ Disjoint state nodes with different labels express mutually exclusive conditions.

◆ State hierarchy expresses logical implication.

13.8 Time

A final semantic issue is time. I introduced the absolute and relative temporal events when(t) and after(t) in Chapter 12. In when(t), the variable t denotes a point in time. When this time point occurs, the event when(t) occurs. But what is a time point? We have seen examples in which a time point is a second, an hour, or a day. A time point viewed at one level of granularity becomes an interval when viewed at a lower level of granularity. Any behavior description must state what is to be considered a time point for that description. A **time point** simply is a time interval whose length is not significant for the description.

This means that the time points mentioned in our behavior descriptions are abstractions from real time (Figure 13.13). If our time points are minutes, then the triggering expression when(31st January 2001, 5:00 p.m.)/start jogging describes an action that is triggered by the occurrence of the abstract time point January 31, 2001, 5:00 p.m., but that in real time is some abstract mathematical point anywhere during the minute between 5:00 and 5:01 p.m.

In after(t), the variable t does not denote a time point but instead a time period. When this period ends, the event after(t) occurs. In the abstraction of time used in this description, the period consists of a sequence of abstract time points. When the last time point occurs (i.e., anytime during the real time period that this point abstracts from), the event after(t) occurs.

Just as time points are abstractions from real time periods, so our events are abstractions from real events. Our abstract events are instantaneous. But now we must point out another ambiguity in STTs and STDs. Take again the STT in Figure 13.3. Suppose the behavior is in state P(3) and e(3, 4) occurs. According to the STT, the behavior should perform action a(3, 4) and move to state Q(3). But *when* should it do so? Immediately? As soon as possible? Any time soon, but before the next event occurs? One possibility is to use a **clock-driven semantics,** in which the behavior responds at the next abstract time point (Figure 13.14). Clock-driven semantics is appropriate in the description of hardware systems that work in synchrony with a real-time clock.

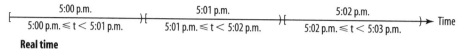

Figure 13.13 Time advances in discrete units. Each unit is an interval of real time that is closed on the left and open on the right.

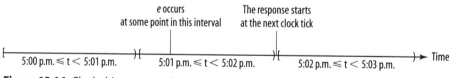

Figure 13.14 Clock-driven semantics.

In **event-driven semantics,** the behavior does not respond in synchrony with the clock, but it does respond as soon as possible. But when is as soon as possible? That depends on whether we want to describe requirements or an implementation. At the requirements level, "as soon as possible" is "now." McMenamin and Palmer (1984) introduce the **perfect technology assumption,** which says that in the specification of system requirements, we should ignore any limitations that any implementation has. According to this assumption, the system produces its responses instantaneously. Because it is an assumption made by a requirements specification, the perfect technology assumption means that any implemented system must produce its response fast enough to be ready when the next environment event occurs. If the real system is fast enough, then for the environment the system behaves as if it were infinitely fast. The perfect technology assumption also implies that, in any implementation, all actions performed to produce the response to a stimulus should behave as if they use the same time value.

The perfect technology assumption is a generalization of the **perfect synchrony hypothesis** introduced by Berry and Gonthier (1992), which says that the response to a stimulus occurs at the same time as the stimulus. The perfect technology assumption is more general because it says in addition that any other hardware limitations, such as restricted memory, should be ignored at the requirements level.

The statement that a stimulus occurs "at the same time" as the response has the paradoxical consequence that cause and effect occur at the same time. This paradox is resolved if we realize that the perfect technology assumption is compatible with the fact that in any real implementation any effect occurs after its cause. The assumption merely says that the effect should occur so soon after the cause that, for the environment, it is as if it happened at the same time.

Statemate makes the perfect technology assumption. If we make the perfect technology assumption, then event-driven response behavior produces a response immediately when an event occurs (Figure 13.15). And because an event is responded to immediately, event-driven behavior with perfect technology implies that a superstep semantics is used. The reason is that if a generated action triggers another transition, then, according to the event-driven semantics, that transition should be responded to as soon as possible. And with perfect technology, as soon as possible is immediately. So

Event-driven semantics + Perfect technology ⇒ Superstep semantics

The UML does not make the perfect technology assumption. When actions are performed, time advances. If actions take time, then the system may be busy when an event occurs and, as defined in the UML, the event is then added to a queue of outstanding events. Temporal events are added to the queue just as other events

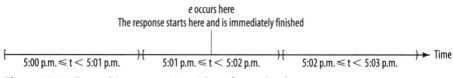

Figure 13.15 Event-driven semantics with perfect technology.

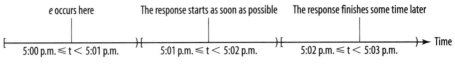

Figure 13.16 Event-driven semantics without perfect technology.

are. The response will occur as soon as possible, and it will take time to produce (Figure 13.16). This semantics is appropriate for the implementation level.

13.9 SUMMARY

The STTs and STDs discussed in this chapter can be used to describe discrete behavior. If the described behavior is continuous, this means that we must make a list of discrete events, introduce atomic transitions and stable states, and separate the effect of an event from anything else that may happen at the same time. States may be wait states or activity states. In a wait state, the behavior is waiting for an event to occur; in an activity state, the behavior is performing some activity. If an event occurs that triggers a transition leaving an activity state, then we may choose to respond to the event as soon as the activity has terminated (deferred response) or we may choose to force termination of the activity (forced termination semantics). A final state in an activity state may denote global termination or local termination of the activity.

We interpret state descriptions in an entry of an STT as pre- and postconditions that constrain the current and next state but do not completely describe it. To save ourselves from writing very large entries, we can use derivation rules and the frame rule, which have to be written only once. STDs can be used as graphical representation of some derivation rules—nodes with different labels represent mutually exclusive properties, and node hierarchy represents implication.

There are several interpretation rules for the situation in which an event is not defined for a state. The event may be impossible in that state, it may be possible but will be ignored, it may have to be inhibited, or it may break the entity that we are describing. We use the ignore semantics in this book unless otherwise stated.

There are several choices to make in an execution semantics.

- ◆ Execute all triggered transitions in one step (step semantics), or perform them in some sequence (single-transition semantics).
- ◆ Respond to all events not yet responded to concurrently (concurrent-event semantics), or respond to them in some sequence (sequential-event semantics).
- ◆ Respond to events generated in a step together with any other events generated by the environment (single-step semantics), respond to internally generated events before responding to external events (superstep semantics), or respond to internally generated events some time later (delayed-step semantics).
- ◆ Execute all actions along a transition concurrently (concurrent-action semantics), or execute them in sequence (sequential-action semantics).

In the sequential-action semantics, we may choose to use a run-to-completion semantics of certain actions.

Time points in our descriptions are really time intervals that we choose to treat as points. Time periods are sequences of these time points. In a clock-driven semantics, the behavior responds to events exactly at the tick of a clock. In event-driven semantics, the behavior responds as soon as possible to an event. If we do not assume perfect technology, "as soon as possible" means just that—as soon as possible. But if we assume perfect technology, "as soon as possible" means "immediately." Event-driven semantics with perfect technology implies that events are responded to immediately, which in turn implies a superstep semantics.

13.10 QUESTIONS AND EXERCISES

QUESTIONS FOR REHEARSAL

1. Explain how derivation rules and the frame rule save us writing when we describe state transitions.

2. For step semantics,
   ◆ Describe what happens when one event triggers two transitions (a) in the step semantics and (b) in the single-transition semantics.
   ◆ Describe what happens when several events each trigger a transition (a) in the step semantics and (b) in the sequential-event semantics.

3. Explain the difference between a superstep and a run-to-completion semantics.

4. Explain the difference between a clock-synchronous and a clock-asynchronous semantics.

5. The perfect technology assumption can never be satisfied. Explain what the assumption means in practice.

6. Explain why clock-asynchrony and perfect technology imply a superstep semantics.

EXERCISES

7. Write the derivation rules represented by the diagram in Figure 13.17.

8. Figure 13.18 shows a statechart with broadcasting that we have seen before. Show what happens when in configuration S11, S21, S31 first e1 and, immediately after that, e5 occurs, according to
   a) the step semantics
   b) the superstep semantics

9. Figure 13.19 shows two Mealy diagrams with the same state names.
   a) Two diagrams are called **trace-equivalent** if the same sequence of inputs generates the same sequence of outputs. Are the two diagrams in Figure 13.19 trace-equivalent?

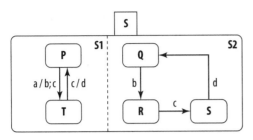

Figure 13.17 A statechart.

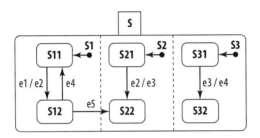

Figure 13.18 A statechart with a multistep response.

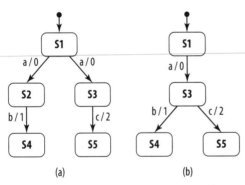

Figure 13.19 (a) A nondeterministic STD. (b) A deterministic STD.

   b) Does the node labeled S3 in both diagrams represent the same state? Why or why not?

10. Suppose that in Figure 13.17 the current configuration contains P, Q and event a occurs. Show what happens according to

   a) the superstep semantics. What is the final basic configuration at the end of the superstep?

   b) the nested step semantics. What is the final basic configuration at the end of the nested step?

CHAPTER 14

Behavior Modeling and Design Guidelines

The SuD is part of a composite system (see Figure 14.1 on page 166.). The desired properties of the SuD should be motivated by the system engineering argument that

S and A entail E

where S is a specification of desired system behavior, A is a description of the collection of assumptions about the external entities, and E is a specification of the desired emergent properties of the composite system. Correspondingly, we use behavior descriptions for three different kinds of subjects:

◆ The desired behavior of the composite system.

◆ The desired behavior of the SuD.

◆ The assumed behavior of the environment.

The structure of the system engineering argument tells us where to start—with the desired emergent behavior of the composite system. To make this clear, Section 14.1 provides two examples in which we describe, in this order,

◆ The behavior properties E of the composite system.

◆ The desired behavior properties S of the SuD.

◆ The assumed behavior properties A of the environment of the SuD.

Section 14.2 then extracts behavior modeling and design guidelines from these examples.

14.1 Two Examples

14.1.1 *The Training Department*

The Training Information System (TIS) is used by a company department whose task it is to train new employees. The training department is a composite system

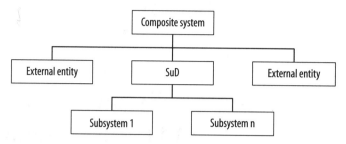

Figure 14.1 The system hierarchy.

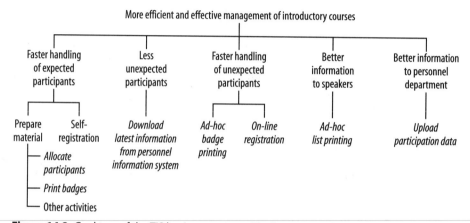

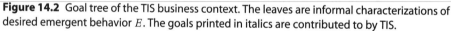

Figure 14.2 Goal tree of the TIS business context. The leaves are informal characterizations of desired emergent behavior E. The goals printed in italics are contributed to by TIS.

that contains, among other things, people, course material, material resources, and software. One of these software systems is the TIS, which is used specifically to manage the introductory course for newly hired employees. The relevant business goal of the training department is identified in Chapter 5 as **More efficient and effective management of introductory courses**. This is a high-level characterization of the desired emergent property of the business. Through a business goal tree, this was reduced to a number of more specific goals to which the TIS can contribute, such as online registration and badge printing. The goal tree is repeated in Figure 14.2. The leaves of the goal tree are sufficiently operationalized to be achieved with the help of software technology. The tree summarizes the argument that the realization of the leaf goals is sufficient to achieve the root goal.

We can now describe this business solution more precisely by means of a state-chart that describes the desired workflow for managing introductory courses. Figure 14.3 shows the part of this workflow that deals with the registration of participants during the course. The diagram says that, first, the badges of expected participants and lists of these participants must be given to the registration desk.

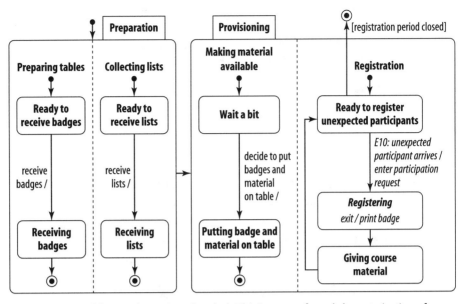

Figure 14.3 Workflow at the registration desk. This is a more formal characterization of desired emergent behavior E. Activities written in italics are to be supported by the TIS. The final states within the activity states have local termination semantics.

As soon as the two components of the Preparation state are both terminated, the unlabeled transition to Provisioning is taken. In that state, registration desk personnel take their time before they decide to make badges and course material available on tables, to be collected by the participants themselves (thus avoiding queues). At the same time, an online registration desk is opened that can register participants not on the lists. Registration closes when no registration activity is busy and the time for registration has passed. We assume that by that time the Making material available process has already reached its final state. The registration and badge-printing activity of the registration desk is to be supported by the TIS. All the other activities are manual.

The STD in Figure 14.3 makes clear which activities are to be performed by the environment of the TIS and which are to be performed, or at least supported, by the TIS itself. It identifies an event labeled E10 that should lead to some desired behavior of the TIS, namely registering a participant and printing a badge. This is our lead to find (part of) the specification S of TIS.

Figure 14.4 lists the desired event-action pair. To realize this desired event-action pair, we must connect the TIS to its environment and specify the desired stimulus-response pairs of the TIS. Figure 14.5 shows how the TIS is connected to its environment. The diagram ignores the technology by which registration desk personnel communicates with the TIS and the technology by which the TIS is connected to the printer. This means that we consider delays and errors in these connection impossible or irrelevant. The events at the interface of the TIS are summarized in

Event	Desired action
E10 Unexpected participant arrives	If there is still room, the participant should be registered and a badge should be printed.

Figure 14.4 Desired behavior of the training department when an unexpected participant arrives. This is part of desired emergent behavior to be supported by the TIS.

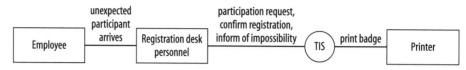

Figure 14.5 Embedding the TIS in its environment.

Stimulus	Current state	Response	Next state
S10 Request to register participant is entered.	According to the data of the system, there is still room.	Allocate participant, inform registration desk personnel, and send badge printing command to printer.	System contains updated list of participants.
	According to the data of the system, there is no room.	Inform registration desk personnel of impossibility.	System contains same list of participants.

Figure 14.6 Part of desired behavior of the training department when an unexpected participant arrives. This is an informal specification of desired system behavior.

the diagram. They are the stimuli and responses of the TIS. Figure 14.6 shows the desired stimulus-response behavior of the TIS.

To summarize, we start with the business goal tree and refine the desired activities in the form of a workflow model (Figure 14.3). This model identifies the desired event-action behavior to which the TIS must contribute. For clarity, we list this separately as an event-action table (Figure 14.4). From this table, it is then trivial to derive a specification S of the desired stimulus-response behavior of the TIS itself (Figure 14.6).

To give the argument that this leads to the desired emergent properties, we still need the assumptions A about the environment. There are two groups of assumptions in this example. First, we assume that the manual activities of the workflow model are allocated to personnel of the training department and that this personnel works according to this model. Second, we need to assume that the connections between the TIS and the relevant events as indicated in Figure 14.5 are reliable: Registration desk personnel do try to register unexpected participants, and print badge commands do arrive at the printer, which executes them correctly. With these assumptions, the argument that S (Figure 14.6) entails E (Figure 14.4) is credible, even though it is not a proof with mathematical certainty.

14.1.2   *The Heating Controller*

The heating controller is used by a fruit-juice-production plant whose relevant business goal is Juice pasteurization, which is refined in a business goal tree into achievable goals such as heating a batch according to recipe. The goal tree is discussed in Chapter 5 and is repeated in Figure 14.7. Operationalizing this further, we get the simple workflow for the operator of the heating controller shown in Figure 14.8. Focusing on the batch-heating activity, the relevant event-action pair is shown in Figure 14.9. Compared to the TIS, we see here a shift of behavioral complexity from the human environment to the SuD.

Figure 14.10 places this event-action pair in the context of the heating controller. The desired action triggered by the start heating command is a scenario involving the controller, the heater, and the thermometer that ends with a notification to

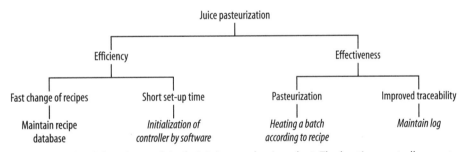

Figure 14.7 Partial goal tree of the fruit-juice-production plant. The heating controller must contribute to the goals in italics.

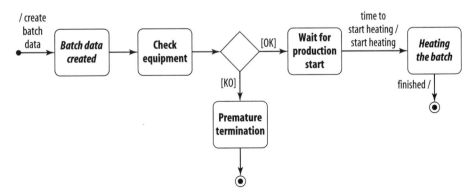

Figure 14.8 Workflow of the operator of the juice-heating controller. The activities in italics are to be supported by the heating controller.

Event	Desired action
Operator gives command to start heating batch b.	A heating process for the heating tanks of b is started. If at the start of the process, temperature in a tank is too low, the heater of that tank is switched on. When during the process, a tank becomes 5 degrees Celsius warmer than the desired temperature, its heater must be switched off. When it becomes 5 degrees Celsius colder than the desired temperature, its heater must be switched on. When the heating process has lasted for the duration of the recipe, heating must stop and the operator must be notified of this fact.

Figure 14.9 The primary event-action pair of the heating control. The description of the start heating action of Figure 14.8 has been refined here into the more detailed event description: Operator gives command to start heating batch b. The desired effects consist of the effects to be achieved by the heating controller in the juice plant.

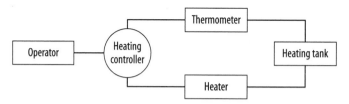

Figure 14.10 Embedding the controller in its environment.

Event	Subject domain state	Desired action
E1 Operator gives command to start heating batch b.		Heaters of tanks of b that are below recipe temperature, are switched on.
E2 Temperature in tank t rises 5 degrees above recipe temperature.	The juice in t is being heated.	The heater of t is switched off.
E3 Temperature in tank t falls 5 degrees below recipe temperature.	The juice in t is not being heated.	The heater of t is switched on.
E4 The heating duration has passed, counted since the start of heating of b.	b is being heated.	• Heaters of b that are on, are switched off. • Operator is informed.

Figure 14.11 Transactional event-action pairs that jointly make up the complex action in Figure 14.9. This decomposes the desired action into desired atomic state transitions to be caused by the controller.

the operator. Figure 14.11 decomposes this into a list of transactional event-action pairs. Note that we need a subject domain state to determine what the desired action triggered by an event is. It is now simple to transform this into a stimulus-response list of the heating controller.

1. We trace events and actions to stimuli and responses at the interface of the controller. This may require replacing an external event by a temporal event.

Stimulus	Current controller state	Desired response	Next controller state
S1 Operator gives command to start heating batch *b*	Not heating *t* and not heating *b*	Heaters of tanks of *b* whose measured temperature is below recipe temperature, are switched on	Heating *t* and heating *b*
S2 Every 60 seconds	Heating *t* and measured temperature > desired temperature + 5	Controller switches off the heater of *t*	Heating *t*
	Heating *t* and measured temperature < desired temperature − 5	Controller switches on heater of *t*	Heating *t*
S4 Timer indicates that recipe time since the start of heating of *b* has passed	Heating *b*	• Switch off heaters of *b* that are on • Inform operator	Not heating *b*

Figure 14.12 Stimulus-response list that describes the desired behavior of the heating controller. This is a specification S of desired system behavior.

It may also involve the addition of a connection domain to connect events and actions in the environment to the stimuli and responses of the controller.

2. We replace the subject domain state with the controller state and add state updates that ensure that the controller represents the subject domain state correctly.

The result is shown in Figure 14.12. Note that we replaced the events that the fluid becomes too hot and too cold by a temporal event in which a condition on the state of the controller is checked. This corresponds to replacing push communication (the fluid tells controller that it is too hot/cold) by pull communication (the controller periodically checks the measured temperature). That means that the controller does not respond to a too hot or too cold event at the exact moment that it occurs. We can do this because we can safely assume that the fluid behaves according to the laws of nature, so that it does not change its temperature so much in 60 seconds as to require the immediate response of the controller.

Another assumption made here is that when the temporal event occurs, the controller state contains information about the measured and the desired temperature. The communication specification should make clear how this state is kept up-to-date with the temperature measured by the thermometer.

We now have a stimulus-response list that can act as a specification S of desired system behavior that will contribute to desired emergent properties E. The desired emergent properties have been operationalized as a simple operator workflow (Figure 14.8) and desired subject domain causality (Figure 14.11). What assumptions A must be made to argue that A and S suffice to produce E? To find these we can use the guidelines already given in Chapter 7, and we can also go back to Chapter 3 to find examples of typical assumptions.

> - The operator works according to the operator workflow.
> - The operator only gives the start command when the batch is in its heating tanks.
> - The heater of a tank never breaks.
> - The controller is connected to the heaters of the tanks.
> - The thermometer of a tank never breaks.
> - The controller is connected to the thermometers of the tanks.

Figure 14.13 Some fallible assumptions made about the environment of the heating controller.

Figure 14.13 gives an informal list. The assumptions may all be described in more detail by means of STDs. We recognize the assumption that human operators do their work as specified and the connection domain assumptions that connect stimuli and responses to the relevant events and actions in the environment. These are only the fallible assumptions. Infallible assumptions, which we do not bother to list, are the laws of nature, such as that heat is propagated through the fluid in a tank when a heater is switched on.

This way of arriving at the specification of desired SuD behavior makes the system satisfy the system engineering argument by construction. We derive the stimulus-response list (S) from a description of desired emergent behavior (E) and then add any assumptions A about the environment to fill in the gap between S and E.

14.2 **Guidelines**

14.2.1 *The System Engineering Argument*

The system engineering argument is produced at various levels of detail (Figure 14.14). The system purpose, stated in the mission statement, is a general indication that the system will probably contribute to the business goal. The list of responsibilities makes this more concrete by summarizing the contributions of the system to the solution goals. Once we have described the system services, which are close to the leaves of the function refinement tree, we start collecting assumptions about the environment under which we expect the system to contribute to the solution goals. Behavior descriptions add more detail. Solution goals are described in detail as desired user workflow and desired subject domain behavior, and system functions are described in detail as stimulus-response behavior. The assumptions needed to argue from S to E are more detailed too and may be described behaviorally.

This added detail brings the formal validation of the specification within reach. For example, we could formally specify the behavioral assumptions A, the desired system behavior S, and the desired emergent behavior E and then use a

Assumptions	Specification	Emergent properties
	System purpose	Business goal
	System responsibilities	Solution goals
Assumptions about environment	System services	Solution goals
Assumed environment behavior	System behavior	Emergent behavior

Figure 14.14 The system engineering argument at various levels of detail. Each line as we go toward the bottom of the list repeats the argument at a lower level of detail.

model-checking tool to show that $A \wedge S \models E$. Formal specification is outside the scope of this book. Suffice it to say that if we follow the system engineering argument in our derivation of S correctly, then S is correct by construction. That is, if we follow the argument correctly, then we are able to show that A and S entail E.

Figure 14.14 shows that we may want to make behavior models of three kinds of things:

◆ Desired composite system behavior

◆ Desired system behavior

◆ Environment behavior
   —Desired environment behavior
   —Assumed environment behavior
   —User workflow

The guidelines in the next section are common to these kinds of behavior models. In Section 14.2.3, we look at the relationships between the models.

14.2.2   *Finding a Behavior Description*

We have two starting points to find a behavior description: states and events.

Starting from states. To start from states, look for wait states and activity states.

√ Look for states in which the behavior is doing nothing but waiting for an event to occur.

√ Look for states that are really modes of behavior, that persist until they terminate of themselves or until they are interrupted by a higher-priority event.

For example, in the registration desk workflow (Figure 14.3), ready to register unexpected participants is a wait state in which a resource (the registration desk employee) is idle until something happens (an unexpected participant arrives). The Registration state as a whole, on the other hand, is an activity state in which registration takes place until the registration period closes.

Starting from events. To start from events, look for the three kinds of events (see Chapter 3).

√ Look for the three kinds of events: named events, condition change events, and temporal events.

√ An event is relevant if some kind of response is required, namely a state change or the performance of an action (or both).

For example, the heating controller should respond to (1) a start heating command, the event that the fluid in the heating tank (2) becomes too hot or (3) too cold, and to (4) the occurrence of the recipe end time.

Once you have events and states, you can connect them in a STD and fill in the details such as the relevant guards and the actions to be performed in response to an event. Finding guards and actions is not the difficult part. The difficult part is connecting events and states because here we have to deal with parallelism and hierarchy.

Parallelism. To find parallelism, you should not concentrate on events that can occur in parallel but on events that occur in sequence.

√ Any pair of events that you *cannot* show with mathematical certainty to occur in sequence can occur in parallel.

For example, there is no way we can argue that, in the registration desk workflow, receive badges and receive lists must occur in some order. Therefore, in Figure 14.3 we describe them as parallel events. On the other hand, we can be certain that registration cannot start unless badges and lists are available, and so Provisioning follows receive badges and receive lists.

But are we really certain about this? What if the badges or lists are not there and the time to register occurs? Participants will be arriving even if not all material is ready. The workflow model in Figure 14.3 does not deal with this possibility. This is OK if either the problem truly does not exist or we can define it away:

◆ The company is so well-run that it is absolutely impossible, now and forever, that badges and lists are not available when registration starts.

◆ The dictionary defined registration as the process in which badges are given to participants and lists are available to check whether a participant is unexpected. According to that definition, whatever takes place when participants come in and material is not available is not registration.

If neither of these statements is true, we should go back to the drawing board and adapt our workflow model to deal with the realistic situation that registration could start when material is not available.

The heating controller behavior also contains parallelism (Figure 14.12). Is there a pair of stimuli in the stimulus-response list that we can be certain occur in a certain order? We can be sure that the start heating command precedes all other stimuli, but there is hardly any other sequence that we can be sure of. For example, the recipe duration may pass at exactly the moment that temperature in a tank becomes too cold. Our stimulus-response list describes inconsistent responses to this situation. One response says that the heater should be switched on and the other says that it should stay off. Clearly, we have to refine our description to deal with these situations. I leave it as an exercise to the reader to see what can be done about this and to check whether there are other sets of events that can occur together.

Hierarchy. Hierarchy is introduced if we want to express that a number of states respond the same to a certain event.

√ Introduce hierarchy to express commonality in behavior among a number of (sub)states.

For example, in Figure 14.3, the condition [registration period closed] defines a change event that takes the workflow to a final state. When this transition is taken, all substates of the provisioning state are left.

As another example, for the heating controller the event that the recipe time ends has priority over the event that the temperature in a tank becomes too hot or too cold. Using the Statemate semantics of priority, in which higher-level transitions have priority over lower-level transitions, this can easily be expressed by using a state hierarchy.

14.2.3 *From the Environment to the System*

There are several ways to arrive at a description of stimulus-response behavior of a system, which all start at a description of desired emergent behavior of the composite system (Figure 14.15). There are two major routes, one through an event-action list and one through system functions. It is recommended that you follow one of these routes, and possibly even two:

√ If you are uncertain about the result, follow a different route and see if you get the same result.

Through desired causality to system transactions. The two examples at the beginning of this chapter took this route. The key steps are as follows.

√ Identify in the business goal tree the solution goals to be supported by the SuD.

√ Identify the solution activities that realize these goals. This may result in a simple list of activities or in a detailed workflow description.

√ Identify the relevant event-action pairs in the environment to be supported by the system.

√ Transform this event-action list into a system stimulus-response list by
  ◆ Expanding scenarios into transactions
  ◆ Replacing events and actions by system stimuli and responses. This may require the introduction of a connection domain.

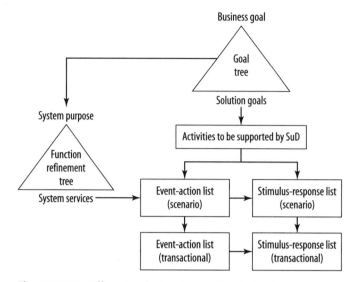

Figure 14.15 Different paths to a transactional stimulus-response list (the arrows represent design steps). An event-action list describes behavior in the environment to be caused by the system. A stimulus-response list describes behavior at the interface of the system.

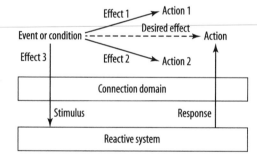

Figure 14.16 The role of a reactive system is to achieve desired effects in the environment by responding to stimuli that originate from events and conditions in the environment.

The event-action list describes the desired causality to be brought about by the SuD. Figure 14.16 (repeated from Chapter 3) shows the role of the system in bringing about this causality. In the part of the TIS example discussed here, there is one event-action pair to be realized—registering a participant if there is still room (Figure 14.4). In the heating controller example, we identify four atomic event-action pairs to be realized—starting a heating process, switching heaters on, switching heaters off, and finishing the heating process (Figure 14.11). Note that in both cases, the system supports the desired causality in the user workflow. In order to realize this causality, the heating controller engages in an interaction with the heater and thermometer. This tells us that there are two places in particular to look for desired event-action pairs:

√ Look for desired event-action pairs in the user workflow.

√ Look for desired event-action pairs in the subject domain.

Systems with directive functionality always control part of subject domain behavior. Systems with informative functionality never do so, at least not in their information-provision function. Systems with manipulative functionality do not control the subject domain, but they realize part of it and they therefore realize part of the desired event-action pairs. For example, the Electronic Ticket System (ETS) implements electronic tickets as well as the rules for buying, using, and refunding these tickets. In all three cases, the system supports user workflow, but only systems with directive and manipulative functionality enforce or realize the desired event-action causality in the subject domain.

Once you have a list of the desired event-action causality, it is fairly straightforward to transform this into a list of desired stimulus-response behavior of the system. We have seen these rules before:

√ Transform a scenario event list into a transactional event list by introducing states and describing a scenario as a collection of states and state transitions.

√ Transform an event-action list into a stimulus-response list by connecting events to stimuli, and responses to actions (Figure 14.16).

Applying the first transformation to an event-action list forces us to refer to domain states in each list entry. Applying it to a system stimulus-response list, it causes us to refer to system states. These system states represent domain states. For example, the TIS and the heating controller contain data that represent the subject domain state, and the stimulus-response rules for these systems use this data. The second transformation causes us to add assumptions about the connection domain. This is particularly well illustrated by the heating controller example. We also have seen that in the interest of observability, external events may have to be replaced by temporal events in which an observation is made.

In the case of systems with manipulative functionality that create part of the subject domain, the connection of events to stimuli and of responses to actions is trivial for events and actions that are to be implemented by the system. For these events and actions, there is no connection domain. For example, Figure 14.17 shows three desired event-action pairs for the ETS. Because tickets are virtual entities implemented in the ETS itself, there is no connection domain. The event is the stimulus, and the response is the action.

Through system services to system transactions. The path through system functionality is different, but it should lead to the same result. From a business goal tree, we can derive a list of desired system services, in which we describe each system service by indicating its triggering event, the added value for the environment, and

Event	Current domain state	Desired action	Next domain state
Request to buy ticket	Any	Ticket created and paid for	Ticket and payment exist
Request to see tickets	Any	All tickets are displayed	Unchanged
Request to use ticket for a rail segment	Ticket exists and is valid for that rail segment	Create ticket stamp for that rail segment	Ticket exists and ticket usage stamp exists for this rail segment and ticket
Request to refund ticket	Ticket exists and not completely used	Create refund stamp	Ticket refunded and ticket is no longer valid

Figure 14.17 Four desired event-action pairs in the subject domain of the ETS.

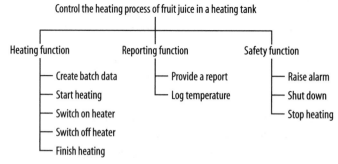

Figure 14.18 Function refinement tree of heating controller.

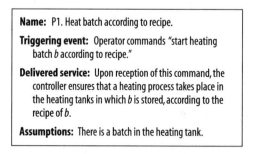

Figure 14.19 The heating service.

any assumptions made about the environment. If we go the route through desired system functionality, we start from the function descriptions.

√ Refine the description of system services into stimulus-response pairs, where the responses may be scenarios.

√ Expand the scenario into transactions by introducing states to get a system transactional stimulus-response list.

For example, Figure 14.18 shows the function refinement tree of the heating controller and Figure 14.19 shows a description of the heating service. It is simple to extend the heating service description into the stimulus-response scenario or even directly into a transactional stimulus-response list such as shown in Figure 14.12.

14.3 SUMMARY

We can refine the system engineering argument by using behavioral models of desired composite system behavior, of the SuD, and of its environment. Whatever the subject of the description, there are some general guidelines for making discrete behavior models. We can start by looking for states or for events. If we are looking for states, we search for wait states and activity states. If we are searching for events, we look for named events, condition change events, and temporal events. To identify parallelism, we search for combinations of events whose sequence we cannot determine with certainty. These events are to be modeled as parallel events. To identify hierarchy, we identify states that respond similarly to the same event. We can introduce a superstate to handle this event.

To find a behavior description of the system, we start with the desired activities of the composite system to be supported by the system. From these, we derive the desired event-action pairs. These can be expanded into sets of transactional pairs that can be transformed into system stimulus-response pairs by linking events to stimuli and responses to actions. Alternatively, we can build a function refinement tree of the system first and extend the service descriptions with scenario descriptions of the desired system behavior. From these, we can construct a transactional system stimulus-response list.

14.4 QUESTIONS AND EXERCISES

EXERCISES

1. Which states are wait states and which are activity states in Figure 14.3?

2. Which events can and which cannot occur at the same time in the event-action list of the heating controller (Figure 14.11)?

3. Make a STD of the behavior in Figure 14.11. Use hierarchy to deal with the possibility that two events with inconsistent responses can occur at the same time.

4. This exercise is about the bug-fixing database example introduced in Chapter 1. Figure 14.20 shows a STT for bugs. Extend this to allow for the fact that a manager can, in any state of a bug but Fixed, close the bug, causing it to transition to a state NFBC (not fixed but closed). Make a hierarchical statechart of the resulting behavior.

5. This exercise is about the tea-bag-boxing controller example introduced in Chapter 1. Figure 14.21 shows a STT for tea-bag removal. required is the

Initially		Bug identified
Event	**Current bug state**	**Next bug state**
Assign programmers	Bug identified	Fixing bug
Propose fix	Fixing bug	Fix proposed
Start testing	Fix proposed	Testing
Report problem	Testing	Fixing bug
Report fix	Testing	Fixed
Release	Fixed	Released

Figure 14.20 State transition table of bugs.

required: Rational

current, max: Natural

Initially		current := 0	Ready to receive tea bag.
Stimulus	**Current controller state**	**Controller response**	**Next controller state**
tea bag arrives(w)	Ready to receive tea bag, w = required	put in box, current := current + 1	Waiting for tea bag to be put in box
	Ready to receive tea bag, w ≠ required	remove teabag	Waiting for tea bag to be put in container
tea bag removed	Waiting for tea bag to be put in box, current ⩾ max	stop belt, replace box	Waiting for box to be replaced
	Waiting for tea bag to be put in box, current < max		Ready to receive tea bag
	Waiting for tea bag to be put in container		Ready to receive tea bag
box replaced	Waiting for box to be replaced	start belt, current := 0	Ready to receive tea bag

Figure 14.21 State transition table for the removal of tea bags.

required tea-bag weight, max is the maximum number of tea bags in a box, and current is the current number of bags in a box. For simplicity, we do a straightforward comparison of the weight w with the required value.

a) Transform this into a Mealy diagram with local variables. Start by listing the states of the diagram.

b) Although there is a definite sequence among the events, we nevertheless for clarity decide to split the STD into two, one for tea-bag removal and one for box replacement. Transform the Mealy diagram into a statechart with a

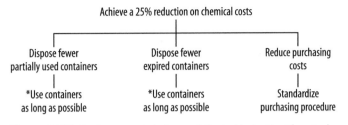

Figure 14.22 Business goals to be contributed to by the Chemical Tracking System.

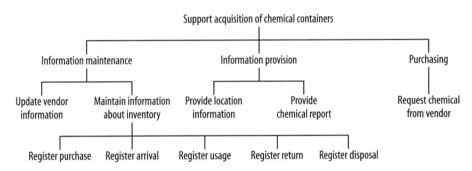

Figure 14.23 Function refinement tree of the Chemical Tracking System.

parallel component that deals with tea-bag removal and a parallel component that deals with box replacement. Is your statechart equivalent to the Mealy diagram?

6. Consider the following events in the subject domain of the Chemical Tracking System (CTS). A chemical container is purchased, a chemical container arrives, a chemical container is used, it is returned, and it is disposed of.

a) Draw a statechart for the life cycle of a container and one for the life cycle of a chemical as they have to be tracked by the CTS. Use state hierarchy where necessary.

b) Why is it not possible to combine the two statecharts into one?

7. Consider again the CTS. Figure 14.22 shows the relevant business goals and Figure 14.23 shows a function refinement tree.

a) Which business activities are supported by the system?

b) What are the transactions to be performed by the system?

c) Show, by following the system engineering argument, that a system with this functionality will contribute to the solution goals. Note any assumptions about the environment of the CTS that you need for this and any desirable properties of CTS unstated in Figure 14.23.

PART V

Communication Notations

Two complementary functional aspects of the services provided by the system are behavior and communication. Behavior concerns the ordering of interactions in time; communication concerns the information exchange between systems during interactions. This part of the book describes communication notations.

◆ Chapter 15. Data flow diagrams (DFDs) are the flagship notation of Yourdon-style structured analysis. DFDs represent the system as a collection of communicating data stores and processes.

◆ Chapter 16. DFDs are generalized to communication diagrams by adding a few notational conventions. These diagrams are also related to a systems engineering approach that traces system properties to component properties that realize them.

◆ Chapter 17. I discuss the semantic options we have in formalizing communication diagrams (including DFDs). This chapter can be skipped if you do not want to make the meaning of communication descriptions precise.

◆ Chapter 18. Communication diagrams can be used to represent the communication structure of the environment of the system. The resulting diagram is called a context diagram. Structuring the context is modeling, not design. Here I give guidelines for context modeling and relate this to classes of problems we might want to solve with the SuD.

◆ Chapter 19. Communication diagrams can also be used to represent communication structures inside the system. Here I present guidelines for defining the requirements-level architecture of a system, which is the architecture it would have if perfect implementation technology were available. The requirements-level architecture of a system is defined in terms of the environment and of system requirements.

CHAPTER 15

Data Flow Diagrams

D ata flow diagrams (DFDs) are a well-known technique from structured analysis that is used to represent the decomposition of the SuD into processes and data stores. A DFD shows two things:

◆ Which processes and data stores can exist in the SuD

◆ Which communications among processes, stores, and external entities can exist

A DFD does not give behavioral information, such as when processes are created or deleted and when these communications take place.

Figure 15.1 shows a decomposition of the heating controller into four processes numbered 1–4 and a data store called Batch data. (The store is shown twice, as indicated by the asterisk in the upper left corner.) These are embedded in an environment that consists of an operator console, a heater, and a thermometer. The diagram shows which of these elements communicate with one another and gives some information about the direction and type of communication.

There are almost as many different conventions for DFDs as there are authors writing about them. In this respect I am no different from all the other authors. You can expect to find differences between the notation introduced here and those of other authors. However, I do make the DFD notation as precise as possible without becoming formal. In the next four sections, I discuss the elements of a DFD: external entities in Section 15.1, flows in Section 15.2, stores in Section 15.3, and processes in Section 15.4. I also show how control processes can be specified by STTs or STDs and that DFDs can be simplified by introducing variables in the behavior description of a control process. Finally, in Section 15.5 I discuss ways to parameterize a DFD so that multiple instances can be described.

15.1 External Entities

Entities in the environment of the SuD are represented by labeled rectangles and stick figures, according to our fancy. Assumptions about the behavior of external

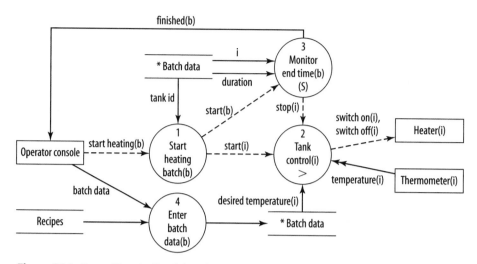

Figure 15.1 Controlling the Batch heating process.

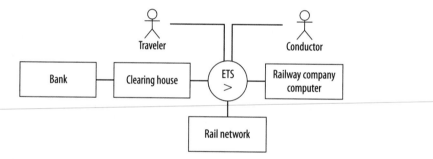

Figure 15.2 Communication context of ETS.

entities are not usually documented in a DFD, but as we have seen many times, these are actually very important if we want to specify and motivate desired SuD behavior. They play a crucial role in the system engineering argument that A and S entail E. DFDs, however, concentrate on the specification of a system decomposition, not on modeling the environment, and so users of DFDs have the habit of excluding entities that are not directly connected to the system. Because of the importance of the effect of the SuD on external entities, we depart from this habit by including sufficiently many external entities to be able to show that the behavior of the SuD and that of the external entities suffice to produce desired emergent behavior of the composite system. Contrary to what is customary in DFD modeling, this means that in our DFDs, external entities may communicate with one another. Figure 15.2 gives an example using the Electronic Ticket System (ETS).

15.2 **Flows**

A **flow** is an instantaneous and reliable communication channel between two elements. It is instantaneous because it introduces no delay. It is reliable because it introduces no distortion or misdirection of communications. If we want to introduce the possibility of delay or unreliability, then these should be represented explicitly, as shown in Figure 15.3.

A flow is represented in a DFD by an arrow or simply by an unlabeled line. If we want to stay at a high level of abstraction, we use unlabeled lines to represent a communication channel. If we want to express more detail, we can use arrows; and if we want to say more about the contents of a communication, we can give labels to the arrows.

Figure 15.2 shows a DFD of the environment of the ETS in which the system is represented a single process and some external entities, people and machines, are shown. The lines are not labeled, so the only thing they represent is that there is a possibility of communication between two elements.

Note that the word "flow" is misleading because it suggests that the sender enters information in the flow line, then the information flows through the line, and then some time later it is received by the receiver. That is not how we interpret a DFD. Our interpretation of a flow line is that a sender influences a receiver instantaneously. A better term would be "communication channel," but because the term "flow" has been in use for more than 25 years in connection with DFDs, we continue to use it here.

But what does an arrow mean if the contents of a flow are available to all communication partners at conceptually the same time? There are two interpretations of arrows, a causal and a semantic one. To express this difference, we distinguish two kinds of arrows to represent the two kinds of flows.

Causal flow. An **event flow** is a channel through which the sender can cause the receiver to do something. An event flow is represented by a dashed arrow. The direction of the arrow represents the direction of causality. Event flows are often named after the effect caused by the communication. For example, in Figure 15.1, the dashed arrow labeled start heating(b) from the operator console to the process Start heating batch(b) represents a communication channel in which the console can cause an occurrence of the event start heating(b). In other cases, an event

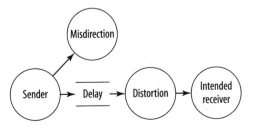

Figure 15.3 Introducing delays and unreliability.

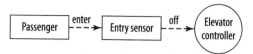

Figure 15.4 Event flow with causal naming.

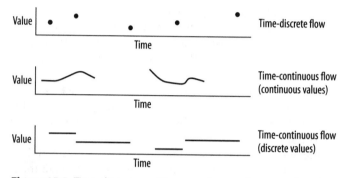

Figure 15.5 Time-discrete and time-continuous flows as a function of time.

flow is named after the event that causes a communication. Figure 15.4 gives two examples.

Semantic flow. A **data flow** is a channel through which a sender can share information with a receiver. A data flow is named after the data that is communicated. It is represented by a solid arrow. The direction of the arrow indicates the direction of the flow of data, not the direction of causality. Data flows may be push or pull communications. For example, in Figure 15.1 the arrow labeled finished(b) from process 3 to the operator console represents a push communication of a data item, caused by process 3. The direction of the arrow represents the flow of information—the operator console learns something that process 3 already knows. On the other hand, the arrow labeled tank id from the data store Batch data to process 1 represents a pull communication caused by process 1. The direction of the arrow again represents the flow of information—process 1 learns something that the data store already knows.

This way of making the distinction is nonstandard, but I think it is the only way in which the distinction can be made to make sense. An important feature of our concept of an event flow is that it may contain parameterized events. This contrasts with Yourdon approaches, in which an event flow only contains parameterless signals. See the Bibliographic Remarks for a discussion of the different interpretations by different authors of the distinction between data and event flows.

A second distinction to be made concerns the period during which a flow contains data or events (Figure 15.5).

◆ A **time-discrete flow** is a channel that contains a value only at discrete moments in time. When a value is present in such a flow, the receiver must respond immediately, because otherwise, the value has disappeared. Note that the value that passes through the flow may have a continuous or discrete data type. For example, it may have type *Real* (which is continuous) or *Integer* (which is discrete). A time-discrete flow is represented by a single-headed arrow. Both data and event flows may be time-discrete.

◆ A **time-continuous data flow** contains values for nonzero periods of time. Again, the value present in the flow may have a continuous data type or a discrete data type. A time-continuous flow is represented by a double-headed arrow. Only data flows can be time-continuous; the concept of a time-continuous event flow makes no sense because events are instantaneous by nature. The arrow labeled temperature(i) in Figure 15.1 represents a time-continuous data flow.

Note that both kinds of flows may have no content at some times. Even time-continuous flows may be empty at some times.

Figure 15.1 also shows that flow names may have parameters. The meaning of the parameters must be defined in the dictionary. For example, the dictionary of the heating controller DFD should contain an entry such as the following:

start heating(b: Batch). Start heating a batch of juice b.

If two flow names in a DFD have the same parameters, we cannot conclude that in an execution of the DFD these parameters have the same value. We should read the process specifications to see whether this is the case. For example, process 2, Tank control(i), has input and output flows all parametrized by i. When we look at the specification of process 2 later, we see that i identifies a heating tank and that all flows interfacing with Tank control(i) should have the same value for i.

Finally, Figure 15.1 shows that some flow arrows may have two or more names. The arrow from Tank control(i) to the external entity Heater(i) is labeled switch on(i), switch off(i). This means that the arrow really represents two distinct event flows, one in which switch on(i) is communicated and one in which switch off(i) is communicated. As an alternative, we may draw two dashed arrows representing the two event flows.

Yet another alternative is to summarize this into a higher-level **composite flow** as shown in Figure 15.6. Now the dictionary should contain an entry

Heater commands. switch on(i), switch off(i).

A composite flow is represented by a solid single-headed arrow—this makes it indistinguishable from a basic data flow! Its name indicates which flows it summarizes. A composite flow can contain event flows as well as data flows.

Figure 15.6 A composite flow.

15.3 **Stores**

A **data store** remembers the data written to it until it is deleted. A data store is represented by a pair of parallel lines enclosing the name of the store. The name of a store must be a noun. Figure 15.1 contains one data store, represented twice to avoid crossing lines. (As in all diagrams shown in this book, a diagram node shown twice is indicated with an asterisk in the upper left corner.)

Access to a data store can be represented by a data flow or by an event flow (Figure 15.7). A data flow indicates the direction of data movement and is labeled by the name of the data. An event flow indicates the direction of causality and is labeled by the name of the access event. An event flow can never depart from a data store because a data store is a passive element. However, an event flow can point to a data store. It is not standard to allow an event flow to interface with a data store, but this follows from our conventions in the previous section.

The DFDs that we use are designed to represent stimulus-response processing independently from any implementation. That means that the data stores do not contain any implementation information but do contain data about the subject domain of the system. The reason is that the store should contain just enough data to be able to compute the system response and no more. To support information-provision functions, a store should contain data about the subject domain of these functions; to support directive functions, the stores should contain data about the subject domain of those functions; and to support manipulative functions, the stores should contain the lexical items to be manipulated. The contents of a data store can therefore be defined by the subject domain ERD, possibly supplemented by verbal definitions in the dictionary. For example, the contents of the Batch data store of Figure 15.1 is documented by the ERD in Figure 15.8. The ERD shows the meaning, and therefore the conceptual structure, of the data in the store.

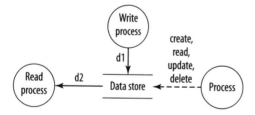

Figure 15.7 Different ways to represent access to a store.

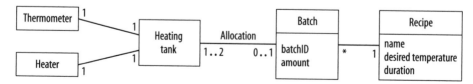

Figure 15.8 ERD of the subject domain of the juice-heating controller.

15.4 **Processes**

A **process** is some system activity. Because structured analysis commonly performs functional decomposition, processes are often called functions. But because I want to also allow other kinds of decomposition, in which processes correspond to devices, events, or subject domain entities, I use the term "process."

Each process has a name that indicates its activity and an **index** that is unique within the DFD. The index identifies a node in the graph. We use numbers as indices. The ordering of these numbers has no significance, but we require different nodes in one diagram to have different numbers.

15.4.1 *Kinds of Processes*

We distinguish three kinds of processes.

◆ A **data process** transforms input data into output data. A data process may interface with data flows as well as event flows. A data process is represented by a solid circle.

◆ A **control process** transforms input events into output events. It is always specified by a STD or STT that tells us how the control process responds to events. A control process can interface only with Boolean data flows and with event flows. (A Boolean data flow is a data flow that can contain True and False as values.) A control process is represented by a dashed circle.

◆ A **composite process** is a process specified by a lower-level DFD. It is represented by a solid circle labeled with a >.

For example, in Figure 15.1, processes 1 and 3 are data processes and process 2, Tank control(i), is a composite process. The lower-level DFD that specifies process 2 is shown in Figure 15.9. The hierarchy introduced by a composite process is visible by a hierarchical numbering scheme of node indices. The nodes labeled 2.1 and 2.2 in Figure 15.9 are the children of the node labeled 2 in Figure 15.1.

15.4.2 *States of a Process*

To specify a process, it is important to distinguish stateless from stateful processes. A **stateless process** is a process without memory. Provided with the same inputs, it produces the same outputs. A stateless data process is also called a **data transformation.** (We ignore stateless control processes here because these are better represented as data processes specified by a decision table.) A stateless process can be triggered by an event flow labeled T, called a **trigger.** When a stateless process receives a T, it reads its inputs and performs its data transformation.

A **stateful process** is a process with memory. Its response to inputs depends not only on these inputs but also on its state. A stateful data process is exactly an object in object-oriented modeling—it has an identity that remains constant, an

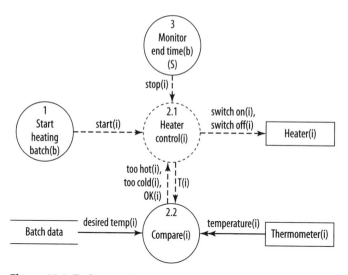

Figure 15.9 Tank control(i).

Figure 15.10 Prompts.

interface, and a state. A stateful data process is labeled **(S)**. All control processes that we consider are stateful.

A stateful process can be in the enabled or disabled state. In the enabled state, it responds to inputs, but in its disabled state it does not respond to any input other than an enable prompt. An **enable prompt** is an event flow labeled E; a **disable prompt** is an event flow labeled D. Where there is an enable prompt, there usually is a disable prompt, and the two flows are usually combined into a single flow labeled E/D. The meaning of the flow is as follows.

◆ If a process has an E or an E/D prompt as input, it starts its life in the disabled state and then moves between its enabled and disabled states under the control of the E and D prompts.

◆ If a process has no E or E/D prompt as input, it starts in its enabled state. If it has no incoming D prompt, it is always enabled.

The T, E, and D event flows are called **prompts.** For each prompt, a special **prompting action** is defined. In Figure 15.10, the action T: Q sends a trigger from P to Q and the actions E: R and D: R send enable and disable prompts to R. These actions can be used in the process specification of P.

15.4.3 *Data Process Specification*

A stateless data process specification describes how input is transformed into output. For example, Figure 15.11 shows a specification of the Compare(i) transformation of Figure 15.9. It simply defines the output in terms of the input.

The figure also contains a specification of the stateful data process Monitor end time. Stateful data processes are specified in three parts:

◆ A declaration of local variables, which hold the state of the process

◆ A specification of the initialization of the local variables

◆ A specification of the process that is then performed

If a stateful data process receives an E prompt, it performs its initialization and then starts processing its inputs (if any).

We do not use a formal language for process specification, but note that a process specification should be clear and unambiguous. The important rules of the game concern consistency between the process specification, on the one hand, and the interface as defined by the DFD, on the other.

◆ Input data flows may be used in the process specification as read-only variables.

◆ Output data flows may be used in the process specification as updatable variables.

◆ Input event flows, except prompts, can be used in the process specification as triggers of actions. (Prompts trigger a process as a whole, not one action in it.)

◆ Output event flows, except prompts, can be used in the process specification as actions to be performed.

2.2 Compare *i*.

When triggered, then let d = i.batch.desired_temperature from Batch data:
- if temperature $i < d - 5$ then too cold *i*,
- if temperature $i > d + 5$ then too hot *i*,
- otherwise OK *i*.

---

3 Monitor end time.

Local variable: current_batch
- This process is started by the reception of *b* and then is active until a temporal event occurs.

When *b* is received, then
- Read b.duration from Batch data and set end_time := now + b,
- current_batch := b..duration.

When end_time occurs, then
- read tank_id's of current_batch from batch data,
- for each tank_id, send "stop(tank_id),"
- send "current_batch finished".

Figure 15.11 Data process specifications.

All flows are identified by name. For example, in the specification of Monitor end time, we can simply say send finished(b) because there is an output data flow named finished(b). In other words, the destination of the output is determined by naming the communication channel, not the receiver. By reading the specification of Monitor end time we cannot find out that the message finished(b) has the operator console as destination; we have to look at the DFD to find that out. This concept is so important that we give it a name: **channel addressing.** It represents a decoupling of a process from its environment. We can reuse the specification Monitor end time in every context in which it is connected to channels with the right names, even if the further end of these channels are connected to different processes in different contexts. This contrasts with communication in object-oriented models, where we have to address the destination, not the channel.

The only exception to channel addressing is the use of triggers and E/D prompts. As we have seen, the prompting actions contain a reference to the destination process rather than to the channel.

To illustrate an event-oriented data process specification, consider the DFD fragment for the elevator controller shown in Figure 15.12. A data store contains data about the allocations of elevator cages to requests. When a button is pushed, a new allocation should be created unless an unserved request from this button has already been allocated. Figure 15.13 contains the specification. It says that when the trigger

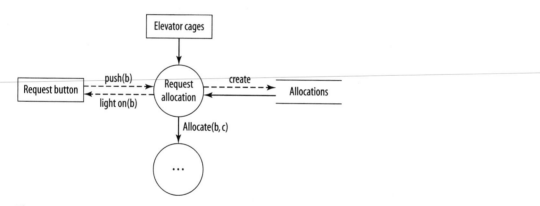

Figure 15.12 Fragment of a DFD for the elevator controller.

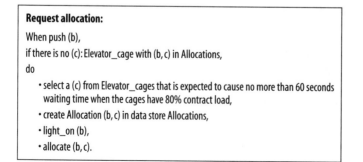

Request allocation:

When push (b),

if there is no (c): Elevator_cage with (b, c) in Allocations,

do

- select a (c) from Elevator_cages that is expected to cause no more than 60 seconds waiting time when the cages have 80% contract load,
- create Allocation (b, c) in data store Allocations,
- light_on (b),
- allocate (b, c).

Figure 15.13 Specification of Request allocation.

occurs and there is no elevator cage already allocated to this button, then select a cage, create an allocation, confirm this, and send a signal about it to some other process. The specification mentions waiting time and contract load, concepts that must be specified before this transformation can be implemented. There is specialized literature about elevator-scheduling algorithms, and this falls outside the scope of this book. Note that the specification consists of three parts that play the roles of triggering event, guard, and action, just as if it were an entry in an event list.

15.4.4 *Control Process Specification*

A control process is specified by means of a STT or STD. In all Yourdon variants of structured analysis, this is done without local variables. This means that data storage, computations, and tests must all be performed by other elements of the DFD. This is exactly how the DFD is constructed:

◆ Data storage is done in data stores.

◆ Computations and tests are performed by data processes.

◆ Behavior is modeled by control processes.

For example, the Heater control(i) process of Figure 15.9 is specified by the STD of Figure 15.14. When Heater control(i) starts, it triggers Compare(i) and waits for the answer in state Comparing(i). Depending on the answer, it switches the heater on or off and enters the appropriate state. Every 60 seconds, it repeats this procedure. The control process uses the Compare(i) process to perform a test. While Compare(i) does its work, the control process waits in the decision state Comparing(i).

The STT or STD that specifies a control process must be kept consistent with the DFD. The rules of the game are simple.

◆ Input event flows correspond to the triggering events of the behavior description.

◆ Boolean input data flows correspond to the guards of the behavior description. I recommend that only time-continuous Boolean input data flows be used.

◆ Output event flows correspond to the actions of the behavior description.

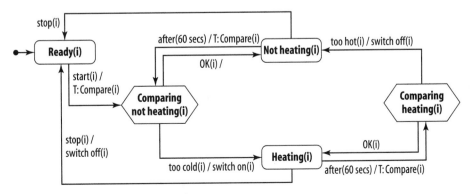

Figure 15.14 STD of Heater control(i).

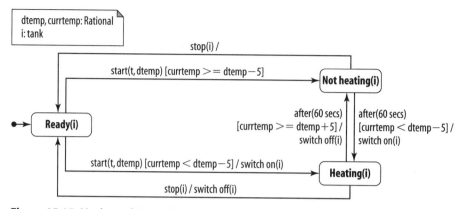

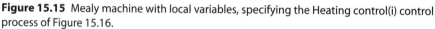

Figure 15.15 Mealy machine with local variables, specifying the Heating control(i) control process of Figure 15.16.

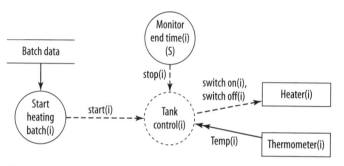

Figure 15.16 Encapsulating the Compare(i) transformation in the control process with local variables.

If a control process receives an E prompt, it enters its initial state, performing an initialization action if specified.

Consider what happens if we allow the use of variables in a control process specification. In this case, we could do away with the decision state and perform the test in the guards of state transitions, as shown in Figure 15.15. In the DFD, we could encapsulate the Compare(i) transformation in the control process, as shown in Figure 15.16. The DFD has been simplified further by having Start heating(i) read the desired temperature from the Batch data store, passing it as a parameter d to the control process. By the inclusion of variables in the STD, we have passed over the line from process-orientation to object-orientation. The Heater control(i) process has really become a software object with a local state and behavior.

15.5 Parameterized DFDs

A DFD is an instance-level technique. It says that particular processes and data stores can exist in a software decomposition and that these can communicate with one another. However, often we want to show several processes with the same

Figure 15.17 An attempt to represent multiple copies of a process.

structure, such as the heating processes of different heating tanks. We can do this by parameterizing the process names in a diagram by a **process identifier.** A process identifier identifies the various copies of a process. A diagram with process identifiers must be instantiated before it is executed.

The difference between a process identifier and an index is that a process identifier identifies a process and an index identifies a node in a graph. For example, one instance of the diagram in Figure 15.1 may have b = b123 and i = tank_456, and another instance may have b = b123 and i = tank_654. Then, in one instance of the diagram, the node with index 2 represents process Tank control(tank_456); in the other diagram, the node with index 2 represents process Tank control(tank_654).

Perhaps we would like to express that the process Start heating(i) sends a start(i) message to several Tank control(i) processes, with different values for i. This is not expressed by the DFD of Figure 15.1 or by the two instantiated DFDs just mentioned. We may invent a notation to express this, such as the circle with the double line in Figure 15.17. However, this causes more trouble than it solves because now we must specify the cardinality relationships among all processes that can be multiplied this way. In addition, it extends the DFD beyond its limits. A DFD should simply represent the communication channels between processes and refrain from including control information such as multiple instantiation of processes or even the creation and deletion of processes. If there is an arrow from node *A* to node *B* in a DFD, this means that process *A* influences process *B* through an instantaneous reliable communication channel. It does not tell us when processes *A* and *B* are created, when they are deleted, or how many of these communications exist at the same time.

15.6 SUMMARY

A DFD shows the decomposition of a software system into a collection of communicating processes and stores. The DFD merely represents the fact that these processes and stores can exist, but not when or for how long they exist. It also represents possible communications, but not how many of them take place nor when they take place. Our DFDs may also include communications between external entities. We represent sufficiently many external entities in a diagram to be able to show how the SuD behavior plus the assumed behavior of external entities leads to the desired emergent composite system behavior.

There are three kinds of processes: data processes, control processes, and composite processes. Data processes may be stateful or stateless. A stateless data process is also called a data transformation. Stateless data processes can be triggered by a

T prompt. A stateful process can be enabled and disabled by E and D prompts. If a stateful data process receives an E prompt, it performs its initialization before processing its input.

We ignore stateless control processes here. A stateful control process is specified by an STD or STT. When it receives an E prompt, it enters its initial state, performing an initialization action if specified.

A composite process is specified by a lower-level DFD. Whether it is stateful depends on this DFD.

A flow is a communication channel. There are three kinds of flows: time-discrete, time-continuous, and composite. A time-discrete flow contains values at discrete points in time and a time-continuous flow contains values during periods of time.

A data flow contains shared data from the sender to the receiver. The flow may be initiated by the sender or by the receiver. The direction of the flow represents the direction in which the information is passing. Data flows may be time-continuous or time-discrete.

An event flow may contain an event caused by the sender. The direction of the arrow represents the direction of causality. The name of the flow may be the name of the causing event or the name of the event caused. Event flows are always time-discrete.

Data stores are passive elements that remember the data written to them until deleted. They can have data flow interfaces that represent data entering and leaving the store and event flow interfaces that represent create, read, update, and delete actions.

A DFD is an instance-level technique, but it can be parameterized to represent multiple instances of the same process. This is done by including process identifiers in the process names and in the data flow names.

15.7 QUESTIONS AND EXERCISES

QUESTIONS FOR REHEARSAL

1. Define the following concepts:
   Data flow
   Event flow
   Time-discrete flow
   Time-continuous flow

2. For values and time:
   ◆ Can an event flow be time-continuous? Why or why not?
   ◆ Can a time-discrete flow contain continuous values? Why or why not?

3. Define the following concepts:
   Data process
   Control process

Stateless process

Stateful process

4. What is the difference between an index and a process identifier?

EXERCISES

5. Figure 15.18 shows a DFD for a controller of the tea-bag-packaging cell. (See Chapter 1 for the case example description.) The process Control tea-bag removal is specified by an STD with variables, shown in Figure 15.19.

a) Make a list of the local variable(s) used by the STD and of the updates and tests performed on them.

b) Eliminate all variables, updates, and tests from the STD by defining data stores for variables, defining a data process for each update and test, and redirecting flows in the DFD accordingly. Draw the resulting DFD and STD.

6. Exercise 5 in Chapter 9 lists the functions of the bug-fixing support system and asks you to make an ERD of the subject domain.

a) Use the function list and ERD to make a DFD of the bug-fixing support system, in which the data stores contain data about the subject domain.

b) Extend the DFD with a bug-monitoring function as follows. Exercise 4 in Chapter 14 gives a STT for the life cycle of bugs. Include a data process in your DFD that monitors the state of each bug and only updates the bug data according to this life cycle.

QUESTIONS FOR DISCUSSION

7. Is there a difference between a process and an activity state?

8. A composite process may or may not be stateful. State exactly when it is stateless.

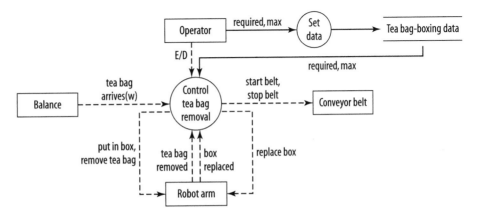

Figure 15.18 DFD of tea-bag boxing. Control tea-bag removal is specified by Figure 15.19.

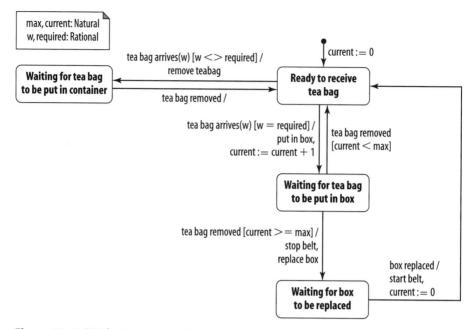

Figure 15.19 STD for the removal of tea bag, with local variables. It contains a simplistic test of the tea-bag weight.

9. Is it meaningful to enable or disable a stateless process? If so, explain the meaning; if not, explain why.

10. Some people like to include material flows and material stores in a DFD that transports and holds material items, defined as items that have a physical mass, size, and location in space. For example, a material flow from a process to a material store would represent the production of a material item by the process and the placement of this item in store. An arrow from the store to a process would represent the use of a material item from the store by the process.

a) What is the differences between material and data?

b) What are the differences between a material flow and a data flow?

c) What are the differences between a material store and a data store?

d) Suppose we represent material flows by bold arrows and material stores by bold parallel lines. Make a DFD in which you represent the processes, material, and data flows in the following situation:

A bank customer writes an order to transfer money from bank account A to bank account B. He posts this order by ordinary mail. When it arrives at the bank, it is put into the in-box of a desk clerk, who then enters the transaction in the bank's information system, which executes the order. The bank sends a confirmation of the execution back to the customer by mail.

CHAPTER 16

Communication Diagrams

C ommunication diagrams generalize DFDs by adding some notational conventions that allow us to represent type-level components, component hierarchy, and closely coupled components. They are intended to be used to represent the **requirements-level architecture** of the SuD, which is the architecture it would have if perfect implementation technology were available. The requirements-level architecture is one of the many architectural views of a software system; other architectural views are the module structure and the physical architecture. It is also called "conceptual architecture" by some authors (Bass, Clements, and Kazman 1998; Hofmeister, Nord, and Soni 2000). Because all architectural views are conceptual structures projected onto a system, I do not use this term. The term "requirements-level architecture" makes clear that this architecture is defined in terms of the requirements.

Figure 16.1 gives a communication diagram of the requirements-level architecture of the heating controller. The nodes in a communication diagram represent components; the edges represent communication channels. The enclosure of one node inside another represents decomposition. Figure 16.1 shows that the heating controller interacts with the operator console, heaters, and thermometers and at the requirements level consists of five components that jointly realize its functionality.

Section 16.1 defines the concept of component used in this book and introduces icons for the different kinds of components. Section 16.2 discusses the representation of communication channels between components, and Section 16.3 discusses the representation of decomposition. Section 16.4 relates communication diagrams to the concepts of allocation and flowdown known from system engineering.

16.1 Requirement-Level Components

There are many different definitions of software component. In this book, we take a simple commonsense view and define a **component** as any part of the executing SuD that delivers a service to its environment. For requirements-level components,

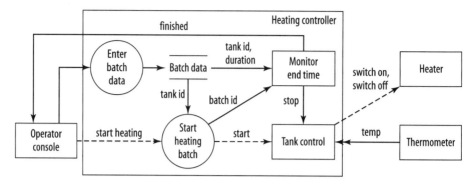

Figure 16.1 Communication diagram of a heating controller.

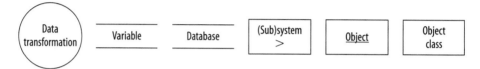

Figure 16.2 Icons used in a communication diagram for various kinds of components.

we assume that the implementation technology is perfect, that is, that it has no memory limitations, has infinite processing speed, and offers all the services we need to execute requirements-level components.

The environment of a component consists of other components and of external entities of the SuD. In this very general sense of the word "component," databases, processes, software objects, procedures, and even variables are components of the SuD. And the SuD itself is a component of a larger composite system, just as the devices and people with which it interacts are components of the composite system.

We distinguish three kinds of requirements-level components, classified according to the way data storage and data processing are encapsulated. The three possibilities are:

◆ Data stores store data but do not process them.

◆ Data transformations process data but do not store them.

◆ Objects store data and process them.

To deal with a time-varying number of components of one software system, we introduce object classes as types components. Because in our decompositions the number of types of components is fixed, we can represent component types in a diagram. This gives us the following classification of components; Figure 16.2 shows the icons used for these kinds of components in communication diagrams.

Data transformations. These are stateless transformations whose output is a mathematical function of their input. Given the same input, they compute the same output in one step. Note that a data transformation may receive a stream of discrete input data and will then iteratively perform its transformation, producing a stream of output data.

Data stores. A data store is a container for data that offers a transactional interface. Data can be written to and read from the store in atomic transactions. It is useful to distinguish two kinds of data stores, which have different interfaces.

◆ *Variables.* A variable is a data store containing one value that can be read and updated in a transactional interface.

◆ *Databases.* A database is a data store that contains a set of tuples that can be created, read, updated, and deleted through a transactional interface.

The two kinds of data stores are represented by the same icon.

Subsystems. These are components with state and behavior. Their output depends on their input and their local state. They have an identity that does not change. A subsystem is decomposed into lower-level subsystems that are themselves represented by a communication diagram. This is indicated by adding a > to the label of the subsystem. The entire SuD can be represented with a (sub)system rectangle. If the system rectangle contains icons that represent its components, the > is not shown. (In a DFD, a subsystem is called a composite process and is represented by a circle.)

Objects. These are subsystems that are not further decomposed by means of a communication diagram. To indicate that an object is an individual, the name of an object is underlined. (In a DFD, an object is called a stateful data process.)

Object classes. An object class is not a component of a system but a type of component. During the existence of the system (i.e., when it executes), a varying number of instances of the class can be components of the system.

We have seen examples of all these kinds of components. Some of the data stores in our examples are really just variables, such as Batch data in Figure 16.1, which holds recipe data and device data of a batch. Others are databases, such as Rail network database in the Electronic Ticket System (ETS). Although a database could be viewed as a variable with a very complex data type, it has a different interface. In our diagrams, a database offers a transactional interface to create, read, update, and delete tuples whereas a variable offers a transactional interface in which it can simply be read and written.

Unlike hardware systems, software systems often contain a time-varying set of components. The introduction of classes allows us to represent this in a diagram of fixed finite size. So Figure 16.1 says that there are components called Tank control, but it does not say how many of them there are in any particular heating controller.

If we include object icons in a communication diagram, we also call it an **instance diagram.** Figure 16.3 shows an instance diagram that represents a batch b0 and two heating tanks t1 and t2. There is still one type box—Operator console. So the diagram says that some unspecified number of operator consoles can send a message start heating(b0) to heating controller(b0). Note that now that there is one box per instance, we must also duplicate the number of arrows. For example, there are three arrows from Batch data(b0) to Monitor end time(b0), summarized as one arrow with three labels.

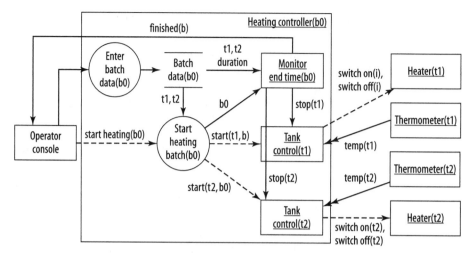

Figure 16.3 Instance diagram of a heating controller.

16.2 **Communication Channels**

A component delivers its services to its environment—other components and external entities—by means of communication channels. A **communication channel** is a way in which one component can influence another, by causing the other to do something or by providing the other with information. Our communication channels introduce no delay and are reliable; that is, they do not distort a communication and no communication gets lost.

Channels in communication diagrams are the same thing as flows in a DFD. Just as in DFDs, we can represent channels at various levels of abstraction. At the highest level, a channel is represented by an undirected line. This merely represents the possibility of interaction, without telling what the interaction is. At a more detailed level, we can add a direction and a name to the interaction. At this level, a channel is represented by a labeled arrow. We distinguish two ways in which communication channels can be named.

◆ An **event channel** connects two components so that one of them can cause the other to deliver a service. The channel is represented by a dashed arrow. The direction of the arrow is the direction of causality. There are two ways to give a name to the arrow: by cause or by effect.
   —*Naming by effect.* All dashed arrows in Figure 16.1 are named after the effect caused by a communication. The operator console causes the Start heating batch component to start heating; in turn, this component causes the Tank control component to start, which in turn asks the Heater components to switch on or switch off. When the arrow is labeled by the name of the effect, it is always the name of the service to be performed by the receiver.
   —*Naming by cause.* Figure 16.4 contains two event arrows named by the causing event: An entry sensor experiences an enter event caused by a passenger, and the controller experiences an off event caused by the entry sensor.

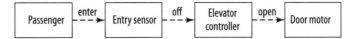

Figure 16.4 Naming an event channel after the cause or after the effect of a communication.

Whatever the naming convention, the sender causes the receiver to do something useful (i.e., to perform a service).

◆ A **data channel** connects two components so that one of them can get information about the other. The channel is represented by a solid arrow. The direction of the arrow is the direction of information flow; the name of the arrow is the name of the information passed through it. The communication can be caused by the sender or by the receiver. A data channel can be time-discrete or time-continuous.

— In a **time-discrete data channel,** the data are present for discrete instants in time. This is represented by a single arrowhead. An example is the arrow labeled batch id in Figure 16.1.

— In a **time-continuous data channel,** the data are present for nonzero periods of time. This is represented by a double arrowhead. An example is temp in Figure 16.1.

Communication channels may support channel addressing or destination addressing. In **channel addressing,** the sender sends something to a channel, which is then received by whatever component(s) are connected at the other side. In **destination addressing,** a sender identifies the components that receive a communication and then sends a communication directed at these components only, using a channel as communication medium.

16.3 Decomposition

Decomposing a system S into components $C_1, \ldots, C_n$ means that the services of the components jointly realize the services of S. Decomposition is represented by enclosing the component rectangles inside the composite rectangle. For example, Figure 16.1 shows that a heating controller contains components of five types: Enter batch data components, Batch data components, a Monitor end time component, Start heating batch components, and Tank control components. Figure 16.3 represents a particular heating controller that contains two Tank control components and one of each of the other four components.

The representation of decomposition by containment makes it possible to draw diagrams such as the one shown in Figure 16.5, in which arrows terminate at a composite box. This means that a channel that connects to a composite, but not to a component, is accessible to all components. In Figure 16.5, this means the following:

◆ C1 and C2 can both be triggered by an occurrence of event e.

◆ C1 and C2 can both read the value of x.

◆ C1 and C2 can both write a value to y.

Figure 16.5 Channels accessible to all components of S.

Figure 16.6 Representing closely coupled components by an AND-component.

Sometimes, objects are closely coupled even though they provide distinct services. We can simplify the communication diagram by representing these using a notation borrowed from statecharts. Figure 16.6 shows a component, called an **AND-component,** containing three closely coupled components. Each of these three can read channel x and can write to channel y. In addition, an event generated by any of these components is received by all three components, so closely coupled components broadcast events to each other.

For example, the elevator controller discussed in Appendix D has four classes of components that control the motor, doors, direction indicators, and buttons. These have many interfaces with one another and also are triggered by the same events. Figure 16.7 shows a communication diagram with an AND-component. The points where the arrows are attached to the AND-node have no significance; for example, all four subcomponents can be triggered by the arrive(b, c) event.

16.4 **Allocation and Flowdown**

Components can be specified in the same way as the SuD can. Each component can be specified by a mission statement, a function refinement tree, and value-oriented service descriptions, and its behavior can be specified in detail by event lists, STTs, and STDs.

This raises the question whether the conjunction of the specifications of the components entails the specification of the SuD. This is exactly the system engineering argument, applied at the SuD level. It now has the form

C_1 and ...C_n entail S

where $C_1, \ldots, C_n$ are specifications of components and S is the specification of the SuD.

A simple way to check the argument is to see whether the SuD functions have been allocated to the components. For example, Figure 16.8 shows the functions

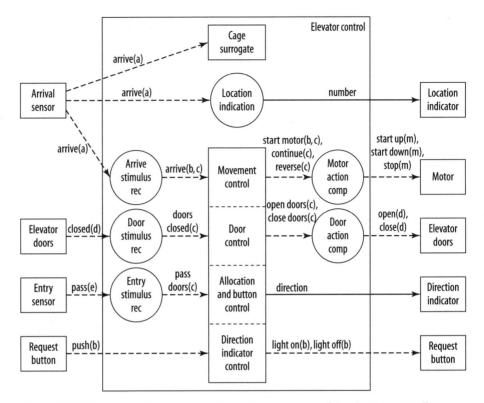

Figure 16.7 Closely coupled requirements-level components of the elevator controller.

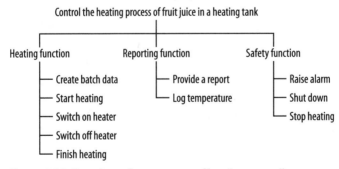

Figure 16.8 Function refinement tree of heating controller.

of the heating controller, and Figure 16.9 shows the allocation of SuD functions to SuD components. The table sets the system functions (horizontally) against system components (vertically) and contains an entry in a cell when a component contributes to a function. When there are several crosses in a column, several components each take care of part of the function. When there are several crosses in

Components	Functions				
	Create batch data	**Start heating**	**Switch on heater**	**Switch off heater**	**Finish heating**
Enter batch data	×				
Batch data	×	×			
Start heating batch		×			
Tank control			×	×	
Monitor end time					×

Figure 16.9 Allocation of SuD functions to components. The top row represents system functions; the leftmost column represents system components. An entry in a cell means that this component contributes to this function.

Components	Functions				
	Create batch data	**Start heating**	**Switch on heater**	**Switch off heater**	**Finish heating**
Enter batch data	Accept batch data and send to store.				
Batch data	Store batch data	Provide batch data			
Start heating batch		Start heating			
Tank control			Switch heater on when too cold	Switch heater off when too hot	
Monitor end time					Stop heating when time is up, and inform operator

Figure 16.10 Flowdown of SuD functions to components. Each entry specifies a function of a component.

a row, one component takes care of several functions. The table allocates external functions to internal components and is therefore called an **allocation table.**

An allocation table represents only the allocation of functions to components. We can go further and also represent **flowdown**—this is the translation of system-level functions to component functions. Figure 16.10 gives an example. Note that some system functions are refined into several lower-level functions, whereas others are simply copied to the component.

Specifying more external functionality at the component level than at the system level is not allowed. For example, Finish heating is refined into the function Stop heating when time is up, and inform operator. Informing the operator is not mentioned in the function refinement tree, but it should be mentioned in the function specification of Finish heating.

Allocation and flowdown tables trace external system functions to the functions of components. They are also called **traceability tables.** They are useful in checking that every function is taken care of (no column without an entry) and that every component has a function (no row without an entry). They are also useful in estimating the impact of changing a function or of changing a component. For realistic systems, traceability tables are too large to draw by hand—or even to draw on a single sheet of paper. There are tools that can store and manipulate the table for you; the Bibliographic Remarks give some pointers.

Allocation and flowdown tables are useful tools to check the system engineering argument. When the SuD and its components have been specified in more detail, the argument gets more complicated. For example, if we have a STT for the SuD as well as STTs for the components, we probably need formal tool support to check that the conjunction of the component STTs entails the STT for the entire SuD. There are tools available that can do this kind of checking. These tools often can also check other properties, such as freedom from deadlock and the preservation of certain desired state properties. The discussion of these techniques falls outside the scope of this book; see the Bibliographic Remarks for some pointers to the literature on this.

16.5 SUMMARY

A communication diagram shows the components of a system and their interconnections by boxes and arrows. A component is an element of the system that delivers a service to its environment. Components are represented by rectangles. The decomposition relationship between components is represented by the containment relationship between rectangles.

A communication channel between components is a connection between components through which one component can cause another component to do something. An event channel is a connection through which one component can cause another component to provide a service. The channel is named after the service itself or after the event that the service is caused. An event channel is represented by a dashed arrow, where the direction of the arrow represents the direction of causality.

A data channel is a connection through which one component can get information about another one. A data channel is represented by a solid arrow, where the direction of the arrow represents the direction of information flow. A data channel can be time-discrete (single arrowhead) or time-continuous (double arrowhead). We can document the allocation and flowdown of system functionality to component functionality by means of traceability tables.

16.6 QUESTIONS AND EXERCISES

QUESTIONS FOR REHEARSAL

1. Define the following concepts:

Component

Communication channel

Event channel

Data channel

2. For traceability:

- ◆ What is the difference between allocation and flowdown?
- ◆ How does a traceability table help with giving the system engineering argument?

EXERCISES

3. The functions of the tea-bag-boxing controller have been identified as follows (the list of functions is basically the list of controller responsibilities):

- ◆ Allow operator to set required tea-bag weight.
- ◆ Allow operator to set maximum tea-bag count.
- ◆ Place tea bag in box or in waste container according to weight.
- ◆ Replace full box by empty box.

Exercise 5 in Chapter 15 gives a DFD for the tea-bag-boxing controller. Transform this into a communication diagram and make an allocation table.

4. The functions of the bug-fixing support system have been identified as follows:

- ◆ Register assignment of bug to programmer and tester, and inform them by email.
- ◆ Register bug fix and inform tester by email.
- ◆ Register test report and inform programmer and bug manager by email.
- ◆ Register bug release.

We take registration to include monitoring; that is, the system will not register a state change in a bug if this is not possible according to the life cycle of the bug. Now suppose you are given the following components:

Manage assignments. Register and store assignments of programmers and testers to bugs and inform them.

Programmer data. Store data about programmers and testers.

Bug monitor. Store data about bugs and check that the current action is permissible in the bug life cycle.

Release. Release a bug.

Manage fixes. Register and store fixes, and inform tester of fix.

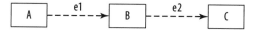

Figure 16.11 A chain of cause and effect.

Manage test reports. Manage and store test reports, and inform programmer and manager about this.

Assemble a bug-fixing support system from this. Draw a communication diagram to show the communication channels, and an allocation table to show that all functions have been implemented.

QUESTIONS FOR DISCUSSION

5. Enable and disable the input prompts of a component C that itself has lower-level components, which are really global input channels available to all components of C. A trigger input is, however, local like any other channel and must be connected to particular components of C. Explain.

6. Figure 16.11 shows a chain of cause and effect involving three components and two event channels. A causes e1, which causes B to cause e2. In which cases can we take out B and let A cause e2 directly?

CHAPTER 17

Communication Semantics

Like behavior descriptions, communication diagrams can be used at various levels of precision. Used as a rough sketch, a communication diagram just says that several components can communicate; at a very precise level, a communication diagram is an instruction for executing a set of communicating processes. When moving from the rough to the very precise level, we have to make a number of semantic choices in the interpretation of the diagram. In this chapter, we review the choices to be made. The choices are applicable to DFDs, too, because these are a special case of communication diagrams.

There are many choices to be made in communication semantics and this chapter merely scratches the surface of a complex topic. Nevertheless, the cumulative number of possibilities I describe here and earlier for behavioral semantics (see Chapter 13) give rise to a bewildering number of combinations. This is unavoidable if we want to get enough information from a communication description to be able to execute the description. However, not all applications of communication diagrams need this level of detail. Read this chapter up to the point where you think the choices are too detailed for your application of the techniques.

To give a semantics to a communication diagram, we replace any composite component by its lower-level components until we have a diagram containing only basic components of the SuD (Figure 17.1). Section 17.1 describes the options in the behavioral semantics of a component that are relevant for communication semantics. Section 17.2 looks at the possible semantics of communication channels, and Section 17.3 looks at some issues that we must decide for the communication diagram as a whole. Section 17.4 explains that none of these semantic choices constrains the environment.

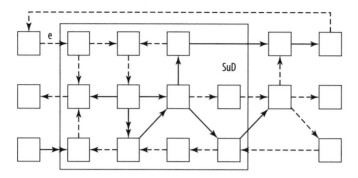

Figure 17.1 What is the response to e?

17.1 **Component Behavioral Semantics**

Components can be specified using the same techniques as are used for the SuD itself. Just as the SuD as a whole, a component can respond to three kinds of events:

Temporal events. These are not offered to a component through a channel. (But an implementation of a component may use a clock to discover that a temporal event occurred.)

Named events. These correspond to input event channels of the component.

Change events. These correspond to changes in time-continuous input channels of the component.

In Chapter 13, we review the choices to make when interpreting behavior descriptions. Some of these impact communication semantics.

◆ In a step semantics, a component can respond to more than one event at the same time. In a sequential-event semantics, it can respond to only one event at a time.

◆ In a superstep semantics, a component first responds to all internally generated events before it is ready to respond to an incoming event. This may bring it into a loop from which it never emerges.

◆ In a clock-driven semantics, a component only responds to events at the tick of a clock. In an event-driven semantics, it responds immediately when an event occurs.

◆ The perfect technology assumption says that a component produces its response immediately. Without this assumption, producing a response takes significant time; that is, a component may still be busy producing a response when the next event arrives.

Semantic options listed in the same entry of this list are mutually exclusive. Semantic options listed in different entries are independent from one another, except the following: The event-driven semantics in combination with the perfect technology assumption implies a multistep semantics.

Most combinations of semantic choices require a component to deal with a backlog of events that have occurred but have not been responded to. For example, with imperfect technology, a component may be busy when receiving an event. And with a clock-driven semantics, a component simply waits until the next clock tick before it responds to an event. The first semantic option concerning communication, then, is whether or not a component has an **input buffer** that contains events not yet responded to. Both Statemate and the UML assume that components have an input buffer. If there is no input buffer, then an event not yet responded to will be lost when the next event arrives.

If there is an input buffer, then several more choices must be made.

◆ What is the size of the buffer? Can it hold more than one event at the same time or is it simply a register that holds the most recently received event?

◆ If the buffer can contain more than one event, what is the structure of the buffer? Is it a queue or a set?

◆ If the buffer is not a queue, in which order are the events removed from it? Is there a fairness assumption (an assumption that an event in the set is responded to after a finite time)?

Statemate assumes there are buffers of finite size because in Statemate only a finite set of events can occur and so there is an upper bound to the number of events not yet responded to. The UML assumes buffers of unlimited size because events may have parameters and, at any point in time, there may be an arbitrarily large set of event instances not yet responded to. Statemate buffers are sets, and a component responds to all events in its input buffer in one step. UML buffers are multisets of event instances, but they are called queues in the UML literature and the events in a buffer are responded to one by one in an unspecified order. This combines well with a sequential-step semantics. However, it opens the possibility that some event will stay in the buffer forever, and so we should consider adding a fairness assumption that any event in the set will be responded to after a finite time.

During a step, a component may need to read more input data values or produce some of its output data values and actions. This raises the question of when input is read and output is written. There are two options.

Eager read/lazy write: All input values are read eagerly, at the start of the step, and all output (actions and data) is written lazily, at the end of the step.

Lazy read/eager write: All input values are read lazily, when needed, and all output is written eagerly, immediately when available.

Statemate takes the first choice, the UML takes the second.

17.2 **Communication Channels**

The edges in our communication diagrams represent communications with the following properties:

◆ There is no delay between sending and receiving.

◆ The message always arrives at its destination(s).

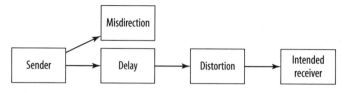

Figure 17.2 Channels do not introduce delays, misdirections, losses, or distortions, but components can.

◆ The message arrives at no other destinations.

◆ The message is never distorted.

If we want to drop one or more of these properties, we should add a component to do this, as illustrated in Figure 17.2.

A DFD shows instance-level communication flows where we can see exactly which components communicate with which. A communication diagram in general, on the other hand, can show which types of components can communicate with which other types of components, but does not show which individuals communicate with which.

This is related to whether a communication diagram supports channel addressing or destination addressing. DFDs support channel addressing; communication diagrams in general allow both. Statemate, which uses a variant of DFDs, therefore uses channel addressing. Channel addressing by its nature is a multicast operation. It says, "Deliver this communication to all components at the other side of the channel." If the communication is intended for one particular component only, then this information should be part of the communication. Even then, channel addressing delivers the message to all components at the other side of the channel.

The UML uses destination addressing. Destination addressing is by its nature a point-to-point operation because a sender addresses a particular receiver. However, by encapsulating this in a complex operation, we can simulate a multicast by repeating a set of point-to-point communications.

An important semantic option is channel capacity. The options are as follows:

Zero channel capacity: A data value or event must immediately arrive at the receiver. If the receiver has no buffer, a channel represents a **synchronous communication** in which the sender cannot put an item in a channel if the receiver does not take it out at the same time.

n-item channel capacity: A channel can contain *n* items at the same time.

Overwrite semantics: If there is a nonzero but finite channel capacity, the further semantic choice to be made is what happens when a sender wants to write something to a channel that is full. Does the channel refuse to accept the communication or does it overwrite its contents?

Statemate and the UML both assume a one-item channel capacity with overwrite semantics. A value or event written to a channel overwrites any value or event that was in the channel.

In the case of synchronous communication, a sender may have to wait until a receiver is ready to receive a communication. Alternatively, it may discard the communication and continue with something else. And in the case of finite channel capacity without overwriting, we have to consider what happens when a sender cannot put an item in a channel. Again, it may wait until the channel is available or it may discard the communication. The **blocking semantics** of a communication is the amount of time that a sender waits before it can place a message in a communication channel. There are three possibilities.

No blocking: The sender discards the communication attempt and goes on doing something else.

Finite blocking: The sender waits for a finite time and then discards the communication attempt and goes on doing something else.

Infinite blocking: The sender waits until it can put a message in a communication channel. If the channel never gets in the state where it can accept a communication, the sender is deadlocked.

Statemate and the UML do not need to make this choice because they use channels with overwrite semantics. Their channels always accept communications.

17.3 The Network

As illustrated in Figure 17.1, the SuD is a network of communicating components. When we look at this network as a whole, one important choice is whether all components have access to the same global time. In a single-processor system we can expect all components to use the same clock, but in a distributed system we cannot expect this. The **global time assumption** says that all components have clocks that indicate the same global time. Without this assumption, clocks may drift. Statemate and the UML both make the global time assumption.

When an event arrives at the interface of the SuD, it triggers a component according to the behavioral semantics of that component. If the component uses a clock-driven semantics, it will wait until the next clock tick before it responds. If it uses an event-driven semantics, it will respond immediately. In either case, if it behaves according to the perfect technology assumption it produces its response immediately, but if it does not behave according to the assumption it takes some time to produce a response. The response may consist of updating its state, sending an event back to the environment, and sending an event to another component. The other component will behave according to *its* semantics, and so on. At what time is the network ready to respond to the next external event? We can make the same distinctions as for the components separately.

Network step semantics: The SuD is ready to respond to an input event when any of its components is ready. When a ready component receives an input, it responds to it.

Network multistep semantics: The SuD is ready to respond to an input event when all the components connected to an input channel are ready. As long as some component must still produce a response to some external or internal event, the network is not ready.

The UML chooses the first option; Statemate allows both. In either case, the response of a component may trigger several other components. Each of these will respond according to its behavioral semantics, but, in addition, we have another choice to make—in which order are the triggered components executed? The two major options are the following.

Breadth-first semantics: A triggered component will not be executed until all components that were triggered earlier have been executed.

Depth-first semantics: If a component C_1 triggers another one C_2, then C_2 will be executed before C_1 returns control.

Statemate chooses the breadth-first semantics; the UML chooses the depth-first semantics. This agrees with the run-to-completion semantics discussed in Chapter 13.

17.4   The Environment

The semantics of the part of the diagram that represents the SuD differs from the semantics of the part of the diagram that represents the environment. The part of the diagram that represents the environment represents assumptions that may be true or false, whereas the part of the diagram that represents the SuD is a specification that must be implemented. The diagram places no restrictions on the environment, except that we assume that the environment is always allowed to provide stimuli to the system and is always able to absorb responses.

At the input of the system, we must deal with the fact that the SuD is a discrete system that behaves in computation steps, but that the environment behaves continuously and may produce inputs at any time. Depending on the semantic choices made for the system, the system may not be ready to process this input. This occurs, for example, when computation steps take time (imperfect technology) and also when a clock-driven semantics is used. Whatever the reason, if two stimuli occur when the system is not ready to respond to either of them, then the SuD may not be able to distinguish the order in which they occurred. For example, if input buffers are not queues, the order of arrival of two stimuli through the same channel within the same time unit is lost. If there is a lower bound on the time interval between two external events, this can be avoided by speeding up the behavior of the system; if there is no such lower bound, the loss of ordering information is unavoidable.

The environment may offer time-continuous data to the SuD. Because the SuD behaves in a discrete stepwise manner, most of the time these values will not be noticed by the system. In practice, the SuD accesses the contents of a time-continuous input flow by means of a sampling technique. The implication is that the SuD may miss the most up-to-date value in the channel, but it uses some very recent value. At the interface of a time-discrete and a time-continuous system, that is as good as it gets.

17.5 SUMMARY

Components of the SuD may behave according to a step or a multistep semantics, and they may behave synchronously or asynchronously with their clock. In addition, they may behave according to the perfect technology assumption. This yields a range of possible behaviors that may cause a component to have a backlog of events not yet responded to. The semantics of a communication diagram may therefore include an input buffer for each component to hold events not yet responded to. The buffer may have finite capacity and it may have an internal structure, such as a queue. If it is not a queue, we need a fairness assumption to guarantee that an event in the buffer is responded to in finite time.

During a step, a component may need to read input values and it may produce output values and events. In an eager read/lazy write semantics, reading is done at the start of a step and writing at the end. In a lazy read/eager write semantics, reading is done as late as possible and writing as early as possible.

Our communication channels introduce no delay, misdirection, loss, or distortion in the communications. They may represent point-to-point, multicast or broadcast communications, and they may carry communications addressed to a channel or addressed to a particular destination component.

Channels may have zero capacity, in which case they allow only synchronous communication. If they have a finite but nonzero capacity, they may become full. An attempt to write an event or data value written to a full channel will block for a period d, after which it is discarded. If $d = 0$ there is no blocking, and if $d = \infty$ there may be a deadlock.

The network as a whole may have one global clock or many local clocks, which may or may not drift. In a network step semantics, the SuD is ready to respond to input from the environment whenever one of its components is ready to respond to this input. In a network multistep semantics, the network is ready when all of its components are ready. In both cases, we can choose between a depth-first and a breadth-first way of traversing the network. One particular way of depth-first traversal is based on the UML nested-step semantics.

All of these semantic choices apply to the SuD. We do not apply them to the environment. The only thing we assume about the environment is that it is at any time allowed to produce input and is at any time able to absorb output. Depending on the semantic choices we make for the SuD, the SuD may miss some inputs or may not notice the temporal ordering of some events. In addition, most values in a time-continuous input are missed, and when the system responds to events it uses a very recent value but not the actual current value.

17.6 QUESTIONS AND EXERCISES

QUESTIONS FOR REHEARSAL

1. For input buffers:
   - ◆ Does the system as a whole have one input buffer or does each component have an input buffer?
   - ◆ Describe the semantic options for input buffers.

2. What is the difference between lazy read/eager write and eager read/lazy write?

3. Consider the following two incompatible definitions of synchronous communication:
   - ◆ A sender cannot proceed until the receiver has received the message.
   - ◆ A sender cannot proceed until the receiver has processed the message.

   Which one is equivalent to the definition given in this chapter?

4. If there is an overwrite semantics, we do not need to choose a blocking semantics. Explain.

5. Explain why both the network step and the network multistep semantics can be executed in a breadth-first or depth-first way.

EXERCISES

6. Explain what a data store does in an eager read/lazy write semantics and what it does in a lazy read/eager write semantics.

7. Execute the network in Figure 17.1:
   a) According to a breadth-first semantics until you enter an infinite loop. Assume that on all output channels, a component sends some message every time it receives one on any input channel.
   b) According to a depth-first semantics, choosing a shortest path from e to some output. Explain why this leads to different output responses of the SuD.

QUESTIONS FOR DISCUSSION

8. The communication between processes and data stores should be as follows: At the start of a step, the process performs all its read operations from a data store, and, at the end of a step, it performs all its updates to the data store. Describe this semantics from the point of view of a data store and explain what the difference is with the eager read/lazy write semantics discussed in this chapter.

9. When can we dispense with input buffers?

10. "A time-continuous value stays in a channel until it is replaced, and therefore the channel introduces delay in the transmission." Show why this argument is false.

11. What is the relationship between a nested-step semantics of component behavior and a depth-first semantics of network behavior?

12. What are the possible causes for the loss of ordering of input events? For each possible cause, give a way to avoid this loss.

CHAPTER 18

Context Modeling Guidelines

W e can use communication diagrams at two levels: to model the context of the system and to design a decomposition of the system. Context modeling is a descriptive activity because we as designers are not designing the system context but are describing our assumptions about the environment. System decomposition, on the other hand, is a prescriptive activity because we are designing the system. This chapter reviews the guidelines for context modeling. Section 18.1 looks at ways to find the system boundary. Section 18.2 discusses context diagrams that describe the system environment. Section 18.3 gives guidelines for finding the context boundary, and Section 18.4 shows that the context of different kinds of reactive systems can be structured in different ways.

18.1 The System Boundary

The system boundary separates the part of the world to be designed from the part of the world that is given. In other words, the system boundary is the boundary of our design freedom. In terms of Figure 18.1, we can design the components of the SuD, but we cannot design the external entities of the SuD.

The system boundary is best viewed as the set of stimuli and responses of the SuD. Once we have a stimulus-response list of a system, we know what the system boundary is. If we redraw the boundary so that a component becomes an external entity or an external entity becomes a component, then the stimulus-response list of the system changes. We can look at several sources to find the system boundary.

√ The function refinement tree describes a boundary on system functionality. Each service description mentions events and entities in the environment and indicates an added value to be delivered to the environment.

√ By identifying stimuli, responses, and external entities involved in system inter-actions, a description of a system boundary can be made more precise.

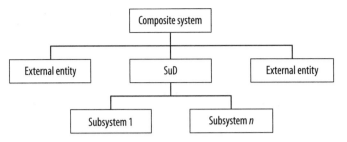

Figure 18.1 The system hierarchy.

The search for a system boundary can be related to the system engineering argument,

  A and *S* entail *E*

where *A* is a list of assumptions about the environment, *S* a list of the desired properties of the SuD, and *E* lists the desired emergent properties of the composite system. Applying the same kind of argument to the system components, we get

  C entails *S*

where *C* is a specification of a system decomposition. Plugging this into the system engineering argument, we get

  A and *C* entail *E*

This looks like letter-juggling, but it means something important: The components of the SuD and the external entities of the SuD should jointly realize the desired emergent properties *E* of the composite system. If the external entities are less intelligent, then the components will have to produce more, and vice versa.

For example, an elevator door may have some intelligence, so that the close command causes it to close its doors gently, taking care that if someone passes through the door while it is closing, it will open to avoid crushing the person, as in Figure 18.2(a). Such an intelligent door should have built-in sensors that, when activated, cause the doors that are closing to open again. This contrasts with a dumb door that crushes anything that gets in its way when it is closing. Such a dumb door needs some extra intelligence to be useful. If we decide to allocate the responsibility of providing this intelligence to the elevator controller, then designing this intelligence becomes a task of the elevator controller designer. The designer may decide to add a component dedicated to door control that makes up for the dumbness of the door, as in Figure 18.2(b). To the rest of the elevator controller, the dumb door plus its control looks just as smart as the other, intelligent door. Alternatively, we may allocate design responsibilities differently and ask the door manufacturer to add a controller to the door that provides it with the required intelligence. This keeps the responsibility of providing intelligence to the door outside the design responsibilities of the elevator controller designer and places the door controller in the environment of the elevator controller, as in Figure 18.2(c). In terms of the

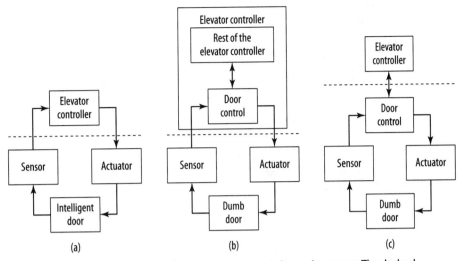

Figure 18.2 Allocating functionality to the system or to its environment. The dashed line indicates the system boundary. Above the dashed line is the system; below it is the environment.

system engineering argument, solution (b) allocates the responsibility for realizing E to one of the components of the SuD and solution (c) allocates it to one of the external entities. The conclusion is:

√ The responsibility of the SuD for realizing the desired emergent properties E is inversely proportional to the responsibility of the external entities for realizing E.

18.2 Context Diagrams

A **context diagram** is a communication diagram that represents the SuD and the entities and communications in its context. The diagram represents the entities given to us, not designed by us. If we use a DFD as context diagram, the diagram represents instances. If we use a communication diagram, we can represent types as well as instances. In either case, a context diagram represents the SuD as a black box.

We can draw a context diagram at various levels of abstraction. Figure 18.3 shows a context diagram of the Teaching Information System (TIS), using only unlabeled lines to represent flows. Figure 18.4 shows a context diagram of the heating controller using labeled flow lines.

There are a number of different kinds of entities in the environment of the system. We have listed these already in Section 2.3, but we repeat them here.

√ The environment of the SuD may consist of
  — Physical entities, such as devices, natural objects, and people
  — Conceptual entities, such as organizations, promises, and vacation rights
  — Lexical entities, such as contracts and specifications.

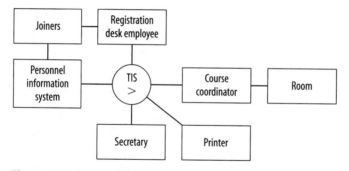

Figure 18.3 Context diagram of the Teaching Information System. (The > indicates that the system bubble has a decomposition.)

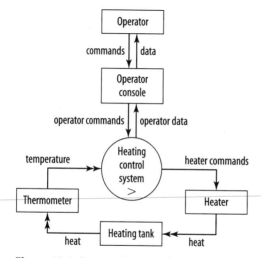

Figure 18.4 Context diagram of the heating controller.

Examples of natural entities are the fluid in a heating tank, the passengers entering an elevator cage, and the course coordinator using the TIS. Natural entities have a weight and size and have properties described by the laws of nature—fluids expand when heated, passengers add to the loads of the cage, and a course coordinator has an attention span and information processing capacity. Devices are natural objects because they behave according to the laws of nature. But, in addition, they behave according to their technical specifications, assuming they behave properly. They may also break, in which case they still behave according to the laws of nature but not according to their technical specification. People are natural objects, but, in addition to behaving according to the laws of nature, they should behave according to human laws, organizational procedures, and policies or simply the user instructions that go with the SuD. As we all know, they may not do so. They then still behave according to the laws of nature (the coordinator does not change his attention span or eyesight by not following procedures).

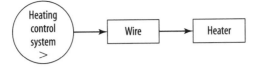

Figure 18.5 Reducing the abstraction level of the context diagram by including a communication channel.

Examples of legal entities are businesses, committees, and government institutions. They are created by human laws and custom.

Flows and channels in a context diagram represent possible communications. As indicated in Chapter 17, we do not assume any particular semantics of communication in the environment, except that communications introduce no delays or distortions and that they never get misdirected or lost. This gives us the following guideline:

✓ A communication channel (flow) represents an abstraction from delay, distortion, misdirection, and loss of communication.

For example, in Figure 18.4, we abstract from the hardware that connects a console to the controller, but we explicitly include the console to allow errors and delays introduced there. The choice of communication channels is really a choice of an abstraction level at which to model the environment. There is always some abstraction level at which we write a description; we always omit things. For example, we may choose to include the physical wires that connect the heating controller to the heater, as shown in Figure 18.5. Now we can talk about wires that break. However, in Figure 18.5 we abstract from the mechanism by which the wire is connected to the heater and to the controller, and these are places where distortion or loss of communication can occur. So we may choose to include these too in the picture, and so on. At a certain point we have to abstract from some communication channel.

18.3 **The Context Boundary**

Our context diagrams include more entities than those the SuD directly interacts with. But ultimately, everything in the world is related to everything else, so the question is how much to include in the environment. For every event that the SDuD must respond to, there is an earlier event that caused it; and for every effect that the SuD causes, there is a further effect caused by it. How large is the relevant part of the context?

The place to look for the environment boundary is the composite system of which the SuD is a part and its goals. For example, the heating controller is part of a human-machine system that contains heaters, thermometers, a heating tank, an operator console, and an operator. This human-machine system has a goal—to pasteurize fruit juice—and it is the task of the heating-control system to contribute to the achievement of this goal. So we include all of this in the context diagram.

Similarly, the TIS operates in a context of registration desk employees, the course coordinator, and the other entities shown in Figure 18.3 to achieve a goal of the training department—the efficient and effective management of introductory courses. And the Electronic Ticket System (ETS) interacts with the traveller, conductor, and the central railway computer to achieve the composite system goal of selling and using rights to transport with the railway company. In all these examples, we see that the SuD contributes to a composite system goal by receiving messages from entities in its environment and by trying to achieve a certain effect in its environment (see Chapter 2). The guidelines extracted from this are the following:

√ Include in the context the entities in the composite system that, jointly with the SuD, achieve the goals of the composite system.

√ Include in the context the entities in which the SuD attempts to cause a desired effect.

√ Include in the context the entities from whom the SuD receives the information it needs to achieve its desired effect.

By implication, these guidelines tell us what to exclude from the context:

√ The part of the world where the effects of the SuD do not contribute to the goal of the composite system falls outside the context boundary.

√ The part of the world whose behavior does not have to be known by the SuD to achieve the goal of the composite system falls outside the context boundary.

For example, it is not necessary for the TIS to have a causal connection with the managers of new employees or with their clients in order to achieve the goal of efficient and effective management of introductory courses, so these entities fall outside the context boundary.

18.4 Structuring the Context

In Chapter 2, we identified three major functions of a reactive system:

Informative/Information provision. To answer questions, produce reports, or otherwise provide information about the subject domain.

Directive. To control, guide, or otherwise direct its subject domain.

Manipulative. To create, change, display, or otherwise manipulate lexical items in the subject domain.

We can find structures in the context that correspond to these three major functions. Figure 18.6 shows typical communications in the context of a system with an information-provision function. Each of the communication channels can, if necessary, be decomposed into one or more connection domains. Note that we now treat the entire domain as a single entity in the context diagram. This does not violate the syntax or meaning of context diagrams because we can choose to treat

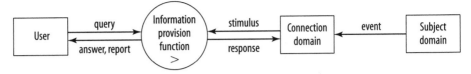

Figure 18.6 Typical structures in an information-provision function.

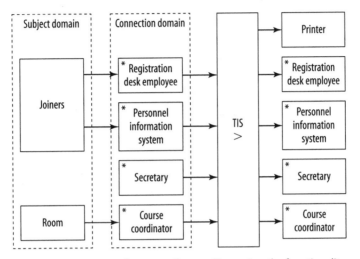

Figure 18.7 Structured context diagram illustrating the functionality of TIS.

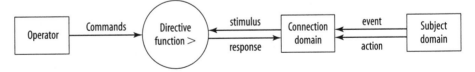

Figure 18.8 Typical structures in a directive function.

a system of any complexity as a single entity in the context diagram. Figure 18.7 illustrates this by structuring the context of the TIS in this way, which has a pure information-provision functionality. The arrows leaving the subject domain may represent push or pull communications, and they may or may not pass through an explicitly modeled connection domain. An interesting case here is the information passed by the secretary to the system, which consists of observations of the non-occurrence of subject domain events; the secretary informs TIS that certain joiners did not arrive to register for the course.

Figure 18.8 shows a typical structure of the context of a system with a directive function. Each of the communication channels can, if necessary, be decomposed into one or more connection domains. The heating controller is an example of this

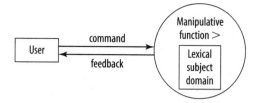

Figure 18.9 Typical structures in a manipulative function.

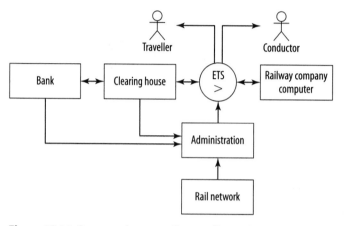

Figure 18.10 Structured context diagram illustrating the functionality of ETS.

(see Figure 18.4). A system with directive functionality is usually part of a feedback loop that runs through the subject domain. The elevator controller example has a directive function (to control the behavior of elevator cages) and a tiny information-provision function (to show where an elevator cage is).

Figure 18.9 shows the typical structure of the context of a manipulative function, which manipulates a lexical part of the subject domain. (This is not a context diagram because context diagrams treat the SuD as a black box.) Each of the communication channels can, if necessary, be decomposed into one or more connection domains. The ETS has manipulative and informative functionality. Figure 18.10 shows that there is an administration that acts as connection domain that provides the ETS with the necessary information about banks, clearing houses, and the rail network. The other external interactions of the ETS manipulate lexical items stored in the ETS, namely tickets, use stamps, and refund stamps.

In all three kinds of context structures, we can find entities with special roles, which may appear as external entity in the context diagram.

◆ *Subject domain entities* are monitored or controlled by the system.

◆ *Connection domain entities* pass information between the system and the sources and destinations in the environment.

- *Users* consume the services of the system.
- *Support staff* keeps the data in the system up to date.
- *Operators* keep the system running.
- *Maintenance personnel* repair and upgrade the system.

These examples show that the subject and connection domains usually show up in the context diagram in ways that are typical for the functionality of the SuD. They also illustrate that several structures may be superimposed in the context diagram of the entire SuD. We can derive the following guideline from this:

√ Look for context structures that correspond to system functionality.

The complete context diagram may be too complex to show in a single diagram. More often than not, we show **partial context diagrams** that show one significant and coherent part of the context. We can project the complete context diagram onto partial ones by several criteria:

√ *Function:* Choose a level in the function refinement tree and show a context diagram for each function.

√ *External entity:* Choose one or more external entities and show only the interactions with those entities.

√ *Subject domain:* Choose one or more subject domain entities and show only interactions that are about those entities.

Context structuring is a new topic in requirements engineering introduced by Jackson (1995). References to the literature on context structuring are given in the Bibliographic Remarks.

18.5 SUMMARY

A context diagram is a communication diagram (DFD or architecture diagram) that represents the SuD and the entities in its context. The boundary of the SuD is best characterized by its stimuli and responses. It can be found by analyzing the function refinement tree. Drawing the system boundary involves an allocation of functionality to the SuD or to external entities, so that they jointly realize the desired emergent composite system properties. If they are allocated to external entities, they fall outside the design responsibility of the SuD designer.

The environment of the SuD consists of nature, people, devices, and other software. We should include the part of the environment in our context model that contributes to the desired emergent properties of the composite system. This includes the entities that must be affected by the SuD and the entities about which it must have information.

We can structure a context diagram according to its functionality. This can be represented by drawing one partial context diagram per function. Other ways to project the context diagram are to show only the part that involves certain external entities and to show only the part that involves certain subject-domain entities.

18.6 QUESTIONS AND EXERCISES

EXERCISES

1. Identify the information-provision, directive, and manipulative context structures in the following examples:

a) The tea-bag-boxing system

b) The bug-fixing support system

2. Make a context model of the Chemical Tracking System (CTS) (see Chapter 1). Ask the following questions to find the context boundary:

a) What is the composite system of which the CTS is a part?

b) About which entities does the CTS need information? How will this information get to the CTS?

c) Where should the desired effects of the CTS take place? Through which channel will the system cause this effect?

d) Who are the users?

Which structure(s) does this context have?

QUESTIONS FOR DISCUSSION

3. Figure 15.18 shows a DFD for the tea-bag-boxing system, including external entities. The functions of the system are the following (the list of functions is basically the list of controller responsibilities):

- ◆ Allow operator to set required tea-bag weight.
- ◆ Allow operator to set maximum tea-bag count.
- ◆ Place tea bag in box or in waste container according to weight.
- ◆ Replace full box by empty box.

a) Discuss ways in which functions could have been reallocated from the tea-bag-boxing system to the operator.

b) Could the pieces of the functionality of the system have been reallocated to the balance, robot arm, and conveyor belt?

4. The context of the TIS contains communications not modeled by Figure 18.3, such as information that the registration desk and coordinator get from the printer.

a) Give an argument why these communications should be included.

b) Give an argument why these communications should not be included.

Which argument do you prefer? Why?

5. Figure 9.10 shows part of the subject domain of the ETS.

a) How would you decide that some of these entities are to be stored and manipulated by the system itself?

b) A ticket represents a right to passage. Why are these rights not represented by the context diagram?

CHAPTER 19

Requirements-Level Decomposition Guidelines

T his chapter gives guidelines for defining a requirements-level system architecture based on a functional requirements specification. A functional requirements specification defines the desired functions, behavior, and external communication of the SuD, and the requirements-level architecture is a decomposition that assumes a perfect implementation technology. The requirements-level architecture is one of the architectural views of the system. Other relevant views are the module structure, the execution structure, and the physical network structure. This chapter discusses only the requirements-level architecture. See the Bibliographic Remarks for literature on other architectural views.

Section 19.1 briefly discusses the concepts of architecture and architectural style. Section 19.2 compares the two major architectural styles (encapsulation and layering). Section 19.3 then distinguishes the three major encapsulation styles (the data flow style, the Von Neumann style, and the object-oriented style) and their variants. Section 19.4 then collects the major decomposition guidelines that can be used with any of these styles. Section 19.5 summarizes the ways in which we can evaluate a software architecture.

19.1 Architectures

An **architecture** of a system is a structure of elements and their properties and the interactions between these elements that realize system-level properties. The architectures used in this book as illustrations are all requirements-level architectures. They show a set of requirements-level components and interactions that realize system-level properties. A description of an architecture should make clear how system-level properties are caused by the interactions of the components of the architecture. Thus, an architectural view is a systemic view that shows how emergent properties arise.

A system can have many architectures, each showing a particular view of the system. For example, for reactive systems we can define a requirements-level architecture that shows which abstract structure should be realized by any imple-mentation. The requirements-level architecture shows how we realize the require-ments when we have perfect implementation technology. To realize this abstract architecture on the available implementation technology, we can in addition define a module architecture in which each module encapsulates data and services defined abstractly in the requirements-level view and map this to an execution architecture consisting of run-time entities such as tasks, libraries, memory, and queues. If we de-fine multiple architectures for a system, the relationships among these architectures must be described too.

An **architectural style** is a set of constraints on an architecture. Each architec-tural style defines a particular set of components from which to assemble an archi-tecture and a particular set of constraints on the way these components interact. For example, in a pure pipe-and-filter architectural style, the system consists of transfor-mations connected in a pipeline; in a pure Von Neumann style, the system consists of data stores and data transformations.

19.2 Encapsulation versus Layering

The first and foremost architectural choice to make is between encapsulation and layering. The decomposition of a system into components involves two relationships between the components and the composite system.

◆ The components deliver services to the composite system. This means that the services of the composite system cannot be realized without using the services of the components.

◆ The composite system encapsulates the components. This means that external entities cannot interact with components except through the interface of the composite system.

We can disconnect these two relationships and define a service-provision rela-tionship that does not entail encapsulation. We then get a layered structure in which lower-level entities provide services to higher-level entities, as illustrated in Figure 19.1. In a layered structure the lower-level entities can provide services to several higher-level entities, instead of to just one higher-level entity—this gives us a **layered architectural style** of Figure 19.1(b) as opposed to the **encapsulation**

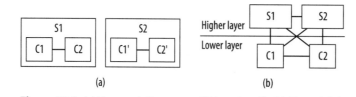

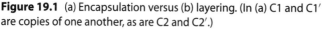

Figure 19.1 (a) Encapsulation versus (b) layering. (In (a) C1 and C1′ are copies of one another, as are C2 and C2′.)

Application layer		
Presentation layer	Presentation layer	
Session layer	Application layer	
Transport layer	Middleware layer	User interface layer
Network layer	Network layer	Business process layer
Data link layer	Operating system layer	Application layer
Physical layer	Physical layer	Database layer
(a)	(b)	(c)

Figure 19.2 Examples of layered architectures.

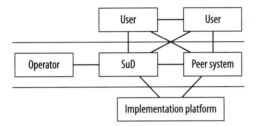

Figure 19.3 Layered context.

architectural style of Figure 19.1(a). In an encapsulation style, a system such as S1 in Figure 19.1(a) realizes its services by using only services from its encapsulated components, which provide services to no other system. In a layered style, a system such as S1 in Figure 19.1(b) realizes its services by using services from lower-level components, which may provide these services to other systems, too. Layering is more efficient in terms of the number of entities used, but the price paid for this is that a change in a lower-level entity may influence many higher-level entities.

Layered architectures are widely used in computer science. The Open Systems Interconnection (OSI) seven-layer stack shown in Figure 19.2(a) is a widely cited example. Figure 19.2(b) shows an alternative often used in practice, and Figure 19.2(c) shows a four-tier client-server architecture. All three examples illustrate that each layer concerns a particular abstraction level that offers a platform on which to implement higher-level services.

The choice between encapsulation and layering exists at all design levels. The composite system of which the SuD is a part may itself be layered. This can be represented in a context diagram as shown in Figure 19.3. For example, Figure 19.4 structures the context of the Training Information System (TIS) into layers. This forces us to make clear who provides a service to whom.

Layering comes in many variants. In a strict variant, entities in one layer can provide services only to entities in the next higher layer; in a loose variant, they can

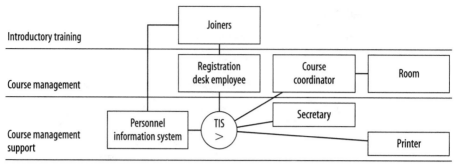

Figure 19.4 Layered context diagram for the TIS illustrating service levels.

provide services to entities in any higher layer; and in an unrestricted variant, entities at any level can provide services to entities at any other level. In the unrestricted variant, layers still correspond to abstraction levels, but there is no service provision hierarchy. The reason for the existence of loose and unrestricted variants is that the real world often cannot be disciplined into one-way single-step service provision layers.

The advantages of layering are:

◆ Simplification of the design of higher-level systems S1 and S2.
◆ Simplification of the operation of these higher-level systems.
◆ Increased operational flexibility due to the possibility of switching among lower-level service providers.

Layering and encapsulation have reverse properties with respect to intellectual manageability. Layering makes life simpler for the system itself because it does not have to care about how lower-level services are provided. Encapsulation makes life easier for the environment because all the complexity is hidden in the system. (See Chapter 18 where we discuss the trade-off of allocating intelligence to external entities or to the SuD.)

The disadvantages of layering are:

◆ Increased processing cost due to standardized interfaces between layers.
◆ Possible decreased performance when lower-level entities get overloaded.
◆ Possible decreased performance when response computation must pass through all layers.
◆ Possible decreased maintainability if a function is decomposed into entities at all layers.

The first disadvantage cannot be countered, but the others can be dealt with by providing sufficient lower-level resources for the desired top-level performance and by finding a decomposition into layers that restricts response processing to higher layers and that restricts changes in functionality to one layer only.

Note how these advantages and disadvantages refer to quality attributes such as performance and modifiability. At the requirements level, we assume perfect implementation technology and performance is not a problem. If we assume in addition a perfect development team, then modifiability is not a problem either. In a perfect world, all quality attributes are realized without effort. However, even if we ignore quality attributes, there are reasons to choose between a layered and an encapsulated architecture, for example, when the structure of the environment and the requirements is itself layered or encapsulated. At the requirements level, the problem structure dictates the solution structure. At the implementation level, the implementation platform (i.e., the solution technology) determines much of the solution structure.

Layering and encapsulation can be applied recursively. Any component of a composite system S, and any entity in a layer, can itself be layered internally, where these layers are all encapsulated in S (i.e., are not accessible from the environment of S). The only unbreakable rule of the game is that layering and encapsulation cannot be applied to the same component. It is impossible for a component to be encapsulated in a composite while at the same time providing services to peer systems of the composite. For example, in Figure 19.1(a) it is impossible for C1 to be part of S2 and at the same time to provide services to S1.

If we assume as given that the SuD will be decomposed into a number of components, the design question is what the relationship between these components is going to be: Should each component hide its internal complexity from other components or should some of it be factored out and placed in lower layers? We can extract the following guidelines from the discussion.

√ Use a layered architecture for the SuD to factor out services needed by several components of the SuD.

√ If a lower-level component C_1 in a layered architecture is used by only one higher-level component C_0, then C_1 should be encapsulated as a subcomponent inside C_0.

√ Consider change scenarios for the system. Choose layers such that changes in functionality are likely to be restricted to one layer of the architecture.

19.3 Architectural Styles

Encapsulation and layering are mutually exclusive because it is impossible for a component to be encapsulated and at the same time provide services to entities outside the one in which it is encapsulated. But, as we have seen, a component encapsulated within a composite system can itself be layered internally.

Encapsulation and layering can be combined with any of the styles discussed in this section. The terminology of architectural styles is not standardized. Different authors distinguish different styles and give different names to them. In addition, the list discussed here is not exhaustive—other authors discuss other styles. The list

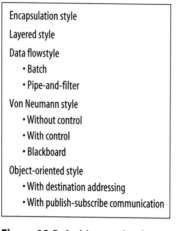

Encapsulation style

Layered style

Data flowstyle
- Batch
- Pipe-and-filter

Von Neumann style
- Without control
- With control
- Blackboard

Object-oriented style
- With destination addressing
- With publish-subscribe communication

Figure 19.5 Architectural styles.

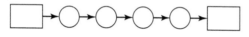

Figure 19.6 Data flow style.

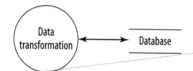

Figure 19.7 The Von Neumann style.

discussed here contains the basic distinctions relevant for requirements-level archi-tectures; Figure 19.5 summarizes them.

In the **data flow style,** data flows through a network of data transformations. The topology of the network can be anything from linear (Figure 19.6) to arbitrary, including cyclic. Control flow can vary from batch (the next transformation starts when the previous one is finished) to pipe-and-filter style (all transformations exe-cute concurrently). The data flow style is natural for transformational systems that perform a stateless transformation. The transformations in the architecture are a functional decomposition of the overall transformation. The pure data flow style is not applicable to reactive systems because these must maintain a model of their environment to compute a response.

A basic architecture for reactive systems is a combination of data transfor-mations and data stores, as illustrated in Figure 19.7. This is what I call a **Von Neumann architectural style,** in which data storage and data processing are strictly separated—data transformations have no memory and data stores do no processing. There may be many data transformations, but these should not have interfaces to one another. If they communicate, they do this via a data store. The

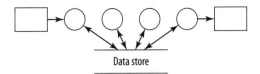

Figure 19.8 Von Neumann style with many transformations.

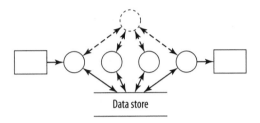

Figure 19.9 Von Neumann style with control.

transformations can be triggered by external events and condition changes and by temporal events. For example, transformations may scan the repository periodically and, when triggered, a transformation reads data from the repository, processes them, and puts them back in the repository.

In Figure 19.8, there is no predefined control flow. For systems with control functionality, the **Von Neumann style with control** is used widely (Figure 19.9). In this variant, there is a control process that determines the order in which the other processes access the repository. In another variant, the **blackboard style,** transformations can respond to changes in the repository, which is now called a blackboard. All these variants are refinements of the Von Neumann style because they maintain the basic principle of separation of data processing and data storage.

In the **object-oriented style,** processing and storage are encapsulated in objects. The Von Neumann and object-oriented styles are mutually exclusive; it is not possible to separate processing and storage in different components and at the same time encapsulate them in these components. Objects encapsulate data transformations as well as behavior. In other words, each object is a discrete state machine with local variables. There is no restriction on the topology of communication channels. Objects send messages to one another using **destination addressing,** which requires the sender to know the identity of the receiver. This causes close coupling between the object and its environment, and this in turn inhibits the reuse of objects and negatively affects maintainability.

In a variant of the object-oriented style that avoids this problem, destination addressing is replaced by the more flexible mechanism of **publish-subscribe communication,** in which objects can publish their ability to perform certain events and can subscribe to certain kinds of events. If an object has subscribed to an event then it will receive the event when it occurs and can therefore respond to it. This allows objects to communicate without having to know one another's identity, thus decreasing the coupling between an object and its environment. Publish-subscribe communication resembles channel addressing in DFDs because, in both mechanisms, a sender sends a message to a communication medium rather than to a destination. The difference is that in DFDs the topology of the channels is fixed, whereas in publish-subscribe communication the topology can change dynamically because objects can dynamically change their publication behavior and their subscriptions.

The architectural styles mentioned here are extremes that can be mixed in practice. For example, we can design a blackboard architecture using subsystems rather than data transformations to access the blackboard and structure the result in various layers.

The styles have different properties with respect to quality attributes. For example, the blackboard style may be very inefficient because many components may just be checking the blackboard without doing anything useful, but it can also be very flexible because components may be added and deleted on the fly. The object-oriented style with publish-subscribe communication can be inefficient due to an expensive communication mechanism, but it can be very reliable because there is no single point of failure and faults can be broadcast to all components. Efficiency, flexibility, and reliability are quality attributes.

This book is not about quality attributes or about evaluating architectures and their properties with respect to quality attributes, and we further restrict ourselves to the support of functional properties by an architecture. Even in this restricted context, there are significant differences among architectural styles:

√ Do not use a pure data flow style for reactive systems because this architecture cannot maintain state across external interactions.

√ Consider a Von Neumann or blackboard style for systems with information-provision or manipulative functionality. The stores hold data about which information is provided or the lexical items to be manipulated. The transformations encapsulate functionality.

√ Consider an object-oriented style for systems with directive functionality. Objects can be used to encapsulate behavior to be enabled or enforced in the environment.

Many systems have a mix of these functionalities, so in practice styles are mixed.

19.4 Requirements-Level Architecture Guidelines

There are two sources for decisions concerning the decomposition of the SuD: the requirements of the SuD and the environment of the SuD. Taking a layered view of the context (Figure 19.4), we partition the environment into a **use environment,** consisting of peer systems and higher-level systems, and an **implementation platform,** consisting of the lower-level layers on which the SuD is implemented. Corresponding to this partitioning of the environment, there are two kinds of architecture: requirements-level architecture and implementation-level architecture.

A **requirements-level architecture** is a decomposition that makes the perfect technology assumption. This means that we assume a perfect implementation

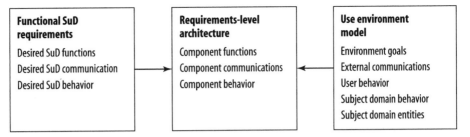

Figure 19.10 Design approach. The arrows represent the justification of design decisions. A decomposition can be motivated in terms of the requirements, the use environment, and the implementation platform.

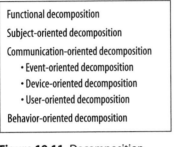

Figure 19.11 Decomposition guidelines for a requirements-level architecture.

platform that offers all the services we need to realize the requirements and that has unlimited memory, unbounded parallel processing activity, and any processing speed we need. A requirements-level architecture is based on functional requirements and use context only, and it ignores the actual implementation platform (Figure 19.10).

An **implementation-level architecture** of a system is an architecture that takes the properties of the implementation platform into account. There are many implementation architectures, including a module architecture, an execution architecture, and a code architecture. Each of these architectures takes some aspect of an actual implementation platform into account, such as finite processing speed, limited memory, libraries with a given functionality, available programming languages, a limited set of execution primitives, and available communication primitives. Any implementation architecture defines some aspect of the mapping from the requirements-level architecture to the available implementation platform. When defining an implementation architecture, the architect must take quality attributes into account because these set targets for the performance of the given finite implementation platform. If the implementation platform were perfect, quality attributes would not be necessary because any quality target is reached by a perfect platform.

Figure 19.11 lists the major decomposition guidelines for defining a requirements-level architecture. Note that the guidelines follow the dimensions of functional specification of reactive systems identified in Chapter 4: services, communication and behavior, and the subject domain.

19.4.1 *Functional Decomposition*

The primary decomposition guideline based on the functional requirements is functional decomposition.

√ In **functional decomposition,** each system function is allocated to a different component.

Figure 19.12 shows the allocation table for pure functional decomposition. There is a one-to-one mapping from functions to components. Figure 19.13 shows a

Components	Functions				
	Function 1	**Function 2**	**...**	**...**	**Function *n***
Component 1	×				
Component 2		×			
...			×		
...				×	
Component m					×

Figure 19.12 Allocation table for pure functional decomposition.

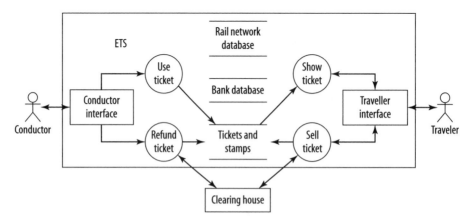

Figure 19.13 Requirements-level functional architecture of the Electronic Ticket System—blackboard style (not all data store accesses are shown).

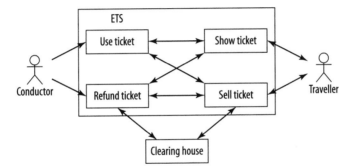

Figure 19.14 Pure functional architecture of the Electronic Ticket System. Each component has a complex internal structure containing a database—object-oriented style.

decomposition of the ETS with functional components (the data processes). It is not a pure functional decomposition because some components are identified using other guidelines, such as subject-oriented decomposition (explained in Section 19.4.2). A pure functional decomposition for the ETS contains four functional subsystems, each encapsulating the databases that they need, as shown in Figure 19.14. Such a decomposition involves the unnecessary duplication of data stores, which is inefficient in operation and hard to maintain. The decomposition is not modular because each functional component must inform the others of any update to its data. Note that this is an object-oriented style because each component encapsulates the data and the operations on this data. The architecture chosen in Figure 19.13 factors out the shared databases and chooses a blackboard style, in which a number of stateless transformations access shared data stores.

Functional decomposition is a good decomposition technique if:

◆ Functions have no interfaces to one another or at least very few, as in Figure 19.13.

◆ Changes to the system are restricted to the addition, deletion, and change of separate functions.

19.4.2 *Subject-Oriented Decomposition*

The primary decomposition criterion based on the use environment is based on the subject domain:

◆ In **subject-oriented decomposition,** each group of subject domain entities corresponds to a system component.

The ETS also contains subject-oriented decomposition. The rail network and bank databases in the decomposition contain data about parts of the subject domain, and the tickets and stamps database actually contains part of the subject domain.

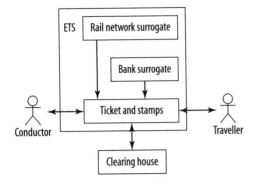

Figure 19.15 Pure subject-oriented architecture of the Electronic Ticket System—object-oriented style. The ticket and stamps components encapsulate several functions.

Figure 19.15 shows a pure subject-oriented decomposition for the ETS in which every component corresponds to a subject-domain entity. To indicate that the system contains data about the rail network and banks, the components that hold data about them are called Rail network surrogate and Bank surrogate. The architecture again uses an object-oriented style, but this time with a subject-oriented decomposition criterion. Whereas the functional decomposition of Figure 19.14 encapsulates all subject-domain data with functions, the subject-oriented decomposition of Figure 19.15 encapsulates all functions with subject-domain data—that is, precisely the reverse.

In the blackboard style of Figure 19.13, we do not worry about style but just apply functional decomposition to the functions and subject-oriented decomposition to the data. The object-oriented style of Figure 19.15 hides the fact that the sets of instances of the surrogate components are just databases of passive data. Also, the Ticket and stamps objects in this architecture have a complex internal structure because they embody a ticket and its possible use and refund stamps. In this decomposition, they also encapsulate the dialog with external entities.

Subject-oriented decomposition is usually called "object-oriented decomposition." I avoid this term here because, as we have seen, objects are a particular kind of component and subject-oriented decomposition can be used with any kind of component. For example, we can partition a collection of data stores and processes in a subject-oriented way by making them correspond to subject-domain entities.

Heating controller decompositions also contain both functional and subject-oriented decomposition. In Figure 19.16, Tank control encapsulates the desired behavior of a heater and Batch data contains data about the batch to be heated. The heater and batch are subject-domain entities. The other components of the heating controller encapsulate some function of the controller: entering batch data, starting the heating process, and monitoring the end time. Just as we did for the ETS, we can transform this architecture into a pure functional and a pure subject-oriented decomposition and combine this with various mixes of the Von Neumann and object-oriented styles. This is left as an exercise for the reader.

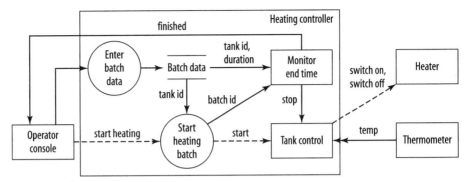

Figure 19.16 Communication diagram of a requirements-level architecture of a heating controller—mixed Von Neumann and object-oriented styles.

We can draw several lessons from these examples.

√ The choice between functional decomposition and subject-oriented decomposition is independent from the choice between a Von Neumann decomposition style and an object-oriented decomposition style.

√ The choice between functional decomposition and subject-oriented decomposition is not global but local—some components encapsulate functions; others represent subject-domain entities.

√ The object-oriented style allows us to encapsulate functions that pertain to one subject-domain entity into an object that represents this subject domain entity.

√ The Von Neumann style allows us to encapsulate all data about a class of subject-domain entities into one data store and to separate a stateless function that needs data from several stores into one data transformation.

This does not tell us which decomposition guideline is better than others. We should not evaluate decomposition guidelines but rather the resulting decompositions. Evaluation guidelines for decompositions are given in Section 19.5.

19.4.3 *Communication-Oriented Decomposition*

The SuD is connected to its use environment by means of communication channels. Focusing on these channels, we obtain the following three decomposition criteria.

√ In **event-oriented decomposition,** each event is handled by a different component.

√ In **device-oriented decomposition,** each device is handled by a different component.

√ In **user-oriented decomposition,** communications with one kind of user are handled by one component.

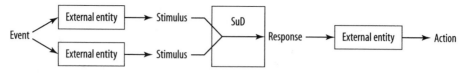

Figure 19.17 Different starting points for communication-oriented decomposition. External entities can be devices or users.

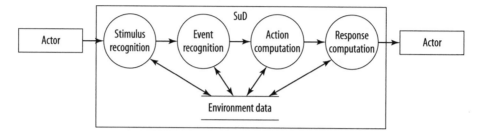

Figure 19.18 Detailed communication-oriented architecture.

Figure 19.17 illustrates the starting points for these criteria. One event may be sensed by several devices leading to different stimuli. The system should recognize this and produce the desired response. To handle a stimulus is to recognize which event occurred; to handle an event is to produce the desired response. For example, Enter batch data and Monitor end time in Figure 19.16 are event-oriented components, the first responding to an external event, the second to a temporal event. The functional components in the ETS decomposition of Figure 19.13 are event-oriented because each handles the response to one event. The two interface components are user-oriented because each handles the interaction with one particular kind of user.

Typical tasks that must be performed on the way from stimulus to response are the following:

Stimulus recognition: Determine which stimulus has occurred.

Event recognition: Based on one or more stimuli and a model of external entities that provided these stimuli, determine which event has occurred in the environment.

Action computation: Based on a model of the subject domain and on the recognized event, determine which action is to be caused.

Response computation: Based on the desired action to be caused and a model of the external entities in the environment, determine which response is to be produced.

If each of these tasks is performed by a different component, we get the architecture in Figure 19.18. In our examples, most of these tasks are performed by a single component. Stimulus recognition shields the rest of the system from the peculiarities of the device through which the stimulus arrives at the system. Event recognition hides the way in which information about an event arrives at the system. If information about an event arrives at the system through different channels, this is invisible after the event recognition process. Action computation abstracts from the devices through which the action is to be caused, and response computation hides the details of these devices from the rest of the system.

19.4.4 *Behavior-Oriented Decomposition*

The SuD interacts with its environment by engaging in a certain behavior that enables or enforces desirable effects in the environment. We can use this as a decomposition guideline.

√ In **behavior-oriented decomposition,** monitoring assumed behavior in the environment or enforcing desired behavior in the environment is allocated to one component.

For example, Sell ticket in the ETS is behavior-oriented because it encapsulates a dialog with the traveler. The Tickets and stamps data store is not behavior-oriented. It contains the state of a ticket, but it does not encapsulate the life cycle of the ticket.

Using behavior-orientation, we encapsulate the different aspects of batch behavior in the heating controller into one object, left scattered around in Figure 19.16. The result is shown in Figure 19.19. The Batch control and Tank control components are behavior-oriented because they encapsulate the behavior to be enforced in the environment: pasteurizing a batch and heating a tank according to recipe.

This example illustrates one guideline that does not belong to one particular aspect of the system but that really results from an architectural ontology in which components have a fixed aggregation level:

√ Separate components that can occur in different multiplicities.

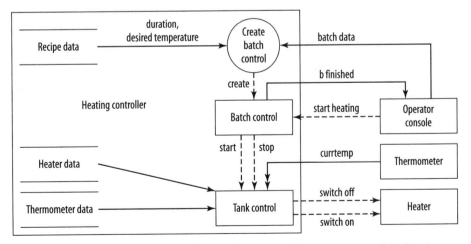

Figure 19.19 Another requirements-level subject-oriented decomposition of the heating controller—mixed Von Neumann and object-oriented styles. Create batch control is a stateless transformation and is therefore represented by a circle.

For example, in the heating controller decomposition, monitoring the end time is a function applicable to all heating tanks of a batch. This is because one batch can be stored in many heating tanks. This indicates that in a subject-oriented decomposition, such as that in Figure 19.19, the batch control component should be different from the heating control component. The multiplicity principle is, however, independent from subject-oriented decomposition. The same principle applies to a process that iterates over multiple data instances or a process that creates several other processes. At any place in the decomposition of the SuD where multiplicity changes, there is a potential separation between components.

In a special case of behavior-oriented decomposition, we look at real-time aspects:

√ In **real-time-oriented decomposition,** the events with the same real-time properties are handled by one component.

An example is the Monitor end time component of the heating controller in Figure 19.16, which recognizes and responds to the occurrence of a temporal event. Stimuli that occur at the same time or with the same frequency may be handled by the same component too. For example, processes that must be performed every midnight may be performed by the same component.

19.4.5 *Choosing Decomposition Guidelines*

With so many decomposition guidelines, where should you start? The answer is that it does not matter, as long as you check any decomposition against all the guidelines. Because any software product design should have its functional requirements available, it is a good idea to start with functional decomposition. But remember that no software decomposition uses one decomposition approach only. In addition, as we have seen, some components will be identified using several guidelines, so you may end up with different components identified according to one or more different guidelines.

√ Use *functional components* for functions that have no interfaces to other functional components.

√ Use *subject-oriented components* if many functions must access information about subject domain entities.

√ Use *communication-oriented components* to perform tasks in stimulus-response processing. Examples are:
  — *Event-oriented components* that handle events
  — *Device-oriented components* that handle all interaction with a device
  — *User interface components* that handle all interaction with a particular kind of user

√ Use *behavior-oriented components* to encapsulate behavior in the environment that is to be monitored or to be enforced.

For example, the life cycle of a ticket is to be enforced by the ETS (e.g., a ticket cannot be refunded after use). We could have chosen a decomposition that encapsulates this behavior in one component. Note that one component may simultaneously satisfy several criteria, that is, be at once functional, event-oriented, and behavior-oriented.

19.5 Evaluation

There are two ways to evaluate a decomposition: by implementing it and using the resulting system in real life and by predicting some of its properties and comparing these predictions with the requirements. The first approach is part of system evolution. It constitutes a feedback loop from experience to (re)design. The second approach is part of a system engineering approach, in which we predict properties of a system before it is built. It has the form of a feed-forward loop. The methods discussed in this section are all of the second kind.

19.5.1 *Syntactic Coherence Checks*

A minimal evaluation of a communication diagram is to see whether it is syntactically coherent with other diagrams. The details of the checks depend on the diagrams used in the specification method. A full list of consistency rules is usually very detailed and hides the purpose of the list. Here I describe what such a list should accomplish.

√ The specification of the components of the SuD should be consistent with respect to the specification of the external properties of the SuD.

√ The specifications of the different functional aspects of a system (functions, behavior, and communication) should be mutually consistent.

For example, if a context diagram of the SuD shows a communication channel called c to external entity E, then a communication diagram of the architecture of the SuD should also show a channel c to external entity E. And if the behavior description of a component shows that the component responds to event e, then a communication diagram of the architecture should show the channel through which e arrives at this component. Checks like these should be performed by a Computer-Aided Software Engineering (CASE) tool upon the request of the analyst.

19.5.2 *Traceability Check*

Syntactic coherence checks only check whether a collection of diagrams could possibly represent a system. A traceability check tells us whether that system is likely to satisfy the requirements previously written down. It consists of drawing tables that set off external functionality against internal components and checking whether each function is allocated to a component and, conversely, whether every component contributes to at least one function.

✓ Use traceability tables to check whether all functional requirements have been accounted for.

Traceability tables are discussed in Chapter 16. A traceability check is essentially informal because function descriptions are essentially informal. Due to the large number of functions and components in a system of any size, software tools should be used for traceability checks.

19.5.3 *Data Access Check*

If the decomposition contains data stores, we can check whether these data are created, used, and deleted by drawing a CRUD (create, read, update, delete) table. Figure 19.20 shows the CRUD table for our ETS example. It shows that two functions read the rail network and bank databases, but that no function creates, updates, or deletes these data. It also shows that tickets and stamps data are created and used, but no function deletes them. We should alter or extend the ETS specification to take care that data are properly maintained. In general, the CRUD table can be used to check the following.

✓ Data in data stores should be created and deleted. In extreme cases, creation occurs when the system is created and deletion occurs when the system is destroyed.

✓ Data stores should be read or updated by some components. A data store that is not read or updated is not used.

CASE tools should offer the option to perform CRUD checks on communication diagrams that contain data stores. However, in order to be able to do that, the components must be specified in such a way that the tool can know that a component performs a C, R, U, or D access to a data store.

Data stores	Other components					
	Use ticket	Refund ticket	Show ticket	Sell ticket	Traveler interface	Conductor interface
Rail network database		R		R		
Bank database		R		R		
Tickets and stamps	U	U	R	C		

Figure 19.20 A CRUD table (C = Create, R = Read, U = Update, D = Delete).

19.5.4 *Executing the Model*

One way to check whether a collection of components creates the desired emergent properties is to execute the model. A low-tech way of doing this is to gather a collection of people, each of whom impersonates one component, and let them collectively act out a number of scenarios. Each scenario consists of a sequence of stimuli for the system. The purpose of the execution is to find out whether the desired functions, behavior, and communication are realized by the system. This way of executing the model may be hilarious, but it is also very informative and it is cheaper than building a prototype manually.

An alternative to executing through role-playing is to execute the model by a CASE tool. This requires specifying the executable part of the model in a language that can be understood by the CASE tool, thus making the execution semantics of this part of the model totally explicit.

19.5.5 *The System Engineering Argument*

Instead of executing the model, we can reason about it. If C is a specification of the components and their interconnections and S a specification of the SuD, does C entail S? This is the system engineering argument at a lower level; the traceability check is really an informal version of this argument. If we have the formal specifications of S, its components, and their interconnection, then we can use formal techniques such as model checking or bisimulation checking to see whether a collection of communicating components realizes overall SuD behavior. Formal specification falls outside the scope of this book, but some pointers to the literature are given in the Bibliographic Remarks.

19.5.6 *Generating a Throw-away Prototype*

Given the appropriate CASE tool, we can generate executable code for part of the system and then run this code. The difference between this and executing the model is the same as between interpretation and compilation. To execute the model is to interpret it on a high-level machine. To generate a prototype is to translate it into something that a lower-level machine can run. The prototype can be used to check that the desired functions, behavior, and communication are indeed present and that certain quality attributes such as usability are present.

19.5.7 *Quality Attributes Check*

All other checks to be performed concern the degree to which the decomposition satisfies quality attributes. We can evaluate the product attributes such as efficiency, safety, and reliability of the decomposition using quantitative or qualitative arguments. And we can evaluate process attributes such as maintainability and interoperability by running through change scenarios. Quality attributes are not within the scope of this book, and I do not discuss the techniques that currently exist in this field here. See the Bibliographic Remarks for pointers to the literature.

19.6 SUMMARY

The architecture of a system is a structure of elements that interact to create system-level properties. An architectural style is a set of constraints on an architecture. The two basic architectural styles are encapsulation and layering. In encapsulation, components are dedicated to one composite and deliver services to realize the emergent properties of that composite. In layering, lower-level components offer services to higher-level components. There are several other decomposition styles for reactive systems; these fall into two groups.

◆ In the Von Neumann styles, data processing is separated from data storage. If data processing is performed by a collection of data transformations that have no interfaces to one another, this is called the blackboard style. Von Neumann styles are useful for systems with information-provision and manipulative functionality.

◆ In the object-oriented styles, objects encapsulate data and behavior. The original object-oriented style employs destination addressing. In a variant with dynamic channel addressing, a publish-subscribe mechanism allows objects to communicate with a dynamically varying set of unknown partners. Object-oriented styles are useful for systems with directive functionality.

A third decomposition style, data flow, is not useful for reactive systems in its pure form because it only uses stateless data transformations.

Our decomposition guidelines are based on a separation of requirements from the use environment and the implementation environment. Functional requirements can be analyzed to give a functional decomposition. This is useful if the resulting functional components have few or no interfaces with each other. The subject domain and its assumed and desired behavior can be analyzed to give subject-oriented decomposition. The resulting components can be used for the encapsulation of functions that deal only with one subject-domain entity. The interface of the system can be analyzed to give communication-oriented decomposition, which includes partitioning the system by event or by external entity. This can be used to encapsulate device interfaces and protocol handling. Finally, we can analyze the assumed or desired behavior in the environment or at the interface of the system and define a behavior-oriented decomposition. This can be useful to encapsulate the desired SuD behavior into a component. A special case of this is decomposition, based on real time, distinguishes components that deal with timeouts or with periodic events. In all these cases, a general principle is that a jump in multiplicity in the tasks to be performed by the SuD indicates a possible separation between components.

All of these guidelines identify a requirements-level decomposition, which is independent from any implementation platform. Mapping a requirements-level decomposition to a platform that consists of multiple physical resources and a stack of available software usually involves a many-to-many mapping from the requirements-level architecture to some implementation architecture.

An architecture is primarily evaluated on its properties with respect to quality attributes (this falls outside the scope of this book). Functional checks include a minimal coherence check across diagrams and a traceability check to see if all functions have been accounted for. A CRUD check can be used to see if all data are created, used, and deleted. The traceability check is an informal way to apply the system engineering argument to the SuD and its components.

19.7 QUESTIONS AND EXERCISES

QUESTIONS FOR REHEARSAL

1. What is the difference and relationship between an architecture and an architectural style?

2. What is the difference and relationship between encapsulation and layering?

3. There are really two basic architectural styles for reactive systems at the requirements level, and each have some variants.
   - ◆ Describe these styles and variants.
   - ◆ Relate these styles to the three basic reactive system functions of information provision, direction, and manipulation of lexical items.

4. Decomposition guidelines are related to the different functional aspects of a system—functions, behavior, and communication—and the subject domain. Give these guidelines.

5. Explain the difference between requirements-level architecture and implementation-level architecture. What is the use of this distinction?

EXERCISES

6. Figure 19.21 shows a function refinement tree of the Chemical Tracking System (CTS). Design a functional decomposition of the system.

7. Exercise 5 in Chapter 15 gives a DFD for the tea-bag-boxing controller. Transform this into a communication diagram using a hybrid style. Explain

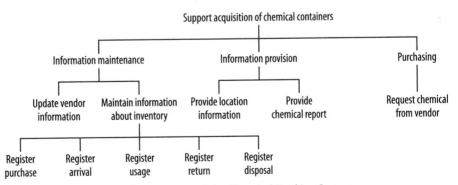

Figure 19.21 Function refinement tree of the Chemical Tracking System.

which decomposition guidelines have been used in the resulting decomposition.

8. Figure 19.22 shows a decomposition of the elevator controller. Classify each component according to the guidelines given in Section 19.4.5.

9. Figure 19.23 shows a decomposition of the bug-fixing support system, using a hybrid style. The Bug component monitors the life cycle of bugs. (Exercise 4 in Chapter 14 gives a STT for this.) Assigning, fixing, testing, and releasing a bug are all represented in Figure 19.23 as data transformation (i.e., stateless components that produce their output in one step). Explain why it is a design mistake to model these events as data transformations and give two possible solutions.

10. Design a decomposition of the ETS that encapsulates the ticket life cycle in an object but also retains the necessary databases. Draw a STD for the ticket life cycle.

11. The architecture of the heating controller shown in Figure 19.19 uses a Von Neumann style. Change it into one with a pure object-oriented style.

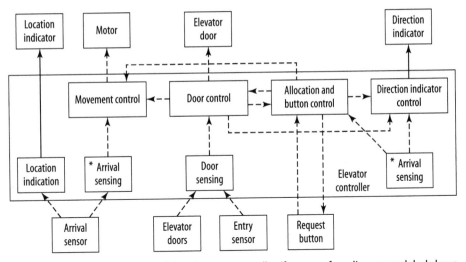

Figure 19.22 Decomposition of the elevator controller (for ease of reading, arrow labels have been omitted).

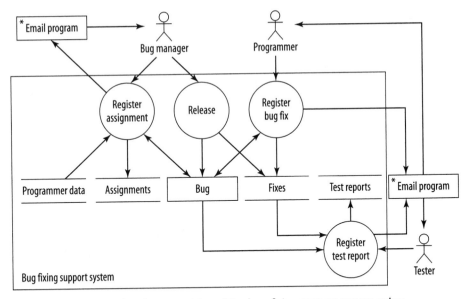

Figure 19.23 Yet another decomposition of the bug-fixing support system, using a hybrid style.

PART VI

Software Specification Methods

A software specification method offers a collection of notations, coherence rules for the notations, and a preferred order of using the notations.

◆ Chapter 20. Postmodern Structured Analysis (PSA) is a revitalized version of Yourdon-style structured analysis in which two environment descriptions are made: an ERD of the subject domain and an extended context diagram that shows where events come from and where responses go to.

◆ Chapter 21. Statemate is a collection of techniques and a software tool for building and executing structured analysis specifications of the SuD. It is included here because it contains an execution algorithm for statecharts.

◆ Chapter 22. The Unified Modeling Language (UML) is a collection of diagram techniques proposed by the Object Management Group as industry standard for object-oriented design. Whereas PSA and Statemate use techniques already described in the book, the UML adds several more. This chapter shows the relationship between these added notations and the ones treated earlier in the book.

◆ Chapter 23. After so many notations and methods, we take a step back and survey what we have done. This chapter puts the notations treated in the book in a simple framework and shows how to use these with varying degrees of weightiness, ranging from flyweight to heavyweight. The result is Not Yet Another Method (NYAM).

CHAPTER 20

Postmodern Structured Analysis (PSA)

S tructured analysis arose in the 1970s out of structured programming. The basic idea of structured analysis and structured programming is that the high-level structure of a software system should match the structure of the problem to be solved rather than the structure of the implementation technology that happens to be available. Despite its name, structured analysis offers techniques and guidelines to design a high-level system structure but not to analyze this structure. The most influential school of structured analysis is the Yourdon approach, in which DFDs, ERDs, and Mealy diagrams without local variables are used to represent the structure of the SuD.

Yourdon-style structured analysis does not include the environment in its models. However, for the design of reactive systems, environment models are crucial and, in this chapter, I discuss an updated version of structured analysis called Postmodern Structured Analysis (PSA), in which two environment models are produced: an ERD of the subject domain and an extended context model that includes the part of the world where the desired effects of the SuD are to be felt and the part that must be monitored by the SuD in order to achieve its desired effect. Another important difference between PSA and classic structured analysis is the particular brand of DFDs used, in which event flows can contain data. This is illustrated using the heating control example.

I call the version of structured analysis presented here "postmodern" because it combines design approaches from several schools, some of which oppose one another, namely Yourdon-style structured analysis, Jackson System Development, and object-oriented analysis. Section 20.1 lists the notations used by PSA and relates them to the design level at which they are used. Section 20.2 summarizes the coherence rules for these notations. Section 20.3 sketches a variety of uses of PSA, ranging from a flyweight to heavyweight use of the notations.

20.1 **Notations**

Figure 20.1 lists the notations used by PSA.

Environment. Communication in the environment is represented by a context diagram. Part of the environment is the subject domain, whose decomposition is represented by an ERD. If the system has directive functionality, an event list can be used to describe desired causality in the environment.

Requirements. The desired functionality is described by a mission statement, refined by a function refinement tree into a number of base functions. The desired behavior at the interface of the system can be represented by a stimulus-response list.

SuD decomposition. A system decomposition is represented by a DFD. Event flows in this DFD represent causality and may include data. Systems with directive functionality may include control processes as components, which are specified by means of some behavior description technique such as STTs or STDs. We allow local variables in a behavior description.

The specifications are supported by a dictionary.

Each of these techniques can be used to represent one aspect of the environment, requirements, or decomposition. The initial versions of these specifications may be fragmented and be incoherent, but, at a certain point of design maturity, we want to produce a coherent specification.

Design level	Notation
Environment	Context diagram ERD of subject domain Event-action lists of desired subject domain behavior Event-action lists of assumed subject domain behavior
Requirements	Mission statement Function refinement tree Service descriptions Stimulus-response list of desired system behavior
SuD decomposition	DFD SuD decomposition STTs or STDs of control processes
	Dictionary

Figure 20.1 Notations used in Postmodern Structured Analysis.

20.2 **Coherence Rules**

Here is an informal list of coherence requirements for each of the three groups of models.

Environment models.
◆ The context diagram must show how information about the subject domain reaches the system and how information from the system reaches the subject domain, for example, by showing a communication path between the subject domain and the SuD.
◆ The descriptions of desired and assumed event-action pairs must mention which subject-domain entities are involved in these events and actions.

Requirement specifications.
◆ The mission statement corresponds to the root of the function refinement tree.
◆ Service descriptions describe the leaves of the function refinement tree.
◆ Each function is triggered by a stimulus in the stimulus-response list.
◆ Each stimulus-response pair is part of a function.

Decomposition specifications.
◆ Each control process is specified by a behavior description (STT or STD).
◆ Each behavior description describes a process in the DFD. The interface of the behavior description is as follows (Figure 20.2):
  — An event in the behavior description corresponds to an input event flow in the DFD.
  — An action in the behavior description corresponds to an output event flow in the DFD.
  — A guard in the behavior description corresponds to a time-continuous Boolean input flow of the process in the DFD.
  — A variable in the behavior description that is read either corresponds to an input event parameter or an input data flow of the process in the DFD or is a local variable.
  — A variable in the behavior description that is written either corresponds to an output data flow of the process in the DFD or is a local variable.

There are also very important coherence requirements across the three models. Here they are.

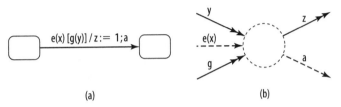

(a)   (b)

Figure 20.2 Coherence between behavior description and control process interface.

Environment and requirements. (See also Chapter 3.)

◆ Each stimulus at the interface of the system is caused by an event in the environment, and each system response causes an action in the environment.
◆ Each link from event to stimulus, and from response to action, is a communication path in the context diagram.

Requirements and decomposition. For each stimulus-response pair, there is a path through the DFD that shows how the stimulus leads to the response.

Decomposition and environment. If we collapse all components of the DFD into one composite process, we get the context diagram.

Dictionary. The dictionary defines at least the relevant subject domain terms for entities and events.

Most of these rules can be formalized and implemented in a CASE tool. CASE tools should offer the option of checking the formalized rules upon the request of the analyst.

20.3   Choosing Notations

The weight of professional boxers is classified according to the following scheme:

flyweight $\leq$ 112 pounds
bantamweight $\leq$ 118 pounds
featherweight $\leq$ 126 pounds
lightweight $\leq$ 135 pounds
welterweight $\leq$ 147 pounds
middleweight $\leq$ 160 pounds
heavyweight $>$ 160 pounds

We can learn two things from this classification:

1. Lightweight is not the lightest weight.
2. Heavyweights can be as heavy as they want.

We can apply this scale to the use of software engineering notations (Figure 20.3).

Flyweight. In a flyweight use of PSA, we use only a context diagram and a mission statement. The context diagram is needed to structure the context and understand how the SuD is connected to relevant events in the environment. It is also needed to relate the desired properties of the system to the desired emergent properties of the composite system. The mission statement is the minimal SuD specification that bounds the desired functionality of the system. It can be used to classify the system as informative, directive, or manipulative (or a combination of these), and the context can be structured to correspond to this functionality.

Featherweight. In a featherweight use, we add information about the subject domain and about system functions. The function refinement tree and descriptions make the desired functionality explicit and the subject-domain ERD shows which

Flyweight	Featherweight	Middleweight	Heavyweight
Context diagram	Context diagram	Context diagram	Context diagram
	ERD	ERD	ERD
			Event-action list
Mission statement	Mission statement	Mission statement	Mission statement
	Function refinement	Function refinement	Function refinement
	Service descriptions	Service descriptions	Service descriptions
			Stimulus-response list
		DFD	DFD
			Behavior descriptions
	Dictionary	Dictionary	Dictionary

Figure 20.3 Flyweight to heavyweight uses of the notations.

subject-domain entities can be identified by the system. The service descriptions describe the added value of each function for the environment, but do not contain behavioral information. They do, however, specify which stimulus triggers which function.

Middleweight. In a middleweight use, we add information about the decomposition of the system by making a DFD. This forces us to show how every function is going to be realized by the system. The specification of the Training Information System (TIS) is an example (see Appendix A).

Heavyweight. In a heavyweight use, we add behavioral information. This is crucial for systems with directive functionality. For these systems, we can proceed as follows.

1. Make an event-action list of desired subject domain behavior.
2. Derive from this a stimulus-response list of desired system behavior.
3. Complement the DFD with behavior descriptions of the control processes.

See the heating controller and elevator controller specifications as examples (Appendices C and D).

This progression of weightiness focuses first on the context and functionality, next on the high-level decomposition, and finally on behavioral aspects. You are free to choose other combinations and sequences. If anything, Figure 20.3 makes clear that the availability of a notation does not make its use obligatory and that particular notations are useful for particular purposes. The need for a certain notation is determined by the kind of functionality of the SuD. For example, for information-provision and manipulative systems, the subject-domain ERD is important because information-provision systems must store data about the domain and a manipulative system must store a lexical part of the domain. In both cases, the requirements include a representation of the entity structures in the domain. For directive systems, the event-action list, stimulus-response list, and component behavior descriptions are important because these systems must monitor and enforce behavior in their environment.

20.4 **SUMMARY**

Yourdon-style structured analysis uses DFDs, ERDs, and Mealy diagrams to represent requirements and a high-level decomposition of the SuD. PSA extends this with a more elaborate representation of the context, which includes all entities relevant for achieving the goal of the composite system and the desirable behavior to be caused by the SuD. PSA also contains more powerful behavior descriptions that may use local variables. There are coherence rules for the notations. Particular notations are useful for particular purposes; which notations we use is determined by the desired functionality of the system.

20.5 **QUESTIONS AND EXERCISES**

QUESTIONS FOR REHEARSAL

1. Consider the three basic reactive functionalities: information provision, direction, and manipulation. Describe and explain which notations you would use for which kind of functionality.

EXERCISES

2. Figure 20.4 shows a DFD of the bug-fixing support system obtained by functional decomposition.

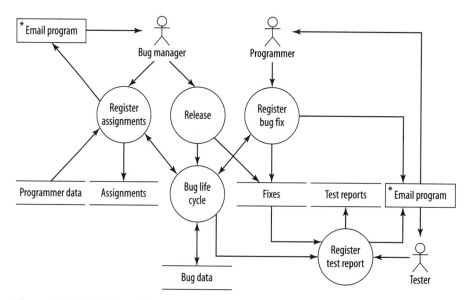

Figure 20.4 DFD of bug-fixing support system.

a) Make a function refinement tree that corresponds to this DFD.

b) The Bug life cycle process can respond to the following events: assign to programmers, propose fix, report problem, report fix, and release. Indicate through which flows these events reach the Bug life cycle process and through which flows the process sends responses.

3. Appendix A contains a specification of the TIS. Check whether the following coherence rules are satisfied:

a) Coherence of the requirement specification.

b) Coherence between the environment model and the requirement specification.

c) Coherence between the decomposition (DFD) and the context model.

CHAPTER 21

Statemate

S tatemate is a tool that offers a collection of notations for structured analysis. It was developed in the early 1980s by Harel and others out of a need to specify requirements for complex reactive systems. The two basic notations developed for Statemate are statecharts and activity charts. These play the role that Mealy diagrams and DFDs play in Yourdon-style structured analysis, and they can be used instead of Mealy diagrams and DFDs in combination with the other PSA techniques. The distinguishing features of Statemate models and the reason to treat it here are:

- The use of statecharts in combination with hierarchical activity charts
- The execution semantics of combined statechart-activity chart models

Section 21.1 reviews two of the three notations used by Statemate: activity charts and statecharts. Activity charts are variations of DFDs. The combination of activity charts and statecharts provides a lot of expressive power, in which we can represent activity hierarchy and parallelism in various ways. Section 21.2 discusses the trade-offs between using activity charts and using statecharts to express activity hierarchy and parallelism. Section 21.3 presents the execution semantics of Statemate.

21.1 Notations

Statemate uses three notations:

Activity charts. Syntactic variants of DFDs that, just like DFDs, are used to represent an essential decomposition of the SuD.

Statecharts. Used to specify the control activities of the SuD.

Module charts. Used to represent the decomposition of the SuD in computational resources that will run the software.

Here I discuss the use of only activity charts and statecharts. The differences between activity charts and DFDs are that in activity charts processes are called activities and they are represented by rectangles. Control processes, called **control activities** here, are represented by rectangles with rounded corners. Data processes, called **regular activities** here, are represented by rectangles with sharp corners. Each regular activity can have at most one control activity as child.

Figure 21.1 shows an activity chart for the heating controller and Figures 21.2 and 21.3 show the statechart of Tank control. The Enter batch data activity reads the relevant data from the operator and the recipes and fills a data store with batch data. The operator sends a start message to the Tank control activity, which responds by entering a control process for each controlled tank. This process is identical to the one we saw earlier: It checks if the current temperature is too high or too low and switches on the heater accordingly. Note that we use state hierarchy to represent

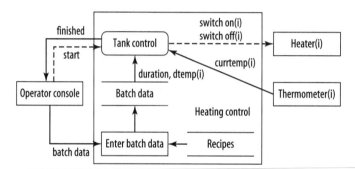

Figure 21.1 Activity chart of the heating controller.

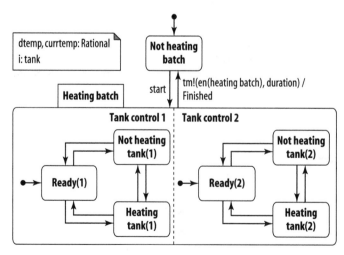

Figure 21.2 Statechart of the control activity. Tank control 1 and 2 have the same behavior, shown in Figure 21.3.

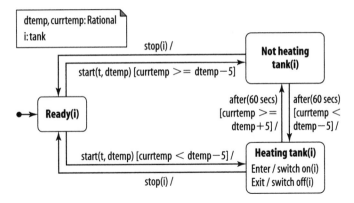

Figure 21.3 Tank control 1 and 2.

the fact that one batch is stored in several heating tanks and state parallelism to represent the fact that the two heating tanks work independently of one another.

21.1.1 *Temporal Events*

Instead of the temporal event **after**, seen earlier, Statemate offers a timeout event.

◆ For each event e and natural number n, timeout(e, n), abbreviated to tm(e, n), occurs n time units after the most recent occurrence of the event e.

Statemate also contains entry and exit events of a state:

◆ When a statechart enters a state S, Statemate generates the event en(s).
◆ When a statechart exits S, it generates the event ex(S).

An after(n) event that leaves state S can now be defined as tm(en(S), n).

Instead of the **when(t)** event that we saw earlier, Statemate offers the possibility of scheduling actions:

◆ For each action a and natural number n, the action schedule(a, n), abbreviated sc"!(a, n), schedules the action a to occur exactly n time units later.

when(n)/a can now be expressed as sc!(a, n).

21.1.2 *Starting, Suspending, Resuming, and Stopping Activities*

Each activity has an interface through which it can send events to any sibling activity and can receive events from any sibling activity. Figure 21.4 shows an important part of this interface. The diagram shows that a control activity can send certain actions to

Figure 21.4 Standard interface of an activity A (these are not shown in an activity chart).

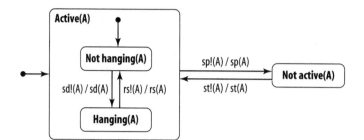

Figure 21.5 Different states of activity A.

a sibling activity, which responds by sending certain events to its environment. These events are received by all sibling activities, including the control activity, which can respond to it. The interfaces are not represented in an activity chart because they are always present. Figure 21.5 shows what these events and actions do. A starts in the state Active(A).

◆ If the control activity performs the action stop(A), abbreviated sp!(A), then A moves to the inactive state Not active(A) and it generates the event stopped(A), abbreviated sp(A).

◆ If the control activity then performs action start(A), abbreviated st!(A), then A moves to the active state Active(A) and it generates the event started(A), abbreviated st(A).

When an activity is active, it responds to any event as indicated in its specification, but it is also possible to suspend its activity.

◆ If the control activity performs action suspend(A), abbreviated sd!(A), then A moves to the state Hanging(A) and it generates the event suspended(A), abbreviated sd(A).

◆ If the control activity then performs action resume(A), abbreviated rs!(A), then A moves back to the state Not hanging(A) and it generates the event resumed(A), abbreviated rs(A).

The difference between resuming and starting an activity is that, when resumed, the activity continues from the state in which it was suspended, whereas, when it is started, it starts from its initial state.

If A has subactivities but no control activity, starting A implies starting all its subactivities. If A has a control activity, then starting A implies starting its control activity. In all cases, suspending, resuming, and stopping are inherited by all subactivities.

21.2 Choosing Notations

As explained in Chapter 12, statecharts differ from Mealy diagrams in their ability to represent state reactions, state hierarchy, and parallelism. In this section I discuss the choice of modeling these aspects in a statechart or in an activity chart.

21.2.1 Placing Activity in a Statechart or in an Activity Chart

State reactions and state hierarchy are two ways to represent activity states because an activity state is a state in which state reactions are defined or in which a sub-statechart is defined. However, activity states can be represented in an activity chart as well.

For example, in Figure 21.6 S1 is an activity state. In Figure 21.7, we moved its subactivity to a separate statechart innerSC that is encapsulated in a sibling activity B. The behavior of the two models is equivalent in a superstep semantics, as well as in a step semantics. We must encapsulate innerSC in B because Statemate does not allow two control activities to be children of the same parent.

We can do this with state reactions too. If S1 contains a list of state reactions, we can remove these and place these in B as we did in Figure 21.7.

If there is a transition that crosses an activity state boundary hierarchy outward, as in Figure 21.8, we can still find an equivalent pair of statecharts that jointly produce the same behavior. See Exercise 2 at the end of this chapter and Appendix E for a way to do this.

If there is a transition that crosses a state inward (Figure 21.9), it is not possible to find an equivalent pair of communicating statecharts. The reason is that we cannot

Figure 21.6 A statechart with an activity state S1.

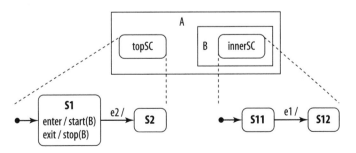

Figure 21.7 Moving the activity in S1 to another statechart. The start and stop interfaces are not shown in an activity chart.

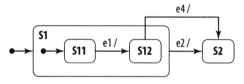

Figure 21.8 A statechart with a transition that crosses an activity state boundary outward.

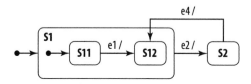

Figure 21.9 A statechart with a transition that crosses an activity state boundary inward.

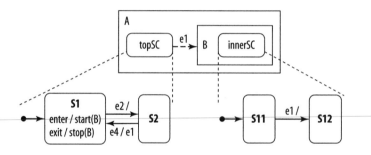

Figure 21.10 Moving the activity in S1 to another statechart. The resulting specification is similar, but not equivalent to the one in Figure 21.9.

factor out the substatechart without depriving e4 of the knowledge of where to go to. Figure 21.10 shows an attempt. When e4 occurs in state S2, then topSC moves to state S1, starting B and sending it event e1. innerSC is waiting in state S11 and responds in the next step by moving to S12. This is a two-step process, whereas in the single statechart in Figure 21.9 it takes only one step to move to (S1, S12). This behavior is not equivalent even in a superstep semantics because before the second step is taken, internal events can occur that affect behavior.

The reason why we cannot split behavior into two statecharts when there is a transition that crosses the activity state S1 inward is that the behavior outside S1 must know something about the behavior inside S1, namely which state to jump to. If we remove the substatechart, then there is no way that e4 can know where to jump to. By contrast, if there are no transitions that cross state boundaries, then the substatechart can be removed and placed in a separate control activity. And if there is an upward transition that crosses the boundary of S1, then, as shown in Exercise 2 (at the end of this chapter and Appendix E), we can still separate the behavior inside state S1 from the behavior outside S1 because the substatechart does not have to know where the outward transition must go.

21.2.2 *Representing Parallelism in Statecharts or in Activity Charts*

Parallelism in a statechart can always be replaced by parallelism in an activity diagram. For example, the diagram in Figure 21.11 is equivalent to the one in Figure 21.12. This means that we can use the decomposition guidelines for DFDs to determine the parallel subprocesses in a statechart. We may, for example, define parallel subprocesses corresponding to external devices, external events, and desired system functions.

The advantage of factoring all parallel subprocesses out as separate activities is that it forces us to make communication explicit. To illustrate, Figure 21.12 represents

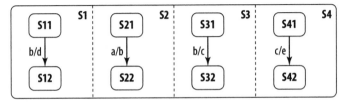

Figure 21.11 A statechart with four parallel substates.

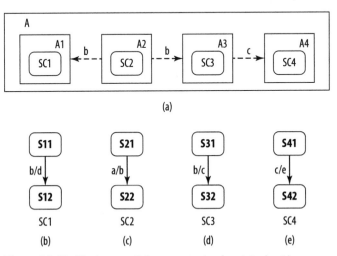

Figure 21.12 Placing parallel components of a statechart in parallel activities. The resulting specification is equivalent to the one in Figure 21.11. (a) An activity chart with four communicating activities. (b) SC1. (c) SC2. (d) SC3. (e) SC4.

explicitly which activity communicates with which other activity and by which event. In Figure 21.11, this is implicit—each action in a statechart is broadcast to all parallel processes in the statechart, and those that can respond to it do so. To understand the behavior of a statechart, we must check all parallel components (transitions and static reactions) to see whether some transition is triggered by an event generated by the statechart.

The disadvantage of factoring out all parallel subprocesses from a statechart is that it clutters up the activity chart. Conversely, including too many levels of concurrency in a statechart clutters up the statechart.

21.3   Execution Semantics

Statemate makes the following semantic choices. See Chapters 13 and 17 for a discussion of the options.

Channel capacity. Flows have capacity 1.

Time-continuous flows. All flows are time-continuous. Even if the receiver is deactivated, a flow keeps its contents until it is overwritten. (So flows behave as if they were data stores.)

Input buffer. Each activity has an input buffer, which is a set.

Priority. If a state transition conflicts with a state reaction (i.e., they cannot both be taken at the same time), then the transition has priority. If two transitions are in conflict, then the highest-level one has priority. (See Section 13.2 for a precise definition of priority.)

Step semantics. In a step, the system responds to all events that have occurred since the start of the previous step.

Perfect technology. Steps do not take time.

Breadth-first semantics. Activities are executed breadth-first.

Statemate offers a choice between clock-driven and event-driven execution. In the clock-driven case, there is an additional choice between a step execution and a superstep execution. As we have seen in Chapter 13, in the event-driven case, only superstep execution is logically possible.

The input to a step has the following components:

◆ The status of the system, which consists of the following items:
   —The current configuration of the statecharts
   —The values of all variables
   —The truth-values of all conditions
   —The activation state of each activity
   —A list of internal events generated during the previous step
   —A list of outstanding timeout events
   —A list of outstanding scheduled actions

◆ The time currently indicated by the system clock

◆ A list of external events that have occurred since the beginning of the previous step

From this input, a step produces a new status. Figure 21.13 shows the algorithm to perform a step. The algorithm computes maximal sets of nonconflicting transitions. In a deterministic system there is only one such set, but in a nondeterministic system there may be more than one. To each set, all state reactions that do not conflict with it are added. The algorithm then selects one of the resulting sets and performs the actions generated by these transitions and state reactions in the selected set.

1. Construct the set E of events to be responded to. First, set $E := 0$. Then:

    (a) Collect all external events generated by the environment since the beginning of previous step and add them to E. If several discrete events occurred in one input flow, take the most recent one. For time-continuous input data flows, take a recent value.

    (b) Collect all events generated in the previous step and add them to E.

    (c) Collect all events generated by the events in E, and add them to E (recursively). For example, if an activity has started, at least one subactivity is started too.

    (d) Execute all scheduled actions whose time is due in the next clock interval, namely the interval $(T, T+1]$, and remove these from the list of scheduled actions.

    (e) Process the list of timeout events. For each $tm(e, n)$ in the list,

        if $e \in E$, compute and record the time at which $tm(e, n)$ is to be generated;

        else if the time for $tm(e, n)$ to occur falls in the interval $(T, T+1]$, then generate the event e and deactivate the timeout event.

2. Construct from E a maximal step S to be executed. First, set $S := 0$. Then:

    (a) Compute the set En of enabled transitions and state reactions, i.e. those whose triggering event occurred and whose guard is true. Remove from En those transitions or reactions that are in conflict with a transition of higher priority in En.

    (b) Compute from En maximal nonconflicting sets S of transitions. Add to each set the state reactions that do not conflict with it. Each resulting set is called a *step*.

    (c) Select a step S to be executed.

3. Execute S.

    (a) Add scheduled actions in the step to the list of scheduled actions.

    (b) Perform all other actions in the step.

    (c) Update the information on the history of states.

    (d) Update the current configuration.

Figure 21.13 Outline of the algorithm to select and execute a step of a statechart in Statemate. In the state preceding the system step, time and all clocks have been advanced at least one unit, but never beyond an outstanding timeout or scheduled action. During the step, time is T.

---

1. Construct the set *E* of events to be responded to as in Figure 21.13.
2. Repeat the following until *E* = ∅:
   2.1 Construct from *E* a maximal system step *S* to be executed as in Figure 21.13. (There are no internal events at the beginning of a superstep.)
   2.2 Execute *S* as in Figure 21.13.
   2.3 Reconstruct the set *E* of events to be responded to. First, set *E* := ∅. Then:
      (a) Collect all events generated on internal flows and add them to *E*.
      (b) Generate derived events from the events in *E* and add these to *E* (recursively).

Figure 21.14 Superstep algorithm. In the state preceding the step, time and all clocks have been advanced some positive real number, but never beyond an outstanding timeout. During the step, time is T.

In a superstep semantics, execution iterates over a step until no more steps are generated. Figure 21.14 lists the superstep algorithm.

21.4 SUMMARY

Statemate uses activity charts, which are a syntactic variant of DFDs, and statecharts to build executable models. All flows in an activity chart are time-continuous and have capacity one. These models can be used in combination with all other PSA techniques to build structured analysis models. In Statemate models, an activity state of a statechart can be removed from the statechart and modeled as an activity in the activity chart instead, provided there is no transition entering the activity state to a substate. Parallel substates of a statechart can be removed from the statechart to be modeled as parallel activities in an activity chart.

Statemate has a well-defined execution algorithm that makes the perfect technology assumption and uses a step semantics in which an activity responds to the set of events that has occurred since the start of the previous step. The activity chart is traversed breadth-first. Statemate offers the option of clock-synchronous or clock-asynchronous semantics. In the first case, there is a choice between a step algorithm and a superstep algorithm.

21.5 QUESTIONS AND EXERCISES

EXERCISES

1. When the statechart in Figure 21.6 is started, it enters the initial configuration {S1, S11} in one step and then waits for an event. Describe the step(s) that occur(s) when activity A in Figure 21.7 is started, using the step execution algorithm.

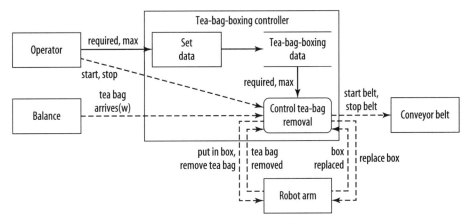

Figure 21.15 Activity chart of the tea-bag-boxing controller.

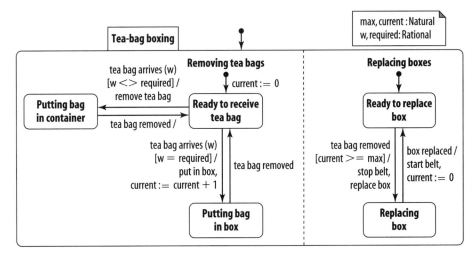

Figure 21.16 Statechart for the Control tea-bag removal activity.

2. Give a pair of communicating statecharts that represent the same behavior as that of Figure 21.8.

3. Figures 21.15 and 21.16 show an activity chart and a statechart for the tea-bag-boxing controller. Suppose the statechart is in configuration {Ready to receive tea bag, Ready to replace box} and current = max − 1. Describe the sequence of steps and states triggered by the following sequence of events:

   E1 tea bag arrives(w) with w = required

   E2 tea bag removed

   E3 box replaced

CHAPTER 22

The Unified Modeling Language (UML)

The Unified Modeling Language (UML) is a collection of diagram techniques adopted by the Object Management Group (OMG) in 1997 as standard notation for object-oriented software designs. The UML was to bring an end to the enormous diversity of notation used in many different object-oriented methods. The initiative to defining the UML was taken by Booch, Rumbaugh, and Jacobson. The version finally adopted by the OMG, however, was defined by a large group of people from many different companies, and at the time of writing the standard is still being updated and, in addition, many variants are being defined.

The UML itself is not a method, but a collection of techniques found in many different object-oriented analysis and design methods that have been proposed since about 1990. The intention is that the UML can be used in these and other object-oriented methods. Different methods will find different uses for these techniques, and some methods will not use all UML techniques. This chapter discusses a lightweight version of the major UML techniques. Section 22.1 gives an overview of all UML notations and explains why they are not all treated here. Section 22.2 shows how to use activity diagrams for workflow modeling. Section 22.3 discusses static structure diagrams, which are an extension of ERDs used to represent a decomposition of the SuD in software objects. Section 22.4 explains how the behavior notations discussed earlier in this book can be used to specify object behavior. Section 22.5 then shows how to use communication diagrams to ensure coherence between static structure diagrams and behavior descriptions. Section 22.6 gives guidelines for designing the static structure of an object-oriented SuD. Section 22.7 discusses the major semantic choices made by the UML. Finally, Section 22.8 shows how we can illustrate a scenario during an execution of a UML model by means of a collaboration or sequence diagram.

22.1 **Notations**

The UML contains the following notations.

Use case diagrams. Used to represent system functions and external communications.

Activity diagrams. Used to represent flow of control; not to be confused with Statemate activity charts.

Static structure diagrams. Used to represent the decomposition of a software system into software objects.

Statecharts. Used to represent the reactive behavior of a software object.

Collaboration diagrams. Used to represent message-passing scenarios among a collection of objects.

Sequence diagrams. Used for the same purpose as collaboration diagrams, but with an emphasis on the passage of time during the scenario.

Component diagrams. Used to represent the decomposition of a software system in a set of executable components.

Deployment diagrams. Used to represent the network of computing resources on which the software runs.

I do not discuss use case diagrams here because they are best viewed as a variant of context diagrams. Recall that a use case is called a *function* in this book; the techniques discussed in Chapter 7 can be used to describe use cases. Component and deployment diagrams are implementation notations that are simple to use, so I will not discuss them. In this chapter, I discuss lightweight versions of the other notations.

22.2 **Activity Diagrams**

22.2.1 *Wait State and Activity States*

Activity diagrams are a late addition to the UML collection of techniques that are very useful in describing business workflows. Suppose we want to express the fact that an action, performed during a state transition, takes time. We can do this by introducing an **activity state** for this action, as represented in Figure 22.1.

In an activity state, the behavior represented by the diagram performs some activity. In a wait state, the behavior represented by the diagram performs no activity but is waiting for an external or temporal event. Activities are represented by ellipsed

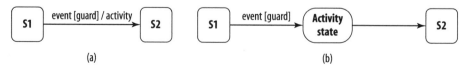

Figure 22.1 Representing an activity that takes time by an activity state.

boxes, that is, a box whose two opposing sides are semicircles. To indicate that the box represents an activity, we give it a name in the –ing form, such as Printing or Giving lists to speakers.

Wait states are, as always, represented by rectangles with rounded corners. A transition leaving an activity state is triggered by the termination of the activity, called a **completion event.** A transition leaving a wait state is triggered, as always, by an external or temporal event.

22.2.2 *Sequence*

Sequencing of activities is represented simply by connecting them with an arrow (Figure 22.2). When the first activity terminates, the second starts immediately. If there is a waiting period between the two activities, a wait state should be added after the first activity, and an event should be added that causes the behavior to leave the wait state and start the second activity.

22.2.3 *Hierarchy*

Activities can themselves be specified by an activity diagram, leading to a hierarchical activity diagram. This is no different from hierarchy in statecharts.

22.2.4 *Parallelism*

Activity diagrams represent parallelism by using bars that represent and-splits and and-joins (Figure 22.3). The arrows connecting the source nodes of an and-join with

(a)   (b)

Figure 22.2 Representing sequence. (a) When activity 1 terminates, activity 2 starts. (b) When activity 1 terminates, the workflow waits for e to occur when g is true, before starting activity 2.

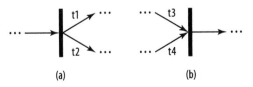

(a)   (b)

Figure 22.3 Representing parallelism. (a) And-split, t1 and t2 are executed simultaneously. (b) And-join, t3 and t4 are executed simultaneously.

the destination node form one complex transition. Therefore, they are executed in a single step. This means that it is not possible in Figure 22.3(a) for t1 and t2 to be executed at different times. Similarly, the arrows connecting the source node of an and-split with the destination nodes form one complex transition, so it is impossible in Figure 22.3(b) for t3 and t4 to be executed at different times.

Figure 22.4 represents the workflow at the registration desk of the training department as an activity diagram. Earlier, we saw a statechart representing the same workflow (see Figure 14.3). Note that to allow receiving badges and receiving lists to start at different times, they are preceded by two wait states. To allow them to finish at different times, they are also succeeded by two wait states. When the workflow is in state Badges received, the change event [Lists received] causes it to take the next composite transition to the next two parallel wait states.

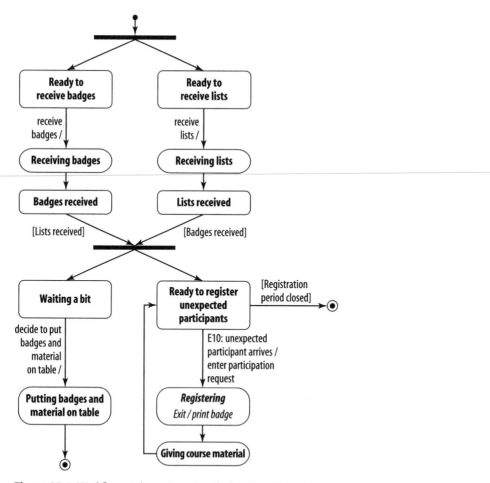

Figure 22.4 Workflow at the registration desk in the TIS. Activities written in italics are to be supported by TIS.

Figure 22.5 Representing choice. (a) Or-split. (b) Or-join.

22.2.5 Choice

Choice is represented by a small diamond, called an or-node. Figure 22.5(a) shows a choice between two branches. The guard g is assumed to be set by previous activity, for example by the activity represented by the node Activity. Any number of branches may enter and leave an or-node. At most one of the guards leaving an or-node may be [else]; this branch is taken when all other branches are false.

Activity diagrams can be used for any flow of control among terminating activities, but, as illustrated by the examples, we use activity diagrams to represent the business workflows in the context of the SuD.

22.3 **Static Structure Diagrams**

The UML is intended for representing the decomposition of a software system into a time-varying collection of objects. An **object** is a software entity with a fixed identity, a local state, and an interface through which it offers services to its environment. When it is executing, a software-system consists of a variable number of objects that can grow and shrink over time. The decomposition of a software system into objects is therefore usually represented on the class level because the number of classes in a program is fixed. A **static structure diagram** (SSD) represents the objects, or the classes of objects, into which a software system is decomposed and their multiplicity properties. If a SSD represents objects only, it is also called an **object diagram.** If it contains classes only, it is called a **class diagram.** Figure 22.6 shows an SSD of a decomposition of our old friend, the heating controller, into types of software objects.

22.3.1 SSDs and ERDs

SSDs are similar to ERDs, but they use a different terminology. Instead of object type, we talk of object class. We transfer the terminology of types to classes: A class instance is an object of the class, the extension of a class is the set of all its possible instances, the current extent of a class is the set of all its currently existing instances, and the intension of a class is the set of all properties shared by all possible class instances. The rest of the terminology is changed as shown in Figure 22.7.

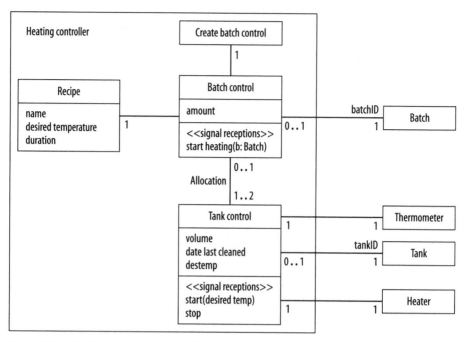

Figure 22.6 Static structure diagram of the heating controller and its environment.

ERD	SSD
Entity type	Class
Entity type extent	Class extent
Entity type extension	Class extension
Entity type intension	Class intension
Entity	Object
Relationship	Association
Tuple	Link
Association entity	Association object
Association entity type	Association class
Cardinality property	Multiplicity property

Figure 22.7 Comparison of terminology in ERDs and SSDs.

22.3.2 Representing Classes and Objects

Figure 22.8 shows the symbols used to represent classes and objects. A class rectangle is partitioned into three compartments that contain, from the top down, the class name, a list of attribute names, and a list of service names. In this book, we do not represent implementations by a SSD, so there are no "private" services. Just as

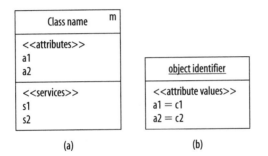

Figure 22.8 Representing classes and objects.

for entity types, the upper right corner of the name compartment may contain a multiplicity expression.

An object rectangle is partitioned into two compartments that contain an identification of the object and a list of attribute values. To indicate that a name is used to identify an object, we underline it. Objects can be identified in three ways.

◆ By a simple identifier, as shown in Figure 22.8.

◆ By a typed identifier, as in <u>1234 : Tank</u>.

◆ By an existential quantifier as in <u>:Tank</u>. The meaning of <u>:Tank</u> is "some instance of Tank." Two occurrences of <u>:Tank</u> in the same diagram may or may not indicate the same instance of Tank.

22.3.3 *Stereotypes*

The labels ≪attributes≫, ≪services≫, and ≪attribute values≫ in Figure 22.8 indicate **stereotypes.** A stereotype is a diagram element that has a special meaning, usually indicated by a ≪label≫ or by a special shape. The stereotypes in Figure 22.8 are superfluous because the middle and lower compartments of a class box are always used to represent attributes and services, respectively. But we may introduce stereotypes to clarify the meaning of some diagram element. For example, if some attributes of an object are not updatable, we may prefix this list of attributes by the stereotype ≪fixed≫. The analyst may simply invent his or her own stereotypes in a diagram.

22.3.4 *The Meaning of a SSD*

A SSD specifies:

◆ Which types of software objects can exist in the system

◆ How many of them can exist

This is analogous to the meaning of an ERD of the subject domain. We may enclose the software objects by a rectangle that represents the SuD, as I did in Figure 22.6, and also represent external entities in the context. This allows us to also represent relative multiplicity properties of the software objects in the SuD with respect to the external entities.

The important difference between SSDs and ERDs is that an ERD is used to represent entities in the subject domain of the SuD, whereas a SSD is used to represent the software objects that make up the SuD. This has important consequences for the meaning of attributes, associations and multiplicity properties, and services.

Attributes. There are two possible interpretations of attributes in a SSD.

1. Attributes are implementation variables that hold part of the state of a software object. Because they are part of the implementation, they may be changed in any way as long as the object provides the same services. And because an attribute is part of the implementation, attributes should be hidden from other objects. If an attribute a should be read or written by another object, then there should be services get_a and put_a to read and update the attribute, respectively.

2. Attributes represent the observable state of an object, which is not part of the implementation. The observable state of an object is a memory of its past and determines its possible future behaviors. Attributes are therefore part of the interface of the object.

I use the second interpretation because I use a SSD to represent the properties to be implemented but not to represent the implementation itself.

Associations. Associations are used to represent the relative multiplicity properties of objects, just as relationships are used in an ERD to represent relative cardinality properties of entities. However, in a SSD, associations also represent access paths. An **access path** is a series of connected links and objects, by which the object at one end of the path can retrieve the identifier of the object at the other end of the path. The representation of the access paths that allow objects to get the information they need to do their work is really the most important function of a SSD.

Associations in a SSD represent the fact that an implementation must contain an access path, but it does not say how it is implemented. A one-to-one association between two objects may be implemented as a pointer in either object to the other, as a separate link object, or by other means. It may even mean that one object is a parameter of an operation of the other object. An association in a SSD merely says that in an implementation, one object should have access to the identifier of another by some means.

We can generalize the concept of an access path to many-to-many associations, in which each object at one side has access to the identifiers of a set of objects at the other side. We use path expressions (see Chapter 10) to traverse access paths.

Services. Objects as represented by a SSD can offer services in two ways: by performing an operation or by receiving a signal. An **operation** is a computation performed by an object that is intended to deliver a service to whomever calls the operation. An example is the operation update floor(c: Elevator cage, a: Arrival sensor) defined in

Figure 22.9. A Cage surrogate is a software object that represents an elevator cage and a Floor surrogate is a software object that represents a floor of the building. These objects are called surrogates because their sole purpose is to represent subject-domain objects and maintain information about them. Within the software system, they are surrogates for the real-world entities that they represent. Note that the specification of an operation is not shown in a SSD. We specify operations as part of the behavior description (see Section 22.4).

A **signal** is a named data structure, instances of which can be sent to objects. A signal is very much like an entity type in software. It has a name and attributes, called parameters. Its instances can be created and destroyed, and an instance has parameter values. Signals can be structured in a taxonomic hierarchy, as illustrated in Figure 22.10.

The ability of an object to receive signal instances is called a **signal reception.** For example, the SSD in Figure 22.6 shows that Batch control objects can receive instances of the signal start heating(b: Batch). A SSD does not show what happens when an object receives a signal instance. The effect of receiving a signal instance is described in a behavior specification.

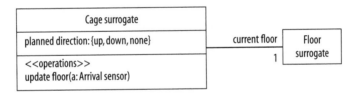

Dictionary:

update_floor(c: Elevator cage, a: Arrival sensor).

   c.current_floor := a.floor

Figure 22.9 Fragment of an elevator controller SSD and the relevant dictionary entry.

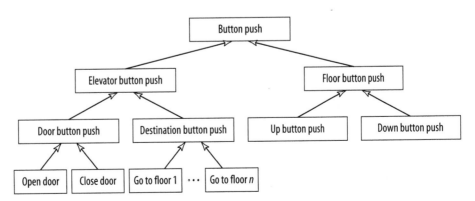

Figure 22.10 A generalization hierarchy of signals.

22.4 **Behavior Specification**

22.4.1 *Specifying the Effect of Operation Calls*

The UML does not provide a notation for specifying the effect of an operation. The usual way to specify an operation is to give an implementation in some programming language, called a **method;** the explanation of this name is that the implementation describes a method to compute the effect of the operation. An operation may or may not return a result that is passed back to the caller of the operation. The update floor operation does not return a result.

An operation may also be specified by means of a state transition in a statechart, as illustrated in Figure 22.11. Now an occurrence of update floor causes a transition, and the method to compute the effect is given as action of the transition. Note that according to this specification, update_floor(c, a) is an event that triggers an action, namely the action of updating the current_floor link, whereas in Figure 22.9 update_floor(c, a) *is* the update. In Figure 22.11, the execution of update_floor(c, a) is a call event that triggers a transition, but in Figure 22.9 the execution of update_floor(c, a) is the action that is called.

There is no restriction on the possible effects that an operation can have. An operation may change the attribute values of the object that executes the operation, but it may also change values in any other object in the system, and it may create or delete objects in the system.

22.4.2 *Specifying the Effect of Signal Receptions*

The effect of a signal reception is always specified by means of an event-action pair in a STT or STD of the behavior of the object because the only thing that a signal instance can do to an object is trigger an action. An object with a signal reception should therefore always have a behavior description (STT or STD) defined for it in which at least one action is triggered by the signal. Figure 22.12 gives an example that shows that when a Batch control object is in its initial state, the reception of the signal start heating(b) causes a transition to the state Heating(b) and execution of the operation start tanks(b).

22.4.3 *Specifying Object Life Cycles*

In addition to specifying the effect of an operation or signal reception, we may use a behavior description to specify the properties of the behavior of an object from

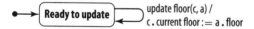

Figure 22.11 Specifying an operation by means of a transition in a statechart.

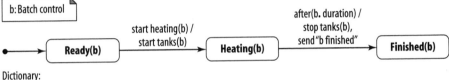

Dictionary:

start_tanks(b: Batch).
 • For all tanks t in b.heating_tank, send start(t, b.recipe.desired_temperature).
stop_tanks(b: Batch).
 • For all tanks t in b.heating_tank, send stop(t).

Figure 22.12 Statechart for Batch control in Figure 22.6.

c: Elevator cage,
a: Arrival sensor

arrival(a) / update_floor(c, a)

Figure 22.13 Cage surrogate event-action pair.

creation to destruction. The behavior of an object from birth to death is called its **life cycle.** It can be specified by means of an event list or statechart. Figure 22.12 shows the life cycle of Batch control objects.

In simple cases, statecharts are an overkill and we can give a simple event list to specify an object life cycle. Figure 22.13 gives an event list entry for Cage surrogate objects that tells us when the current floor association of the surrogate is updated—when an arrival sensor tells the surrogate that the elevator cage has activated it.

Because the UML forces us to think about the details of operations and signals, there are also detailed decisions to be made about events, guards, and actions in a behavior description. Here are the options. First, the trigger in an event-action pair (event list or statechart) can be one of the following kinds of events.

Signal event. Reception of a signal instance.

Call event. Reception of an operation call.

Change event. Change in the truth value of some condition. The syntax for this is when C for a condition C.

Temporal event. An absolute deadline (when t) or a relative deadline (after t).

Completion event. An activity state reaches its final state.

Second, a guard can be any Boolean expression; the guard may test the state of any object in the SuD accessible to it. Third, the action of an event-action pair can be one of the following.

Send action. A signal instance is created and sent to its destinations by means of a statement of the form send objectset.signalname (parameters). objectset is a path expression that evaluates to a set of objects and each object in this set receives a signal instance.

Call action. An operation is called by a statement of the form objectset.operationname (parameters). objectset is a path expression that evaluates to a set of objects and each object in this set executes the operation.

Return action. An operation executes a statement return v, where v is an expression that computes a value.

Assignment action. An attribute is assigned by a statement of the form attribute := v where attribute is a patch expression that evaluates to an attribute and v is an expression that computes a value.

Create action. A software object is created by a statement of the form new classname (parameters).

Destroy action. A software object is destroyed by a statement of the form object. destroy, where object is a path expression that evaluates to an object identifier.

Terminate action. An object reaches a top-level final state.

These actions may be combined using the constructs of the programming language available, such as sequence, choice, and iteration.

22.4.4 *Differences between Operations and Signals*

Operations and signals seem to be roughly the same thing—receiving an operation call or a signal instance leads to a computation that may change the state of software objects. However, there are some important differences between the two.

◆ An operation is defined by a method or by an event-action pair in a behavior description (event list or statechart transition). A signal, on the other hand, is always defined by an event-action pair in a behavior description.

◆ An operation may return a value. A signal instance never returns a value.

◆ Communication by means of an operation call may be synchronous or asynchronous, whereas communication by means of a signal instance is always asynchronous. In synchronous communication, the caller waits for the operation to complete its computation, whereas in asynchronous communication, the operation caller or signal sender continues its own computation after the message is sent.

◆ Operations are not generalizable, but signals can be generalized in a taxonomy of signals.

◆ An operation is called by some software object in the system. A signal instance may be sent and received by an external entity or by a software object in the system.

22.5 **Communication and Coherence**

The statecharts that specify object life cycles are closely coupled to the SSD because the interface of the life cycle must agree with the interface as defined in the SSD. To

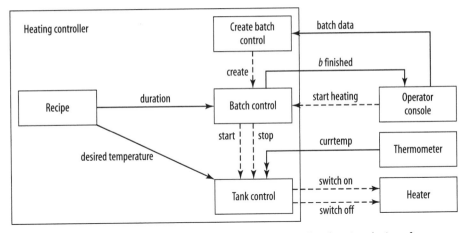

Figure 22.14 Communication diagram of the heating controller showing the interfaces of the objects.

assure that the SSD and behavior specifications are consistent, it is useful to draw a communication diagram that shows the interfaces. Figure 22.14 gives an example.

First, compare this with the statechart in Figure 22.12. The communication diagram shows where the start heating signal comes from—from the operator. It also shows that a Batch control object sends start and stop messages to Tank control objects. The dictionary in Figure 22.12 shows that these messages are sent by the actions start tanks and stop tanks, respectively.

Next, compare the communication diagram with the SSD in Figure 22.6. There we see that Batch control objects have a signal reception start heating declared for them and that Tank control objects can receive the signals start and stop. This agrees with the communication diagram too. So the communication diagram binds together the SSD and the behavior description, providing a context for both.

Figure 22.15 shows the coherence rules between SSDs and communication diagrams. Data passed between objects are called **messages.** As shown in the figure, a message can be a signal instance, an operation call or a return value, or a creation or destruction message. A message is created by an action, and the reception of a message is called an event.

22.6 **Static Structure Design Guidelines**

A SSD adds a new kind of documentation of the system decomposition, in addition to communication diagrams. A SSD shows which classes of objects can exist in the SuD, how many of them can exist, and what the access paths between them are. This forces us to be precise about object identification. We regard the SSD as additional documentation to the communication diagram that provides more detail about object identification and access.

To find a SSD, we first need an adequate environment model that contains at least a system context diagram and a subject domain ERD. In addition, we should

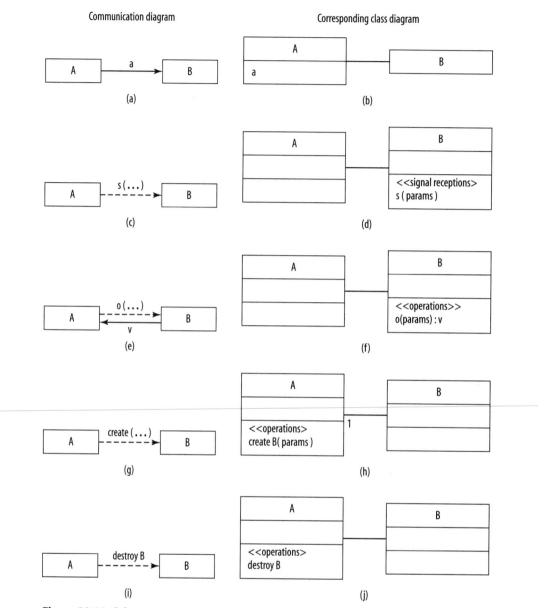

Figure 22.15 Coherence requirements between communication diagrams and SSDs.

have a communication diagram of the requirements-level architecture. The SSD then indicates how each of the components can get the information that it needs to do its job. It also summarizes the interface and observable state variables (attributes) of each component.

For example, Figure 22.16 shows an architecture for the elevator controller. The central components are a cage surrogate class whose instances represent the current

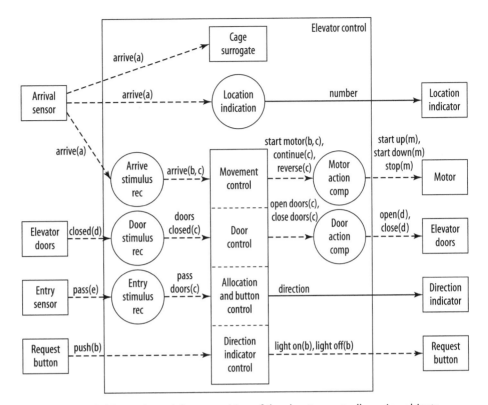

Figure 22.16 Subject-oriented decomposition of the elevator controller, using objects and data transformations.

state of each cage, a location indication transformation that indicates the current floor in each cage, and four closely coupled control processes that control different aspects of desired elevator system behavior. At the input side there are stimulus-recognition transformations, and at the output side there are action-computation transformations. These implement dictionary definitions. For example, the term arrive(b, c) is defined in the dictionary and the transformation Arrive stimulus rec implements this definition. All event interfaces are shown, but to avoid cluttering the diagram almost all the data flow interfaces have been omitted.

Before we can build a SSD that shows the information needed by each component to do its job, we must first specify the job done by each component. In other words, we must specify the behavior of each component. The behavior of cage surrogate objects is:

c: Cage surrogate

arrive(a) / update_floor(c, a), where update_floor(c, a) = c.current_floor := a.floor.

See Figure 22.17 for the access paths. Looking at the specification of update_floor, we see that this operation contains identifiers of the cage surrogate c and of an arrival sensor surrogate a as parameters. From c it needs to access the current floor and from

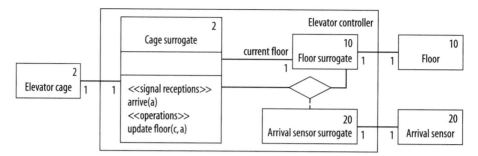

Figure 22.17 SSD showing the access paths needed by Cage surrogate objects.

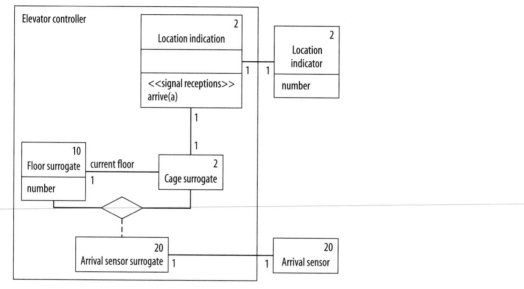

Figure 22.18 SSD showing the access paths needed by the Location indication transformation objects.

a it needs to access the floor. This gives us the SSD fragment shown in Figure 22.17. The SSD fragment mirrors a fragment of the subject-domain ERD. Each surrogate has a one-to-one relationship to the external entity that it represents.

As another example, the specification of the location indication transformation is as follows.

Location indication:

◆ When arrive(a),

◆ do set number(a.cage.location_indicator, a.cage.current_floor.number).

This tells us that the location indication transformation receives the identifier a of an arrival sensor surrogate, from this identifier needs access to the cage whose arrival is sensed by a, and then to the appropriate location indicator as well as to the current floor number. Figure 22.18 shows the access paths needed.

Note that the SSDs include surrogate classes not included in the communication diagram. The reason for this is that these surrogates contain data that are read by other objects but they do not perform the operations or receive the signals of other objects. In a communication diagram that shows data flows, these classes would be included.

To summarize, a SSD provides access path details for components, so before drawing a SSD, we find a decomposition and document this in a communication diagram. Next, we specify the behavior required of each component. This gives us sufficient information to find SSDs using the following guidelines.

√ To find a SSD, identify the access paths needed by each component to do its job.

√ Draw a SSD for each component in the communication diagram.

√ The classes in the SSDs include surrogate classes that represent subject-domain entities. The multiplicity properties of these classes mirror the cardinality properties of the subject-domain entities.

22.7 Execution Algorithm

At the time that I write this (summer 2001), the UML is still being extended and refined, and there is currently no fully defined execution semantics for it. I here summarize some of the choices that have been made already and outline an execution algorithm compatible with those choices. See also Chapters 13 and 17 for a discussion of these choices.

Mixed-step and single-transition semantics. If several transitions are triggered in one thread of control, choose one nondeterministically and execute it. If they are triggered in different threads of control, perform transitions in the different threads concurrently.

Sequential-event semantics. Input events are responded to in sequence. If the environment produces several events simultaneously, then the system chooses to respond to them in some sequence.

Delayed-step semantics. An object responds to events generated internally or externally at some later time, when it is ready for them.

Sequential-action semantics. The actions along a transition are executed in sequence.

Run-to-completion semantics. When an action calls an operation, this operation is executed to completion before the rest of the action is executed.

Input buffer. At each moment during the execution of the system, there is a set of messages that have been sent but not yet processed by their receiver. The UML does not require this set to be a queue. Depending on the degree of parallelism of the system, there is one global set or there are several sets, one for each parallel thread of computation.

Imperfect technology. The UML does not make the perfect technology assumption. Actions may take time to execute.

Compute the maximal sets of transitions that are triggered by the current event and whose guards evaluate to true.

Remove conflicting transitions from each of these sets, such that no transition outside the set has a higher priority than a transition inside the set.

Select one of these sets for execution.

Perform the transitions in the set in arbitrary order. For each of these, do the following:

- First perform all exit actions of states exited by the transition, where exit actions of lower-level states are performed before those of higher-level states. Exit actions of concurrent states at the same level are performed in arbitrary order.
- Next, perform all actions of the transition in sequence.
- Finally, perform all entry actions of states entered by the transition, where entry actions of higher-level states are performed before those of lower-level states. Entry actions of concurrent states at the same level are performed in arbitrary order.

Figure 22.19 An algorithm to compute a step of an object, which is compatible with the UML semantic choices.

The resulting semantics is quite complex. There are several implementations compatible with these choices. See the Bibliographic Remarks for pointers to existing implementations.

Figure 22.19 shows an algorithm to compute a step of the SuD, which is compatible with the semantic choices. The algorithm starts with one event, called the current event, to be responded to by an object. Due to nondeterminism or parallelism in an object, the event may trigger several transitions. The algorithm constructs a step from this and then serializes the transitions in this set, respecting the constraint that exit actions are performed first, transition actions next, and entry actions last. Note that executing an operation call may cause the execution of a nested step.

22.8 Collaboration and Sequence Diagrams

The execution of a software system can be illustrated by means of sequence and collaboration diagrams. A **sequence diagram** consists of a set of time lines that represent the passage of time in an object or external entity and a set of message exchanges between these objects and entities. Figure 22.20 shows the sequence diagram of one possible scenario that results from the start heating message. At the top, the individual software objects and external entities involved in the scenario are shown. The arrows represent messages. Time increases from top to bottom. Because a sequence diagram shows only communication by messages, the data flows duration and curr_temp (Figure 22.14) have been replaced by a get followed by a return of the requested value. Sequence diagrams can be annotated with temporal information about the time that a message is sent or received and about the interval between two send or receive events on one time line.

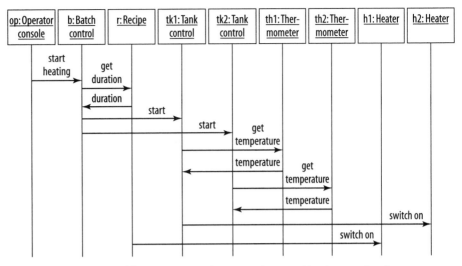

Figure 22.20 One possible message-passing scenario caused by the start heating message.

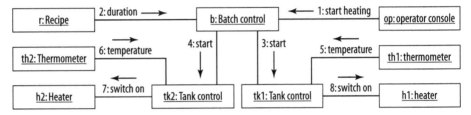

Figure 22.21 Collaboration diagram of the scenario of Figure 22.20.

It is important not to attach too much meaning to a sequence diagram. A sequence diagram expresses two kinds of sequences:

◆ The sequence of message sending and receptions along one time line is totally ordered.

◆ A message is received after it has been sent.

No other temporal ordering is represented by a sequence diagram. This means that in Figure 22.20, the switch on message from tk1 to h1 may very well have been sent before tk2 sends switch on to h2.

The UML offers an alternative notation to represent scenarios, namely collaboration diagrams. A **collaboration diagram** is an object diagram (a SSD representing only objects) that shows the objects and links involved in a scenario and shows the messages passed in the scenario. Figure 22.21 shows a collaboration diagram that expresses the same scenario as Figure 22.20. It shows a part of the heating controller SSD (Figure 22.6) instantiated to a number of individual objects and shows the messages passed along the links. Message sequencing is indicated in this diagram by numbers. A collaboration diagram makes clear which access paths are used to retrieve the identifier of the object to which a message must be sent. The UML offers a complex numbering scheme to indicate the partial ordering of messages and even parallel threads of computation in a collaboration diagram. You are referred to the standard literature on the UML to learn more about this scheme.

Sequence and collaboration diagrams can be used not only to illustrate a scenario, but also to specify a behavior. The difference is that an illustration describes what happens in one particular possible computation, whereas a specification describes what must be present in all possible computations. When used for specification, sequence and collaboration diagrams do not represent individual objects and external entities but instead classes of objects and entities. The appearance of the diagrams is the same, but their use is radically different. When Figures 22.20 and 22.21 are used as specifications, they say that all possible responses to start heating should contain this sequence of message exchanges. As illustrations, they merely say that one possible response to start heating consists of this scenario.

Yet another use of sequence and collaboration diagrams is to represent typical patterns of computation. Now the diagram does not represent individual objects nor classes but instead roles that can be played by objects and external entities. These roles are just like classes, except that in a particular system these roles are played by objects of a particular class.

If a collaboration diagram is used as specification or to express a pattern, it is a type-level diagram and it looks somewhat like a communication diagram. There are, however, two important differences.

◆ A collaboration diagram is a SSD that shows the structure of a collection of object classes. A link in a collaboration diagram means that a sender knows the identity of the receiver. A communication diagram, by contrast, shows the communication channels between a collection of object classes. An arrow in a communication diagram means that a message can get from a sender to a receiver, but this may use channel addressing instead of destination addressing.

◆ A collaboration diagram shows the sequencing of messages in a scenario. A communication diagram, by contrast, does not show sequence; it just shows possible communications.

To support all these uses, the UML offers techniques to represent control structures, such as choice, iteration, and parallelism in sequence, and collaboration diagrams. These techniques drive the expressive power of sequence and collaboration diagrams in the direction of statecharts, providing us with yet another alternative for the specification of behavior.

22.9 **SUMMARY**

UML activity diagrams are a useful technique for modeling workflows. They distinguish wait states, in which the workflow is waiting for an external or temporal event, from activity states, in which the workflow performs a (hopefully) terminating activity. Activity diagrams contain constructs for sequence, choice, parallelism, and hierarchy.

SSDs represent the (classes of) software objects into which the SuD is decomposed and the multiplicity constraints on those objects. A SSD can also represent external entities and the system boundary. An object has attributes that represent its observable state and offers services to its environment. In the UML, these services are operations or signal receptions.

For each object class in the SSD, an object life cycle can be specified using an event list or statechart. To check the coherence between the service declarations in the SSD and the interface of an object statechart or event list, a communication diagram can be drawn that shows the context for each object behavior.

The UML execution semantics is not yet fully defined, but it makes at least the following choices. The system responds to one event at a time. Operation calls are executed to completion before execution continues with the next action. For each thread of computation in the system, there is a set of messages sent to an object that runs in that thread, but not yet processed by their receiver. And the UML does not make the perfect technology assumption, so actions may take significant time.

An execution of the system may be illustrated by means of a collaboration or sequence diagram. These diagrams may also be used to specify possible behavior or to specify patterns of computation.

22.10 QUESTIONS AND EXERCISES

QUESTIONS FOR REHEARSAL

1. For activity diagrams,
  - ◆ What is the difference between a wait state and an activity state?
  - ◆ Can a wait state be decomposed into a lower-level activity diagram?
  - ◆ Can an activity state be decomposed into a lower-level activity diagram?
  - ◆ What is a completion event?

2. Define the following concepts.
  Object
  Class
  Class extension
  Class extent
  Class intension
  What is the difference between an object and an entity?

3. Define the following concepts.
  Operation
  Method

Signal

Signal reception

4. Define the following.

Operation

Signal

What are the differences between an operation and a signal?

5. For messages,

◆ List the five types of messages that can be sent between objects.

◆ Are there actions that do not lead to a message?

◆ Are there events that cannot be caused by a message?

EXERCISES

6. Figure 22.22 shows a statechart for tea-bag boxing.

a) Give a communication diagram for the tea-bag-boxing controller with two components: a controller of the robot arm, whose behavior is specified in Figure 22.22, and a data container that contains the required tea-bag weight and maximum number of bags in a box. The data container is initialized by the operator and read by the control object. Assume that the tea-bag-removal controller is created and destroyed by the operator.

b) Make a SSD of the system and its context.

Take care that the communication diagram and SSD are consistent with the statechart.

7. Figure D.25 (Appendix D) lists the specifications of the transformations Arrive stimulus rec, Door stimulus rec, and Motor action comp of the elevator controller

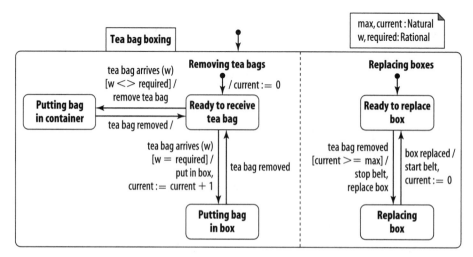

Figure 22.22 Statechart for removal of tea bag.

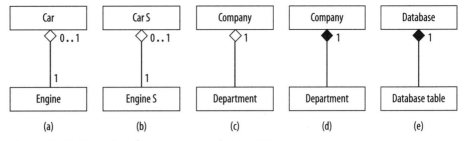

Figure 22.23 Examples of aggregation and composition.

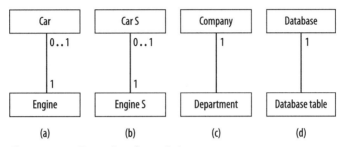

Figure 22.24 Examples of association.

architecture. Figure D.32 (Appendix D) shows a SSD for the relevant access paths needed by these components and by Movement control.

a) Check that the SSD defines all access paths needed by these components.

b) Define the transformations Entry stimulus rec and Door action comp of the elevator controller, using the dictionary in Appendix D.

c) Draw a SSD that defines the access paths needed by Entry stimulus rec, Door action comp, and Door control.

QUESTIONS FOR DISCUSSION

8. The UML allows the representation of aggregation and composition relationships. Figure 22.23 gives four examples. Car and Engine are physical entities in the subject domain; Car S and Engine S are software objects in a software system. The open diamond represents a whole-part relationship: An engine is a part of a car. The black diamond represents strong composition, which means that the part cannot exist outside the whole: A database table cannot exist outside a database. Discuss the differences in meaning between the models in Figure 22.23 and Figure 22.24 in:

a) The creation, update, or deletion of the part or whole.

b) Any meaning attached to the diamond that is not already conveyed by the multiplicity constraints.

CHAPTER 23

Not Yet Another Method (NYAM)

T here is only a small number of notations that a software engineer can remember. Sooner or later, an engineer gets exasperated with so many alternative ways of describing a design, each with many fine details of expression, and gets on with the business of designing software. In this chapter, I summarize the design approach taken in this book, summarize the notations that we have reviewed, and provide a road map for using these notations. I sketch the spectrum from flyweight to heavyweight use of the notations. The resulting approach is NYAM—it is Not Yet Another Method; it is simply the gist of existing methods.

Section 23.1 summarizes the design approach taken in this book. Central elements in this approach are the distinction among the functions, behavior, and communication of systems, and the identification of an aggregation hierarchy in which reactive software design is embedded in a larger composite system design process. Section 23.2 summarizes all software design notations treated in this book and shows how they can be used in our design approach. The use of the notations is arranged in a sequence from flyweight to heavyweight use. Section 23.3 presents a method that starts with problem analysis and ends with the decomposition of the SuD. Section 23.4 shows the role that the notations can play in the system engineering argument and Section 23.5 discusses the difference between formality and precision, arguing that in software design we need precision before formality.

23.1 Software Design Context

In Chapter 19, architecture decisions are divided into four groups:

- ◆ Decisions based on functional requirements
- ◆ Decisions based on quality requirements
- ◆ Decisions based on the use environment
- ◆ Decisions based on the implementation platform

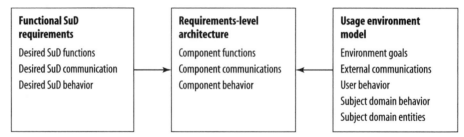

Figure 23.1 Design approach, shown earlier as Figure 19.10 (the arrows represent justification of design decisions).

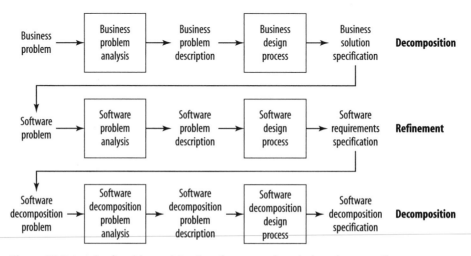

Figure 23.2 Levels of problem solving in software product design, shown earlier as Figure 5.3.

In this book, we do not consider decisions based on quality requirements. The other decisions are summarized in Figure 23.1.

But where do the functional requirements and the use environment model come from? From a composite system design process. Figure 23.2 shows the situation in which the composite system is a business. A business solution consists of a number of interacting entities, one of which is the SuD, which is a software system. The SuD specification is obtained by analyzing the use environment and refining it by identifying:

◆ The desired functions of the SuD

◆ The desired external behavior of the SuD

◆ The desired external communication of the SuD

This is a design process because decisions are made about what the SuD should do.

The business solution is also the source for the use environment model, which refines descriptions that are already given in rough form in the business solution

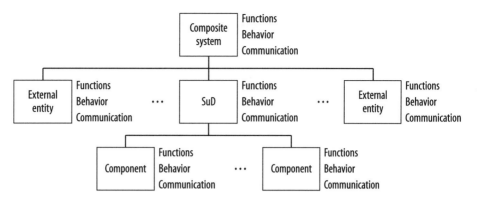

Figure 23.3 Recurrence of aspects at different levels in the hierarchy, shown earlier as Figure 4.3.

specification. Depending on the kind of SuD, the use environment model describes one or more of the following elements:

◆ Relevant business goals

◆ Relevant communication in the business

◆ The business workflow

◆ Subject domain entities

◆ Assumed and desired subject domain behavior

At each level in the hierarchy, we encounter the same aspects (Figure 23.3). This is reflected in the use of notations.

23.2 From Flyweight to Heavyweight Use of Notations

Figure 23.4 summarizes the specification notations discussed in this book and the system aspects that they can be used for. I have also briefly discussed UML collaboration and sequence diagrams as illustration techniques. As explained earlier, those notations can also be used as specification techniques.

The different aspects recur at every level in the system hierarchy (Figure 23.3), so we may choose to use some notation from the business level down to the software object level. This may not be a bad idea for the mission statement, which can be useful to give for the business, the SuD, and its components down to the level of software objects. But most notations have their natural aggregation level. Figure 23.5 indicates a possible use of the notations at the different aggregation levels.

There are several degrees of weightiness with which we can use these notations. A flyweight use has:

◆ The SuD context diagram

◆ The SuD mission statement

	Functions	Behavior	Communication	Decomposition
Mission statement	×			
Function refinement tree	×			
Service description	×			
State transition list		×		
State transition table		×		
State transition diagram		×		
Activity diagram		×		
Data flow diagram			×	
Communication diagram			×	
Entity-relationship diagram				×
Static structure diagram				×

Figure 23.4 Specification techniques.

Use environment of SuD	Context diagram
	Subject domain ERD
	Activity diagram of user workflow
	STT or STD of desired subject domain behavior
	STT or STD of assumed subject domain behavior
Functional properties of SuD	Mission statement
	Function refinement tree
	Service descriptions
	Stimulus-response descriptions
Decomposition of SuD	Communication diagram
	STT or STD of component behavior
	Static structure diagram

Figure 23.5 Possible use of specification techniques.

This bounds the composite system to which the SuD should contribute some useful behavior, and it bounds the desired functionality of the system.

A bantamweight use extends this with more information about functionality:

◆ The function refinement tree
◆ The service descriptions
◆ The dictionary

The service descriptions contain information about the events that trigger a function and the added value delivered by a function to the environment. The dictionary documents the meaning of key terms in the service descriptions.

For systems with information-provision functionality, such as the Training Information System (TIS), and with manipulative functionality, such as the Electronic Ticket System (ETS), it is important to supplement the dictionary with an ERD of subject-domain entities. This brings us to the featherweight use of the techniques—extend the descriptions with

◆ A subject-domain ERD

This makes the classification, identification, and cardinality properties of subject-domain entities precise. The examples show that this can also be useful for systems with directive functionality.

Many systems make certain assumptions about user workflow, which are relevant to document because it is only while interacting with this workflow that desired composite system behavior emerges. Documenting this behavior raises the weightiness of our descriptions to lightweight:

◆ An activity diagram of user workflow

The assumed workflow of users of the TIS is nontrivial, and the assumed workflows of the users of the ETS and of the operator of the heating controller system are trivial. The elevator controller makes no assumption about elevator-passenger behavior.

For directive systems, we need more information about the desired behavior to be enforced, prevented, or enabled in the subject domain, as well as about the behavior assumed by the SuD in achieving this desired behavior. This brings us, for directive systems, to a welterweight use of the techniques, in which we add the following behavior descriptions:

◆ A STT or STD of desired subject domain behavior
◆ A STT or STD of assumed subject domain behavior

For example, the heating controller needs a model of desired behavior of the heater and thermometer, and the controller behaves under the assumption that its response will have certain behavioral effects in the subject domain. See Appendices C and D for the complete case studies of the heating controller and elevator controller, including their use of behavior description techniques.

Moving to a documentation of the system decomposition, we get to a middle-weight use and add:

◆ A communication diagram
◆ STTs or STDs of component behavior

This involves a choice mix of Von Neumann and object-oriented architectural styles. STTs and STDs are useful for systems with directive functionality, such as the heating and elevator controllers, and for systems with nontrivial interface protocols, such as the ETS.

Moving finally to a heavyweight use of techniques, we add detailed information about multiplicity and access paths:

◆ A static structure diagram

As I remarked earlier, heavyweights can be as heavy as they want, and we can add an almost unlimited amount of information to a SSD, such as messages sequences, exact timing information, object composition, implementation details, name visibility, the details of identification, object creation and destruction, and threads and parallelism. See the standard UML literature for information on how to specify all this.

The set of notations that we can use ranges from flyweight to heavyweight. But for each of the notations, too, we can choose to use it in a manner that ranges from flyweight to heavyweight. For example, a lightweight use of the communication diagram notation does not show all the interfaces and does not label the communication channels. This is useful for sketching the desired properties and architecture of the system. We have done this in several diagrams. If, on the other hand, we want to execute a model or generate an executable program from it, we have no choice but to use the heavyweight version of the notation, including all the necessary syntactic details, in our descriptions.

23.3 Design Approach

Computer scientists love recipes. As long as there have been books written about software-design methods, there have been recipes that instruct the software engineer precisely when to deliver which design model. This book tries to be an exception to this rule, and so I try not to provide something that looks like a software-design recipe. However, there is a loose sequencing constraint on design tasks:

> In order to build a design model of a component, the engineer often needs a more refined model of the composite system first.

This is expressed in Figure 23.6. To **refine** a description is to provide more detail about the subject of the description. The very loose sequence expressed in Figure 23.6 is the following.

> *Problem bounding.* The starting point is a business solution specification, which is a description of the desired business situation that is precise enough for business designers but which does not provide enough detail for software designers. In any software-design process, the business solution description should be refined into a mission statement and context diagram. These characterize the software-design problem.

> *Service description.* If we want to provide more detail about the system, we should refine the mission statement into service descriptions. But to identify the desired functions of the SuD, we often need to refine our environment model by modeling the workflow to be supported.

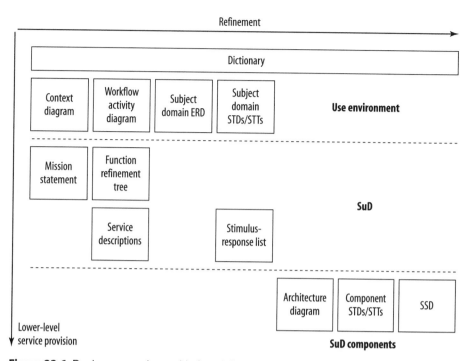

Figure 23.6 Design proceeds roughly from left to right, which is a progression from flyweight descriptions to descriptions of increasingly heavier weight. Often, in order to make a lower-level design model, the designer has to first make a more refined higher-level description. Not all notations need to be used for all kinds of systems.

Defining key terms. If we have sufficient certainty about the desired functionality, we should fix the meaning of the key terms in the dictionary, supported by an ERD of the subject domain. This is again an environment model.

Identifying desired and assumed behavior. In order to describe the desired stimulus-response behavior of the SuD, we first need a description of the desired and assumed behavior in the subject domain. This may also involve the addition of more detail to the context diagram.

Decomposition. Using the descriptions of the use environment and the SuD requirements, we can define a SuD decomposition. For directive systems, we have to add more detail to this by describing the desired behavior of the components. We may wish to supplement this with a SSD that gives the details about access paths and multiplicity constraints on objects.

This list illustrates that software design is at the same time top-down and middle-out. We start with a rough description of a business solution, which is top-down, but we have to refine the environment description at the same time as we are designing the SuD, which is middle-out.

23.4 **Engineering Arguments**

Why do we need descriptions of software systems at all? Why not simply go ahead and write or buy the software? One reason why we need descriptions of the system is to coordinate the work of building or buying it. Builders of custom-made products make plans based on system specifications. If there are subcontractors, these coordinate their activities based on system descriptions. And if the product is to be bought, the buyer needs a description of the environment and requirements in order to select a product. The descriptions provide a conceptual model of the system that is shared by the different stakeholders involved in making or buying the system and that is used to plan and coordinate their work.

A related reason why we need descriptions is to manage the evolution of the system. System use leads to change requests, and, to see whether and how these requests can be honored, they are interpreted using a description that relates the system requirements to system architecture.

But the reason that I am focusing on here is that we try to engineer the system. And the essence of engineering design is the ability to predict the properties of a product before it is built. To do that, we need a description of the product before it is built. When we build a house, the architect produces a number of documents that describe the mechanical structure, the plumbing systems, the electrical system, the esthetic appearance, and so on. From these descriptions, the architect is able to predict the strength of the walls and floors, the ease of use for the inhabitant, the cost of the materials, and so on. Some of these predictions can be made using calculations backed up by a knowledge of the materials used. Others are estimates based on the expectations of the preferences of the inhabitants or even esthetic judgments based on an artist's impression. Still other estimates are based on previous experience. Whatever the prediction technique, if we cannot provide some kind of prediction of the product properties based on a product specification, then we have no clue what the product will do in advance of building it. And in that case, we are not engineering the product but we are growing it. The product then evolves with experience.

Engineering involves a feed-forward loop from specification to product properties. Product evolution, by contrast, involves a feedback loop from experience with the product back to an improved product specification. Both processes happen in the life of any product. We are concerned here with the feed-forward part: predicting product properties from a product specification. How can we use the description techniques discussed in this book to predict product properties?

First, the environment models are not used to derive product properties but to express assumptions about the environment. We need the environment models to provide the system engineering argument that the SuD together with its environment creates the desired emergent behavior of the composite system. This is part of engineering at a higher level. Presumably, the business solution specification has been used by business designers to argue that this solution will improve the achievement of the current business goals. As indicated in Figure 23.6, the software design activity has resulted in more refined models of the business environment. Using these more refined models, we can refine the system engineering argument.

Second, the decomposition specification of the SuD should be used to argue that a product that implements this decomposition will satisfy the functional software specification. Minimally, the decomposition is specified by means of a communication diagram. In a heavyweight approach, all the functions, behavior, and communications of all components are specified in detail. Which tools are available to produce an argument that the decomposition realizes the desired properties?

Engineering knowledge. We can use knowledge based on our experience designing similar products. This experience is built up by the engineer and extended by exchanging experiences with other engineers in professional meetings and in the professional literature. It may also be extended by visits to sites where similar products are built. The reasoning is:

> Products with this kind of decomposition usually have properties *P.*
> Since this product will have this kind of decomposition,
> It will probably have properties *P.*

The role of description techniques such as treated in this book is to ascertain informally that the current system is similar to the ones that the engineer knows of. To do this, the specification language should allow the representation of the system structure so that the engineer can see its differences from and similarities to other systems.

Throw-away prototyping. We can simply build a prototype of the system and experiment with it to see if the prototype has the desired functional properties. The reasoning now is:

> Since the prototype has properties *P,*
> And the prototype is similar to the final product,
> The final product probably has properties *P.*

The role of description techniques is to write a specification from which we can build or generate a prototype. To do this, the system specification should have a precise execution semantics and, preferably, there should be a tool that can generate a prototype from a specification.

Model execution. We can describe the model in a language so that it can be executed by a machine. Statemate is one example of a tool that provides an executable specification environment. Now the reasoning is:

> Since the model execution has properties *P,*
> If the system implements this model exactly,
> Then the system will have properties *P.*

The role of description techniques is to write a specification of the SuD that can be executed. To do this, the specification language should have an execution semantics and there should be a tool that can execute the specification according to this semantics.

Model checking. We can describe the decomposition formally as a finite set of states and state transitions, formalize the desired properties, and then check by exhaustive search whether the state transition graph satisfies these properties. There are tools, called model checkers, that can do this for us. The engineering argument is:

Since the state transition graph has properties *P*,
If the system implements this graph correctly,
Then the system will have properties *P*.

The role of description techniques is to write a specification of the SuD from which a finite state transition graph can be generated. Preferably, there should be a tool that can generate a state transition graph from the specification and that is suitable as a model checker.

Theorem-proving. We can specify the decomposition in a formal logical language with an effective proof system and derive the desired SuD properties as theorems. The argument now is:

Since the decomposition has been proved to have properties *P*,
If the system correctly implements this decomposition,
Then the system will have properties *P*.

The role of description techniques is to write the specification of the SuD so that logical inferences can be drawn from it. To do this, the specification language should come with a formal logic and a theorem-proving tool.

We can use different approaches for different parts of the system. For safety-critical systems, we may want to use model execution, model checking, or theorem-proving. For systems with a complex user interface, we may want to use throw-away prototyping. And in all cases, these approaches are supplemented by engineering knowledge.

23.5 Formality and Precision

Software engineering notations should be as simple as possible—not simpler, but certainly not more complex. Notations get in the way of the software engineer when they are too complex for their purpose. More often than not, the semantics of complex notations is undefined, ambiguous, or ill-understood. As a result, such a notation is:

◆ Difficult to use because there are no coherent guidelines

◆ Easy to use because every model satisfies the fuzzy criteria for good models

◆ Difficult to understand because it contains too many symbols whose meanings are undefined, ambiguous, or ill-understood

◆ Easy to understand because every interpretation is compatible with the fuzzy semantics of the notation

There is room for notations with semantics ranging from informal to formal, but in all cases the semantics of a notation should be defined with a precision that matches its intended use. A description is **precise** if it expresses as briefly as possible what is intended. It is **formal** if it uses a language for which formal meaning-preserving manipulation rules have been defined. For example, a description written in elementary arithmetic is formal. The description

$$a + 3 = b \qquad \text{where } a, b \in N$$

is formal. An example of a formal manipulation rule is the $x + y \Rightarrow y + x$, which allows us to derive the description

$$3 + a = b$$

Note that this manipulation rule is defined only in terms of the form, or more generally the physical appearance, of the symbol occurrences. Second, note that the manipulation rule is sound with respect to some intended semantics, namely the semantics in which the letters stand for natural numbers and the + stands for addition. The game of formalization consists of separating symbol manipulation from meaning, at the same time maintaining a relationship between the two by demanding soundness of the manipulation rules. This allows us to manipulate symbols without regard for their meaning, but by looking only at their physical form, which is a prerequisite for automation. It also allows us to generalize the applicability of the notation by assigning different possible meanings to it, taking care to choose only meanings that are respected by the manipulation rules.

The notations discussed in this book range from essentially informal to formalizable. The mission statement is essentially informal; statecharts, by contrast, can be formalized. Formalization consists of a boring part and an interesting part.

◆ The boring part is fixing the precise manipulation rules for the notation. The demand of formality forces us to introduce a certain amount of bookkeeping and bureaucracy in the notation that is great for computers but boring for people.

◆ The interesting part is fixing the precise semantics of the notation. In this book, I discuss the issues involved in the semantics of statecharts and communication diagrams.

The emphasis in this book is on precision, not on formality. We can give a very precise but informal mission statement of a system. On the other hand, we can give a formal but imprecise description of a system. For example, we may draw a statechart with a formally defined execution semantics of desired system behavior and include a nondeterministic choice at every point where we are not sure what the system should do; and we can include descriptions of superfluous behavior that will never occur in practice because the relevant guards will always be false. Such a description is formal but imprecise.

It is possible to use formalization as a tool to achieve precision, but there are numerous examples of formal specifications that are wrong. The attempt to be precise should always have priority over the attempt to be formal.

23.6 SUMMARY

The design approach of NYAM separates decisions about system decomposition into those based on the functional requirements, those based on the use environment, and those based on the implementation platform (see Chapter 19). The functional requirements and use environment model, in turn, are derived from a previous design of a composite system. In our examples, the composite system is a business. Design decisions thus take place at three levels:

1. The business
2. The SuD
3. The decomposition of the SuD

At each of these levels, the systems that we encounter have desired functions, desired behavior, and desired communications that we can use the notations described in this book to create specifications for.

The user of the notation has a range of weightiness choices from flyweight to heavyweight use. The choice made depends on the kind of functionality of the SuD and on the intended use of the notation: sketching desired properties, building a prototype, executing the model, checking the model, or proving a theorem.

There is no particular order in which the specifications are written, but there is a general principle that in order to make a lower-level system specification we need to produce more refined environment descriptions first. The specifications are used to coordinate and plan the building or buying process and also to predict properties of the finished product. In these processes, the use of notations should focus on precision before formality.

Appendices

- ◆ Appendix A describes a Training Information System. This is a classic data-intensive information system.

- ◆ Appendix B describes an Electronic Ticket System. This is an example of a communication-intensive system that manipulates virtual entities.

- ◆ Appendix C describes a heating controller. This is a simple example of a behavior-intensive system that is used as illustration in many chapters.

- ◆ Appendix D describes an elevator controller. This is a less trivial, behavior-intensive system with a nontrivial dictionary.

- ◆ Appendix E contains answers to selected exercises in the text.

The specifications in Appendices A to D have different structures. This has been done on purpose to illustrate that there is not a single specification structure that suits all kinds of systems.

A Training Information System

A.1 Case Description

Each second and third working day of a month, a large multinational company provides introductory training to employees who have joined the company in the previous month, called joiners. In this course, a member of the Group Board and members of the National Board give talks, and teachers introduce the joiners to the philosophy and operational processes of the company. Usually the joiners are divided into four to nine groups, which follow the course in parallel. The Training Information System (TIS) supports the course coordinator and other personnel of the Training Department in preparing and organizing the course.

The course coordinator uses the system to retrieve joiners from the Personnel Information System through an online connection. On request, the system assigns the joiners to groups for the 2 days, trying to avoid allocating joiners from the same office to the same group and trying to ensure that the groups on the second day consist as much as possible of people who were not in the same group on the first day. This way, each participant meets as many people from different offices as possible.

On the request of the coordinator, the TIS prints the lists of participants per day per room and includes the total number of people on each list. The coordinator then gives these lists to the speakers. The system also prints badges, which are prepared the day before the course starts.

Before the course starts, all badges plus course material are laid out on a desk. Between 7:30 and 8:30 in the morning of the first day, joiners arrive and collect their badge and other material. Usually, some people turn up who are not on any list; these were not yet registered in the personnel information system when data were downloaded. These are directed to a registration desk, where their data must be entered in the system and a badge printed. The system also allocates these unexpected participants to a group.

The day after the course, all badges that are left are collected by a secretary, who uses the TIS to register absenteeism. The registration desk sends the participation record to the Personnel Information System.

At any time during the course, a speaker may request that the coordinator provide an updated list of participants for his or her course. The coordinator then prints this list on the spot and hands it to the speaker.

The specification has the following structure.

Business context.
◆ Business goal tree
◆ Workflows

High-level system functionality.
◆ Mission statement
◆ System-level context diagram

Subject domain. Entity-relationship diagram

System functions. For each system function:
◆ Service description
◆ Transaction descriptions
◆ Context diagram

A.2 Business Context

The goal tree (Figure A.1) terminates in activities to be performed in the redesigned business context. This is part of the business solution specification (see Chapter 5, Figure 5.3). The coordination and registration workflows are more detailed models of this business solution. They may be made as part of the analysis of the software problem analysis or in a parallel detailed business design process. The upload activity is not modeled in an activity diagram because it consists of an iteration over a single activity. The activities at the leaves of the goal tree are stated in more general terms

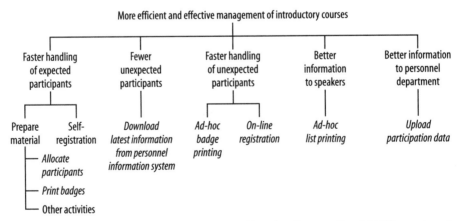

Figure A.1 Goal tree of the TIS business context. (See also Chapters 5 and 14.) The root goal is one of the goals of the training department. The tree is the outcome of a business design process in which a proposal for a new way of organizing introductory courses was proposed. The activities printed in italics are to be supported by the TIS.

than the activities in the workflow models, but it is straightforward to trace the one to the other.

The activities in the workflows are performed by entities in the environment of the TIS: the coordinator and the registration desk (Figures A.2 and A.3). These can be found in the context diagram.

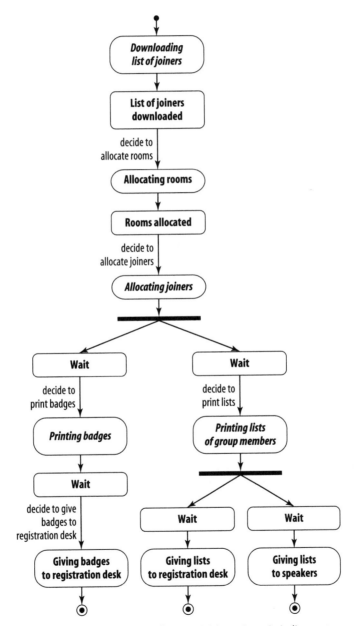

Figure A.2 Coordinator workflow. Activities written in italics are to be supported by the TIS.

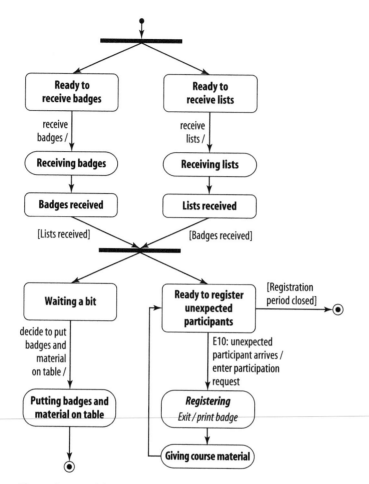

Figure A.3 Workflow at the registration desk. Activities written in italics are to be supported by the TIS. (See also Chapter 22.) A statechart model of this workflow is discussed in Chapter 14. When the workflow is in state Badges received when the parallel branch enters state Lists received, the transition to the parallel bar pseudo-node will be taken. At the same time, because [Badges received] is true, the transition from Lists received to the parallel bar pseudo-node will be taken. This combines in a transition to {Waiting a bit, Ready to register unexpected participants}.

A.3 **High-Level System Functionality—Mission and Context**

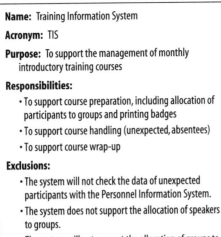

Name: Training Information System

Acronym: TIS

Purpose: To support the management of monthly introductory training courses

Responsibilities:
- To support course preparation, including allocation of participants to groups and printing badges
- To support course handling (unexpected, absentees)
- To support course wrap-up

Exclusions:
- The system will not check the data of unexpected participants with the Personnel Information System.
- The system does not support the allocation of speakers to groups.
- The system will not support the allocation of groups to rooms.

Figure A.4 Mission statement of the TIS, summarizing the function refinement tree and relating TIS functions to business goals. (See also Chapter 5.) This statement was actually made after the function refinement tree was made. The phrase in the Purpose "the management of monthly introductory training courses" summarizes the activities printed in italics in the goal tree.

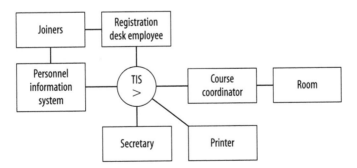

Figure A.5 Context diagram relating the TIS to entities in the business environment. (See also Chapter 18.) Figure 18.7 shows a structured version of the context diagram, which brings out the information-provision functionality of the TIS. Chapter 19, Figure 19.4 shows a layered version, indicating who gives a service to whom. The choice of which presentation of the context diagram to use is determined by the intended readership.

A.4 **Subject Domain**

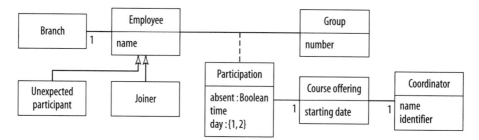

Figure A.6 Subject domain model. Participation is really a ternary relationship among Employee, Room, and Course, but we assume that at any moment the TIS contains data about one course offering only—so the Course entity type has been dropped from the model. There is an unstated constraint that day 1 and 2 are always the second and third working days of the month.

A.5 **System Functions**

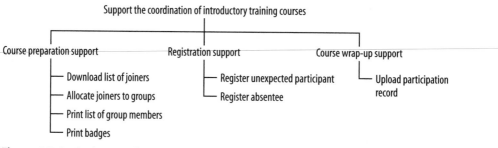

Figure A.7 Desired system functions. (See also Chapter 6.) Each function can be linked to a business goal in Figure A.1. The layout of the tree has no implication for the structure of the system but is chosen to be meaningful to stakeholders. Chapter 6, Figure 6.4 gives an alternative layout.

Download joiners

Service description

Triggering event: The coordinator requests to download list of joiners from the Personnel Information System.

Delivered service: Download the list of people who have joined the company since the previous training.

Assumptions: The data in the Personnel Information System accurately reflects the situation with a time lag of not more than one working day.

Transaction descriptions

Event	Stimulus	Current system state	Response	Intended action	Next system state
E1 Time to download list of joiners.	Receive event "download list of joiners" from coordinator.	System contains no list of joiners.	Send event "send me a list of joiners" to Personnel Information System.	Personnel Information System knows that list of joiners is requested.	System is waiting for list of joiners.
E2 Personnel Information System sends list of joiners.	Receive list of joiners.	System is waiting for list of joiners.	Confirm to coordinator.	Coordinator knows that list has been downloaded.	System contains list of joiners.
E3 System has been waiting for list of joiners too long.	A timer times out.	System is waiting for list of joiners.	Inform coordinator of problem.	Coordinator knows that list has not been downloaded.	System contains no list of joiners.

Decomposition

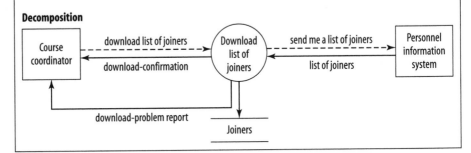

Figure A.8 The function Download. (Service descriptions are discussed in Chapter 7.)

Upload participant record

Service description

Triggering event: The coordinator requests an upload list of joiners to the personnel information system.

Delivered service: Upload to the Personnel Information System the list of people who participated in the training.

Assumptions: The Personnel Information System is able to process data about unexpected participants, including any remaining errors in that data.

Transaction descriptions

Event	Stimulus	Current system state	Response	Intended action	Next system state
E4 Time to upload participation record.	Receive request "upload list of joiners" from coordinator	System contains participation record, and participation record not sent before.	Send participation record to Personnel Information System.	Personnel information system receives participation record.	System contains participation record; System is waiting for upload confirmation.
E5 Personnel information system sends upload confirmation.	TIS receives upload confirmation.	System contains participation record; System is waiting for upload confirmation.	Send upload confirmation to coordinator.	Coordinator knows that upload succeeded.	System contains participation record; Participation record sent.
E6 System is waiting for upload confirmation too long.	A timer times out.	System contains participation record; System is waiting for upload confirmation.	Inform coordinator of problem	Coordinator knows that list has not been uploaded.	System contains participation record; Participation record not sent.

Decomposition

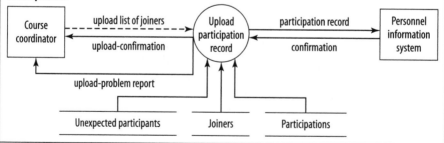

Figure A.9 The function Upload.

Allocate joiners to groups

Service description

Delivered service: TIS allocates all joiners to groups, subject to the following constraints:
- In each group, as many people as possible should come from different branches.
- In each group of day 2, as many people as possible should not have participated in the same group in day 1.
- A group should fit in a room.

If there is not enough room, TIS notifies the coordinator of this.

Triggering event: Coordinator requests to allocate joiners

Relevant assumptions about the environment: None

Transaction descriptions

Event	Stimulus	Current system state	Response	Intended action	Next system state
E7 Coordinator requests to allocate joiners to groups	Receive request "allocate joiners" from coordinator	System contains list of joiners, list of available rooms and their size. There are enough seats.	Create list of participations, subject to the constraints listed above.	Obligation for joiners to participate in groups is created.	System contains list of participations.
E7 Coordinator requests to allocate joiners to groups	Receive request "allocate joiners" from coordinator.	System contains list of joiners, list of available rooms and their size. There are not enough seats.	Send problem report to coordinator.	Coordinator understands what the problem is.	(Same state.)

Decomposition

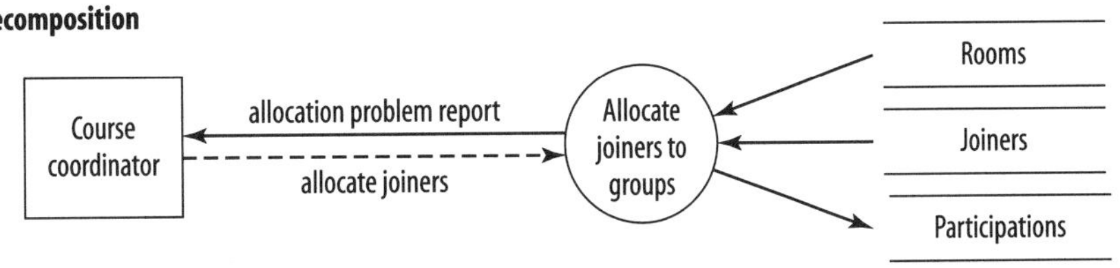

Figure A.10 The function Allocate joiners to groups.

Print badges

Service description

Delivered service: TIS prints badges for all participants. If there are insufficient badges in the printer, TIS asks the coordinator to put in more.

External entities involved: Course coordinator

Triggering event: Course coordinator requests to print badges.

Relevant assumptions about the environment: None

Transaction descriptions

Event	Stimulus	Current system state	Response	Intended action	Next system state
E8 Course coordinator requests that badges be printed.	Receive request "print badges" from coordinator	System contains list of participations	Send "badge data" to printer.	Coordinator gets complete set of printed badges.	(Same state)

Decomposition

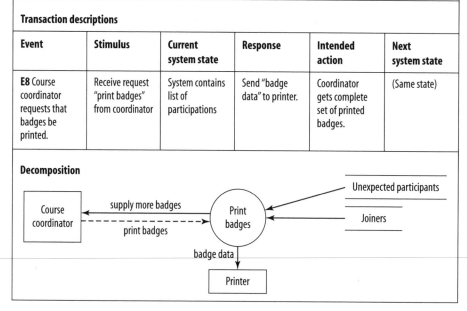

Figure A.11 The function Print badges.

Print list of group members

Service description

Delivered service: Print a list of members and the total number of members, one list for each group.

External entities involved: Course coordinator.

Triggering event: Course coordinator requests to print group lists.

Relevant assumptions about the environment: None.

Transaction descriptions

Event	Stimulus	Current system state	Response	Intended action	Next system state
E9 Course coordinator requests list of group members.	Receive request to print group lists.	System contains list of participations.	Send formatted and totalled group lists to printer.	Course coordinator gets lists of group members.	(Same state)

Decomposition

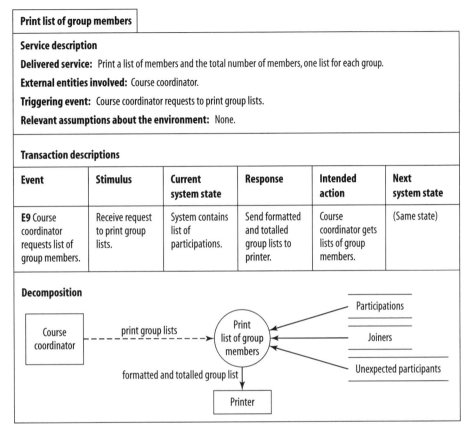

Figure A.12 The function Print list of group members.

Register unexpected participant

Service description

Delivered service: If there is still room, register an employee not on the list of joiners for the course, allocate the employee to a group and print badge.

External entities involved: Registration desk personnel

Triggering event: Unexpected participant arrives at registration desk.

Relevant assumptions about the environment: None

Transaction descriptions

Event	Stimulus	Current system state	Response	Intended action	Next system state
E10 Unexpected participant arrives at registration desk.	Data of unexpected participant received from registration desk.	System contains list of participations; there is still room, according to the data in the system.	Add participant to a group, subject to the constraints (Figure A.10); confirm to registration desk.	Participant knows he or she is registered.	System contains updated list of participants.
E10 Unexpected participant arrives at registration desk.	Data of unexpected participant received from registration desk.	System contains list of participations; there is no room left, according to the data in the system.	Inform registration desk.	Participant knows he or she cannot register.	System contains same list of participants.

Decomposition

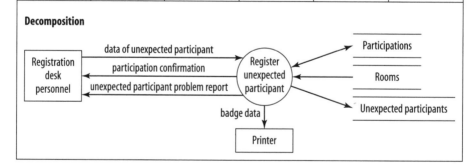

Figure A.13 The function Register unexpected participant.

Register absentee					
Service description					
Delivered service: Register absence of a joiner in the participation list.					
External entities involved: Secretary					
Triggering event: Request from secretary					
Relevant assumptions about the environment: None					

Transaction descriptions

Event	Stimulus	Current system state	Response	Intended action	Next system state
E11 Secretary identifies badge not collected by joiner.	Data about absentee received.	System contains participation record.	Confirm data.	Secretary knows that non-participation has been registered.	System contains updated participation record.

Decomposition

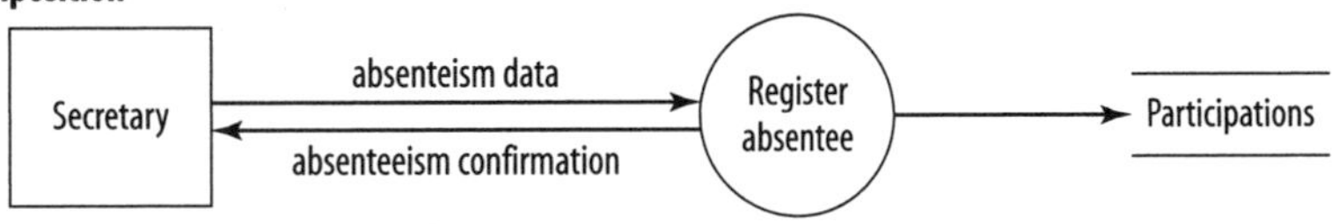

Figure A.14 The function Register absentee.

A.6 Requirements-Level Architecture

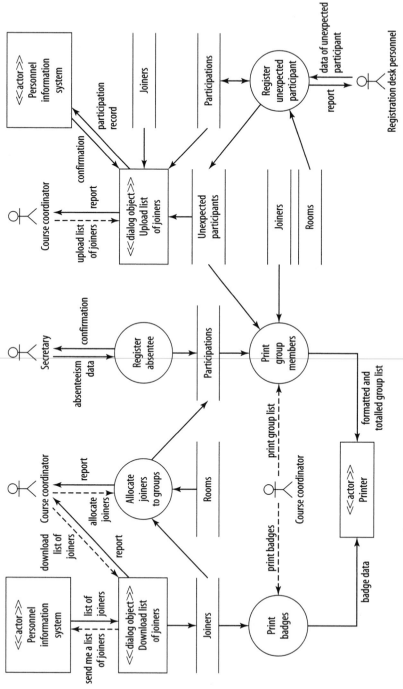

Figure A.15 Communication diagram of the requirements-level architecture that contains all the fragments shown in the previous figures, plus a few user-interface objects. It uses a Von Neumann style. All processes in the diagram should be specified in a few sentences. Some, involving several transactions, can be documented using state transition diagrams for the dialogs with the user.

An Electronic Ticket System

B.1 Case Description

The Electronic Ticket System (ETS) is a software system by which travelers can purchase a railway ticket with a smartcard when it is put into their Personal Digital Assistants (PDAs). The ticket is a virtual entity that can be created on the smartcard itself. Payment is made through a wireless connection with the computer system of the railway company, which itself is connected to the computer systems of a clearing house and a trust center. In our case study, the ETS does not authenticate travelers or conductors. We assume that they are authenticated by some other software system running on their PDAs.

The specification has the following structure.

Activities to be supported. Ticket workflow

Desired functionality.
- Mission statement
- Function refinement tree
- Service description
- Other required properties

Subject domain.
- Entity model
- Some rules for the subject domain
- Subject domain dictionary

Desired ETS behavior.
- Stimulus-response pairs
- Ticket-selling scenario

Architectures.
- Requirements-level architecture
- Allocation of data to data stores
- Physical network

B.2 **Activities to Be Supported**

The relevant composite system consists of the ETS, travelers, conductors, banks, and clearing houses. All these entities, including the ETS, must interact to realize this desired behavior. The entities in the composite system each have their own goal, but there is also a shared goal—to sell and use rights to transport by the railway company. We can draw an activity diagram of the workflow of a ticket as it passes through several states when it is owned and used by a traveler, as shown in Figure B.1.

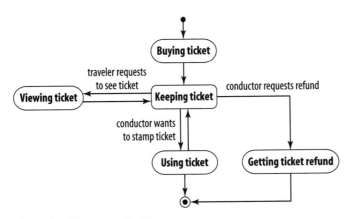

Figure B.1 Workflow of a ticket.

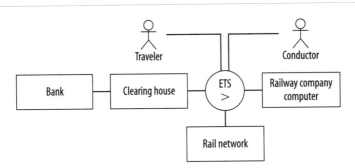

Figure B.2 Context diagram, showing the composite system of which the ETS is a part. (See also Chapter 15.) See Chapter 18 for a structured version of this context diagram.

B.3 Desired Functionality

Name of the system: Electronic Ticket System (ETS)

Purpose: To provide capability to buy and use tickets of a railway company using a Personal Digital Assistant and a smart card

Composition: ETS consists of software distributed over the traveler's smart cart and PDA, the conductor's PDA and a central computer of the railway company

Responsibilities of the system:
- To support ticket buying
- To support ticket usage
- To support ticket refunding

Exclusions:
- The system does not perform travel planning.
- Each ticket sold by ETS is for one person and one trip (single or return).

Figure B.3 Mission of the ETS. (See also Chapter 5.)

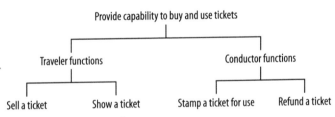

Figure B.4 Function refinement tree.

Name: Sell a ticket.

Triggering event: Traveler requests to buy a ticket.

Delivered service: Allow a traveler to buy a ticket at any time and place chosen by the traveler.

Name: Show a ticket.

Triggering event: Traveler requests to view a ticket.

Delivered service: Display ticket attributes to the user.

Name: Stamp a ticket for use.

Triggering event: Conductor requests to stamp an unused part of a ticket for use.

Delivered service: Mark the requested part of the ticket as used.

Name: Refund a ticket.

Triggering event: Conductor requests to refund an unused part of a ticket.

Delivered service: Cause the unused part of a ticket to be refunded to the traveler and make this part of the ticket invalid.

Figure B.5 Service descriptions. (Used in Chapter 9 to determine the subject-domain boundary.) We assume that travelers and conductors are not authenticated by the ETS (but by some other software system running on their PDAs).

- A traveler cannot get a ticket without paying for it.
- The price of a ticket is withdrawn from the bank account associated with the smart card.
- A traveler who has paid for a ticket gets it.
- A refunded ticket cannot be used any more.
- A fully used ticket cannot be refunded.
- It is not possible to use a ticket twice.

Figure B.6 Other required properties.

B.4 **Subject Domain**

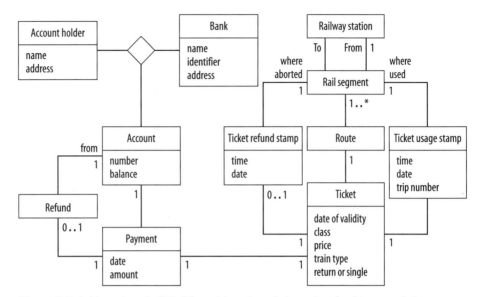

Figure B.7 Subject-domain ERD. (The subject-domain boundary for this example is discussed in Chapter 9.) Because travelers and conductors are not authenticated by the ETS, the system cannot identify them and so they are not part of the subject domain.

- All segments of a route should be connected.
- The price of a ticket depends upon the route and attributes of the ticket, such as class.
- A ticket can only be used on a segment for which it is valid.
  - For all *u:* Ticket_usage_stamp, u.where_used ∈ u.ticket.route.rail segment.
- A ticket can only be refunded for segments for which it is valid.
  - For all *r:* Ticket_refund_stamp, r.where_aborted ∈ r.ticket.route.rail_segment.

Figure B.8 Some rules for the subject domain.

> **Railway station**   Entity type name. Entity used to bound *rail segments*. This may be a physical entity consisting of platforms where passengers can enter or leave a train. It can also be a mathematical point used to bound a segment. For example, the point where the line of rail passes the Dutch-German border is a "railway station," because one can buy a ticket to that point. It can also be a collection of physical stations. For example, a ticket to "Berlin U-Bahn" is a ticket to any subway station in Berlin.
>
> **Rail segment**   Entity type name. A shortest path between two railway stations. Segments are directed and are identified by the two stations they connect. So all shortest paths through the rail network from A to B are considered the same segment, called AB; and all shortest paths from B to A are the same segment, called BA; and AB and BA are two different segments.
>
> **Route**   Entity type name. A path through the rail network that consists of a connected series of *rail segments*, where each segment occurs at most once in the route.
>
> **Ticket**   Entity type name. A lexical item owned by a passenger, that represents the passenger's right to travel a route by train (as far as it is not stamped).
>
> **Ticket refund stamp**   Entity type name. A lexical entity related to a *ticket* and a *railway segment s*. In the presence of this stamp, the ticket does not represent a right to travel a route, but it represents the right on a refund of the price of the railway segment *s*, and all subsequent segments of the route.
>
> **Ticket usage stamp**   Entity type name. A lexical entity related to a *ticket* and a *railway segment s*, which represents the fact that the ticket has been used for all segments of its route up to and including the segments where it is stamped. Since we only consider tickets for one trip (single or return), the ticket does not anymore represent the right to travel this route up to and including the current segment, but it still represents the right to travel the remaining segments of the route.

Figure B.9 Subject-domain dictionary.

B.5   Desired ETS Behavior

Event	Current domain state	Desired action	Next domain state
Request to buy ticket	Any	Ticket created and paid for	Ticket and payment exist
Request to see tickets	Any	All tickets are displayed	Unchanged
Request to use ticket for a rail segment	Ticket exists and is valid for that rail segment	Create ticket stamp for that rail segment	Ticket exists and ticket usage stamp exists for this rail segment and ticket
Request to refund ticket	Ticket exists and not completely used	Create refund stamp	Ticket refunded and ticket is no longer valid

Figure B.10 Stimulus-response pairs of the ETS. (See also Chapter 14.) Each stimulus-response pair can be related to a desired system function (the function that they realize) and to the context diagram (the channels through which stimuli arrive and responses leave the system). The responses are not atomic. Each stimulus-response pair can be refined into a collection of atomic transactions. For example, the ticket-selling response is worked out as a dialog in Figure B.11.

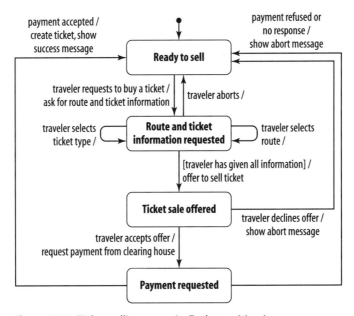

Figure B.11 Ticket-selling scenario. Each transition is a stimulus-response pair of the system.

B.6 **Architectures**

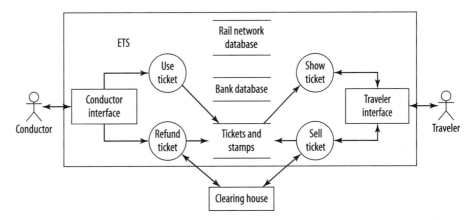

Figure B.12 Requirements-level architecture for supporting the four system functions. (See also Chapter 19.) Not all read accesses to data stores are shown. This is a Von Neumann style containing data transformations and stores and some user-interface objects. Chapter 19, Figures 19.14 and 19.15 show a pure functional and a pure object-oriented decomposition, respectively.

Sell ticket.
  • See Figure B.11.

Show ticket.
  • Retrieve all tickets from Tickets and display them.

Use ticket.
  • Look in Tickets for a ticket for the current route.
  • Create a ticket usage stamp for this ticket and the current rail segment (see Figure B.7).

Refund ticket.
  • Find ticket to be refunded and find all its ticket usage stamps.
  • Create a ticket refund stamp for the remaining part of the ticket and cause a refund on the bank account associated with the ticket.

Figure B.13 Specifications of the transformations in Figure B.12.

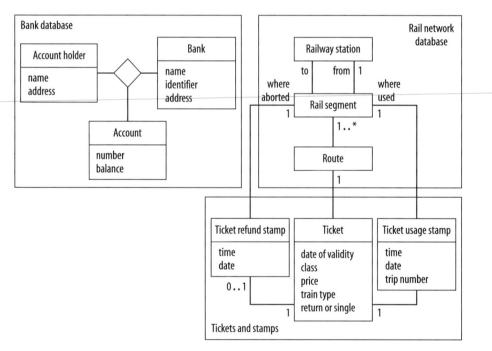

Figure B.14 Allocation of data about the subject domain to data stores. Data about related subject-domain entities are grouped in one store, and the volatile data about tickets are factored out. The system does not need to store data about payments or refunds. Note that we have omitted the initialization functionality of the databases. This should be added in a refinement of the specification.

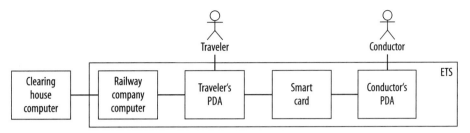

Figure B.15 A physical network architecture.

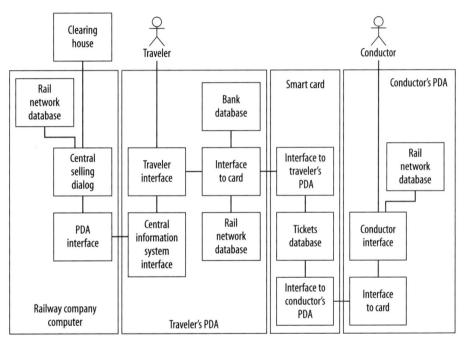

Figure B.16 Allocation of requirements-level components to physical components. This illustrates that the relationship between the requirements-level architecture and implementation architectures can be many-to-many. Interfaces between the physical components are added.

A Heating Control System

C.1 Case Description

In a fruit-juice production plant, storage tanks and heating tanks are connected by a system of pipes. To produce a batch of mixed juice, ingredient fruit juices are transported from storage to the heating tanks, where they are heated according to a recipe to a temperature for a certain duration. The heating process is started and monitored by a human operator. Your job is to design the heating-control software. This case is based on an example of Shlaer and Mellor (1992).

The specification has the following structure.

Business context.
◆ Business goal tree
◆ Operator workflow

Mission and context.
◆ Mission statement
◆ Context diagram
◆ Assumptions

Desired functionality.
◆ Function refinement tree
◆ Service descriptions

Subject domain.
◆ Entity-relationship diagram
◆ State transition diagram of heater behavior

Desired emergent behavior of composite system.
◆ Primary event-action pair
◆ Transactional event-action list of emergent behavior
◆ State transition diagrams of emergent behavior

Desired system behavior. Stimulus-response list

Alternative requirements-level architectures.

◆ Von Neumann–style architecture without objects
— Data flow diagram
— State transition diagram of control process
◆ Von Neumann–style architecture with objects
— Communication diagram
— State transition diagrams of control objects
◆ Pure object-oriented style architecture
— Communication diagram
— Sequence diagram
— Collaboration diagram
— Static structure diagram

C.2 Business Context

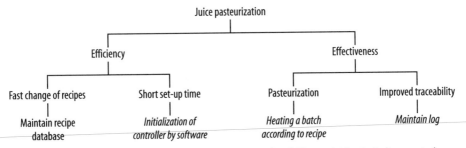

Figure C.1 Business goal tree. (See also Chapters 5 and 14.) The activities in italics are to be supported by the control software.

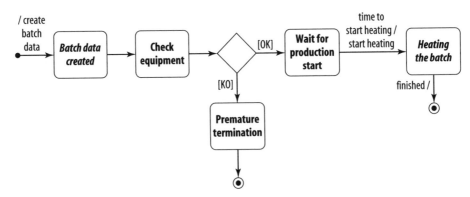

Figure C.2 Workflow of the operator of the juice-heating controller. (See also Chapter 14.)

C.3 Mission and Context

Name: Juice heating controller

Purpose: To control the heating process of fruit juices in a heating tank

Responsibilities:
- To initialize itself with batch data and heat the batch according to recipe
- To report on the heating process
- To maintain safe conditions in a tank

Exclusions:
- Filling the storage tanks with juice
- Transferring pasteurized juice to the canning line

Figure C.3 Mission statement for a heating controller. (See also Chapter 6.)

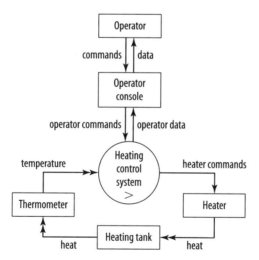

Figure C.4 Context diagram of the heating controller. (See also Chapter 18.) The controller has directive functionality and is connected to the subject domain by a heater and thermometer and to the operator by a console.

• The operator works according to the operator workflow.

• The operator only gives the start command when the batch is in its heating tanks.

• The heater of a tank never breaks.

• The controller is connected to the heaters of the tanks.

• The thermometer of a tank never breaks.

• The controller is connected to the thermometers of the tanks.

Figure C.5 Some fallible assumptions made about the environment of the heating controller. (See also Chapter 14.) These assumptions must be true if the behavior of the controller is to produce desired emergent behavior. Some of these assumptions are likely to be falsified, so they must be dropped in a later version of the design. When we drop these assumptions, we must figure out whether the software can discover that they are falsified (e.g., that the heater or thermometer are broken) and, if so, add alarms for this.

C.4 **Desired Functionality**

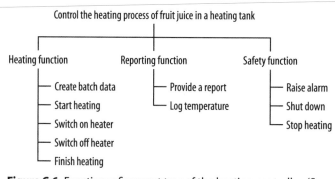

Figure C.6 Function refinement tree of the heating controller. (See also Chapters 6, 14, and 16.) The single primary function is heating; the other two functions are secondary. The tree already shows the refinement of the primary function into more elementary subfunctions that we will identify later when we analyze the interactions between the controller and its environment that take place during an execution of this function.

In the rest of this appendix, we deal with the heating function (P1) only.

Name: P1. Heat batch according to recipe.

Triggering event: Operator commands "start heating batch *b* according to recipe."

Delivered service: Upon reception of this command, the controller ensures that a heating process takes place in the heating tanks in which *b* is stored, according to the recipe of *b*.

Assumptions: There is a batch in the heating tank.

Name: Provide a report.

Triggering event: Operator requests report about batch *b*.

Delivered service: The controller produces a report of the temperature log of the heating process of *b*.

Name: Log temperature.

Triggering event: When an execution of P1 starts, and then every 10 seconds during this execution of P1

Delivered service: The controller records the measured temperature in each tank in which *b* is stored.

Name: P4.1 Raise an alarm.

Triggering event: The pressure in heating tank *t* rises above a critical value.

Delivered service: The controller causes a bell to start ringing and displays a problem report in the operator console.

Name: P4.2 Shut down.

Triggering event: Pressure in heating tank *t* rises above a critical value and the heating process P1 is going on.

Delivered service: The controller causes a bell to start ringing, displays a problem report in the operator console, terminates the heating process, and ensures that the pressure in *t* falls.

Name: Stop heating.

Triggering event: The operator requests to stop heating a batch *b*, which is an instance of P1 now going on.

Delivered service: The controller ensures that the tanks in which *b* is heated, stop heating.

Figure C.7 Heating service description. (See also Chapter 7; P1 is discussed in Chapter 14.) Descriptions of secondary services refer to other functions; primary services do not refer to other functions.

C.5 Subject Domain

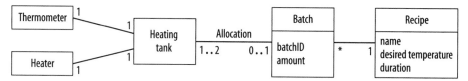

Figure C.8 The function descriptions presuppose a model of the subject domain that consists of heating tanks, batches, and recipes. (See also Chapters 8 and 15.) This is an ERD of the subject domain of the primary juice-heating controller function: Heat batch according to recipe. The subject domain of the entire controller is the union of the subject domains of each function.

Heater behavior

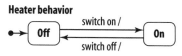

Figure C.9 Assumed behavior of a heater. An example of the kind of discrete behavior presupposed in the subject domain. Only if assumptions like these are valid can the controller achieve its purpose.

C.6 Desired Emergent Behavior of Composite System

Event	Desired action
Operator gives command to start heating batch *b*.	A heating process for the heating tanks of *b* is started. If at the start of the process, temperature in a tank is too low, the heater of that tank is switched on. When during the process, a tank becomes 5 degrees Celsius warmer than the desired temperature, its heater must be switched off. When it becomes 5 degrees Celsius colder than the desired temperature, its heater must be switched on. When the heating process has lasted for the duration of the recipe, heating must stop and the operator must be notified of this fact.

Figure C.10 The primary event-action pair of the heating control. (See also Chapter 14.) This is the desired emergent behavior of the composite system, consisting of the controller, operator, heater, and so on, as indicated in the context diagram (Figure C.4). The controller cannot bring about this desired emergent behavior on its own but needs the cooperation of external entities, as listed by the assumptions in Figure C.5.

Event	Subject domain state	Desired action
E1 Operator gives command to start heating batch *b*.		Heaters of tanks of *b* that are below recipe temperature, are switched on.
E2 Temperature in tank *t* rises 5 degrees above recipe temperature.	The juice in *t* is being heated.	The heater of *t* is switched off.
E3 Temperature in tank *t* falls 5 degrees below recipe temperature.	The juice in *t* is being heated.	The heater of *t* is switched on.
E4 The heating duration has passed, counted since the start of heating of *b*.	*b* is being heated.	• Heaters of *b* that are on, are switched off. • Operator is informed.

Figure C.11 Transactional event-action pairs that jointly make up the complex action in Figure C.10. (See also Chapter 14.) This is desired subject domain behavior.

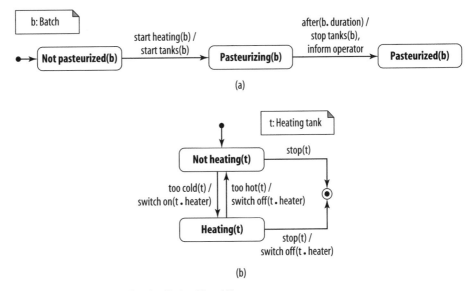

(a)

(b)

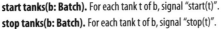
start tanks(b: Batch). For each tank t of b, signal "start(t)".
stop tanks(b: Batch). For each tank t of b, signal "stop(t)".

Figure C.12 Two state transition diagrams that we can use to describe the same behavior as the transactional event list of Figure C.11: (a) desired behavior when batch b is heated and (b) desired behavior when tank t is heated. The diagrams are more informative than the event list because they show that desired subject-domain behavior contains two aggregation levels: at the batch level and at the heating-tank level. We want batch heating to start at the operator's command and to stop when recipe time is over. We want tank heating to occur when the tank is too cold.

C.7 **Desired System Behavior**

Stimulus	Current controller state	Desired response	Next controller state
S1 Operator gives command to start heating batch b	Not heating t and not heating b	Heaters of tanks of b whose measured temperature is below recipe temperature, are switched on	Heating t and heating b
S2 Every 60 seconds	Heating t and measured temperature $>$ desired temperature $+ 5$	Controller switches off the heater of t	Heating t
	Heating t and measured temperature $<$ desired temperature $- 5$	Controller switches on heater of t	Heating t
S4 Timer indicates that recipe time since the start of heating of b has passed	Heating b	• Switch off heaters of b that are on • Inform operator	Not heating b

Figure C.13 Stimulus-response list that describes desired behavior at the interface of the heating controller. (See also Chapter 14.)

C.8 **Alternative Requirements-Level Architectures**

C.8.1 *Von Neumann–Style Architecture without Objects*

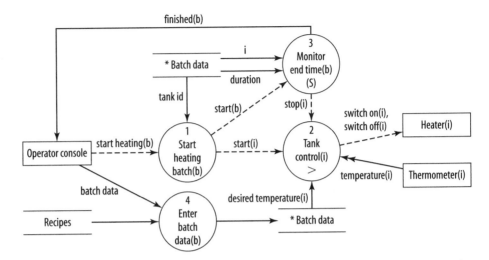

Figure C.14 Von Neumann–style architecture with strict separation of data processing and data storage. (See also Chapter 15.) Note that processes 1 and 3 correspond to the functions Start heating and Monitor end time from the function refinement tree, respectively. The process Tank control(i) encapsulates two functions: Switch on and Switch off. Figure C.15 decomposes Tank control(i).

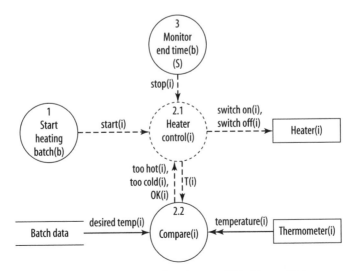

Figure C.15 Decomposition of Tank control(i) in Figure C.14. (See also Chapter 15.) Heater control(i) is defined in Figure C.16.

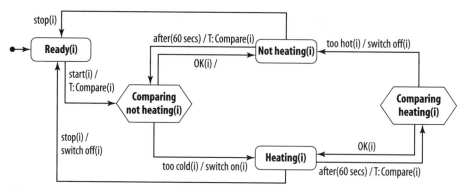

Figure C.16 Specification of Heater control(i) in Figure C.15 using a Mealy diagram without variables. (See also Chapter 15. See Figure C.20 for a version with variables.)

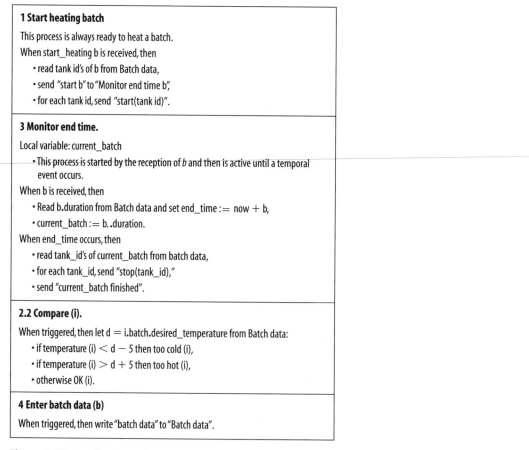

1 Start heating batch

This process is always ready to heat a batch.

When start_heating b is received, then
- read tank id's of b from Batch data,
- send "start b" to "Monitor end time b",
- for each tank id, send "start(tank id)".

3 Monitor end time.

Local variable: current_batch
- This process is started by the reception of b and then is active until a temporal event occurs.

When b is received, then
- Read b.duration from Batch data and set end_time := now + b,
- current_batch := b..duration.

When end_time occurs, then
- read tank_id's of current_batch from batch data,
- for each tank_id, send "stop(tank_id),"
- send "current_batch finished".

2.2 Compare (i).

When triggered, then let d = i.batch.desired_temperature from Batch data:
- if temperature (i) < d − 5 then too cold (i),
- if temperature (i) > d + 5 then too hot (i),
- otherwise OK (i).

4 Enter batch data (b)

When triggered, then write "batch data" to "Batch data".

Figure C.17 Specification of processes 2, 3, 2.2, and 4. (See also Chapter 15.)

The intended execution semantics of the model is:

Step 1. When Start heating batch(b) receives the event start heating(b), it reads the identifiers of the tanks in which b is stored from Batch data, sends the identifier b to Monitor end time, and starts a Tank control(i) instance for each tank in which b is stored (see Figures C.14 and C.17).

Step 2.
- ◆ When it receives a value for b, the process Monitor end time reads the duration of the recipe of b from Batch data, computes the desired end time, and starts watching for that time (see Figure C.17).
- ◆ Each start(i) event is received by a control process Heater control(i) inside the compound process Tank control(i) (see Figure C.15). The control process responds by triggering the data process Compare(i), end enters an unstable state.

Step 3. When triggered, Compare(i) compares the desired temperature of b with the temperature measured by the thermometer of tank i, which is permanently available to it through the time-continuous data flow temperature(i). It sends the answer back to Heater control(i).

Step 4. Reception of too cold or too hot brings Heater behavior(i) into the stable state Heating(i) or Not Heating(i), respectively (see Figures C.16 and C.17).

These four steps, performed in this order, constitute the desired response of the controller to the start heating(b) command. From then on, every 60 seconds, the controller compares the actual with the desired temperature of each heating tank and switches the heaters on and off accordingly. Finally, when the end time is reached, the heaters are switched off if necessary and the operator is informed.

We use a superstep execution semantics with the perfect technology assumption. Thus, when a temporal or external event arrives, the control process is in a stable state, so the stop event cannot arrive in the comparing state. This is good because, in that state, we do not know whether the heater is on or off.

Note that we have discretized a time-continuous controlling process. Switching a heater on or off may be done almost 60 seconds after the point where the stimulus-response list says it should happen.

C.8.2 Von Neumann–Style Architecture with Objects

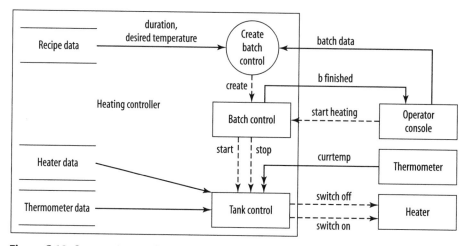

Figure C.18 Communication diagram using a Von Neumann–style architecture. (See also Chapter 19.) Batch control and Tank control are specified in Figures C.19 and C.20. Tank control objects correspond to the Control tank process in the PSA model of Figure C.14. They encapsulate behavior, data processing (comparing values), and the relevant heating data. Batch control objects encapsulate the functions Monitor end time and Start heating batch of Figure C.14. Create batch control corresponds to Enter batch data.

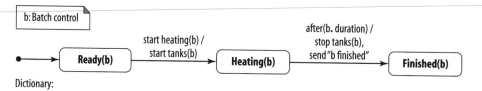

Dictionary:

start_tanks(b: Batch).
   • For all tanks t in b.heating_tank, send start(t, b.recipe.desired_temperature).
stop_tanks(b: Batch).
   • For all tanks t in b.heating_tank, send stop(t).

Figure C.19 Mealy diagram for Batch control in Figure C.18, with local variables. This enforces the desired batch behavior represented in Figure C.12(a).

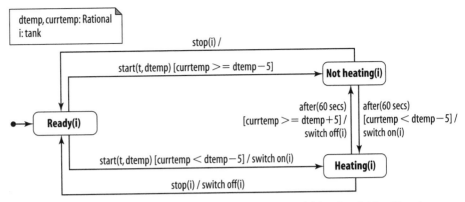

Figure C.20 Mealy diagram for Tank control in Figure C.18 with local variables. (See also Chapter 15.) This enforces desired tank behavior represented in Figure C.12(b).

C.8.3 Pure Object-Oriented Style Architecture

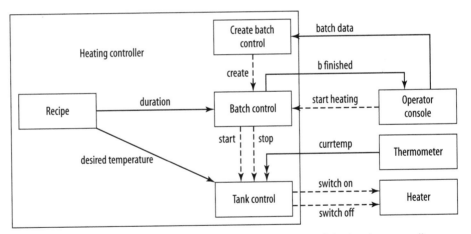

Figure C.21 Requirements-level subject-based decomposition of the heating controller—object-oriented style. (See also Chapter 22.) Batch control and Tank control contain data that in the Von Neumann architecture of Figure C.18 are stored separately in data stores. The behaviors of Batch control and Tank control are unchanged; they are specified in Figures C.19 and C.20. Because in this style we can use objects only, Create batch control is represented by an object class even though it is stateless. Figure C.24 shows a SSD of this architecture that includes objects from the environment to show the relative multiplicity properties of software objects with respect to those external entities.

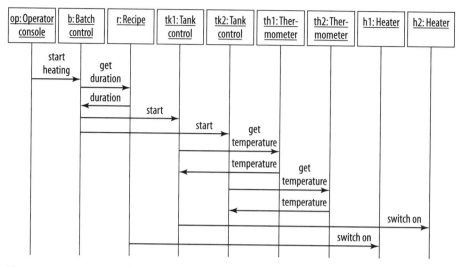

Figure C.22 One possible message-passing scenario caused by the start heating message. (See also Chapter 22.)

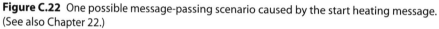

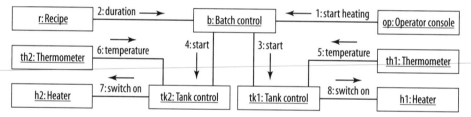

Figure C.23 Collaboration diagram of the scenario of Figure C.22. (See also Chapter 22.)

The intended execution algorithm is:

Step 1. When the Batch_control instance b receives a start heating(b) message, it sends a start(i) message to the tank control software objects for the tanks in which this batch is stored (see Figures C.21 and C.22).

Step 2. When a Tank control instance i receives a start(i) message, it compares its parameter dtemp with its input value currtemp and takes the corresponding transition, sending a switch_on(i.heater.heaterID) message if necessary. This brings the software object in the stable state Heating(i) or Not Heating(i).

These two steps, performed in this order, constitute the desired response of the controller to the start heating(b) command. From then on, every 60 seconds, the controller compares the actual with the desired temperature of each heating tank

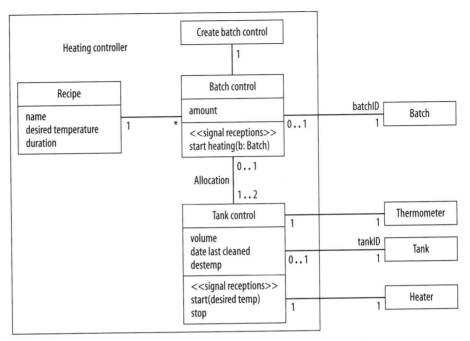

Figure C.24 Static structure diagram of the heating controller and its environment.

and switches the heaters on and off accordingly. Finally, under the control of the **b** object, when the end time is reached, the controller stops, heaters are switched off if necessary, and the operator is informed. The external system behavior of this model is equivalent to that specified by the DFD model if we assume superstep semantics in both cases. In a step semantics, however, the behaviors are different.

An Elevator Control System

D.1 Case Description

An elevator controller must ensure that an elevator system collects and delivers passengers from floor to floor as requested. In this example, the controller must control two elevator cages that can move up and down in two shafts that cross 10 floors. There are floor buttons on the floors by which a passenger can summon an elevator to the floor. Floor buttons indicate the direction in which the passenger wants to travel. There are destination buttons in the elevator cages by which a passenger who is inside an elevator cage can request to be carried to a particular floor. Each floor has a direction indicator for each of the two shafts, which shows the direction of movement of the cage in that shaft. Each cage has a location indicator that tells a passenger at which floor the cage is now.

The specification has the following structure.

Desired functionality.
- Mission statement
- Function refinement tree
- Service descriptions
- Partial context diagram

Subject domain.
- Dictionary
- Entities
- Assumed behavior
- Desired behavior

Alternative requirements-level architectures.
- Functional decomposition, Von Neumann style
  —Data flow diagram
  —Control process

◆ Subject-oriented decomposition, object-oriented style
— Architecture diagrams
— Control processes
— Static structrure diagram fragments

D.2 Desired Functionality

Name: Elevator movement controller

Purpose: To coordinate the movements of a number of elevator cages in order to provide optimal service to passengers waiting for service or traveling in the elevator

Quality of service:
- Each elevator cage should have an average round-trip time of 150 seconds.
- Average round-trip time should be no more than 60 seconds, assuming cage utilization of 80% of the guaranteed load of a cage.

Responsibilities:
- To ensure that, upon request from passengers, the elevator collects and delivers these passengers in a short time
- To ensure that passengers have sufficient information to be able to know when to enter and leave an elevator cage
- To allow and support maintenance activities
- To provide operating information

Exclusions:
- The controller will not take an idle elevator to some home floor.
- The controller will not take the current load of an elevator cage into account.

Figure D.1 Mission statement of the elevator controller. The exclusions have been stated to simplify the problem. Our basic elevator controller will, for example, let a cage stop at a floor to collect passengers, even when the cage is already fully loaded. If upon entry of a person, an elevator cage is loaded too heavily, the hardware is assumed to wait until the load becomes acceptable before closing the doors. The desired service level could be specified more exactly by requiring that a particular elevator-scheduling algorithm be used. See Barney and Dos Santos (1977).

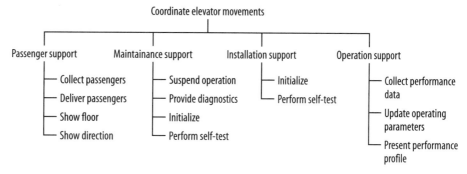

Figure D.2 Function refinement tree for an elevator control.

In the rest of the case study, we restrict ourselves to the passenger support functions.

Name: Collect passengers.

Triggering event: A passenger pushes a floor button at floor F.

Delivered service: The controller ensures that an elevator cage stops at floor F and allows passengers to enter. Average round-trip time when a cage is used at 80% of the guaranteed load should be no more than 60 seconds.

Name: Deliver passengers

Triggering event: A passenger pushes the destination button for floor F in an elevator cage.

Delivered service: The controller ensures that the elevator cage gets to floor F and allows the passenger to leave the cage. Average waiting time at 80% contract load should be no more than 60 seconds.

Name: Show floor.

Triggering event: A cage arrives at a floor.

Delivered service: The controller ensures that any passengers inside the cage are informed of the current floor number.

Name: Show direction

Triggering event: Elevator cage arrives at a floor to service a request.

Delivered service: The controller ensures that the direction of travel of the cage is shown at the floor to passengers waiting outside.

Figure D.3 Descriptions of the basic services. Delivery service description discussed in Chapter 7. See Barney and Dos Santos (1977) for elevator-scheduling algorithms and their expected passenger waiting time.

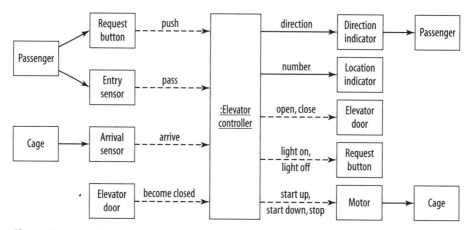

Figure D.4 Partial context diagram showing stimuli and responses. The labels refer to the interfaces of the devices with which the controller interacts. There are two data interfaces, labeled by the name of the data that flow through it. The input event flows are labeled by the events that cause a transfer, and the output event flows are labeled by the events to be caused by the transfer. For example, pushing a button causes the event flow push to transfer information and light_on should cause a request button to light up.

D.3 Subject Domain

D.3.1 *Dictionary*

Terms with an initial uppercase letter stand for predicates (which can be true or false), terms with an initial lowercase latter stand for attributes (which express a property) or events (which may occur at time points). The definitions should be read in conjunction with the subject-domain ERD.

The names of flows in the context diagram are defined in the technical documentation of the devices, and they are not defined here. The following list defines some additional correspondences.

Correspondence rules

allocation(b: Request button, c: Elevator cage). Event. Allocation(b, c) becomes true.

Allocation(b: Request button, c: Elevator cage). Relationship predicate. A request from b has been allocated to c and not yet been served by c.

Arrival sensor. Entity-type predicate. A sensor in an elevator shaft that is activated when an elevator cage approaches a floor. If s is an arrival sensor, we say that Arrival_sensor(s) is true.

Idle(c: Elevator cage). State predicate. c is stationary, its position is such that the cage floor is exactly at the level of a building floor, its doors are closed, there is no allocation to c, and the direction indicator at its current floor is off.

Elevator door. Entity-type predicate. A door connected to an elevator cage. When the elevator is stationary at a floor, an elevator door can only open and close jointly with the floor doors for that cage at that floor. If d is an elevator door, we say that Elevator_door(d) is true.

Indicating(a: Arrival sensor). State predicate. The location indicator of the cage of arrival sensor a is indicating the current floor of the elevator.

Moving(c: Elevator cage). State predicate. c is moving.

planned direction(c: Elevator_cage). Attribute. The preferred direction in which c will depart after closing its doors. If there are requests to be served higher and lower than the current floor of the elevator cage, then it will depart in the planned direction.

Round-trip time. The time in seconds for a single cage trip around a building from the time the cage doors open at the main terminal until the doors reopen when the cage has returned to the main terminal floor after its trip around the building (Barney and Dos Santos 1977).

serve(b: Destination button, c: Elevator cage). Event. After Allocation(b, c) is created, serve(b, c) occurs the first time that Stationary(c), Atfloor(b, c), and Opened(c) occur.

The following list introduces terms for concepts that we could already describe using terms declared in the subject-domain ERD or already defined.

Abbreviations

arrive(b: Request button, c: Elevator cage). Event. arrive(a), where a is the arrival sensor of c at the floor of b.

Atfloor(b: Request button, c: Elevator cage). Predicate. c.current_floor = b.floor.

close doors(c: Elevator cage). Action. close(c.doors).

Closed(c: Elevator cage). State predicate. Closed(c.doors).

Closing(c: Elevator cage). State predicate. c.doors.Closing is true.

continue(c: Elevator cage). Action. Term is applicable only if c.planned_direction ≠ none.
◆ If c.planned_direction = up then start_up(c.motor).
◆ If c.planned_direction = down then start_down(c.motor).
The motor of c is started in the planned direction of c.

Destination request(b: Destination button, c: Elevator cage). Predicate. Allocation (b, c).

doors closed(c: Elevator cage). Event. closed(c.doors).

Downstream(b: Request button, f: Floor, c: Elevator cage). Predicate. Term is applicable only if c.planned_direction ≠ none.
◆ If c.planned_direction = up, then b.floor.number > f.number.
◆ If c.planned_direction = down, then b.floor.number < f.number.
If f is the current floor of c, we write Downstream(b, c).

Downstream required(b: Request button, c: Elevator cage). Predicate.
◆ Allocation(b, c).
◆ Downstream(b, c).
◆ There is no b' with (Allocation(b' c) and Atfloor(b', c)).

Floor request(b: Floor button, c: Elevator cage). Predicate. Allocation(b, c).

Forward request(b: Floor button, c: Elevator cage). Predicate. Allocation(b, c) and c.planned_direction = b.direction.

open doors(c: Elevator cage). Event. open(c.doors).

Opened(c: Elevator cage). State predicate. c.doors.Opened is true.

Outermost reverse request(b: Floor button, c: Elevator cage). Term is applicable only if c.planned_direction ≠ none.
◆ Allocation(b, c).
◆ b.direction ≠ (c.planned_direction).
◆ There is no b' : Request button with (Allocation(b', c) and Downstream(b', b.floor, c)).
Button b is a floor request for the reverse direction of c and there is no request further downstream for c.

pass doors(c: Elevator cage). Event. pass(c.doors.entry_sensor).

Request(b: Request button). Predicate. There is a c: Elevator cage with Allocation(b, c).

reverse(c: Elevator cage). Action. The planned direction of c is reversed, and the motor of c is started in this reversed direction. Term is applicable only if c.planned_direction ≠ none.
◆ If c.planned_direction = up then c.planned_direction := down and start_down(c.motor).
◆ If c.planned_direction = down then c.planned_direction := up and start_up(c.motor).

reverse and show direction(c: Elevator cage). Action. Term is applicable only if c.planned_direction ≠ none.
◆ If c.planned_direction = up, then c.planned_direction := down and set direction(di, down)
◆ If c.planned_direction = down, then c.planned_direction := up and set direction(di, up)
where di is the direction indicator of c at c.current_floor.

set and show direction(b: Floor button, c: Elevator cage). Action. c.planned_direction := b.direction and set direction(di, b.direction), where di is the direction indicator of c at c.current_floor.

set location indicator(a: Arrival sensor). Action. set number(a.cage.location_indicator, s.cage.current_floor.number). The location indicator of the elevator cage in the shaft where a is mounted, is set to the number of the current floor of the cage.

serve(b: Floor button, c: Elevator cage). Event. After Allocation(b, c) is created, serve(b, c) occurs the first time that Stationary(c), Atfloor(b, c), Open doors(c), and c.planned_direction = b.direction occur.

Service required(c: Elevator cage). Predicate. There is some request button b with Allocation(b, c).

show direction(c: Elevator cage). set direction(di, c.planned_direction), where di is the direction indicator of c at c.current_floor.

start motor(b: Request button, c: Elevator cage). Event.

- If b.floor.number > c.current_floor.number then c.planned_direction := up and start_up (c.motor).
- If b.floor.number < c.current_floor then c.planned_direction := down and start_down (c.motor).

The motor of c is started so that c moves in the direction of the floor of b, as viewed from the current floor of c. The planned direction of c is set in this direction.

Stationary(c: Elevator cage). State predicate. not Idle(c).

stop motor(c: Elevator cage). Action. stop(c.motor).

stop showing direction(c). Action. set direction(di, none), where di is the direction indicator of c at c.current_floor.

time to close doors(c: Elevator cage). Event. timeout(Opened(c), 10 seconds). Five seconds after entry of the state Opened(c).

Upstream(b: Request button, f: Floor, c: Elevator cage). Predicate. Term is applicable only if c.planned_direction ≠ none.

- If c.planned_direction = up, then b.floor.number < f.number.
- If c.planned_direction = down, then b.floor.number > f.number.

If f is the current floor of c, we write Upstream(b, c).

Upstream required(b: Request button, c: Elevator cage). Predicate.

- Allocation(b, c).
- Upstream(b, c).
- There is no b' with (Allocation(b' c) and Atfloor(b', c)).
- There is no b' with Downstream required(b', c).

Vacuous request(b: Request button, c: Elevatore cage). Predicate. (Destination_request (b, c) or Forward_request(b, c)) and Atfloor(b, c) and Opened(c).

D.3.2 Entities

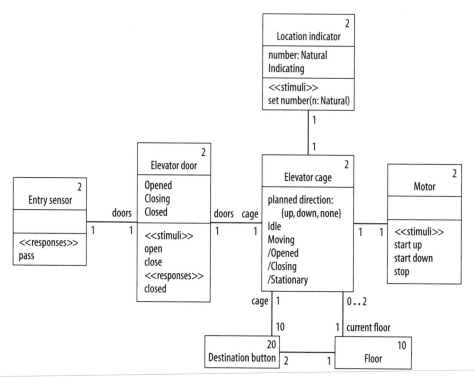

Figure D.5 Partial entity model of the subject domain, including stimuli and responses of subject domain entities (1): Entities related to a cage. (See also Chapter 8.) The entity models use the UML SSD format because all entities are devices with local behavior that is relevant for the operation of the controller. Device behavior is represented as a list of stimuli and responses. Sometimes only device stimuli or device responses are included in the model. Note that the response of one device may be a stimulus of the controller.

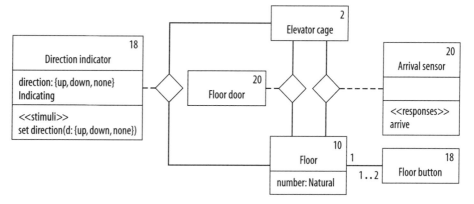

Figure D.6 Partial entity model of the subject domain, including stimuli and responses of subject-domain entities (2): Entities related to a floor. Note that the direction indicator is not represented as an independent entity with its own identity. Instead, it is identified by a cage and a floor. The controller is not interested in the identity of the device that currently acts as the direction indicator for a particular cage and floor. It is interested in the direction indicator for a cage and floor, whatever device is currently used for that role.

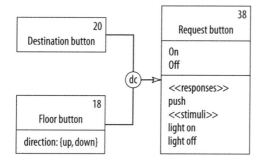

Figure D.7 Partial entity model of the subject domain, including stimuli and responses of subject domain entities (3): Request buttons.

D.3.3 *Assumed Behavior*

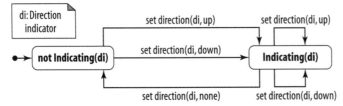

Figure D.8 Assumed behavior of direction indicators. All behavior descriptions are locally closed and globally open, meaning that, viewed at the abstraction level of the model, nothing else can happen in the life of this entity, but that at the same time anything can happen in the life of other entities.

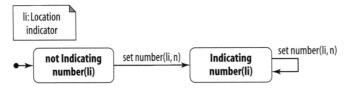

Figure D.9 Assumed behavior of location indicators.

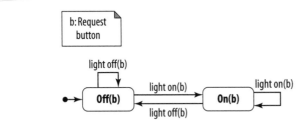

Figure D.10 Assumed behavior of request buttons.

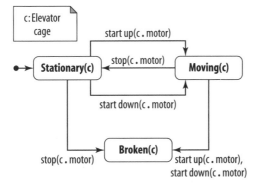

Figure D.11 Assumed behavior of elevator cage and motor. This diagram summarizes the consequences of the fact that the cage is connected to the motor so that the state of the cage can be affected by sending commands to the motor.

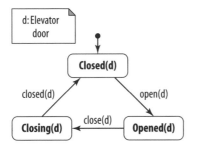

Figure D.12 Assumed behavior of elevator doors.

D.3.4 *Desired Behavior*

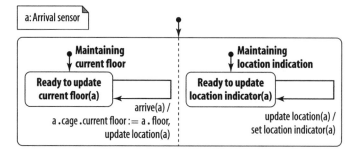

Figure D.13 The desired location indication process. This process must occur independently from other desired behavior and can therefore be independently specified.

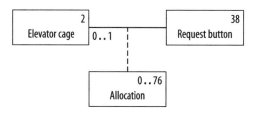

Figure D.14 Allocation of requests to cages introduces a virtual entity type into the subject domain, namely Allocation.

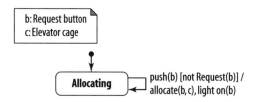

Figure D.15 The desired allocation process. This process too must occur independently from other processes.

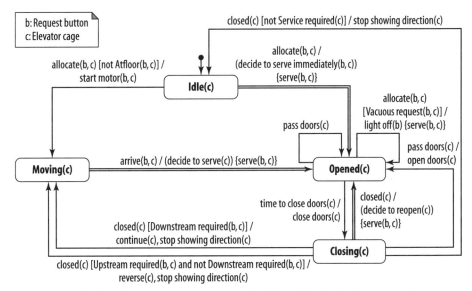

Figure D.16 Desired elevator cage movement. Decision tables for the three complex transitions are given in Figures D.17–D.19. See the dictionary for a definition of terms.

Explanation of desired behavior (see Figure D.16):

Idle(c). If a request is allocated to an idle cage, then this cage will move to the requested floor if it is not already there. Otherwise, it will open its doors and, in the case of a floor request, indicate the requested direction.

Moving(c). When a cage arrives at a floor for which there is a request, it will serve the request (1) if it is a destination request from this cage (someone wants to get out), (2) if it is a floor request in the current direction (someone wants to get in), or (3) if it an outermost reverse request (a turning point).

Opened(c). When doors are opened, they will close when a timeout occurs. The timeout is reset every time someone enters.

Closing(c). Upon closing, the elevator should continue in the current direction until there are no more requests to be served and then turn around. When the doors are closing, they will open again when someone enters the cage or when someone pushes a button for this floor.

At certain points in this behavior, a request is served. According to the dictionary, this happens any time an elevator stops at a floor with a floor request in the current direction, any time it stops at a destination floor, and any time an elevator stops at a floor with an outermost reverse request. An outermost reverse request for a cage is a floor request for the reverse direction at a floor where there is no request further downstream for this cage. Because the diagram describes what should happen in the subject domain, not what the controller should do, the service events happen by implication. They have been added to the diagram as comments between curly braces.

Decide to serve immediately(b, c)

	T	F
Destination request(b, c) and Atfloor(b, c)	T	F
Floor request(b, c) and Atfloor(b, c)	F	T
open doors(c)	×	×
set and show direction(b, c)		×
light off(b)	×	×

Figure D.17 Rules for the decision to serve immediately. This summarizes the possible guard/action pairs in the transition from Idle(c) to Opened(c) in Figure D.16.

Decide to serve(c)

There is a bd with Destination request(bd, c) and Atfloor(bd, c)	T	F	T	F	T
There is a bf with Forward request(bf, c) and Atfloor(bf, c)	F	T	T	F	F
There is a br with Outermost reverse request(br, c) and Atfloor(br, c)	F	–	–	T	T
stop motor(c)	×	×	×	×	×
open doors(c)	×	×	×	×	×
reverse and show direction(c)				×	×
light off(bd)	×		×		×
light off(bf)		×	×		
light off(br)				×	×

Figure D.18 Rules for the decision to serve on arrival. This summarizes the possible guard/action pairs in the transition from Moving(c) to Opened(c) in Figure D.16.

Decide to reopen(c)

There is a bd with Destination request(bd, c) and Atfloor(bd, c)	T	F	T	F	T
There is a bf with Forward request(bf, c) and Atfloor(bf, c)	F	T	T	F	F
There is a br with Outermost reverse request(br, c) and Atfloor(br, c)	F	–	–	T	T
open doors(c)	×	×	×	×	×
reverse and show direction(c)				×	×
light off(bd)	×		×		×
light off(bf)		×	×		
light off(br)				×	×

Figure D.19 Rules for the decision to reopen. This summarizes the possible guard/action pairs in the transition from Closing(c) to Opened(c) in Figure D.16.

D.4 Alternative Requirements-Level Architectures

D.4.1 *Functional Decomposition, Von Neumann Style*

In Figure D.20, each input flow carries the identifier of the device from which it originates as parameter and similarly each output flow contains the identifier of the destination device. All other flow parameters are explained by the specification of the control process. The transformations at the input and output side of the diagram correspond to dictionary definitions; their specifications are not given because they almost literally repeat dictionary definitions. Their function is to use input data to present a more informative signal to the central control process and to transform the output of that process into signals that devices can understand (see Figure D.21).

The functional decomposition of the controller is obtained by replicating the descriptions of the desired subject-domain behavior in the controller and connecting the controller to the subject domain, as shown in the context diagram (Figure D.4). Events and conditions in the subject domain then trigger the controller and the responses of the controller cause actions in the subject domain.

The Collection and delivery control process in Figure D.22 is almost identical to the desired cage behavior in Figure D.16, but there is an important semantic difference between the two figures. Figure D.22 defines desired *software* behavior and refers to the state of software as stored in data stores, whereas Figure D.16 describes desired *subject-domain* behavior and refers to subject-domain states. The definitions of terms in Figure D.22 must now be read as the specifications of values to be computed or actions to be performed by software. Most transformations in the controller decomposition correspond to definitions in the dictionary. They transform inputs into a form understandable by the control process and outputs into a form understandable by the environment.

Note that whereas in the description of desired domain behavior (Figure D.16) we could assume by definition that a request is served when the conditions in its

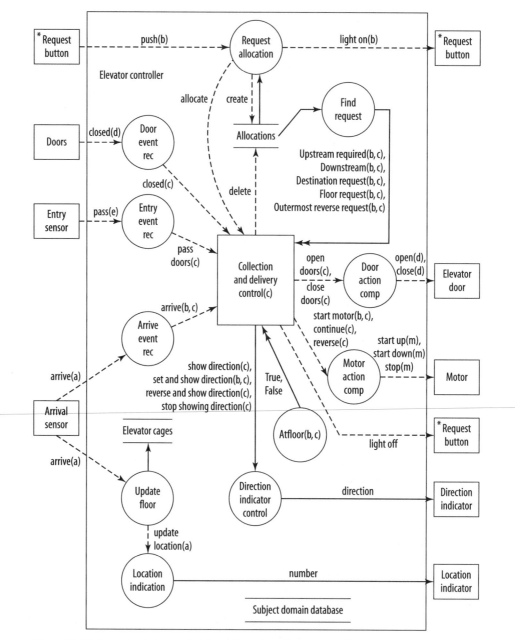

Figure D.20 Functional decomposition using a Von Neumann style with one object. The Allocations database contains instances of the Allocation relationship. The Elevator cages database contains records that represent the cages and their states, each record in the format (c, planned_direction: d, current_floor: f, state: s). To avoid a ravioli diagram, most interfaces to the data stores are not shown. The transformations Location indication, Request allocation, and Update floor are specified in Figure D.21. The control process is specified in Figure D.22.

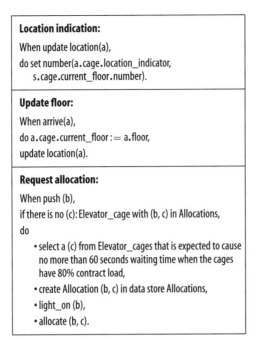

Location indication:

When update location(a),

do set number(a.cage.location_indicator,
    s.cage.current_floor.number).

Update floor:

When arrive(a),

do a.cage.current_floor := a.floor,

update location(a).

Request allocation:

When push (b),

if there is no (c): Elevator_cage with (b, c) in Allocations,

do

    • select a (c) from Elevator_cages that is expected to cause
      no more than 60 seconds waiting time when the cages
      have 80% contract load,

    • create Allocation (b, c) in data store Allocations,

    • light_on (b),

    • allocate (b, c).

Figure D.21 Transformation specifications for the DFD in Figure D.20. Request allocation is discussed in Chapter 15. Path expressions use the subject domain ERD.

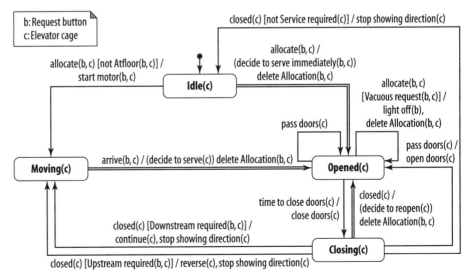

Figure D.22 Collection and delivery control for Figure D.20.

definition are satisfied, we now have to explicitly maintain the **Allocations** data store. This is done by explicit delete statements in Figure D.22.

D.4.2 *Subject-Oriented Decomposition, Object-Oriented Style*

If we partition the controller according to subject-domain entities, we expect components that correspond to the direction indicators, doors, motor, and location indicator. Figure D.23 shows such a decomposition using a hybrid object-oriented

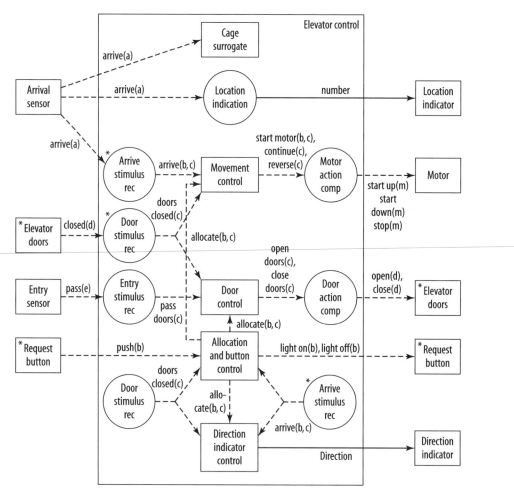

Figure D.23 Subject-oriented decomposition using objects and data transformations. (See also Chapter 19.) At the input side there are stimulus-recognition transformations, and at the output side there are action-computation transformations. These implement dictionary definitions. The objects in the middle are closely coupled because they have many interfaces to one another and they also respond to the same events. The diagram becomes less cluttered if the objects are collected together as parallel processes in one control process, as shown in Figure D.24. To avoid a spaghetti diagram, almost all data flows have been omitted.

style that contains objects that encapsulate behavior and a number of stateless data transformations that present a rationalized view of the outside world to the software objects. The parallelism of the elevator services (two requests may be served simultaneously) is now handled by parallelism across software objects. This means that the complexity in the behavior of Collection and delivery control (functional decomposition of Figure D.20) is traded for complexity in the communication structure (subject-oriented decomposition of Figure D.23).

To get a subject-oriented partitioning, we project the desired subject-domain behavior onto the desired local behavior of the subject-domain entities. Then, just as in the functional decomposition, we use this as a desired behavior specification of the software objects and connect the software objects to the subject domain through a connection domain as indicated in the context diagram.

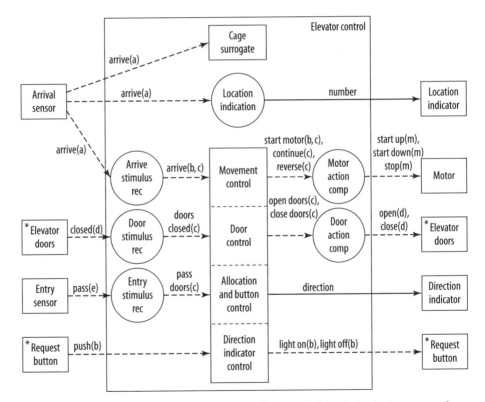

Figure D.24 Subject-oriented decomposition, collecting all object behavior in one set of closely coupled components. (See also Chapters 16 and 22.) Again, to avoid a spaghetti diagram, almost all data flows have been omitted. The components are specified in Figures D.25–D.29. The necessary access paths are represented in the SSDs in Figures D.30–D.32 (see also the answer to Exercise 7 in Chapter 22 in Appendix E).

c: Cage surrogate

arrive(a) / update_floor(c, a), where update_floor(c, a) = c.current_floor := a.floor.

Location indication:

When arrive(a),

do set number(a.cage.location_indicator, a.cage.current_floor.number).

Arrive stimulus rec:

When arrive(a), then

for each b with b.floor = a.floor, send arrive(b, c) where c = a.elevator_cage.

Door stimulus rec:

When closed(d) then

send doors_closed(d.elevator_cage).

Motor action comp:

When start_motor(b, c) then

- if b.floor.number > c.current_floor.number then c.planned_direction := up and start_up(c.motor).
- if b.floor.number < c.current_floor then c.planned_direction := down and start_down(c.motor).

When continue(c) then

- if c.planned_direction = up then start_up(c.motor).
- if c.planned_direction = down then start_down(c.motor).

When reverse(c) then

- if c.planned_direction = up then c.planned_direction := down and start_down(c.motor).
- if c.planned_direction = down then c.planned_direction := up and start_up (c.motor).

Figure D.25 Specification of the behavior of Cage surrogate objects and of some of the data transformations in Figures D.23 and D.24. The stimulus recognizers and action computation transformations all correspond to dictionary definitions. For example, Arrive stimulus rec operationalizes the definition of arrive(b, c) given in the dictionary, and Motor action comp operationalizes the definition of start motor(b, c), continue(c), and reverse(c). Figure E.51 shows the specifications of Entry stimulus rec and Door action comp.

Movement control

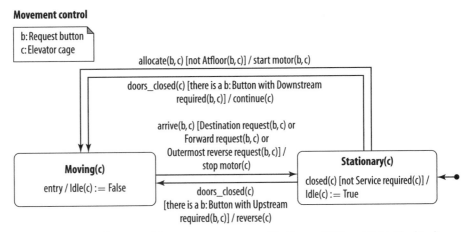

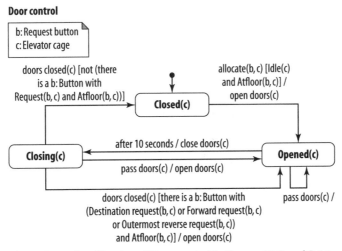

Figure D.26 Specification of Cage movement control in Figures D.23 and D.24. The binding of the identifier variable c is global to the diagram.

Door control

Figure D.27 Specification of Door control in Figures D.23 and D.24. The identifier variable c is global to the diagram.

Allocation and button control

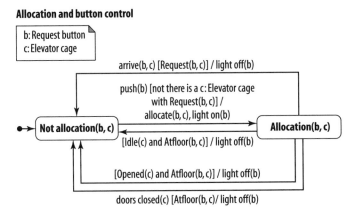

Figure D.28 Specification of Allocation and button control in Figures D.23 and D.24. This merges the allocation process with the button control process because buttons must light up and turn off exactly in step with allocating a request. The identifiers are global to the diagram. Predicates such as Idle(c) are defined in the dictionary.

Direction indicator control

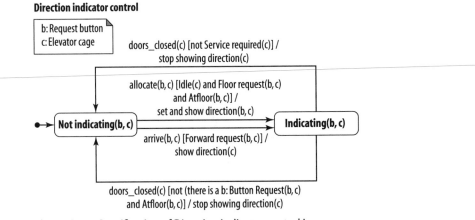

Figure D.29 Specification of Direction indicator control in Figures D.23 and D.24. A direction indicator is identified by a button and a cage identifier. These identifiers are global to the diagram.

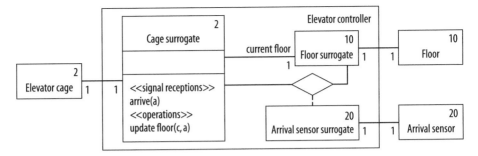

Figure D.30 SSD showing access paths needed by Cage surrogate objects. (See also Chapter 22.) These correspond to the Update floor transformation of the functional decomposition (Figure D.20).

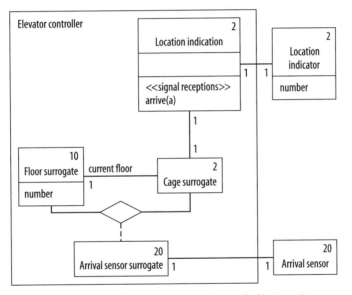

Figure D.31 SSD showing the access paths needed by Location indication transformation objects. (See also Chapter 22.)

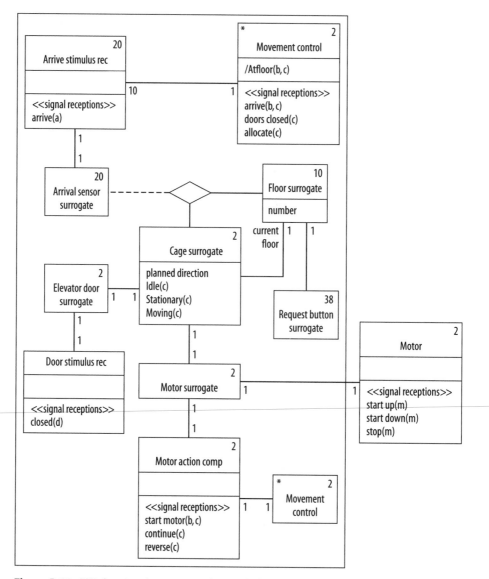

Figure D.32 SSD showing the access paths needed by Movement control objects and by Arrive stimulus rec, Door stimulus rec, and Motor action comp transformations. Each surrogate class has a one-to-one association to the external entity that it represents. The multiplicity properties of the surrogate classes mirror those of the subject domain (Figures D.5–D.7).

Answers to Selected Exercises

A ppendix E contains answers to most exercises in the book. About half of the answers can be found here; the remaining answers are available on the book's web site (*www.mkp.com/dmrs*).

Chapter 1 Reactive Systems

2. The controller is treated as a nonterminating process that is always able to respond to the arrival of tea bags. It does not interact intensively with people, but it is highly interrupt-driven. Its response to the arrival of a tea bag depends on its current state, such as the current value of the maximum tea-bag count. Its response is highly environment-oriented because it tries to maintain a desirable state of affairs in the tea-bag-boxing cell. There is some parallelism because it must be able to respond to input from sensors, whatever other processes are currently executing. However, the number of simultaneous inputs is small because the cell does not contain so many entities that can generate simultaneous inputs for the controller. The controller has strict real-time requirements.

Chapter 2 The Environment

2. Yes, but it will always be a *part* of the subject domain of the entire system.

4. Yes. For example, a financial information system may send and receive messages about salaries and business trips. The salary administration department will exchange information with the system about the first salary domain, and the travel office will exchange information about the travel domain. Employees are part of both domains.

6. ◆ Tea-bag boxing: Pure directive function.

   ◆ Bug-fixing support: Information-provision function. Informing program-mers and the manager of a change of state can be viewed as a directive function because it tells these people what to do next. A pure directive func-tion that it can provide is refusing to accept an event in the life of a bug that deviates from the prescribed workflow. Whether this function is provided is not clear from the case description, which talks of "tracking." The system has a manipulative function because it stores bug descriptions, fixes, and test reports.

   ◆ Chemical tracking system: Information-provision function. Ordering chem-ical containers is a manipulative function because the orders are stored and manipulated by the system.

8. (a) Elevator control system: It depends on how ambitiously you define its func-tions. Assuming that the purpose of the control system is to respond properly to events such as a passenger pushing a button and an elevator arriving at a floor, entities such as buttons, elevator cages, and motors are part of the subject domain. The communication channel connecting the system with this subject domain consists of the wires that connect these entities to the controller. If, however, the purpose of the control system is viewed as re-sponding to the wish by people to go to another floor, then the subject domain is the wishes of the user; but that domain would be unobservable by the control system because there is no reliable communication channel linking these events to the system. This channel would contain the intended passenger, the buttons and lights of the elevator, and the wires connecting these to the controller. Only the part from the buttons and so on to the sys-tem is reliable, and so we take these buttons and so on as the subject domain of the controller and keep the purpose of the controller correspondingly feasible: Respond to button pushes and not to the decisions of a would-be passenger.

   (b) Cruise-control system in a car. Again, this depends on how ambitiously you define its functions. If the mission is to control the speed of the car as requested by the user, then the subject domain consists of the buttons used by the driver to indicate her wishes, the speed of the car, and the state of the engine and gear of the car. However, the speed of the car—presumably with respect to the road—is not observable. Axle rotation, by contrast, is observable. Assuming that the car is on the road, this indicates car speed. And it is not the axle that is controlled by the cruise control but the engine throttle. So we may want to scale down the mission of the cruise control to controlling the engine as indicated by the user. The subject domain now consists of the buttons used by the driver to indicate her wishes, the axle rotation, and the state of the engine and gear of the car. The corresponding connection domain consists of the wires connecting the driver buttons to the cruise control, wires conveying the state of the engine and gear box to the control, and a sensor measuring axle rotation plus the wires connecting it to the control.

(c) Personnel information system. The subject domain consists of the people working for the company and the employment relationships they have with the company. If we take the PCs and workstations used by the personnel department as part of the personnel information system, then the connection domain consists of the people interacting with these devices and talking with the employees. (Assuming that these people are themselves also employees, then the connection domain is part of the subject domain.) Alternatively, if these devices are not viewed as part of the personnel information system, they are part of the connection domain.

(d) Word processing system. The subject domain consists of the text edited by the system, including its markup and its presentation to the user. Observe that the text itself is an abstract conceptual entity of which there can be many physical representations. For example, one and the same text can be represented on a piece of paper, on a screen, in computer memory, and on a disk. The user communicates with the word processor about the text by communicating about the representation of the text on the screen. So the subject domain of the word processor consists of the text (an abstract conceptual entity) and some of its physical representations (on the screen, in memory, on disk). These physical representation are accessible by the computer because they exist in the word processing system. There is no connection domain between the word processor and the text as an abstract conceptual entity because it is not possible to connect to that abstract entity; and there is no distinct connection domain between the word processor and the physical representations of the text in the word processor because it is not necessary to have such a connection.

(e) Your bank. The bank is an information-processing organization implemented in people, machines, procedures, and software. The interactions with you as customer have as their subject domain you and your bank account. The connection domain that connects the bank to you consists of the communication channels used by the bank to communicate with you about your bank account: the post office, telephone, fax, newspapers, TV, radio, and Internet. The bank account is an abstract entity that the bank contains physical representations of, say on paper, disk, and tape. There is no connection domain that connects the bank computer to the abstract bank account because it is not possible to have such a connection; and there is no connection domain between the bank and the physical representations of this account because it is not necessary to have such a connection. These physical representations are part of the bank.

(f) Account database of your bank. This has the same subject domain as your bank. The corresponding connection domain is the same as that of the bank, plus the bank personnel involved in bringing information from the database to you and back again.

(g) Online bookstore. The subject domain consists of books available, users accessing the Web page of the store, click stream of these users, transactions actually performed, Web pages containing links to this bookstore, and so on.

It is connected to this subject domain primarily by means of the Internet, but also by more traditional technology such as the telephone and fax.

(h) Supermarket. A supermarket manipulates goods and processes customers, and it manipulates information about both. Its subject domain therefore consists of goods and their suppliers and transporters, the goods sold, and the people buying them. Information about these entities is obtained through many different channels, including communication channels with suppliers and transporters and familiar devices such as a customer card. The supermarket may also have a Web presence that allows it to collect customer data through the Web.

(i) EDI system. The EDI system interacts with the supermarket itself and with dairy-product suppliers. The subject of these interactions consists of dairy products and their suppliers and transporters, and so those entities make up its subject domain. The system receives information about these entities and outputs messages about them, by means of employees in both companies handling these entities and devices such as bar code scanners. These employees and devices communicate with the system through network technology and data entry and display devices.

(j) Web search engine. The subject domain of a Web search engine consists of all pages on the Web and their contents. The engine is connected to its subject domain through the Internet.

10. (a) The DBS subject domain is the people who have insurance policies with the company, the policies, and the claims they ever made on this policy.

(b) The WFMS subject domain consists of the claims currently being processed by the organization, the people handling those claims, and the relevant databases and applications needed to handle the claims.

(c) The insurance company subject domain includes the (a) and (b) as well as the potential market for insurance, including potential customers and competitors.

12. Software is a symbolic state of a physical computer. At each time point, the parts of the computer are in a physical state. They have a direction of magnetization or an electrical potential. We interpret some of these states symbolically as 0 and others as 1. By this *meaning convention*, these states have turned into lexical items. Additional meaning conventions then interpret patterns of 0s and 1s as more complex lexical items. A lexical item exists in a computer if we can interpret its physical state according to this set of meaning conventions.

Chapter 3 Stimulus-Response Behavior

4. (a) (i) Event: An up button on floor 1 has been pushed. (ii) Subject domain entity in whose life this occurs: An up button on floor 1. (iii) Observer: The wire connecting the button to the controller. (iv) Desired action: The motor in elevator shaft 3 starts rolling down its cable. (v) Subject domain entity

in whose life the action occurs: The motor. (vi) Actor: The wire connecting the controller to the motor. Assumptions: The button has been pushed by a user with the intention of entering the lift, the cable connects to the elevator cabin, the cabin can move through the shaft, the shaft is connected to floor 1, and there is room for one more passenger in the cabin. The controller does not verify this because it cannot verify it. Only under these assumptions is the response a desired response. In this example, we assume there is currently no elevator at floor 1.

(b) (i) Event: The Delete button was pushed. (ii) Subject domain entity: The Delete button. (iii) Observer: The hardware that registers this event and the operating system software that informs the word processor of it. (iv) Desired action: The cursor moves left, erasing the character at the position that it moves to. (v) Subject domain entity in whose life the action occurs: The edited text. (vi) Actor: None; this part of the subject domain (a physical representation of the text) is manipulated as part of the word processor. Assumptions: The Delete button was pushed by a user who wanted to delete the character left of the cursor. The word processor does not verify this, and no one expects it to.

(c) (i) Event: A request to update the bank account was issued. (ii) Subject domain entities: The owner of the bank account. (iii) Observer: There are many ways in which information about the event can reach the database. One possible way is the following. The owner writes the request on a paper form and mails this to the bank. Upon receiving it, the bank routes it to an employee who is authorized to update bank accounts. This employee reads the paper and enters the data in a terminal connected to the database. In this scenario, the observers (i.e., entities that play a role in communicating the subject domain event to the database) are the post office, the employee entering the data, the terminal and the connection between the terminal and the database. Banks communicate with their customer through multiple communication channels, and this is only one possible communication route. The bank includes the bank account owner in the subject domain because it will not accept an update request from someone else. For security reasons, it will probably also monitor parts of the connection domain, such as the bank employee and the terminal used to enter the update request, which thereby are included in its subject domain. So the subject domain event issue an account update request is expected to cause other subject-domain events, such as employee 007 enters an update request in terminal 999, and if these other events do not occur, the update will not take place. (iv) Desired action: 567 is added to the balance field of the bank account record of account 345 and a confirmation is sent to the port connected to terminal 999. Let us say that this is port 888. (v) Subject domain entity: This action occurs in the life of bank account 345. (vi) Actor: None for the bank account; the domain of bank accounts is virtual. The bank account is considered to be updated if the bank account *record* is updated. The actor for the confirmation is the line connecting the database to terminal 999 and the terminal itself. Assumptions: The update request was issued by a bank account owner who can be held accountable for his or her actions. We also assume that port 888 is connected to terminal 999.

(d) (i) Event: The number of milk packages becomes less than 100. (ii) Subject domain entities: The milk packages in the store. (iii) Observer: A program that watches the number of milk packages in the store, as recorded by the information system. (iv) Desired action: An order is placed with the milk-package supplier for 300 packages of milk. (v) Subject domain entities: Milk package (a type of product of which there can be many instances in store) and supplier. (vi) Actor: The network that connects the supermarket information system with the production information system of the supplier. Assumptions: The information system accurately represents the number of milk packages in the store at each time point. The truth of this assumption must be guaranteed by devices that update the information system as soon as the number of milk packages in store changes. This is done by connecting point-of-sale terminals to the information system, by placing a point of entry in the warehouse of the store, and by implementing appropriate organizational procedures. The assumption cannot be fully guaranteed, however, due to events such as theft and breakage in the store not being reported to the system.

6. (a) Patient monitoring system: Would like it to cause the nurse to attend to the patient whenever vital data indicate that the patient is not well. What the system can do is sound audible alarms and show information on a screen when certain events occur. This is done using the nurse's workstation and attached devices. But if the nurse is away, asleep, or attending to another patient, then the nurse will not attend to the patient.

(b) A library document circulation information system: Would like it to cause users to return documents on time. What it can do is help the library send out reminders to return documents. This is done using a clock that counts the indicated time and printing devices.

(c) The information system of a supermarket: Would like it to cause stock to be replenished when it falls below a threshold. What it can do is print a report that stock is low or cause an EDI system to reorder stock. This is done by an interface to the printing facilities or an interface to the EDI system. It is not under the control of the system whether these actions lead to the desired effect of replenishing stock.

(d) A Web shop: Would like it to cause people to buy the company's products. The only thing it can do is offer easy catalog access and show advertisements on the screen, using standard Web servers.

(e) An email system: Would like it to inform a receiver that an important email has been sent. The only thing it can do is set a priority flag or urgency flag in an email that is sent. It depends on the receiver's email system what is done with this.

8. An external event is an event in the environment to which the system is expected to respond. Some event in the environment may, however, trigger an observer, which causes a stimulus, even if the system is not expected to respond to the event. (An event-recognition process performed by the SuD may filter out this

irrelevant stimulus.) Or the observer may be broken and cause a stimulus even if there is no event at all. In both cases, the stimulus is not caused by a relevant external event. And, of course, a stimulus may be a tick caused by a clock, which is not caused by a temporal event.

Chapter 4   Software Specifications

5. *Functions:* The function of the machine is to make coffee from ground coffee and water.

    Behavior: Put in coffee or water (in any order); switch on; take out pot or switch off (in any order).

    Communication events: Switch on, switch off, put in coffee, put in water, take out pot. Each of these events involve several entities and is therefore a communication event.

6. Representing the interests of the user, I argue as follows. We only know that the assumption-requirements specification is not *applicable* in this environment. If the environment does not satisfy the assumption, then the manufacturer cannot know whether or not the system still must satisfy the requirement. In order to find out, he should have asked. Before selling you the system, he should have verified that you knew what his assumptions were.

8. No, it is not the same. An operationalized requirement merely states the observable criteria that the system has to satisfy. A test, on the other hand, specifies a test set-up, including the environment conditions in which the test is to be run and one or more sequences of particular input values and the output values expected for those inputs. An operational requirement describes operations to be performed, but does not specify the other elements of a test.

Chapter 5   Mission Statement

2. (a) The business goal tree is shown in Figure E.1.
    (b) The business activities to be supported by the Chemical Tracking System are
        - Find a chemical
        - Purchase a chemical that is not available in the company itself
        - Provide a report about chemical usage, storage or disposal.
    (c) The purpose of the Chemical Tracking System is to support the acquisition of chemical containers.
    (d) The major responsibilities are to maintain information about vendors and about the location of containers, provide information about the location and use of containers, and purchase containers if requested.

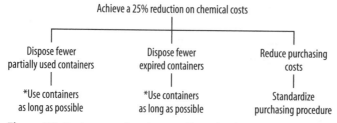

Figure E.1 Business goals to be contributed to by the Chemical Tracking System.

(e) One possible exclusion is that the system will not maintain information about the identity of the users of chemical containers.

4. ◆ **Name.** Bugfix.
   ◆ **Purpose.** To support the workflow of bug fixing.
   ◆ **Composition.** A single program accessible through the company's network.
   ◆ **Responsibilities.**
      —Registering bug status
      —Informing programmers of relevant bug status
      —Maintaining a database of programmers allocated as the fixer or tester to a bug

Chapter 6 Function Refinement Tree

2. The list of functions is basically the list of controller responsibilities:
   ◆ Allow operator to set required tea-bag weight.
   ◆ Allow operator to set maximum tea-bag count.
   ◆ Place tea bag in box or in waste container according to weight.
   ◆ Replace full box by empty box.

4. See Figure E.2.

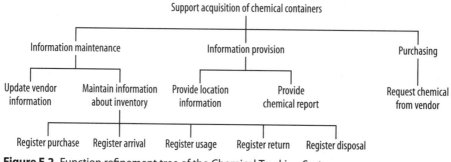

Figure E.2 Function refinement tree of the Chemical Tracking System.

6. *In favor:* You may choose to implement all functions by system components. This gives you a functional decomposition of the system and, as a result, the function refinement tree also represents the decomposition structure. *Against:* The decomposition dimension is independent of the external property dimension. The function refinement tree is merely a representation of the functional properties and belongs entirely to the external property dimension. See Figure 4.2.

Chapter 7   Service Description

4. ◆ **Name:** Register test report.
    ◆ **Triggering event:** Tester enters his or her test report.
    ◆ **Delivered service:** Bugfix stores the report and sends an email to the programmer and manager whether the test was or was not succesful.
    ◆ **Assumptions:** The programmer and manager are reading their email regularly.

    The email system is mentioned because it is mentioned in the problem statement. If using the email system had been a design choice made during the specification of the bug-fixing support system, then it would have been inappropriate to mention it here.

6. A value-oriented description tends to abstract from behavior, communication, and data formats, and so allows you more freedom to design these once the value to be delivered has been determined.

Chapter 8   Entity-Relationship Diagrams

6. In the same order as they are listed in Section 8.2.1: Two teachers cannot use the same book for the same course. A teacher can use a book for any number of courses. A teacher uses at least one book per course.

8. Figure E.8 says that, over time, a heating tank can have several heaters and thermometers, but that each of these devices, after being attached to a heating tank, will not be attached to any other heating tank. In the course of time, a batch is at first not allocated at all and can then be allocated to at most two heating tanks. In its life, a tank will be allocated many different batches. A batch will be treated according to exactly one recipe and this will not change over time. A recipe can be used for many batches.

10. Figure E.9(a) is wrong because it says that all tanks are monuments. Figure E.9(b) allows vehicles to become monuments, which is close. But now all monuments are tanks, which is not what we want either.

    What we want is for tanks to have two states: being-a-monument and not-being-a-monument. We also want to distinguish two kinds of monuments: tanks in the state of being-a-monument and other monuments. Something like

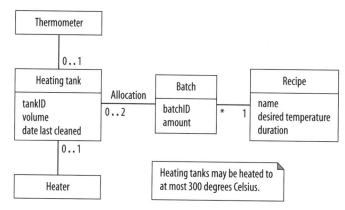

Figure E.8 Historical cardinalities in the subject domain of the heating controller.

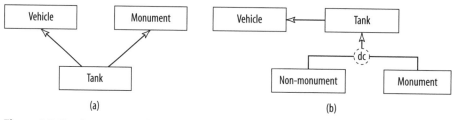

Figure E.9 Two incorrect models of tank, vehicles, and monuments.

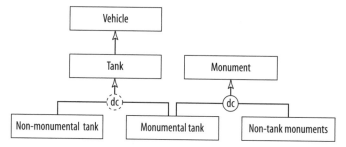

Figure E.10 Another incorrect model.

Figure E.10? Now, when a tank becomes a monument, it does not change its identity but its state. The extension of Monumental tank is the extension of Tank. But Figure E.10 also says that the extension of Monumental tank is a subset of the extension of Monument. The implication is that all tanks are monuments! Again, this is not what we want. There is no model of the situation in terms of classification and specialization.

Chapter 9   ERD Modeling Guidelines

4. See Figure E.11. Note that the controller does not have to know the identity of the tea bags or boxes. If we represent the required tea-bag weight as an attribute of a metaclass TeaBagType, then all tea bags would have the same required weight, whereas the case description implies that the required weight is different for different kinds of tea bags. Note that Figure E.11 is not a database schema but merely helps to define the meaning of some subject-domain terms. The controller is not required to maintain a database of tea bags or boxes.

6. See Figure E.13.

8. See Figure E.15. There are two type-instance relationships in the model: between Flight and Flight instance and between Hop and Hop instance. The relationship between hop and flight is one of aggregation—a flight consists of one or more hops. There is a corresponding aggregation relationship between flight instance and hop instances and between booking and hop booking. A ticket is related to hop bookings by means of seat assignments.

10. (a) Railway station: In the subject domain because the passenger must identify stations to the system. A station is observable by all railway employees (and travelers) and we consider the communication channel by which information about stations reaches the information system reliable, even though it consists of railway employees. (These are very reliable people.) Delays in transferring information through this channel are irrelevant. So we can consider railway stations to be observable by the information system.

    (b) Rail track: Not in the subject domain because the system need not know the identity of the tracks. The system needs only information about connectivity, not about the tracks.

Figure E.11 ERD for the tea-bag-boxing controller subject domain.

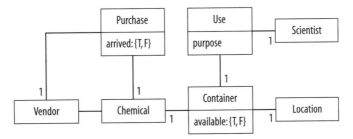

Figure E.13 Subject-domain ERD of the Chemical Tracking System.

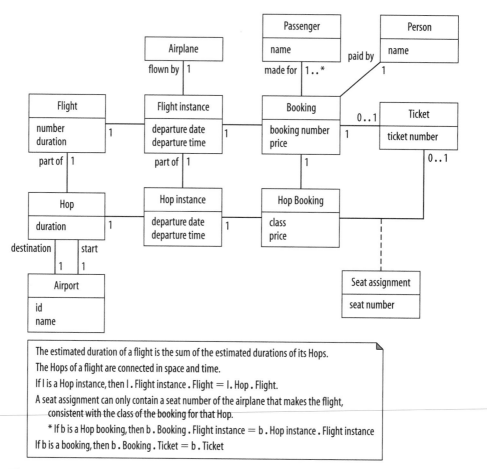

Figure E.15 A model for booking flights.

(c) Traveler: Very relevant, but nevertheless the system need not know the identify of a traveler. Registering individual travelers in a train would be useful for the traveler because it indicates how busy a particular connection is at different times of the day. It would be even more useful for the company because they can then start a personalized marketing campaign. But the current system does not provide this functionality and so travelers are outside its subject domain.

(d) Railway connection: In the subject domain. It is observable by the people who initialize the database and this, as we have seen, is a reliable connection. And the system must be able to identify connections. (They are identified by their end points.)

(e) Rail car. Not relevant. The system does not need to know the identity of a rail car.

12. (a) In Figure 9.14(a), Participation is a relationship between students and exams. That means that each Participation instance is identified by a pair ⟨s, e⟩, where s is a student and e an exam. Because any extent of Participation is a *set*

(which cannot contain duplicate elements), there can at any moment be at most one participation per student per exam. If this is not what we want, then the model in Figure 9.14(b) is better. It can represent any number of participations of one student in an exam.

(b) Figures 9.15(a) and (b) distinguish the different instances of an exam. In Figure 9.15(a), each student can only participate in each exam offering once. This is an improvement (from the student's point of view) on Figure 9.14(a), in which a student can partake in only one offering of an exam. In Figure 9.15(b), each student can participate any number of times in one exam offering. This is nonsense and should be excluded. The difference from Figure 9.14(a) is that participations have their own identifier. It is very unlikely that there is a need for this. Notice how the modeling decision is again guided by consideration of the counting criterion of relationships—how many instances of a type can there be and how are they counted?

14. (a) Owner is a role that some entity (e.g., a person) is playing with respect to some other entity (a car). Person is *not* a role. A person entity is a person in itself rather than with respect to something else. Manufacturer, Car, and Garage are borderline cases. They are artificial entities manufactured with a particular functionality in mind, namely to manufacture cars, to transport people, and to sell and maintain cars. This functionality is provided to users and customers; but these functions are not roles played by these cars and garages with respect to users and customers. Rather, cars and garages essentially have these functions. They cannot exist without these functions. If they did not have these functions anymore, they would cease to be cars or garages.

(b) The model is wrong because not all garages, cars, and manufacturers are car owners.

(c) Figure E.17(a) gives an improved model. The constraint cannot be expressed in the diagram, so we add it as a note. The model has been improved further in Figure E.17(b) by including the player of which manufacturer is a role.

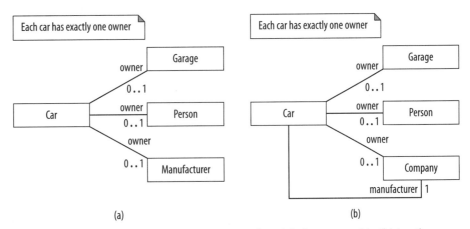

Figure E.17 Models of ownership. (a) An improved model of car ownership. (b) Another improvement.

16. It depends. Perhaps we want to count the number of wrecked cars that we currently own. And perhaps we count wrecked cars by counting the number of cars that have been wrecked. In that case, Wrecked car is a dynamic subtype of Car. But we may count the number of wrecks that look like cars. We then may count two wrecks as different when they actually originated from one car. In this case, Wrecked car is not even a subtype of Car because it has a different identification criterion.

Chapter 10   The Dictionary

4. (a) Chair. This has an open texture. Chairs may have zero, one, two, three, or more legs; they may have a flat surface to sit on, but may also be perfectly round balls; they may stand or hang from the ceiling; and so on. The intensional definition "A device to be used for sitting" comes close, but because I may use devices as chairs that were not intended to be used this way, this is not yet good enough. So I regard this as an open-textured term. The list of examples given here can be used as extensional definition. There is no single authority that determines what is or is not a chair. We all do.

   (b) Assembler. A program that translates symbolic assembly code into a machine language program.

   (c) Employee. How we define this depends on our subject domain model. If we view Employee as subtype of Person, then the definition is "A person who has an employment contract with a company." If we view Employee as a distinct identifiable role of Person, then the definition is "A role played by people, in which the player has an employment contract with a company."

   (d) Car. According to *Webster's*, "A vehicle moving on wheels."

Chapter 11   State Transition Lists and Tables

2. Extract enough of the condition on the current state to distinguish between the different effects that the event can have.

4. Each column corresponds to a combination of truth values of conditions for one event in a stateless transformation table.

6. See Figure E.19. Note that the current state involves the actual event parameter.

Chapter 12   State Transition Diagrams

4. If an action a performed in a transition affects a condition g that is used as guard along a transition, then we need a decision state to sequence the performance of a and the testing of g.

required: Rational

current, max: Natural

Initially		current := 0	Ready to receive tea bag
Stimulus	**Current controller state**	**Controller response**	**Next controller state**
tea bag arrives(w)	Ready to receive tea bag, w = required	put in box, current := current + 1	Waiting for tea bag to be put in box
	Ready to receive tea bag, w ≠ required	remove tea bag	Waiting for tea bag to be put in container
tea bag removed	Waiting for tea bag to be put in box, current ≥ max	stop belt, replace box	Waiting for box to be replaced
	Waiting for tea bag to be put in box, current < max		Ready to receive tea bag
	Waiting for tea bag to be put in container		Ready to receive tea bag
box replaced	Waiting for box to be replaced	start belt, current := 0	Ready to receive tea bag

Figure E.19 State transition table for the box-removal function.

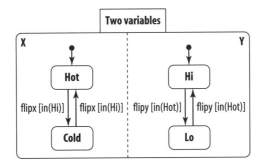

Figure E.20 STD with two explicit variables.

6. A state reaction does not involve exit from or entry into a state. A state transition has priority over a state reaction.

12. (a) See Figure E.20. The important semantic difference between this statechart and the Mealy diagram is that the statechart can respond to a flipx and a flipy event at the same time.

  (b) See Figure E.21. This diagram represents almost the same behavior as Figure 12.26. The only difference is that it does not indicate the initial value of the variables.

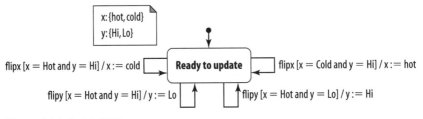

Figure E.21 A trivial STD.

Chapter 13 Behavioral Semantics

8. The superstep response has already been shown in Chapter 12.

Event	Current basic configuration	Action	Next basic configuration
e1	S11, S21, S31	e2	S12, S21, S31
e2	S12, S21, S31	e3	S12, S22, S31
e3	S12, S22, S31	e4	S12, S22, S32
e4	S12, S22, S32		S11, S22, S32

If **e5** occurs at any time during this response, it will be handled in basic configuration S11, S22, S32, which means that it will be ignored (assuming the Ignore semantics). In the step semantics, if e5 occurs during the first transition, then the response is nondeterministic. One possible response is to choose e2 and ignore e5:

Event	Current basic configuration	Action	Next basic configuration
e1	S11, S21, S31	e2	S12, S21, S31
e2, e5	S12, S21, S31	e3	S12, S22, S31
e3	S12, S22, S31	e4	S12, S22, S32
e4	S12, S22, S32		S11, S22, S32

Another response is to choose **e5** and ignore **e2**:

Event	Current basic configuration	Action	Next basic configuration
e1	S11, S21, S31	e2	S12, S21, S31
e2, e5	S12, S21, S31		S11, S22, S31

10. (a) In the superstep semantics, first b, c are generated and then the step to R is taken. The final basic configuration is P, R. See Figure E.25.
    (b) In the nested-step semantics, first b is generated, which triggers transition Q → R, and then c is generated, which triggers the transition R → S. The final basic configuration is T, S. See Figure E.26.

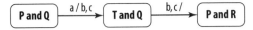

Figure E.25 The superstep response.

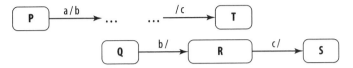

Figure E.26 The nested-step response.

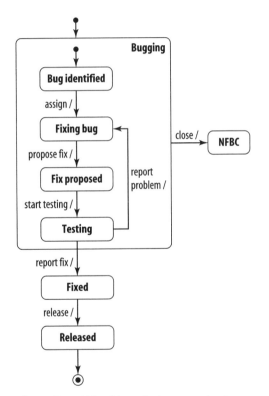

Figure E.27 Using hierarchy in a statechart.

Chapter 14   Behavior Modeling and Design Guidelines

2. E4 can occur jointly with E2 or E3. E2 and E3 exclude one another. E4 can occur jointly with E1 if the duration of a recipe is 0.

4. See Figure E.27.

6. (a) See Figure E.30.

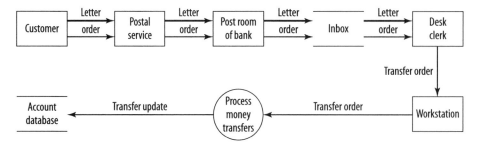

Figure E.35 Material flows.

Remove an item from a store. This is destructive for the store contents because the removed item is no longer present in the store. This differs from data store read, which is not destructive.

(d) See Figure E.35. The material flow from the customer to the desk clerk consists of a piece of paper in an envelope. The model does not show where the envelope goes or where the letter goes after the clerk has read it. The letter is the carrier for a data flow, containing the order.

Note that we stop representing material flows at the desk clerk. In reality, the data flow from the desk clerk to the workstation is implemented by a material flow. Some physical objects move to realize this flow. The workstation then sends electrons—which are physical objects too—to the processor doing the computations and finally to the disk that holds the database. The very idea of a DFD is to abstract from this material flow, and therefore we do so in the lower part of Figure E.35.

Chapter 16 Communication Diagrams

4. Figure E.38 shows the communication diagram, and Figure E.39 shows the allocation table.

6. If **B** always causes **e2** when prompted by **e1** and does nothing else, then it acts as a communication channel and can be removed. To be a useful component, **B** should have to make a decision or introduce a delay.

Chapter 17 Communication Semantics

6. Eager read/lazy write: At the start of a step, it accepts all inputs, and so creates, updates, and deletes items in its memory. At the end of a step, it writes all outputs and so provides all values asked for in a read operation. Lazy read/eager write: It processes its inputs as late as possible; because it has nothing else to do, that

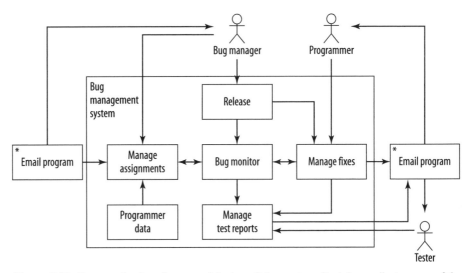

Figure E.38 Communication diagram of the bug-fixing system. Each box collects some of the components of the DFD of Figure E.33.

	Register assignment	Register bug fix	Register test report	Register bug release
Manage assignments	✕			
Programmer data	✕			
Bug monitor	✕	✕	✕	✕
Manage fixes		✕		
Manage test reports			✕	
Release				✕

Figure E.39 Allocation of bug-fixing support functions to components.

is at the end of a step. It writes its outputs as early as possible; because it has nothing else to do, that is at the start of a step.

8. At the start of the step the data store provides all values asked for in this step, and at the end of the step the data store accepts all updates sent to it. The difference with the read/write semantics discussed in this chapter is that in those semantics a data store responds to events generated in the previous step, whereas here we want the data store to respond to events generated by a process in the current step.

10. There is always a value in a time-continuous channel, but any new value is present at the destination immediately.

12. Imperfect technology: Use faster technology. Clock-synchronous semantics: Use a smaller clock cycle. Finite buffer: Use a larger buffer. Events occur within one time point: Use smaller time points that can discriminate their time of occurrence.

Chapter 18   Context Modeling Guidelines

2. See Figure E.41 for a context diagram.

   (a) The composite system crosses organizational boundaries because it includes parts of the company and also external vendors and the government. The emergent properties of the system are valuable for the company.

   (b) The system needs information about vendors, chemicals, containers, scientists, and locations. See also the ERD (Figure E.13). Information about these entities reaches the system through the data processing department.

   (c) The desired effects of the system are that chemical containers are used more efficiently, purchasing takes place in a standard way, and standard reports are produced. These effects involve scientists, the stockroom, and vendors.

   (d) The users are the scientists and the administrators who must produce reports.

   The context structure contains flows for information provision: tracking and monitoring (which are directive) and manipulation (of purchase orders).

4. (a) They should be included because they are part of the effects of the system relevant for the creation of the desired emergent properties of the composite system (efficient and effective management of introductory courses).

   (b) They should not be included because they are not effects of the system. The SuD produces the messages to be communicated, but the communications take place only because external entities decide to do so.

   I prefer (b) because the resulting diagram is simpler.

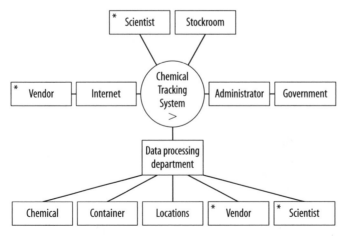

Figure E.41 Context diagram for the Chemical Tracking System.

Chapter 19   Requirements-Level Decomposition Guidelines

6. See Figure E.42. Update vendor information is a function triggered by a temporal event (every night). The contents of the data stores is defined by the ERD you made in Chapter 9. (See Figure E.13 for the ERD.)

8. Location indication: Functional, subject-oriented, device-oriented. Direction indication: Functional, subject-oriented, device-oriented. Arrival sensing: Subject-oriented, event-oriented, device based. Movement control: Functional, subject-oriented, device-oriented, behavior-oriented. Door sensing: Subject-oriented. Door control: Subject-oriented, behavior-oriented. Allocation and button control: Subject-oriented, device-oriented, behavior-oriented.

10. See Figure E.45. Figure E.46 shows the life cycle of a ticket. Any event not conforming to this life cycle is simply ignored.

Chapter 20   Postmodern Structured Analysis (PSA)

2. (a) All processes except Bug life cycle correspond to functions.
   (b) The events arrive from the corresponding processes. See the answer to Chapter 6, Exercise 3 for a brief function description that indicates where the responses go.

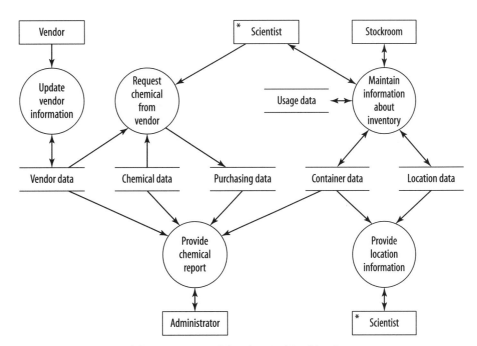

Figure E.42 Functional decomposition of the Chemical Tracking System.

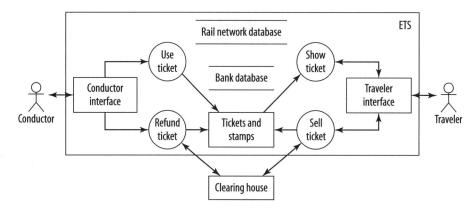

Figure E.45 Requirements-level ETS architecture—hybrid style.

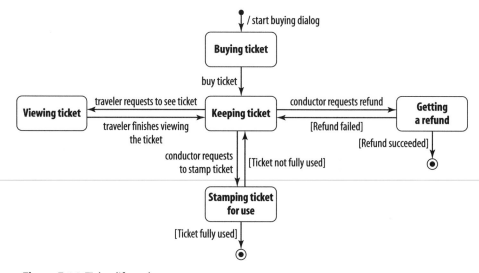

Figure E.46 Ticket life cycle.

Chapter 21 Statemate

2. See Figure E.48. The transition leaving S12 triggered by e4 is replaced by a transition leaving S1 triggered by e4, which can only be enabled when the control activity in B is in state S12. The step behavior of both models is the same.

Chapter 22 Unified Modeling Language (UML)

2. An object is an entity that offers services to its environment. Because it is an entity, it has identity and state.

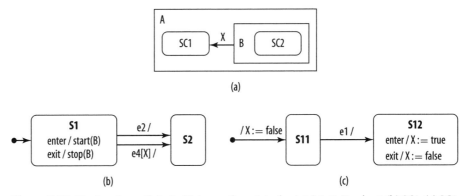

(a)

(b)   (c)

Figure E.48 Moving the activity in S1 to another statechart. (a) Activity chart. (b) SC1. (c) SC2.

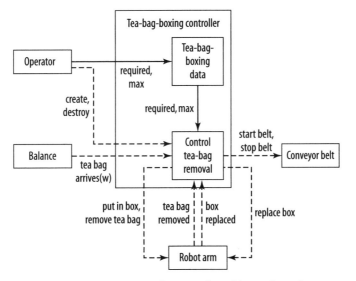

Figure E.49 Communication diagram of an object-oriented architecture of the tea-bag-boxing controller.

6. (a) See Figure E.49. The **create** and **destroy** messages are not visible in the state-chart.
   (b) See Figure E.50. The multiplicities are not particularly interesting. Remember that they characterize snapshots, not histories. The interface for putting and getting the attributes of **Tea-bag-boxing data** is not shown.

8. ◆ *Cars and engines.*
   (a) In both diagrams, a car cannot exist when it is not related to an engine. So in both diagrams,
      —when a car is created, a link to an existing engine must be created at the same time

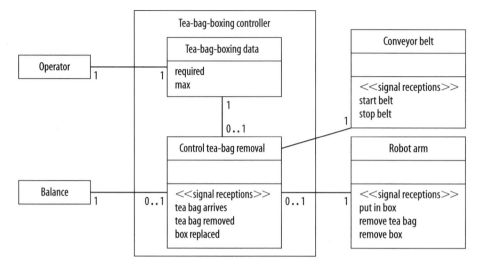

Figure E.50 SSD of the tea-bag-boxing controller architecture in Figure E.49.

— when an engine is destroyed, the car must immediately get another engine or it must be destroyed too

(b) The additional meaning conveyed by the diamond seems to be that a car physically contains an engine and an engine delivers a service to a car.

◆ *Car surrogates and engine surrogates.* Surrogates are software objects that represent real-world objects.

(a) The multiplicity properties are identical to those for cars and engines.

(b) What could the diamond mean?

— A car software object physically contains an engine software object. This is an implementation instruction because it says that the physical executable code of one object must contain the physical executable code of some other object. Even if this would be a useful instruction, in this book we avoid implementation instructions in an SSD.

— An engine software object delivers a service to a car software object. Whatever this service is, it is not the same service that engines provide to cars (providing locomotive power). In fact, I cannot think of a service that an engine software object delivers to a car software object.

◆ *Company and department.*

(a) The multiplicity property in Figures 22.23(c) and (d) and in Figure 22.24(c) is that a department can only exist in relationship to an existing company. This means that

— When a department is created, a link to an existing company must be created at the same time.

— When a company is destroyed, all its departments go with it or else they immediately get a link to an existing company.

(b) This already provides the element of existence dependency conveyed by the black diamond. The additional meaning provided by the black diamond could be:

  — A company physically contains a department. This is nonsense. A company is not a physical object and therefore does not physically contain anything.

  — A department delivers a service to a company. This is true, but we wonder whether we need a black diamond to express this.

◆ *Database and database table.*

  (a) The multiplicity constraints are the same as for departments and companies.

  (b) Any additional meaning conveyed by the diamond could be:

    — A database physically contains a database table. As for car and engine software objects, this is an implementation instruction. But in this case, it is an empty instruction because a database is defined to be a collection of database tables.

    — A database table delivers a service to a database. This is true because a table provides part of the storage capacity of a database.

Surveying these examples, we see that the additional meaning provided by the hollow or black diamond over and above the multiplicity properties differs in different examples. My recommendation is therefore to avoid using the diamond. If you see a SSD drawn by someone else containing a diamond, ask what the diamond means precisely.

Abbreviation A dictionary entry that introduces a shorthand for a concept that can already be described using words from the same dictionary. See also *Correspondence rule*.

Absolute cardinality property The absolute cardinality of an entity type is a set of natural numbers that indicates how many instances of the type can exist at the same time.

Abstraction Omission of detail from a description. The opposite of *Refinement*.

Action Each event is an action when viewed from the initiator of the event.

Activity chart Statemate alternative for data flow diagrams.

Activity diagram UML notation to represent flow of control. We use activity diagrams to represent workflow.

Activity state A statechart or activity diagram state in which the described behavior is performing an ongoing activity. Every superstate is an activity state. See also *Wait state*.

Actor An entity in the environment that can cause actions in the environment when so triggered by the output response of the system.

Actuator An actor device.

Allocation table A table that shows which SuD components play a role in the provision of a SuD service.

And-component Collection of closely coupled components that broadcast information to one another. Each closely coupled component has access to the same communication channels as the other components.

And-state Statechart concept. State of a behavior that has substates. If the behavior is in an and-state, it is in all of its children states simultaneously. See also *Or-state*.

Architectural style A set of constraints on an architecture. Each architectural style defines a particular set of kinds of components from which to assemble an architecture and a particular set of constraints on the way these components interact.

Architecture A structure of system elements and their properties, and the interactions among these elements that realize system-level properties. A system usually has many architectures, each highlighting one aspect of the system.

Arity The number of entity types that a relationship relates.

Aspect A group of product properties.

Association UML term for *Relationship*.

Association entity A relationship with attributes.

Assumption Each product requirement makes assumptions about the product environment such that, if the environment does not satisfy these assumptions, it is not certain whether the product should still satisfy this requirement.

Asynchronous communication Communication through a channel with capacity one or more. The sender and receiver then do not have to wait for one another for the communication to take place. See also *Synchronous communication*.

Attribute A property of an entity that can be represented by a value.

Basic configuration The basic states in a configuration of a statechart.

Basic state A state without substates.

Behavior The ordering of events in time.

Behavior-oriented decomposition Decomposition approach in which each monitored or enforced behavior is allocated to one component.

Binary relationship A relationship of arity two.

Blackboard architectural style Special case of the Von Neumann style, in which a number of data transformations act on a single data store, called the blackboard. The data transformations have no interface to one another.

Blocking communication semantics The amount of time that a sender waits before it can place a message in a communication channel.

Breadth-first semantics Execution semantics of a network of components in which a triggered component will not perform its step before all components that were triggered earlier have performed their steps. See also *Depth-first semantics*.

Call event In the UML, an event in which an operation call is received that triggers a transition in an object life cycle.

Cardinality property See *Absolute cardinality property; Relative cardinality property*.

Change event The term used in the UML for a *Condition change event*.

Channel addressing A mechanism by which a sender sends messages to a communication channel irrespective of what the channel is connected to at the other end. See also *Destination addressing*.

Class diagram UML concept. A static structure diagram that represents only classes and their associations. See *Static structure diagram; Object diagram*.

Collaboration diagram UML concept. Static structure diagram used to represent a message-passing scenario. If used to illustrate a scenario, it is an object diagram. See also *Sequence diagram*.

Communication The ordering of events in space. Each event involves a number of entities that are said to communicate in that event. If a sender sends a message that later arrives at a receiver, we view this as two communication events—one between the sender and the communication channel, and one between the communication channel and the receiver.

Communication channel A way in which one component can influence another by causing the other to do something or by providing the other with information. Our communication channels are reliable and introduce no delay. Synonymous with *Flow*.

Communication diagram A diagram showing the components of the SuD and their communication channels. Generalizes *Data flow diagram*.

Communication-oriented decomposition A decomposition approach in which the system is decomposed into components that deal with handling a communication. See also *Event-oriented decomposition; Device-oriented decomposition; User-oriented decomposition*.

Completion event In the UML, termination of an activity state. See also *Activity state*.

Component A part of the SuD that delivers a service to its environment.

Composite process A process specified by a lower-level data flow diagram.

Conceptual entity An invisible, nonphysical entity that people use to structure their world.

Conceptual event An invisible, nonphysical event that people use to structure their world.

Concurrent-action semantics A semantics of behavior descriptions in which all actions along a transition are executed concurrently. See also *Sequential-action semantics.*

Concurrent-event semantics A semantics of behavior descriptions in which the behavior concurrently responds to all events not yet responded to. See also *Sequential-event semantics.*

Condition A state of the world. Conditions persist for some nonzero period of time.

Condition change event The event that a condition changes its truth value.

Configuration A configuration of a statechart is a largest set of mutually consistent states of the statechart.

Connection domain A domain through which messages travel to or from the system to their senders and receivers. See also *Domain.*

Constraint A desired product property that is imposed by the environment and is a boundary within which the requirements must be realized. See also *Requirement.*

Context diagram A communication diagram that represents the SuD and the entities and communications in its environment.

Control process DFD concept. A process that transforms input events into output events. See also *Data transformation.*

Correspondence rule Dictionary entry that relates a word to observable reality. See also *Abbreviation.*

Counting criterion Criterion by which we can know that two distinct instances of a type are different. See also *Recognition criterion.*

Current extent The current extent of a type is the set of currently existing instances of the type.

Data channel Communication diagram concept. A communication channel through which a sender can share information with a receiver. Named after the data communicated. Represented by a solid arrow, the direction of which represents the flow of information not causality. Can be push or pull communication.

Data flow DFD concept. A *Data channel* in a PSA data flow diagram. See also *Event flow.*

Data flow architectural style Architectural style in which a system is decomposed into data transformations connected by flows.

Data flow diagram (DFD) A PSA diagram that shows which processes and stores can exist in the SuD and which communication channels exist between them.

Data process DFD concept. A process that transforms input data into output data. See also *Data transformation; Object.*

Data store DFD concept. A component that remembers data written to it until deleted. See also *Variable; Database.*

Data transformation DFD concept. A stateless data process that transforms input data into output data in one step. Because it is stateless, equal inputs are always transformed into equal outputs. May interface with data flows as well as with event flows. Synonymous with *Stateless process.* See also *Control process.*

Database A data stores that can contain a set of tuples. It offers a transactional interface to create, read, update, and delete tuples.

Decision state A state in a Mealy diagram in which a decision is made among outgoing transitions based on the evaluation of a condition. The state is entered and exited in one step.

Decision table A table whose columns contain (condition, action) rules.

Default state Statechart concept. The initial substate of a superstate.

Deferred response semantics Interpretation rule for behavior descriptions according to which an event that triggers a transition that leaves an activity state is responded to as soon as the activity has terminated. See also *Forced termination semantics.*

Defining intension The defining intension of a type is the part of the intension listed in the type definition. See also *Intension.*

Depth-first semantics Execution semantics of a network of components in which triggering is performed depth-first. So if C_1 triggers C_2, then C_2 will be executed before C_1 returns control. See also *Breadth-first semantics.*

Derivable property Property whose value can be derived by symbol manipulation alone.

Derivation rule A logical rule that relates the truth value of a derivable property to that of more basic properties.

Destination addressing A mechanism by which a sender sends a message to a named destination, irrespective of the channel by which it is connected to the destination. See also *Channel addressing.*

Device-oriented decomposition Communication-oriented decomposition approach in which each device is handled by one component. See also *Communication-oriented decomposition.*

Disable prompt DFD concept. An event flow that disables a process.

Domain A domain is a part of the world that for the purpose of the design process is conveniently treated as a whole. It usually has more internal than external interactions, often is the subject of a profession, and has special jargon that people use to talk about it. See also *Subject domain; Connection domain.*

Dynamic generalization node ERD concept. A dashed generalization node, which indicates that entities can migrate between subtypes.

Eager read/lazy write A strategy in which all inputs needed in a step are read at the start of the step and all outputs produced by a step are written at the end of the step. See also *Lazy read/eager write.*

Enable prompt An event flow that enables a process.

Encapsulation architectural style An architectural style in which a system encapsulates its components. See also *Layered architectural style.*

Entity A discrete, identifiable part of the world.

Entity-relationship diagram (ERD) Diagram that represents entity types and their absolute and relative cardinality properties.

Entry action An action performed when entering a state.

Event Some discrete happening in the world. An event occurrence is instantaneous; that is, it does not take time. See also *Condition change; External event; Temporal event.*

Event broadcasting Broadcasting of an action to all parallel components of a statechart.

Event channel A communication channel through which the sender can cause the receiver to do something. May be named after the cause or after the effect of the communication. Represented by a dashed arrow, the direction of which represents the direction of causality. See also *Data channel.*

Event-driven semantics A semantics of behavior descriptions in which a behavior responds to events immediately when they occur. See also *Time-driven semantics.*

Event flow DFD concept. An *Event channel* in a data flow diagram. Usually named after the effect caused by a communication. See also *Data flow.*

Event list List that describes for each event its behavioral effect. Each entry has the form (event, state, effect), where the effect is a next state and action (transactional effect) or a scenario. See also *Transactional effect; Scenario effect; Service description.*

Event-oriented decomposition A communication-oriented decomposition approach in which each event (external or temporal) is handled by one component. See also *Communication-oriented decomposition.*

Event recognition A process in the SuD by which it analyzes a stimulus to see whether it was caused by an event and, if so, which event this was.

Exclusion Part of a mission statement in which a responsibility is mentioned that the product will not satisfy.

Exit action Statechart concept. An action performed when exiting a state.

Extension The extension of a type is the set of all possible instances of the type, past, current, and possible future.

Extent See *Current extent.*

External entity An entity in the environment of the SuD.

External event An external event of a system S is an event in the environment of the system to which S is expected to respond. An external event can be a named external event or a condition change event. See also *Named event; Condition change event.*

Feature An incremental product functionality defined on top of a service that the product already offers.

Flow DFD concept. A communication channel between two elements represented by a data flow diagram. As are all communication channels, it is reliable and instantaneous. See also *Communication channel; Event flow; Data flow.*

Flowdown Determination of the function that an SuD component must have to contribute to some SuD function.

Forced termination semantics Interpretation rule for behavior descriptions according to which an event that triggers a transition that leaves an activity state terminates the activity. See also *Deferred response semantics.*

Formalization Definition of a formal syntax and symbol manipulation rules that is sound with respect to an intended meaning. See also *Precision.*

Fragile semantics Interpretation rule for behavior description according to which the effect of an event in a state for which the description defines no effect is unknown. See also *Ignore semantics; Inhibit semantics.*

Frame rule A blanket assumption that anything not mentioned in a state transition description and that is not implied to change by the transition remains unchanged.

Function For a product, the ability of the product to create a desired effect in the environment. See also *Responsibility; Service; Feature.*

Function refinement tree A hierarchical list of desired system functions.

Functional decomposition A decomposition approach in which each system function is allocated to a different component.

Generalization ERD concept. Entity type E1 is a generalization of entity type E2 if every possible instance of E2 is also an instance of E1.

Generalization node A node in an ERD that can be used to indicate whether a collection of subtypes of an entity type is mutually disjoint or whether it jointly covers the supertype. See also *Static generalization node; Dynamic generalization node.*

Global termination semantics Interpretation rule for behavior descriptions in which a final state node represents the termination of the entire behavior. See also *Local termination semantics.*

Global time assumption The assumption that all components of the SuD have clocks that indicate the same global time.

Goal tree A tree that decomposes goals into subgoals.

Identifier A proper name of an individual. Within a subject domain, the name is given to at most one individual and, once given, it is never changed.

Identifier variable A variable that ranges over entities and is used to parameterize an STD that describes the behavior of any of these entities.

Ignore semantics Interpretation rule for behavior description according to which the occurrence of an event in a state for which the description defines no response should be ignored. See also *Inhibit semantics; Fragile semantics.*

Implementation-level architecture An architecture of the SuD that takes properties of the implementation platform into account.

Implementation platform The part of the environment of the SuD consisting of the lower software and hardware layers on which it is implemented.

Induction Derivation of a model that explains observed phenomena.

Inheritance All properties shared by supertype instances are also shared by all subtype instances.

Inhibit semantics Interpretation rule for behavior description according to which the occurrence of an event in a state for which the description defines no effect is inhibited. See also *Ignore semantics; Fragile semantics.*

Input buffer The input buffer of a component C is a second component that is able to accept and remember all inputs arriving from any channel connected to C and to deliver them to C when C is ready to process the input.

Instance An individual that has the properties defined by a type. See also *Type.*

Intension The intension of a type is the set of properties shared by all instances of the type. See also *Defining intension.*

Layered architectural style An architectural style in which the components are organized in layers of abstraction, where the lower layers provide services to the higher layers. See also *Encapsulation architectural style.*

Lazy read/eager write A strategy in which all inputs needed in a step are read when they are needed and all outputs produced by a step are written when they become available. See also *Eager read/lazy write.*

Lexical item A physical entity to which we assign a meaning by convention.

Life cycle The behavior of an object from birth to death.

Local termination semantics Interpretation rule for behavior descriptions in which a final state node represents the termination of the enclosing activity state. See also *Global termination semantics*.

Magic square Commutative square that sets off functionality against decomposition. The horizontal dimension lists different levels of refinement at which functions can be described; the vertical dimension lists the decomposition levels of the product.

Mealy diagram A flat state transition diagram without parallelism and without actions in a state.

Message In the UML, a possibly structure data item passed between objects. A message can be a signal instance, an operation call or return value, or an object creation or destruction message.

Method An implementation of an operation. See also *Operation*.

Mission statement A mission statement of a product is a high-level description of the purpose of the product, refined into major responsibilities and limited by a list of responsibilities that it will *not* have, called exclusions. The mission statement may also contain a list of components from which the system is going to be built. See also *Responsibility*.

Multiplicity property UML term for *Cardinality property*.

Multistep semantics A semantics of behavior descriptions in which the behavior responds to all internally generated events before it can respond to other (external or temporal) events. There are two kinds of multistep semantics: *Superstep semantics* and *Nested-step semantics*. See also *Step semantics*.

Named event An event that has been given a unique name.

Nested-step semantics A multistep semantics in which an internally generated event is responded to immediately when it is generated. That is, an internal event is responded to during the current step, before this step is finished. Also known as *Run-to-completion semantics*. See also *Multistep semantics; Superstep semantics*.

Network multistep semantics Execution semantics of a network of components in which the network is ready to accept input from the environment only when all of its components are ready. See also *Breadth-first semantics; Depth-first semantics*.

Network step semantics Execution semantics of a network of components in which the network is ready to accept input from the environment when any of its components are ready. When that component receives an input, it will take a step. See also *Breadth-first semantics; Depth-first semantics*.

Object A stateful component of the SuD not decomposed further. Synonymous with *Stateful process*. See also *Subsystem*.

Object diagram A static structure diagram that represents only objects and their links. See *Static structure diagram; Class diagram*.

Object-oriented architectural style Architectural style in which the system is decomposed into objects. See *Publish-subscribe communication*.

Observer An entity in the environment that can observe conditions or events and can inform the system about this by means of a stimulus.

Operation A terminating computation performed by an object to deliver a service.

Operational specification A description of a repeatable procedure that yields a definite answer to the question whether or not a product has a property. The procedure yields the same answer even if it is performed by people with conflicting interests.

Or-state Statechart concept. State of a behavior, with substates. If the behavior is in an or-state, it is in exactly one of its children states. See also *And-state*.

Output response An event at the interface of the system caused by the system.

Path expression An expression that navigates from an entity to a set of entities related to it by relationships in an ERD.

Perfect synchrony hypothesis A hypothesis about the implementation platform that the response to a stimulus occurs at the same time as the stimulus. See also *Perfect technology assumption*.

Perfect technology assumption An assumption about the implementation platform that in the specification of system requirements we should ignore any limitations that any implementation will have. This means that we assume that the implementation platform offers all the services we need to realize the requirements and that it has unlimited memory, unbounded parallel processing activity, and any processing speed we need. This implies the *Perfect synchrony hypothesis*. A further consequence is that steps are instantaneous. See also *Step; Perfect synchrony hypothesis*.

Postcondition A condition that is true after state transition has taken place.

Precision Expression of what is intended that is as brief as possible. See also *Formalization*.

Precondition A condition that must be true in the current state before a state transition can take place.

Process In PSA, some activity of the SuD.

Process identifier Identifier used in a DFD to distinguish different copies of a process.

Prompt DFD concept. An event flow that enables, triggers, or disables a process.

Prompting action DFD concept. If P is the name of a process, then the prompting actions E: P, T: P, and D: P enable, trigger, and disable P, respectively.

Publish-subscribe communication A variant of the object-oriented style in which objects communicate through a publish-subscribe mechanism. This is a dynamic form of channel addressing. See *Object-oriented architectural style; Channel addressing*.

Quality property An aspect of product functionality that indicates how valuable or costly the function is for the environment. Also called quality attribute.

Reactive system A system that, when switched on, is able to create desired effects in its environment by enabling, enforcing, or preventing events in the environment.

Real-time-oriented decomposition Decomposition strategy in which events with the same real-time properties are handled by one component.

Recognition criterion Criterion by which we can recognize an individual as an instance of a type. See also *Counting criterion*.

Refinement Addition of detail to a description. The opposite of *Abstraction*.

Relationship ERD concept. A type. Its instances are tuples of related entities.

Relative cardinality property ERD concept. If E1 is related by R to E2, then the relative cardinality of E1 with respect to E2 is a set of natural numbers that indicates how many existing instances of E1 can be related by R to one existing instance of E2.

Requirement A desired product property needed to achieve the desired composite system properties. See also *Constraint*.

Requirements-level architecture A decomposition of the SuD that assumes perfect implementation technology. The decomposition is defined in terms of requirements and the use environment, but not in terms of the implementation platform. See also *Implementation-level architecture; Perfect technology assumption.*

Response The observable result of a system stimulus. A response can consist of a state update and an output response. See also *Output response.*

Responsibility A product responsibility is a requirement that the product contributes to the achievement of some environment goal. Specified in the mission statement. See also *Function.*

Role Each entity related by a relationship plays a role in that relationship.

Run-to-completion semantics See *Nested-step semantics.*

Scenario A nonatomic behavior, consisting of a number of states connected by state transition, and triggered by events.

Scenario effect An event effect that consists of several state transitions, with possible intermediate states. See also *Transactional effect; Service description.*

Scenario list An event list containing scenario effect descriptions.

Sensor An observer device. See also *Observer.*

Sequence diagram UML diagram. Collection of object life lines that represent a message-passing scenario. See also *Collaboration diagram.*

Sequential-action semantics A semantics of behavior descriptions in which the actions along a transition are executed sequentially. See also *Concurrent-action semantics.*

Sequential-event semantics A semantics of behavior descriptions in which the behavior responds to one event at a time, in sequence. See also *Concurrent-event semantics.*

Service An interaction between a product and its environment that is valuable to its environment. The interaction need not be atomic. Services have a *Behavior* and *Communication.*

Service description A description that lists the triggering event of the service, the value of the service for the environment, and any assumptions made about the environment.

Signal In the UML, a named data structure of which instances can be sent to objects.

Single-transition semantics A semantics of behavior descriptions in which the behavior consists of a sequence of single transitions. See also *Step semantics.*

Snapshot property A property that is valid for all possible states of a system. The cardinality properties expressed in an ERD are snapshot properties of the subject domain.

Solution goals Goals that characterize a solution to a business problem.

Specialization ERD concept. Entity type E1 is a specialization of entity type E2 if every possible instance of E1 is also an instance of E2.

Specialization attribute ERD concept. An attribute of a supertype whose values correspond to different subtypes. Instances of different subtypes have different values for this attribute. Instances of the same subtype have the same value for this attribute.

Specification A description of desired product properties.

State reaction Statechart concept. An event-action pair in a state. Performing it does not cause entry in or exit from the state.

State transition diagram (STD) A finite directed graph, possibly with nested and partitioned nodes. The nodes represent states, node containment represents state hierarchy, node partitioning represents parallelism, and edges represent state transitions. See also *Statechart; Mealy diagram.*

State transition table (STT) An event list whose entries have the form (event, current state, action, next state).

Statechart A *State transition diagram* with state reactions, hierarchy, and parallelism.

Stateful process DFD concept. A process with memory. Synonymous with *Object.* See also *Process.*

Stateless process DFD concept. A process without memory. Synonymous with *Data transformation.* See also *Process.*

Static generalization node ERD concept. A solid generalization node, which indicates that entities cannot migrate between the subtypes.

Static structure diagram UML diagram to represent the decomposition of the SuD in (classes of) software objects. See also *Class diagram; Object diagram.*

Step A largest set of mutually consistent transitions triggered at the same time.

Step semantics A semantics of behavior descriptions in which the behavior consists of a sequence of steps, each of which responds to all events that have happened since the start of the previous step. After a step, the behavior can respond to internally generated events, external events, and temporal events. See also *Single-transition semantics; Concurrent-event semantics; Sequential-event semantics; Multistep semantics.*

Stereotype A label used in a UML diagram to indicate that a diagram element has a special meaning.

Stimulus A stimulus of a system is an event at the interface of the system caused by the environment.

Subject domain The subject domain of an external interaction of a system is the part of the world referred to by the message. The subject domain of a system is the union of the subject domains of all its external messages. See also *Domain.*

Subject-oriented decomposition A decomposition approach in which each group of subject-domain entities corresponds to a system component.

Subsystem Part of a system that is treated as a system in its own right. A subsystem is always decomposed into smaller parts.

Subtype See *Specialization.*

Superstate A state with substates.

Superstep semantics A multistep in which steps are ordered sequentially. That is, internally generated events are responded to in the next step within a superstep. See also *Multistep semantics; Nested-step semantics.*

Supertype See *Generalization.*

Surrogate A system component with the purpose to represent information about a subject-domain entity.

Synchronous communication Communication through a channel with zero capacity. The sender and receiver must then share whatever they want to communicate (data or event) for the communication to take place. See also *Asynchronous communication.*

System A collection of elements that interact to form a whole. As a result of the interaction of its components, the system has emergent properties.

System engineering argument The argument that properties S of the SuD and assumed properties A of its external environment cooperate to produce desired emergent properties E of the composite system formed by the SuD and its external entities.

System under Development (SuD) The part of the world subject to the design freedom of the designer.

Temporal event A significant moment in time.

Time point A time interval whose length is not significant for the behavior description under consideration.

Time-continuous channel A communication channel that contains values for nonzero periods of time.

Time-continuous flow A time-continuous channel in a data flow diagram.

Time-discrete channel A communication channel that contains values only at discrete moments in time.

Time-discrete flow A time-discrete channel in a data flow diagram.

Time-driven semantics A semantics of behavior descriptions in which a behavior responds to events at the next time point. See also *Time point; Event-driven semantics*.

Timer A clock that watches for the occurrence of a temporal event.

Traceability table A table showing the allocation or flowdown of SuD functions to component functions.

Transactional effect An event effect that consists of a single-state transition, without intermediate states.

Transactional event list An event list containing only transactional effect descriptions.

Transformation table An event list whose entries have the form (event, current state, action). See also *Decision table*.

Transformational system A system that transforms an input into an output and then terminates.

Trigger An event flow, labeled T, whose sole purpose it is to trigger a process.

Type A concept by which entities are classified.

Use environment The part of the environment of the SuD consisting of users and peer systems.

User-oriented decomposition Communication-oriented decomposition approach in which each user is handled by one component. See also *Communication-oriented decomposition*.

Variable DFD concept. A data store that can contain at most one value. It offers an interface in which this value can be read and written.

Von Neumann architectural style Architectural style in which a system is decomposed into data transformations that are stateless and into data stores that do not process. See also *Blackboard architectural style*.

Wait state A statechart or activity diagram state in which the described behavior is doing nothing but waiting for an event. See also *Activity state*.

Part I Introduction

Reactive Systems. Reactive Systems are defined by Harel and Pnueli (1985). Harel and Politi (1998) also give a brief but useful discussion.

Case Studies and Examples. The sources of the case studies are as follows. The Teaching Information System was done by some of my students for a company. The Electronic Ticket System is based on an example provided by Reif and Stenzel (1999). The heating tank controller is from Shlaer and Mellor (1992). The elevator controller example is ubiquitous. The tea-bag-boxing example is based on an example treated by Goldsmith (1993). The bug-fixing example is taken from Kovitz (1998). The Chemical Tracking System example is based on a case provided by Wiegers (1999, 102).

Systems and the Environment. The importance of the environment for systems design is pointed out in many texts on systems engineering, such as Blanchard and Fabrycky (1990), in which it appears as the concept of an open system, and in Stevens, Brook, Jackson, and Arnold (1998). These are also sources for the concepts of allocation and flowdown of properties, which is the basis for the systems engineering argument. Another source on this is Davis (1993). The concepts of allocation and flowdown appeared in bottom-up form, taking the viewpoint of the software engineer, in the requirements engineering reference model of Gunter, Jackson, and Zave (Gunter, Gunter, Jackson, and Zave 2000; Jackson 1995).

For reactive software systems, the environment is even more important than for general systems because the essential subject of the computations is in the subject domain. Jackson (2000) makes environment analysis the centerpiece of his problem-analysis approach.

Domains. The concept of a domain originated in Shlaer and Mellor (1992). It is the central structuring tool in Jackson's problem structuring approach (Jackson 1995, 2000). The subject domain is often called the Universe of Discourse (UoD) by database people. The source for this is an ISO report on the standardization of conceptual modeling terminology (Griethuysen 1982). The concept of a Universe of Discourse also plays a central role in a conceptual modeling method called Nijssen's Information Analysis Method (NIAM), which is now turning into oblivion (Nijssen and Halpin 1989).

Lexical Items and Virtual Entities. Lexical items can be used to represent virtual entities. I analyze virtual entities in detail in two research papers (Wieringa 1989, 2000). The idea that lexical items, by their mere existence, can declare the existence of certain conceptual entities was introduced by Kimbrough, Lee, and Ness (1983), based on Searle's speech act theory (Searle 1969, 1979).

Lexical items stored in a computer are very similar to Jackson's workpieces (Jackson 2000). The major difference is that Jackson abstracts from the meaning of these items in the social environment of the system. Lexical items get a special treatment in the NIAM method.

System Functionality. The classification of system functions into information provision, direction, and manipulation is derived from Searle's classification of speech acts into descriptive (information-providing), directive, and declarative (Searle 1979). A declarative speech act creates the situation that it describes, provided that certain conditions are satisfied and procedure followed. Examples are "The meeting is opened" uttered by the chairperson at the start of a meeting and "You are now man and wife" uttered by an official at a certain moment in a wedding ceremony. Virtual entities have a very similar function: A virtual entity "declares" the existence of some conceptual entity. Of course, as for declarative speech acts, certain conditions must be fulfilled for this to be effective. For example, the stakeholders must accept certain rules concerning what can be counted as evidence for the existence of conceptual entities. I discuss the interaction between virtual entities and social rules in the context of a software product in Wieringa (2000).

Stimulus-Response Behavior. The concepts of event, temporal event, and response are defined in the literature on structured analysis, especially by Ward and Mellor (1985) and Hatley and Pirbhai (1987). The presentation in Chapter 3 is very much influenced by Jackson (1995, 2000) and Parnas and Madey (1995).

Behavior and Communication. I proposed the partitioning of functional properties into functions, behavior, and communication in a survey paper of approximately 25 distinct methods for software design (Wieringa 1998b). The synchronous view of communication taken here comes from process algebra (Baeten and Weijland 1990; Hoare 1985; Milner 1980) and from the Jackson System Development (JSD) method of software design (Jackson 1983).

Assumptions. In distributed systems specification, we work with assumption-guarantee specifications (Jones 1983), which are used to prove the correctness of composition (Abadi and Lamport 1995). The idea is that if component C_1 has properties R_1 if its environment satisfies A_1, and component C_2 has properties C_2 if its environment satisfies A_2, then their composition will satisfy $R_1 \wedge R_2$ if C_1 satisfies A_2 and if C_2 satisfies A_1. In this argument, $A \Rightarrow R$ is called an assumption-guarantee specification. The builder guarantees that his component satisfies R as long as its environment satisfies A. I have switched the perspective to the user who specifies requirements.

The Three-Mile Island example is taken from Ferguson (1992, 183).

Part II Function Notations

Mission and Goals. The concept of a mission statement comes from structured analysis (Yourdon Inc. 1993). The embedding of software engineering in systems engineering is explained well by Stevens et al. (1998). The use of goals and goal trees is common in Information Engineering (Martin 1982, 1989). Research on patterns in goal analysis is reported by Antón and Potts (1998), Antón, Carter, Dagnino, Dempster, and Siege (2000), and Darimont and Lamsweerde (1996). Yu and Mylopoulos (1996) and Mylopoulos, Chung, and Yu (1999) report on the use of a requirements analysis framework called i* to analyse goals. Goal-directed requirements engineering is discussed from a formal point of view by Dardenne, Lamsweerde, and Fickas (1993), Darimont and Lamsweerde (1996), and Lamsweerde, Darimont, and Letier (1998).

Function Refinement Tree. Function refinement trees are well-known in industrial product design (Roozenburg and Eekels 1995) and in Information Engineering (Martin 1982, 1989). The method of using Post-It notes is suggested by Barker and Longman (1992).

Service Description. Services are similar to use cases because both have a discrete triggering event and both should deliver a value to the environment. The reasons for my avoiding the term "use case" are (1) that I do not understand why this term was introduced anyway, when the term "service" has been part of the English language for ages; and (2) that the term "use case" suggests that each use case must have a user, which is too limited a view for services. The topic of service description receives very little attention in the software engineering community. Software engineers like to immediately dive into the details of possible scenarios rather than first describe what the added value of a service is for the environment. See Cockburn (2001) for ways to do add scenario information to use cases. All his guidelines are applicable to service descriptions as well.

Part III Entity Notations

Notations. Entity-relationship modeling was introduced by Chen (1976). It was introduced in structured analysis by Flavin (1981) and had a pervasive influence on object-oriented analysis, starting with Shlaer and Mellor (1988). Batini, Ceri, and Navathe (1992) give a good book-length introduction to entity-relationship diagrams. Elmasri and Navathe (1989) give a shorter introduction in two chapters. These and other authors define entities in different ways. Five different definitions of an entity are:

A thought. "Let *e* denote an entity which exists in our minds . . ." (Chen 1976, 11).

A type of subject domain entities. "Entities represent classes of real-world objects" (Batini et al. 1992, 31). Instances of these classes are called "entity occurrences."

A subject domain entity. An entity is "A 'thing' with real-world existence" (Elmasri and Navathe 1989, 40).

A record in a database. "A database will usually contain groups of entities that are similar" (Elmasri and Navathe 1989, 42).

A record type in a database. An entity is "a 'thing' of interest in the database, such as STUDENT" (Storey and Goldstein 1988, 328). An instance of such a type is called an "entity occurrence."

These examples also illustrate that the same authors can use two conflicting definitions only a few pages apart.

Modeling Guidelines. This chapter is based on a more detailed exposition given earlier (Wieringa 1996), which uses a different syntax but gives the same guidelines as the ones presented here. The rules of classification are given in nineteenth-century books on logic. I used Joseph (1916) and Copi and Cohen (1990). Batini et al. (1992) give useful tips for deriving ERDs from forms and record structures. An older source is Rock-Evans (1987), summarized a few years later in Rock-Evans (1989). Another source for simple pragmatic guidelines is Barker (1990). Useful subject-domain modeling patterns are given by Hay (1996) and Fowler (1997).

Dictionary. Definition is a classical topic in philosophical logic and argumentation theory that deserves more attention from the software engineering community. I used Copi and Cohen (1990) as a source for the classification of definitions; Jackson (1995, 2000) and Kovitz (1998) show how definitions are essential in requirements engineering. The definition of identifier requirements comes from Wieringa and de Jonge (1995).

Part IV **Behavior Notations**

Event lists are a central tool in structured analysis to specify system-level behavior (Yourdon Inc. 1993; Yourdon 1989). State transition tables have been in use for a long time in software engineering. Hatley and Pirbhai (1987) use them in their version of structured analysis. They are the central technique in the Software Cost Reduction method (Heitmeyer and Labaw 1991; Heitmeyer, Jeffords, and Labaw 1996; Heitmeyer and Bharadwaj 2000; Parnas and Madey 1995).

Mealy diagrams have been in use in software and hardware engineering since the 1950s. Hopcroft and Ullman (1979) and later editions of that book give a formal definition. They are used in most versions of structured analysis. Moore diagrams use entry actions instead of actions placed along state transitions. These are used in the object-oriented analysis (OOA) methods (Shlaer and Mellor 1992). Trace-equivalent expressiveness of Mealy and Moore diagrams is proven by Hopcroft and Ullman (1979).

The extension of STDs with variables is discussed very well by Belina, Hogrefe, and Sarma (1991).

Statecharts have been introduced by Harel (1987). They are used in the Statemate tool (Harel and Politi 1998). The Statemate and UML semantics of statecharts are discussed by Harel and Naamad (1996) and Harel and Gery (1996), respectively. Von der Beeck (1994) lists 20 different semantics for statecharts, in which many more issues are discussed than I am able to do in Chapter 13. Jackson (2000) discusses a number of methodological issues involved in behavior modeling.

The method presented here to find behavioral specifications has some similarity with Parnas's four-variable method (Parnas and Madey 1995) and has its roots in JSD (Jackson 1983) and in the underlying principles of the analysis of structured and object analysis (Wieringa 1998b). I discuss the underlying principles and motivations in detail in Wieringa (1998a, 1999). The combination of this approach with model checking to show the correctness of the specification of desired system behavior with respect to desired emergent behavior is discussed in Wieringa and Jansen (2001).

Part V **Communication Notations**

Data Flow Diagrams. DFDs have been around since the 1970s, when DeMarco (1978), Gane and Sarson (1979), and Yourdon and Constantine (1979) introduced them as high-level representations of structured programs. The basic design guideline of structured programming was to structure the program according to the problem, not according to the solution technology. The problems considered were transformation problems, in which a terminating input-output computation was required, and the most natural problem decomposition technique for these problem is functional decomposition. Hence, functional decomposition was proposed as a decomposition technique for DFDs. Over the years, this was supplemented with many other decomposition techniques.

Flavin (1981) add ERDs to data flow modeling and thereby introduce subject-domain orientation. McMenamin and Palmer (1984) introduce the concept of essential model, adding the design guideline of event partitioning. In order to deal with real-time systems, Ward and Mellor (1985) and Hatley and Pirbhai (1987) add STDs to the repertoire of techniques, and they add device partitioning as a decomposition technique.

Yourdon (1989) summarizes the techniques as known at the time. For many people, this is the end point of structured analysis because, at that time, object-oriented analysis took sway and a new generation of software engineers grew up for which data flow modeling was a thing of the past, to be forgotten. Developments continued for a while, however, with a very good integration attempt by Shumate and Keller (1992) and an encyclopedic compendium published a year later (Yourdon Inc. 1993). Goldsmith (1993) provides the best introduction to structured analysis that I know.

Shumate and Keller (1992) not only integrate the different structured analysis approaches, they also integrate this with their view of object-oriented analysis. Another author that proposed an integration is Gomaa (1993).

In a parallel development, Statemate (Harel et al. 1990) integrated statecharts and activity charts into an executable structured analysis approach. This is best known for its statecharts (Harel 1987), but activity charts, which are a variant of DFDs, have been integrated with them since about 1984. Harel and Politi (1998) describe the complete set of diagram techniques.

Of all these approaches, only the Statemate approach is well defined. All approaches use different terminology and define key concepts such as processes and flows differently. In the various Yourdon approaches, time-continuous event flows are allowed. These are really as Boolean data flows that can contain the Booleans True and False for periods of time. Statemate makes no distinction between event flows and data flows, although it allows the user of the Statemate tool to draw a flow as a solid or dashed arrow. There is no semantics attached to this visual difference. In Statemate, all flows are time-continuous and an event is simple a discrete change in a flow.

Communication Diagrams. Box-and-arrow diagrams to represent communication are used in SDL (Belina and Hogrefe 1988–1989; Belina et al. 1991; Færgemand and Olsen 1994; Sarraco and Tilanus 1987; Saracco, Smith, and Reed 1989), where they are called block specifications. They are also used in the object-oriented analysis method (Shlaer and Mellor 1992) and in every book on software architecture (Bass, Clements, and Kazman 1998; Buschmann et al. 1996; Hofmeister, Nord, and Soni 2000; Shaw and Garlan 1996).

Our notation is actually a higraph notation (Harel 1988), very similar to the Statemate activity chart (Harel and Politi 1998). The use of underlining to indicate instances comes from the UML (Booch, Rumbaugh, and Jacobson 1999; Rumbaugh, Jacobson, and Booch 1999).

Communication Semantics. Sources on communication semantics can be found in the SDL literature given in the preceding paragraph and in work on the Statemate execution semantics. A third important source is formal specification theory, especially process algebra (Baeten and Weijland 1990; Hoare 1985; Milner 1989), and a fourth important source is work on distributed systems (Coulouris, Dollimore, and Kindberg 1994; Polman, Steen, and Bruin 1997, 1998; Tagg and Freyberg 1997; Tanenbaum 1995). Petersohn et al. (1994) gives a detailed formal treatment of a multistep semantics of DFDs.

Context Modeling. Structured and object-oriented analysis have no attention for the system environment. Their context diagrams (called use case diagrams in object-oriented analysis) contain only the external entities with which the system interacts and no more. Usually, they omit the entities that are of interest. The idea of partial context diagrams comes from Goldsmith (1993). Context structuring was introduced by Jackson (1995) as part of framing the design problem, viewing and structuring it in such a way that it is amenable to solution. As shown by Schön (1983), professionals in action engage in the continuous framing and re-framing of design problems until they have a satisfactory solution. Jackson (2000) gives a meticulous introduction to framing and structuring software engineering problems.

Requirements-level Architecture Design. Research architecture on design emerged from earlier work on patterns in software (Gamma et al. 1995; Buschmann et al. 1996). Styles were introduced by Shaw and Garlan (1996). Bass et al. (1998, 95) present a classification of styles based on work by Shaw and Clements (1997). Their data-centered style is called the Von Neumann style in this book and their object-oriented style is called the object-oriented style. Bass et al. (1998) give a detailed taxonomy of communication styles, based on the taxonomy given by Shaw and Clements (1997). Bosch (2000) discusses another classification, which is the basis for the discussion in Chapter 19. In addition, I use a number of the dimensions used by Polman et al. (1997, 1998) to classify communication mechanisms. The dimensions used are data type of the communication channel, capacity of the communication channel, blocking type of the port of the sender, number of receivers (ranging from point-to-point to broadcast), success criterion (in the case of multiple destinations, how many must have received a message for the communication to count as succeeded?) and stride (how large are the groups of messages sent in one shot?).

All of this work on architecture design arose from a bottom-up analysis of existing software architectures and analyzes the architecture in terms of software quality attributes such as efficiency, reliability, and maintainability. With the inclusion of conceptual architectures in the inventory of relevant architecture views (Bass et al. 1998; Hofmeister et al. 2000), architecture research reached common ground with the information system specification community. The concept of conceptual architecture corresponds to the concept of essential decomposition introduced by McMenamin and Palmer (1984). Because in my view all architectural views are conceptual—they are not physical—and to indicate the close relationship with requirements, I refer to this view as "requirements-level architecture."

Gomaa (1993) is one of the first authors to identify software structures in terms of the environment of the system. He identifies objects that correspond to user roles, devices, control, data abstractions, and algorithms and discusses several kinds of cohesion between components, including temporal and behavioral cohesion. Some of these structuring criteria have their background in structured design (Page-Jones 1988).

Jacobson, Christerson et al. (1992) distinguish interface objects, control objects, and entity objects, which are similar to the communication-based components, behavior-based components, and subject-based components introduced in Chapter 19. Cook and Daniels (1994) discuss several domains that can be used to partition the system, such as the concept domain, interaction domain, and infrastructure domain. This corresponds to our subject domain, connection domain, and implementation platform. These external domains are likely to have subsystems or other components in the SuD dedicated to them. The concept of a domain was introduced in system design by Shlaer and Mellor (1992). Awad, Kuusela, and Ziegler (1996) use a similar partitioning into domains to define subsystems of the SuD. The shared feature of all these approaches is that they analyze the environment to get to a suitable system decomposition. This complements the software engineering approach, which analyzes the architecture and derives consequences for the environment in terms of quality attributes.

The concept of a surrogate, important in subject-oriented decomposition, is ancient, as far as computer science goes. It was introduced by Hall, Owlett, and Todd (1976).

The concept of essential model was introduced by McMenamin and Palmer (1984). They also introduce event partitioning as a design strategy, subsumed in Chapter 19 under the heading communication-based design.

Functional Decomposition and Transformational Systems. Functional decomposition was introduced in the 1970s as the major innovation in structured programming (Dijkstra 1972), which allowed us to define the structure of the program in terms of the structure of the problem to be solved rather than in terms of the structure of the implementation. The problem to be solved was, in Jackson's (2000) terms, a transformation problem. To solve the problem, we decompose a complex transformation into simpler parts until we get to the parts that can be implemented on the available implementation platform. This does not work for reactive systems because these systems must respond to stimuli based on a model of the environment. The transformation of stimulus and current state into response and next state is a transformation problem, but to define this transformation we need an understanding of reactive behavior as a whole and, therefore, of the actual behavior in the environment and the desired effects of the system on this behavior. This insight was already brought forward by JSD (Jackson 1983) and it is also stated by Harel and Pnueli (1985).

Evaluation of Architectures. Evaluation of architectures is a current software engineering research topic. Kazman et al. (1994) present an approach to do this quantitavely. Bass et al. (1998) illustrate architecture analysis with numerous case studies. Bosch (2000) discusses architectural transformations to satisfy quality attributes. Smith (1990) gives numerous design principles and methods for measuring and improving software performance.

Lauesen (1998) reports one of the few empirical evaluations of object-oriented styles and finds that in business data processing they are usually Von Neumann styles in disguise.

Model checking and other formal approaches for evaluating a design are concerned with functional properties. A technical introduction to model checking is given by Clarke, Grumberg, and Peled (1999). Bisimulation is a correctness relationship between external behavior e specification and implementation specification. For an entry to the huge amount of literature on the subject, see the references cited earlier (Baeten and Weijland 1990; Hoare 1985; Milner 1980).

Part VI   **Software Specification Methods**

Structured Analysis. Structured analysis began as an outgrowth of structured programming and structured design in the late 1970s with publications by Ross (Ross and Brackett 1976; Ross 1977; Ross and Schoman 1977), DeMarco (1978), Weinberg (1978), Gane and Sarson (1979), and Yourdon and Constantine (1979). This led to Ross's school of structured analysis, called SADT, and to the Yourdon school. Marca and Gowan (1988) give a survey of the current status of SADT. For the Yourdon school, see the bibliographical remarks given earlier about data flow diagrams.

Postmodern Structured Analysis (PSA). The differences between PSA and Yourdon-style structured analysis are the following:

◆ PSA includes a larger part of the context than Yourdon approaches. This approach was borrowed from Jackson (1995).

- ◆ PSA emphasizes the distinction between the subject domain and the SuD. This was taken from Jackson (1983) and Cook and Daniels (1994).
- ◆ PSA uses ERDs to represent the subject domain.

These points are elaborated also in Wieringa (1996).

Statemate. More information on the Statemate tools can be found at *www.ilogix.com*. A brief overview of the Statemate approach is given by Harel et al. (1990). Harel (1987) gives a good overview and motivation of the statechart notation. Harel and Pnueli (1985) are among the first to observe that functional decomposition is OK for transformational systems but not for reactive systems, at least not as sole decomposition principle. The other place where this insight was brought forward is, of course, Jackson (1983).

There are many variants of the statechart technique. Almost all object-oriented methods use their own version of the technique. The UML, discussed in Chapter 22, also contains its own version of the technique. Yet another version is RSML, defined by Leveson et al. (1994). Kesten and Pnueli (1991) define an interesting extension of statecharts with continuous variables. Von der Beeck (1994) gives a thorough survey of statechart variants as of 1994.

The first published version of a formal execution semantics of statecharts is given by Harel et al. (1987). A different semantics, which uses fixpoints, is defined by Pnueli and Shalev (1989, 1991). The Statemate semantics is described by Harel and Politi (1998) and, in more detail, by Harel and Naamad (1996). Damm et al. (1998) give a formal semantics of the Statemate semantics in full detail. The Statemate simulator implements this semantics but also contains a number of variations on it (i-Logix 1997). Von der Beeck (1994) surveys 20 different published semantics of statecharts as known in 1994.

The Unified Modeling Language. This chapter presents only a lightweight version of the UML diagram techniques. To learn about the full UML, access the reference documentation on the UML Web pages at the OMG (*www.omg.org*), which provides full information, albeit in a rather terse form. At the time of writing, the latest version of the standard is UML 1.3 (UML Revision Task Force 1999), and UML 1.4 and UML 2.0 are being prepared.

A good lightweight introduction to the UML is given by Fowler and Scott (1997). More elaborate introductions to the UML are given by Larman (1998) and Douglass (1998), who treat object-oriented design of information-intensive and control-intensive systems, respectively. These two books nicely complement one another. Booch et al. (1999) gives a complete tutorial introduction to UML version 1.3, treating all aspects of the language. Rumbaugh et al. (1999) is a reference manual, and Jacobson, Booch, and Rumbaugh (1999) contains a description of the Rational Unified Process, which uses the UML. You should beware, however—all these books describe slightly differing versions of the UML that precede the version 1.3 that is the basis of this chapter. To give an example of the subtle and not so subtle inconsistencies among these books, here are the definitions of the concept of an operation

Abadi, M., and Lamport, L. (1995). "Conjoining specifications," *ACM Transactions on Programming Languages and Systems* **17**(3), 507–534.

Antón, A., Carter, R., Dagnino, A., Dempster, J., and Siege, D. (2000). "Deriving goals from a use-case based requirements specification," *Requirements Engineering* **6,** 63–73.

Antón, A., and Potts, C. (1998). "The use of goals to surface requirements for evolving systems." In *International Conference on Software Engineering* (ICSE'98). IEEE Computer Society, pp. 157–166.

Awad, M., Kuusela, J., and Ziegler, J. (1996). *Object-Oriented Technology for Real-Time Systems: A Practical Approach Using OMT and Fusion*. Prentice-Hall.

Baeten, J. C. M., and Weijland, W. (1990). *Process Algebra,* Cambridge Tracts in Theoretical Computer Science 18. Cambridge University Press.

Barker, R. (1990). *Case*Method: Entity Relationship Modelling*. Addison-Wesley.

Barker, R., and Longman, C. (1992). *Case*Method: Function and Process Modelling*. Addison-Wesley.

Barney, G. C., and Dos Santos, S. M. (1977). *Lift Traffic Analysis Design and Control*. Peter Peregrinus.

Bass, L., Clements, P., and Kazman, R. (1998). *Software Architecture in Practice*. Addison-Wesley.

Batini, C., Ceri, S., and Navathe, S. (1992). *Conceptual Database Design: An Entity-Relationship Approach*. Benjamin/Cummings.

Belina, F., and Hogrefe, D. (1988–1989). "The CCITT-specification and description language SDL," *Computer Networks and ISDN Systems* **16,** 311–341.

Belina, F., Hogrefe, D., and Sarma, A. (1991). *SDL with Applications from Protocol Specification*. Prentice-Hall.

Berry, G., and Gonthier, G. (1992). "The ESTEREL synchronous programming language: Design, semantics, implementation," *Science of Computer Programming* **19,** 87–152.

Blanchard, B. S., and Fabrycky, W. J. (1990). *Systems Engineering and Analysis*. Prentice-Hall.

Booch, G., Rumbaugh, J., and Jacobson, I. (1999). *The Unified Modeling Language User Guide*. Addison-Wesley.

Bosch, J. (2000). *Design and Use of Software Architectures: Adopting and Evolving a Product-Line Approach*. Addison-Wesley.

Buschmann, F., Meunier, R., Rohnert, H., Sommerlad, P., and Stal, M. (1996). *A System of Patterns: Pattern-Oriented Software Architecture*. John Wiley.

Chen, P.-S. (1976). "The entity-relationship model—Toward a unified view of data," *ACM Transactions on Database Systems* **1,** 9–36.

Clarke, E., Grumberg, O., and Peled, D. A. (1999). *Model Checking*. MIT Press.

Cockburn, A. (2001). *Writing Effective Use Cases*. Addison-Wesley.

Coleman, D., Arnold, P., Bodoff, S., Dollin, C., Gilchrist, H., Hayes, F., and Jeremaes, P. (1994). *Object-Oriented Development: The FUSION Method*. Prentice-Hall.

Cook, S., and Daniels, J. (1994). *Designing Object Systems: Object-Oriented Modelling with Syntropy*. Prentice-Hall.

Copi, I., and Cohen, C. (1990). *Introduction to Logic*, 8th ed. Macmillan.

Coulouris, G., Dollimore, J., and Kindberg, T. (1994). *Distributed Systems: Concepts and Design*, 2nd ed. Addison-Wesley.

Damm, W., Josko, B., Hungar, H., and Pnueli, A. (1998). "A compositional real-time semantics of STATEMATE designs." In W.-P. de Roever, H. Langmaack, and A. Pnueli, eds., *Compositionality: The Significant Difference* (COMPOS 97), Lecture Notes in Computer Science 1536. Springer, pp. 186–238.

Dardenne, A., Lamsweerde, A. v., and Fickas, S. (1993). "Goal-directed requirements acquisition," *Science of Computer Programming* **20,** 3–50.

Darimont, R., and Lamsweerde, A. v. (1996). "Formal refinement patterns for goal-driven requirements elaboration." In *Fourth ACM Symposium on the Foundations of Software Engineering* (FSE4). ACM Press, pp. 179–190.

Davis, A. M. (1993). *Software Requirements: Objects, Functions, States*. Prentice-Hall.

DeMarco, T. (1978). *Structured Analysis and System Specification*. Yourdon Press/Prentice-Hall.

Dijkstra, E. (1972). "Notes on structured programming." In O.-J. Dahl, E. W. Dijkstra, C. A. R. Hoare, eds., *Structured Programming*. Academic Press, pp. 1–82.

Douglass, B. (1998). *Real-Time UML: Developing Efficient Objects for Embedded Systems*. Addison-Wesley.

Elmasri, R., and Navathe, S. (1989). *Fundamentals of Database Systems*. Benjamin Cummings.

Færgemand, O., and Olsen, A. (1994). "Introduction to SDL 92," *Computer Networks and ISDN Systems* **26,** 1143–1167.

Ferguson, E. (1992). *Engineering and the Mind's Eye*. MIT Press.

Flavin, M. (1981). *Fundamental Concepts of Information Modeling*. Yourdon Press.

Fowler, M. (1997). *Analysis Patterns: Reusable Object Models*. Addison-Wesley.

Fowler, M., and Scott, K. (1997). *UML Distilled*. Addison-Wesley.

Gamma, E., Helm, R., Johnson, R., and Vlissideas, J. (1995). *Design Patterns: Elements of Reusable Object-Oriented Software*. Addison-Wesley.

Gane, C., and Sarson, T. (1979). *Structured Systems Analysis: Tools and Techniques*. Prentice-Hall.

Goldsmith, S. (1993). *Real-Time Systems Development*. Prentice-Hall.

Gomaa, H. (1993). *Software Design Methods for Concurrent and Real-Time Systems*. Addison-Wesley.

Griethuysen, J. v., ed. (1982). *Concepts and Terminology for the Conceptual Schema and the Information Base*. Technical Report TC97/SC5/WG3. International Organization of Standards.

Gunter, C., Gunter, E., Jackson, M., and Zave, P. (2000). "A reference model for requirements and specifications," *IEEE Software* **17**(3), 37–43.

Hall, P., Owlett, J., and Todd, S. (1976). "Relations and entities." In G. Nijssen, ed., *Modelling in Database Management Systems*. North-Holland, pp. 201–220.

Harel, D. (1987). "Statecharts: A visual formalism for complex systems," *Science of Computer Programming* **8,** 231–274. Preliminary version appeared as Technical Report CS 84-05, Weizmann Institute of Science, Rehovot, Israel, February 1984.

Harel, D. (1988). "On visual formalisms," *Communications of the ACM* **31,** 514–530.

Harel, D., and Gery, E. (1996). "Executable object modeling with statecharts." In *Proceedings of the 18th International Conference on Software Engineering*. IEEE Press, pp. 246–257.

Harel, D., and Gery, E. (1997). "Executable object modeling with statecharts," *Computer* **30**(7), 31–42.

Harel, D., and Kupferman, O. (1999). *On the Inheritance of State-based Object Behavior*. Technical Report MCS99-12, Weizmann Institute of Science, Faculty of Mathematics and Computer Science, Rehovot, Israel.

Harel, D., Lachover, H., Naamad, A., Pnueli, A., Politi, M., Sherman, R., Shtull-Trauring, A., and Trakhtenbrot, M. (1990). "STATEMATE: A working environment for the development of complex reactive systems," *IEEE Transactions on Software Engineering* **16,** 403–414.

Harel, D., and Naamad, A. (1996). "The STATEMATE semantics of statecharts," *ACM Transactions on Software Engineering and Methodology* **5**(4), 293–333.

Harel, D., and Pnueli, A. (1985). "On the development of reactive systems." In K. Apt, ed., *Logics and Models of Concurrent Systems,* NATO ASI Series. Springer, pp. 477–498.

Harel, D., Pnueli, A., Schmidt, J. P., and Sherman, R. (1987). "On the formal semantics of statecharts." In *Proceedings of the Symposium on Logic in Computer Science*. Computer Science Press, pp. 54–64.

Harel, D., and Politi, M. (1998). *Modeling Reactive Systems with Statecharts: The STATEMATE Approach*. McGraw-Hill.

Hatley, D., and Pirbhai, I. (1987). *Strategies for Real-Time System Specification*. Dorset House.

Hay, D. (1996). *Data Model Patterns: Conventions of Thought*. Dorset House.

Heitmeyer, C., and Bharadwaj, R. (2000). "Applying the SCR requirements method to the light control case study," *Journal of Universal Computer Science (JUCS)* **6**(7), 650–678.

Heitmeyer, C., Jeffords, R., and Labaw, B. (1996). "Automated consistency checking of requirements specifications," *ACM Transactions on Software Engineering and Methodology* **5**(3), 231–261.

Heitmeyer, C., and Labaw, B. (1991). "Requirements specification of hard real-time systems: Experience with a language and a verifier." In A. v. Tilborg and G. Koob, eds., *Foundations of Real-Time Computing: Formal Specifications and Methods*. Kluwer, pp. 291–313.

Hoare, C. (1985). *Communicating Sequential Processes*. Prentice-Hall.

Hofmeister, C., Nord, R., and Soni, D. (2000). *Applied Software Architecture*. Addison-Wesley.

Hopcroft, J., and Ullman, J. (1979). *Introduction to Automata Theory, Languages and Computation*. Addison-Wesley.

i-Logix (1997). *Statemate Trailblazer Reference Manual, Version 1.2*. i-Logix Inc., *www.ilogix.com*.

i-Logix (1999). *Rhapsody Reference Guide, Version 2.1*. i-Logix Inc., *www.ilogix.com*.

Jackson, M. (1983). *System Development*. Prentice-Hall.

Jackson, M. (1995). *Software Requirements and Specifications: A Lexicon of Practice, Principles and Prejudices*. Addison-Wesley.

Jackson, M. (2000). *Problem Frames: Analysing and Structuring Software Development Problems*. Addison-Wesley.

Jacobson, I., Booch, G., and Rumbaugh, J. (1999). *The Unified Software Development Process*. Addison-Wesley.

Jacobson, I., Christerson, M., Johnsson, P., and Övergaard, G. (1992). *Object-Oriented Software Engineering: A Use Case Driven Approach*. Prentice-Hall.

Jones, C. (1983). "Specification and design of (parallel) programs." In R. Mason, ed., *Information Processing '83: Proceedings of the IFIP 9th World Congress*. North-Holland, pp. 321–332.

Joseph, H. (1916). *An Introduction to Logic*. Clarendon Press.

JTC1/SC7/WG6, I. (1995a). *ISO/IEC 9126-1 Information Technology: Software Quality Characteristics and Metrics—Quality Characteristics and Subcharacteristics*. International Organization for Standardization.

JTC1/SC7/WG6, I. (1995b). *ISO/IEC 9126-2 Information Technology: Software Quality Characteristics and Metrics—External Metrics*. International Organization for Standardization.

Kazman, R., Bass, L., Abowd, G., and Webb, M. (1994). "SAAM: A method for analyzing the properties software architectures." In *Proceedings of the 16th International Conference on Software Engineering*. ACM Press, pp. 81–90.

Kesten, Y., and Pnueli, A. (1991). "Timed and hybrid statecharts and their textual representation." In J. Vytopil, ed., *Formal Techniques in Real-Time and Fault-Tolerant Systems*, Lecture Notes in Computer Science 571. Springer, pp. 590–620.

Kimbrough, S., Lee, R., and Ness, D. (1983). "Performative, informative and emotive systems: The first piece of the PIE." In L. Maggi, J. King, and K. Kraenens, eds., *Proceedings of the Fifth Conference on Information Systems*. Pp. 141–148.

Kovitz, B. (1998). *Practical Software Requirements: A Manual of Content and Style*. Manning.

Lamsweerde, A. v., Darimont, R., and Letier, E. (1998). "Managing conflicts in goal-driven requirements engineering," *IEEE Transactions on Software Engineering* **24**(11), 908–926.

Larman, C. (1998). *Applying UML and Patterns*. Prentice-Hall.

Lauesen, S. (1998). "Real-life object-oriented systems," *IEEE Software* **15**(2), 76–83.

Leveson, N., Heimdahl, M., Hildreth, H., and Reese, J. (1994). "Requirements specification for process-control systems," *IEEE Transactions on Software Engineering* **20**(9), 684–707.

Marca, D. A., and Gowan, C. L. (1988). *SADT: Structured Analysis and Design Technique*. McGraw-Hill.

Martin, J. (1982). *Strategic Data-Planning Methodologies*. Prentice-Hall.

Martin, J. (1989). *Information Engineering*. Prentice-Hall.

McMenamin, S. M., and Palmer, J. F. (1984). *Essential Systems Analysis*. Yourdon Press/Prentice Hall.

Meyer, B. (1985). "On formalism in specifications," *IEEE Software* **2**(1), 6–26.

Milner, R. (1980). *A Calculus of Communicating Systems*, Lecture Notes in Computer Science 92. Springer.

Milner, R. (1989). *Communication and Concurrency*. Prentice-Hall.

Mylopoulos, J., Chung, L., and Yu, E. (1999). "From object-oriented to goal-oriented requirements analysis," *Communications of the ACM* **42**(1), 31–37.

Nijssen, G., ed. (1976). *Modelling in Database Management Systems*. North-Holland.

Nijssen, G., and Halpin, T. (1989). *Conceptual Schema and Relational Database Design*. Prentice-Hall.

Page-Jones, M. (1988). *The Practical Guide to Structured Systems Design*, 2nd ed. Prentice-Hall.

Parnas, D., and Madey, J. (1995). "Functional documents for computer systems," *Science of Computer Programming* **25**, 41–61.

Petersohn, C., Huizing, C., Peleska, J., and Roever, W.-P. d. (1994). "Formal semantics for Ward & Mellor's transformation schemas." In D. Till, ed., *6th Refinement Workshop*, Workshops in Computing, BCS-FACS. Springer Verlag, pp. 14–41.

Pnueli, A., and Shalev, M. (1989). "What is in a step?" In J. Klop, J.-J. Meyer, and J. Rutten, eds., *J.W. de Bakker, 25 Jaar Semantiek. Liber Amicorum.* Stichting Mathematisch Centrum, pp. 373–399.

Pnueli, A., and Shalev, M. (1991). "What is in a step: On the semantics of statecharts." In T. Ito and A. Meyer, eds., *Theoretical Aspects of Computer Software*, Lecture Notes in Computer Science 526. Springer, pp. 244–264.

Polman, M., Steen, M. v., and Bruin, A. d. (1997). "Formalizing a design technique for distributed systems." In *Proceedings of the Second International Workshop on Software Engineering for Parallel and Distributed Systems*. IEEE Computer Science Press, pp. 150–159.

Polman, M., Steen, M. v., and Bruin, A. d. (1998). "A structured design technique for distributed programs." In *Proceedings of the 22nd International Computer Software and Applications Conference* (COMPSAC). IEEE Computer Science Press, pp. 308–315.

Reif, W., and Stenzel, K. (1999). *Formal Methods for the Secure Application of Java Smartcards*. Technical report, University of Ulm. Presentation slides. *www.informatik. uni-augsburg.de/swt/fmg/projects/javacard_presentation.ps.gz*.

Rock-Evans, R. (1987). *Analysis within the Systems Development Life Cycle*, Vol. 1. *Data Analysis—The Deliverables*. Pergamon Infotech.

Rock-Evans, R. (1989). *A Simple Introduction to Data and Activity Analysis*. Computer Weekly Publications.

Roozenburg, N., and Eekels, J. (1995). *Product Design: Fundamentals and Methods*. John Wiley.

Ross, D. T. (1977). "Structured analysis (SA): A language for communicating ideas," *IEEE Transactions on Software Engineering* **SE-3**(1), 16–34.

Ross, D. T., and Brackett, J. W. (1976). "An approach to structured analysis," *Computer Decisions* **8**(9), 40–44.

Ross, D. T., and Schoman, K. E. (1977). "Structured analysis for requirements definition," *IEEE Transactions on Software Engineering* **SE-3**(5), 6–15.

Routio, P. (1999). *Arteology or the Science of Artefacts*. Technical report, University of Art and Design Helsinki. *www.uiah.fi/projects/metodi/*.

Rumbaugh, J., Jacobson, I., and Booch, G. (1999). *The Unified Modeling Language Reference Manual*. Addison-Wesley.

Saracco, R., Smith, J. R. W., and Reed, R. (1989). *Telecommunications Systems Engineering using SDL*. North-Holland.

Sarraco, R., and Tilanus, P. A. J. (1987). "CCITT SDL: Overview of the language and its applications," *Computer Networks and ISDN Systems* **13**, 65–74.

Schön, D. (1983). *The Reflective Practitioner: How Professionals Think in Action*. Arena.

Searle, J. (1969). *Speech Acts: An Essay in the Philosophy of Language*. Cambridge University Press.

Searle, J. (1979). *Expression and Meaning*. Cambridge University Press.

Shaw, M., and Clements, P. (1997). "A field guide to boxology: Preliminary classification of architectural styles for software systems." In *Proceedings of the Twenty-First International Computer Software and Applications Conference* (COMPSAC 97). IEEE Computer Science Press, pp. 6–13.

Shaw, M., and Garlan, D. (1996). *Software Architecture: Perspective on an Emerging Discipline*. Prentice Hall.

Shlaer, S., and Mellor, S. J. (1988). *Object-Oriented Systems Analysis: Modeling the World in Data*. Prentice-Hall.

Shlaer, S., and Mellor, S. J. (1992). *Object Lifecycles: Modeling the World in States*. Prentice-Hall.

Shumate, K., and Keller, M. (1992). *Software Specification and Design: A Disciplined Approach for Real-Time Systems*. John Wiley.

Smith, C. (1926). *Synonyms Discriminated*. G. Bell and Sons.

Smith, C. (1990). *Performance Engineering for Software Systems*. Addison-Wesley.

Stevens, R., Brook, P., Jackson, K., and Arnold, S. (1998). *Systems Engineering: Coping with Complexity*. Prentice-Hall.

Storey, V., and Goldstein, R. (1988). "A methodology for creating user views in database designs," *ACM Transactions on Database Systems* **13**(3), 305–338.

Tagg, R., and Freyberg, C. (1997). *Designing Distributed and Cooperative Information Systems*. International Thomson Computer Press.

Tanenbaum, A. (1995). *Distributed Operating Systems*. Prentice-Hall.

UML Revision Task Force (1999). *OMG UML Specification*. Object Management Group, *uml.shl.com*.

Verheijen, G., and Bekkum, J. (1982). "NIAM: An information analysis method." In T. Olle, H. Sol, and A. Verrijn-Stuart, eds., *Information Systems Design Methodologies: A Comparative Review*. North-Holland, pp. 537–589.

Von der Beeck, M. (1994). "A comparison of Statecharts variants." In H. Langmaack, W. d. Roever, and J. Vytopil, eds., *Formal Techniques in Real-Time and Fault-Tolerant Systems*, Lecture Notes in Computer Science 863. Springer, pp. 128–148.

Ward, P. T., and Mellor, S. J. (1985). *Structured Development for Real-Time Systems*. Prentice-Hall/Yourdon Press.

Weinberg, V. (1978). *Structured Analysis*. Yourdon Press.

Wiegers, K. (1999). *Software Requirements*. Microsoft Press.

Wieringa, R. J. (1989). "Three roles of conceptual models in information system design and use." In E. Falkenberg and P. Lindgreen, eds., *Information System Concepts: An In-Depth Analysis*. North-Holland, pp. 31–51.

Wieringa, R. J. (1996). *Requirements Engineering: Frameworks for Understanding*. John Wiley.

Wieringa, R. J. (1998a). "Postmodern software design with NYAM: Not yet another method." In M. Broy and B. Rumpe, eds., *Requirements Targeting Software and Systems Engineering*, Lecture Notes in Computer Science 1526. Springer, pp. 69–94.

Wieringa, R. J. (1998b). "A survey of structured and object-oriented software specification methods and techniques," *ACM Computing Surveys* **30**(4), 459–527.

Wieringa, R. J. (1999). "Embedding object-oriented design a systems engineering approach." In H. Kilov, B. Rumpe, and I. Simmonds, eds., *Behavioral Specifications of Businesses and Systems*. Kluwer, pp. 287–310. Original version appeared in *Second ECOOP Workshop on Precise Behavioral Semantics*, July 1998.

Wieringa, R. J. (2000). "The declarative problem frame: Designing systems that create and use norms." In *10th International Workshop on Software Specification and Design* (IWSSD-10). IEEE Computer Society, pp. 75–85.

Wieringa, R. J., and de Jonge, W. (1995). "Object identifiers, keys, and surrogates—Object identifiers revisited," *Theory and Practice of Object Systems* **1**(2), 101–114.

Wieringa, R. J., and Jansen, D. N. (2001). "Techniques for reactive system design: The tools in TRADE." In K. Dittrich, A. Geppert, and M. Noirie, eds., *Advanced Information Systems Engineering (CAiSE)*, Lecture Notes in Computer Science 2068. Springer, pp. 93–107.

Yourdon, E. (1989). *Modern Structured Analysis*. Prentice-Hall.

Yourdon, E., and Constantine, L. L. (1979). *Structured Design: Fundamentals of a Discipline of Computer Program and Systems Design*. Prentice-Hall.

Yourdon Inc. (1993). *Yourdon*™ *Systems Method: Model-Driven Systems Development*. Prentice-Hall.

Yu, E., and Mylopoulos, J. (1996). "Using goals, rules, and methods to support reasoning in business process reengineering," *International Journal of Intelligent Systems in Accounting, Finance and Management* **5**(1), 1–13. (Special issue on Artificial Intelligence in Business Process Reengineering.)

Note: Boldface pages indicate definitions.